Stock-Market Psychology

Stock-Market Psychology

How People Value and Trade Stocks

Karl-Erik Wärneryd

Professor Emeritus of Economic Psychology,
Stockholm School of Economics, Sweden

Edward Elgar
Cheltenham, UK • Northampton, MA, USA

Published by
Edward Elgar Publishing Limited
Glensanda House
Montpellier Parade
Cheltenham
Glos GL50 1UA
UK

Edward Elgar Publishing, Inc.
136 West Street
Suite 202
Northampton
Massachusetts 01060
USA

A catalogue record for this book
is available from the British Library

Library of Congress Cataloguing in Publication Data
Wärneryd, Karl-Erik, 1927-
Stock-market psychology : how people value and trade stocks / Karl-Erik Wärneryd.
p.cm.
Includes bibliographical references and index.
1. Investments—Psychological aspects. 2. Stock exchanges—Psychological aspects. 3. Investment analysis. 4. Stocks. I. Title.

HG4515.15 .W373 2001
332.63'22'019—dc21 2001031364

ISBN 1 84064 736 1

Printed and bound in Great Britain by MPG Books Ltd, Bodmin, Cornwall

Contents

List of Figures

List of Tables

Preface

'I never thought, when I used to read books, what work it was to write them.' 'It's work enough to read them, sometimes,' I returned. 'As to the writing, it has its own charms, aunt.'

Charles Dickens, *David Copperfield* (1849–50, p.701)

When I was more than half-way through writing this book, stock prices started plummeting, led by the Nasdaq Stock Exchange. On April 13 2000, the Nasdaq index dropped 9.7 percent and the Dow Jones almost 6 percent. Commentators on TV, in several countries, used almost the same expression: 'Now it is all psychology'. What did they mean? They were certainly not thinking of the psychology that dominates behavioral finance and which is primarily based on cognitive problems. It turned out that they were talking about expectations and how these were formed in moments of turbulence and uncertainty and colored by strong emotions. A typical assertion was: 'There are more sellers than buyers and buyers do not know when prices will stop going down. They have no basis for forming expectations.'

Expectations are central to human actions. They push individuals to make or not to make decisions. A few things are known about the formation of expectations and about what factors influence such processes, but much is still open to question. Expectations which are sometimes instantly formed and resemble (instant) scenarios of the future are often strange mixtures of past experience, new information, and feelings. Efficient-market theory is a relatively recent development in the century-old attempts towards understanding expectations in stock markets. Its definition stipulates that all relevant information is immediately reflected in stock prices, which then cannot be predicted on the basis of earlier prices. The theory may be inadequately descriptive of actual financial expectations in its emphasis on rational use of information, but it can be complemented with systematic psychological knowledge about information processing and social influences. What appears as deviations from rationality may to some extent be predictable. This is implied in the heuristics-and-biases approach, set forth by Daniel Kahneman and Amos Tversky. It has been widely adopted in behavioral finance.

Many observations to the effect that professional and private investors do not base their investment decisions primarily on expected fundamentals, that is, future returns – have led to a search for human fundamentals beyond economic rationality which is the firmly rooted human fundamental in economic theory. Human fundamentals have turned out to be multifarious and hard to subsume under simple behavioral laws. One of the difficulties is that humans really are different in many ways, and most, if not all, psychological laws hold only under certain conditions. The quest for fundamentals governing financial behavior has in behavioral finance first and foremost been directed towards cognitive psychology and social psychology with an emerging interest in theories of emotions. A particularly intriguing problem is the role of an investor's expectation of other investors' expectations. Whatever the weaknesses of the theories tried so far, they should not tempt us to go back to mere anecdote-based guesses about the psychology of financial markets.

The main objective of the book is to present ideas of how problems related to stock-investor behavior can be structured and to provide tools for analyzing problems in finance, using psychological theory. The book illustrates how the ideas have so far been applied in analyses of financial behavior. Earlier research gives greater or less credence to the ideas as worthwhile guides for analysis and research. To some extent, it may even be possible to extricate principles that can guide investment decisions in practice. The book is not an attempt to present an integrated theory, for the simple reason that none exists. Such an attempt is hardly possible. Those who feel that they would like to work with global theories may find good starting points in the varied findings covered in the book.

Much of the psychological thinking pertinent to stock-market behavior can be related to the simple concept of *expectation*. It encompasses the influence of all sorts of factors that have to do with the subjectively experienced scenario of the future. Typical investors – who may have a considerable proportion of the total stock value – make scenarios that are cautious and that make them passive traders. They are not like the overactive, profit-seeking trader of many news media and investment guides written by financial advisors.

I have received comments and suggestions from many people and I am most grateful for their interest and willingness to read early, sometimes rough drafts. I want to thank Peter Högfeldt, Horst Müller-Peters, Bertil Näslund, and Ekkehard Stephan. I owe special thanks to my son Jan Erik Wärneryd, who works in the field of finance, for his comments. He has also over many years given me ideas and stimulated my interest in stock-market psychology. No doubt errors and omissions that could have been avoided remain and I am solely responsible for those. I am indebted to CentEr for Economic Research, Tilburg University, and to Helena Flink, Jonas Gunnarsson, and Richard Wahlund for giving me access to their data bases.

Karl-Erik Wärneryd
Stockholm, March 2001

Introduction

THE OBJECTIVES OF THE BOOK

In a nutshell, this book deals with the question of how investors go about ascribing value to stocks, how they view trading with stocks and, to some extent, also with other securities. While it must be admitted that there is not much knowledge about how people actually reason when they make financial choices, there is plenty of material to be found in financial theory writings, innumerable studies of stock prices over time, a few behavioral studies of asset portfolios and abundant, often ad-hoc, suggestions of psychological explanations. In addition, many findings in psychology relating to judgments, valuations, and choices serve to illuminate factors that potentially affect financial behavior. All these sources have contributed ideas for the book.

Many books and countless articles have been written on private investing. Mostly, they give advice in the guise of guidelines and warnings, all based on the author's own success stories and perceptions of others' dealings in financial markets. Little has been written about the behavior of individual investors and segments of investors. There exist only a few investigations of individual factors influencing portfolio choice. The general assumption is that most investors are very active and should be very active traders, buying and selling at the right time. My idea is rather that most investors are relatively inactive, opt for long-term investments and add to their investments rather than sell. I am also convinced that many of those have over time made considerable capital gains. The focus in this book is on the individual investor's perception of the world and efforts to secure a better or at least equally prosperous future. It is an attempt to bring together empirical findings and relevant and potentially useful theories from financial economics and psychology. An interesting, rapidly developing area of empirical research is pursued under the label of *behavioral finance*. This area has furnished much of the material used here. The material has been further complemented by research results from modern cognitive and social psychology.

The book is written in an endeavor to claim investor psychology as an essential area for economic psychology. It may not make stock prices more forecastable, but it should facilitate the understanding of the individual investor and lead to appreciation of the fact that there are bound to be segments of investors with highly varying properties. Even if most of the segments of investors possess properties that financial economists would see as indicators of irrationality, it is likely that there is some system in the deviations from rationality and that some deviations may lead to gains for the individual investor. Few investors are apt to see the whole financial market as opaque and most investors seem to believe that there are ways to beat the market index.

The major theme of the book is the forward-looking thinking of humans and their subsequent behavior. Investors build up expectations on the basis of earlier experience, vicarious experience, the experience of others, and various bits of new information. They infuse more or less emotion in the expectations and they feel that they have varying degrees of control of the situation. Expectations may involve fear of the future or hope for a successful future. Investors are bound to experience both types of feelings as they follow stock-price movements over long periods of time. The hyperactive investor in stocks may bounce between hope and fear even in times when stock indexes in general are moving upwards.

A BACKDROP

Increasing Participation in Securities Markets

While participation in the stock market varies considerably between countries, it is generally very low, meaning that a minority, often less than 10 percent, of households owns stocks directly or indirectly through mutual funds. The data in Figure I.1 emanate from different sources – mostly economic news journals – and are uncertain in many cases, but they probably reflect the main differences. Since the estimates emanate from interview surveys affected by large sampling and systematic errors and the stock definition may sometimes include stock funds, the estimates should be looked at with some circumspection. For some countries, estimates for several years are available. The tendency suggests increasing participation in all Western countries. Over the last few years, rapid increases in stock market participation have occurred, even in countries with already high participation. In a few countries, notably Australia, the USA and Sweden, the majority of households, albeit only slightly more than 50 percent, owns stocks either directly or through funds. In the UK, between one-fifth and one-quarter of the households own stocks. Keeping in mind the years of the big crashes, it is interesting to see the following short series for the USA: 1929, 1 percent; 1987, 10 percent; and 1999, 50 percent. For Germany, the following sequence is illustrative of the current rapid increase in participation: 1978, 10 percent; 1988, 11.4 percent; 1993, 12 percent; 1999, 15 percent; and in 2000, 20 percent of households.

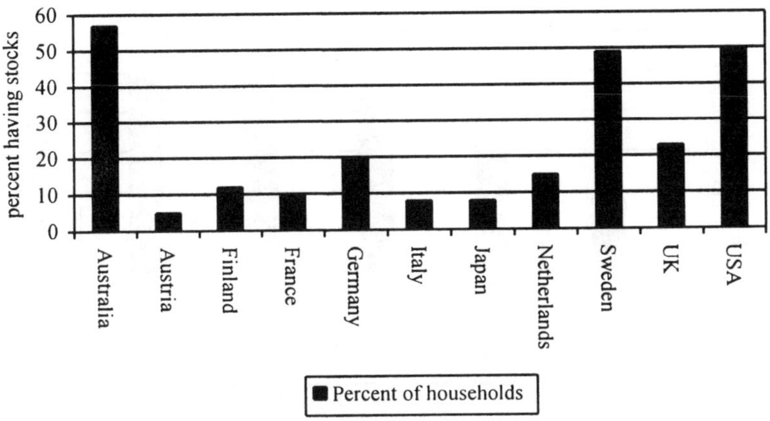

Figure I.1 Households in Eleven Countries Having Stocks (percent)

Why are there such differences? That the US households to a large extent own stocks may come as no surprise, but the fact that Sweden, which has a much lower average per capita GNP than most OECD countries has as high a proportion of stock-owning households as 50 percent is more astounding. The economic systems in these two countries are in many ways different, Sweden being one of the highest taxed countries in the world. Sweden has a comprehensive system of social benefits, including an old-age pension system that is fairly generous to low- and low-middle- income earners. Retirement saving is expected to be lower when there are comparatively generous old-age pensions, which seems to be the case in France. Still, in Sweden people invest much of their savings in stocks or in mutual funds.

The fact that participation in mutual funds was encouraged by tax incentives from the early 1980s probably led many Swedish savers to discover the benefits of investing in stocks. Participation was usually arranged as a monthly deduction from wages and salaries which tended to be perceived as a fixed, unavoidable expenditure. When stock prices rose many people were surprised to find out how much money they had actually saved. In the early 1990s, privatization of government-owned companies served to augment interest in stocks among the general public. In Figure I.2, a comparison is made between Sweden and the Netherlands for frequency of stock holding in age groups (see Wärneryd, 2000b). A distinct picture emerges: stock owning is much more frequent in all age groups in Sweden and the discrepancy is already there in the youngest groups.

While there are relatively few stock owners in many Western countries, those countries evince clear tendencies towards a wider spread of stock ownership. At the same time, in countries such as the USA and Sweden where owner-

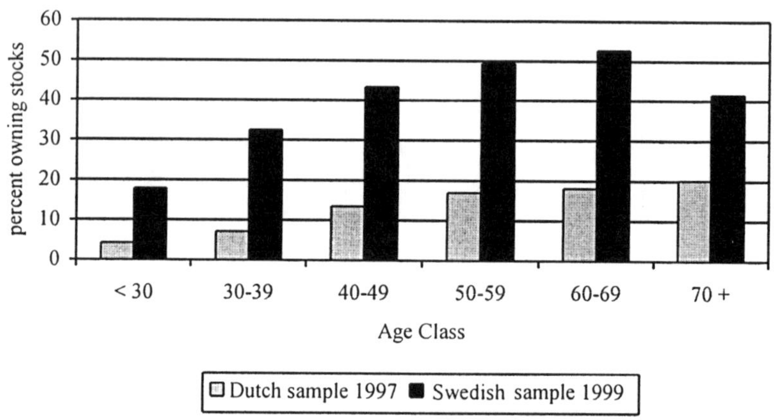

Figure I.2 Ownership of Stocks in Age Classes in the Netherlands and Sweden

ship is already widespread, the portion of wealth placed in stocks and the number of stock owners have been rapidly increasing over the last decade and the increase seems to continue. Apparent reasons for this development are:

1. The long-run profitability of investing in stock for retirement purposes
2. The short-run possibility of becoming rich
3. Low interest rates, which together with taxes on interest make bank savings rather unprofitable
4. Perceived protection against the risk of inflation
5. Expectations (mostly well-founded) of decreasing old-age pensions from public pension systems
6. Intensive advertising and other marketing campaigns for privatization of government-owned stocks.

There seem to be good reasons for expecting increased investment in stocks, at least in the long run, albeit the burst of some so-called bubbles may deter investment for a while. With increasing participation in the stock market a new type of investor emerges. These investors may be even less like the rational investor of financial economics than present investors and the need for psychological interpretations of the stock market will increase.

The Image of the Non-Rational Investor

> *To want more than you have, whether in monetary or other terms, is a basic human instinct. As they sang in 'South Pacific', if you don't have a dream, how can you have a dream come true?*
>
> *The Economist* (September 11–17, 1999, S11)

My starting point for this book was an idea about how private investors in stocks, bonds, and mutual funds tended to behave and the changes in investor behavior that might follow the ongoing recruitment of broad new groups of stock holders. The prevalent picture of speculating, continually active investors looked too simplified, not to say wrong. Many stock holders were now reported to stick to their investments over long periods of time, to tend to favor well-known companies, rarely to sell and rather to add to their holdings. When stock prices have long-term tendencies to go up, such investors become prosperous, which ultimately will increase their propensity to spend money on riskier assets and on more lavish consumption. Many of them save for a 'golden' retirement. Those who make short-term investments to save up for not too distant purchases tend to lose or make lower gains, due to short-term variations in stock rates and bond interest rates. Those who speculate and buy and sell continuously end up with lower wealth than the less-active first category. Those who really gamble on the stock market and freely buy and sell stocks and/or derivatives in a few cases end up very rich but, in many cases, lose everything.

The purpose of the book is to review the evidence for these views of mine and to use both economic and psychological reasoning and findings to establish the case. More as an afterthought, I sketch some possible consequences for financial markets of what may predominantly be prudent investor behavior such as overevaluation of well-known firms on the stock market. In a review of research on German investors, Müller-Peters (1999, p.138) makes a point of the fact that the German stock owner hardly corresponds to the rational investor of financial theory. The typical investor does not diversify, shows low spread of assets and holds on to the assets for long periods of time rather than being active in the market. My focus in this book is on the investors who are not rational in the economic sense and less emotional than in mass media stories. While they may be viewed as disturbances, turbulence-creating nuisances or 'noise traders', which is the preferred term in finance, many of them seem to be doing well and succeed in providing security for their old age or for some shorter-run goals.

Much of the discussion about investing in financial markets presupposes that people are very active traders and make continual adjustments to their portfolios. Only recently, research evidence has appeared indicating that more passive investors may be doing much better than inveterate traders (De Bondt, 1998; Odean, 1998; Barber and Odean, 2000b). Whereas there are many books giving advice to would-be investors and a few good recent attempts at dealing more extensively with psychological factors in investing (Shefrin, 2000; Shiller, 2000; Shleifer, 2000), most of the theory developments and serious applications of modern psychology, notably cognitive and social psychology, are spread out in a large number of journal articles. Thaler (1992) explored some of the implications in an early work in the field. De Bondt (1998) gives a good overview of the issues and reports research results. Shefrin (2000) discusses in great detail implications for practitioners in the finance area. Shiller (2000) gives a coherent account of how psychological and other factors have influenced the stock markets and also makes some – rather gloomy – predictions. Shleifer (2000) integrates findings from cognitive psychology and behavioral finance in an attack on the dominant theory and develops alternative theory.

Judging from casual as well as systematic observations of the stock market, it appears that stock prices are determined by two sets of factors. One set is the actual and expected dividends or returns and includes expected growth of the firm. So-called mispricing of stocks can then be a consequence of bad guesses about future returns, of expectations that do not come true. The psychology of expectation formation can contribute towards explaining why mathematical expectations failed. The other set has to do with what investors believe other investors will be willing to pay for a certain stock. The field is then open for loans of a variety of psychological concepts, from the relative clarity of cognitive research to obfuscating psychoanalysis (cf. Lifson and Geist, 1999). The theories that dominate the thinking about financial market behavior are, however, economic and apply the mathematics of rationality to all reasoning on behavior.

Ordinary private investors who are interested in long-term security on the basis of investments are called 'noise traders' in financial theory and are often held responsible for fluctuations and even crashes in financial markets. They are not driven by instinct to maximize their gains, but to get satisfactory results over the long run. It does not seem right that ordinary investors are looked down upon both in theory and in practical advisory work. Many investors have made money on their investments despite neglecting theoretical and practical rules for financial behavior. They deserve better theory that explains their successes and failures.

Using economic rationality as a benchmark or criterion for judging financial behavior, one easily notes that observed behavior mostly deviates from the ideal model of rationality. Explanations of such behavior may underline the difficulties of being rational due to a lack of information and limited cognitive capacity in humans, or they may suggest that economic considerations are not the only important and relevant considerations made, unless economic utility encompasses a broad set of values and emotions. Psychologists may tend to be misled by such observations and explanations into believing that economic factors lack importance. They should not be. In economic psychology, the prevailing tendency is to combine economic and other factors in attempts at explaining economic behavior; this should include economic motivation, which can be essential even though individual decision makers are not rational in the economic sense.

ECONOMIC PSYCHOLOGY AND BEHAVIORAL FINANCE

Some people think that behavioral finance introduced psychology into finance, but psychology was never out of finance. Although models of behavior differ, all behavior is based on psychology.

Statman (1999, p.19)

In a lecture some years ago, Professor Werner De Bondt, one of the leaders in behavioral finance, submitted – tongue in cheek – that there were three approaches in the history of financial economics. The first approach was characterized by assumptions of perfect markets and perfect people who behaved as rational humans in the way prescribed by von Neumann and Morgenstern. This approach still prevails as modern finance. The second approach comprised imperfect markets and perfect people and was inspired by institutional economics. The approach could be called institutional finance. The third approach gave room for both imperfect markets and imperfect people. It was labeled behavioral finance.

When psychological thinking is applied to financial markets in search of explanations for behavior that apparently deviates from what is expected on the basis of economic theory, and efficient-market theory in particular, the applications are often referred to as *behavioral finance*. While there are several ways of delimiting the field, Statman's (1999) discussion clarifies the difference between standard finance and behavioral finance. He says that market efficiency has two meanings. To some people it means that there is no systematic way to beat the market. To others, it means that security prices are assumed to be rational. If rational, prices reflect only 'fundamental' or 'utilitarian' characteristics which include 'risk'. They do not comprise psychological or 'value-expressive' characteristics such as sentiment. The psychological characteristics include many loans from cognitive psychology such as heuristics and biases and mental accounting, concepts that will be dealt with in later chapters.

In my view, the field of economic psychology covers these phenomena – and many more. This does not imply that behavioral finance is necessarily a subdivision of economic psychology. Based on what has for many years been characteristic of research in economic psychology, some differences as well as similarities between the approaches should be pointed out. In economic psychology, notably financial psychology, more attention is paid to the psychological intricacies of financial behavior and attempts are made to relate the problems to psychological theory.

Financial psychology has long been a branch of economic psychology. It deals with financial affairs and financial management in the household. Saving behavior has been a topic of special interest and, in this connection, household and individual investment has also been included in the study. Once in a while, research on investments and investment decisions has been published in the *Journal of Economic Psychology* in its almost 20 years of existence. Over the last few years, there has been a steadily increasing interest among psychologists to attack problems of financial behavior. In cognitive psychology, judgments and decisions under uncertainty form an important area of study. The problems studied are often close to financial psychology and are sometimes directly relevant to it. The work by Daniel Kahneman and Amos Tversky has drawn special attention and these authors have themselves applied their thinking to financial behavior. Their ideas of loss aversion, framing of decision situations and the use of heuristics have flowed into economists' attention span in the search for explanations of irrational behavior. The ideas have also eagerly been seized upon by practitioners.

Behavioral finance is sometimes defined as the application of (certain) findings in cognitive psychology to financial behavior. De Bondt and Thaler (1985) were early in using the representativeness heuristic to explain overreactions to news. Recently, Thaler (1999a) declared the end of behavioral finance, intimating that all finance must accept some psychological explanations of financial behavior so that the tag 'behavioral' was no longer necessary. Shefrin (2000), who deals primarily with investment in stocks, discusses behavioral finance as an alternative to efficient-market theory and notes that while it is useful for the practitioner to be well versed in cognitive psychology, there is still much truth in efficient-market theory at the aggregate level. He reports on many cognitive psychological concepts developed in the Kahneman–Tversky approach and used in behavioral finance. Fama (1998) downplays behavioral finance as an alternative to efficient-market theory and demands a clearly formulated alternative, for example based on the representativeness heuristic, before accepting the challenge.

There appear to be some differences in approach between economic psychology and behavioral finance. The differences represent different focuses of interest as well as some more fundamental issues. Researchers in economic psychology mostly work in the tradition of empirical psychological research and use well-specified models sparsely. They rely on survey data and on experimental data. Researchers in behavioral finance continue in the economic research tradition with well-specified models and demand a plausible micro model supporting the aggregate model. They tend to accept what psychologists may think of as more flimsy evidence at the market level as confirmation of their micro models. Psychologists prefer to make rather strict tests of their hypotheses at the individual level before those are tentatively accepted.

A notable difference between economic psychology and behavioral finance is the focus on individual differences in the former. In economic psychology, the analyses are often aimed at finding clusters or segments of individuals or households that have minimal variance inside the segment and maximal variance between the segments. While researchers in behavioral finance who are preoccupied with the market level tend to consider the whole market as one entity, researchers in economic psychology tend to analyze possible actions and reactions for each segment separately. One segment may react to a price drop by selling, another by doing nothing, and a third by buying (the same number of stocks are sold and bought). Financial economists and practitioners may recognize such differences, but they apparently prefer to talk about a single, currently dominating, type of stock holder and not about investor segments with maybe different ways of reacting to new information. Unlike reactions of segments may be important for total effect.

CONTENTS OF THE BOOK

The first two chapters comprise modern views of financial markets. In the first chapter, the focus is on financial theories in their pure economic form. In the second, the perspective moves to attempts at modifying the theories as a consequence of market observations that do not agree with the predictions of the theory. Chapters 3 to 7 are based on the major areas of psychology: (1) expectation formation, (2) judgments and decisions, (3) cognitive capacity, (4) emotions, and (5) social psychology. All the time note is taken of applications to finance. Two chapters are then devoted to behavioral research on investing in stocks. The final chapter brings together ideas from the earlier chapters and pushes them a little further towards application in research and in practice.

In efficient markets, traders are assumed to react rationally to new information. This means that they revise their probability judgments when there is new information. They act as Bayes' theorem prescribes. In Chapter 1, a brief review of Bayes' theorem and some simple examples are first given. Then the dominating economic theory, the *efficient-market theory*, is introduced. The theory is founded on the economic postulate of rationality and it presupposes rational expectations. Much of the theoretical thinking on security price developments is based on the Capital Asset Pricing Model (CAPM), which deals with how security prices are formed, and the Mean-Variance Model for the composition of portfolios. A fundamental consequence of the former model is that investors vary their portfolios of assets in accordance with their degree of risk aversion. While more risk-averse investors should have more in riskless cash, all investors should have the same proportion of less risky and riskier risk assets. The chapter reviews some attempts at explaining observed deviations from theory such as financial bubbles, booms, and crashes. It also looks at some of the attempts to elaborate the models to make them better predictors of market behavior. The primary aim of the treatment in Chapter 1 is to ascertain where psychological assumptions are made and how those are handled.

Chapter 2 goes a little deeper into the deviations from efficient-market theory and pays special attention to the assumption that two types of traders are in the market: rational traders and noise traders. Noise traders are characterized by economically irrational behavior in the sense that they are assumed to deal inadequately with financial information. Their behavior may be given many psychological interpretations based on cognitive and social psychology. The Behavioral Capital Asset Pricing Model of Shefrin and Statman (1994) is briefly reviewed. A number of strategies and tactics are discussed, such as contrarian and momentum strategies, which are more or less related to mean-reversion assumptions and are apparently used by some active investors. Attempts to reconcile efficient-market theory with the existence of bubbles and crashes have involved introducing intriguing assumptions about hidden information and diffusion of private information. As a contrast, a behavioral view of information diffusion and use is described.

Decision models in financial economics contain two dominating concepts: expectation and risk. Both of these appear in economics as well as in psychology, but they do not have the same meaning in the two sciences. Mathematical expectation and expectations held by humans tend to be different. Chapter 3 is devoted to a discussion of expectation formation and change. A simple model is presented as a way of structuring the problems and utilizing findings from psychological research. Rational expectations theory stresses the significance of information for forming expectations, albeit information is defined in a rather limited economic–theoretical manner. In stock markets, the interplay between investors' earlier experience, personal or vicarious, that is, mediated by others, and new information is crucial. A persistent question is: when a stock price has been going up or down for some time, what new information can possibly reverse expectations?

Chapter 4 deals with decision making, the psychological concept of risk, and risk attitudes. It introduces some ideas from the research on dynamic decision making. Dynamic decision making is complex; it involves the consideration of earlier decisions, and that many variables in a system may be affected by a single decision. Studies of such decision making using simulation games, so-called microworlds, have shown the many types of errors that decision makers tend to commit. Similar errors can probably occur in financial decision making. Prospect theory, which has had a great influence on thinking in behavioral finance, is briefly presented with a focus on the concept of loss aversion: 'losses loom larger than gains'. Finally, it is noted that brokerage firms and advisors sometimes use regular tests for risk taking to categorize their clients' willingness to take risks in investing. Some methods to study willingness to take risks are reviewed.

It is sometimes said that behavioral finance has its foundation in the psychological approach called 'heuristics and biases'. Chapter 5 exposes the psychological underpinnings of behavioral finance and reports research on so-called cognitive errors or cognitive biases and a number of heuristics. Heuristics are simple behavioral rules of thumb that facilitate decision making. Studies of expert advice to investors as well as studies of portfolio composition suggest that the theoretical rules of market conduct are often broken by both professionals and private investors. Ad-hoc attempts at explanations invoke cognitive biases such as the representativeness heuristic and social influences like herd behavior and the force of fashions. The chapter is primarily based on cognitive psychology and it pays attention to recent challenges to the cognitive-error approach. The new view that is spreading is that man uses fast and frugal heuristics which are smart rather than irrational deviations from an ideal model the goals and rules of which can never be attained.

Chapter 6 brings in a broad topic which can be called 'emotionality', and elucidates the role of what Keynes called 'animal spirits', which lead to overoptimism. Overreactions to information are often ascribed to optimism and overconfidence. The uses of these concepts in finance refer to market-level phenomena. Stock-price curves rather than traders overreact or underreact or display optimism or pessimism. Cognitive findings have in finance been much more used than results from the research on emotions. Explanations that cite emotions as contributory causes of unexpected events are often based more on everyday observation than on systematic research. Mood, affect, and emotion, which are now frequently summed up as 'market sentiment' and which are commonly used when stock-price jumps are discussed in the news media, are defined and their use in psychology is explained. Motivation stands for drives that give direction and goals for action; especially achievement motivation may be essential for risky activities like investment in stocks. Finally, self-control, which is often treated as a matter of volition, has returned to economics and psychology after a long period of oblivion. Some modern trends in the thinking about self-regulation are reviewed.

Chapter 7 approaches the subject of social influence and discusses the many open or more subtle ways in which humans influence other humans. Herd behavior has become a common term in connection with stock-exchange crashes. Attempts to explain crashes have launched theories of information diffusion that involve ideas about crowd or herd behavior. There is more in sociological and social-psychological research in this field than has hitherto been used. The chapter describes humans as members of large and small groups with a view to understanding individuals and investor segments. Small-group research can contribute many ideas for research in finance where social interaction is important. Positive-feedback theories in financial economics presume that investors are influenced by their own and others' successes in the market. These theories get support from causal attribution theory, which has been tested in many contexts. Self-attribution of successes and blaming of others or unlucky circumstances for failures are common findings in psychology, which agree with explanations of financial behavior.

Chapter 8 reviews empirical studies of investor behavior. While there are many studies based on aggregate data, differently interpreted with the help of behavioral assumptions, behavioral studies of investors are few. Two early US studies hinted that stock owners were less active than earlier assumed and, in particular, that they diversified less than they were supposed to. Some data from more recent Dutch and Swedish inquiries are analyzed. The former VSB Panel, now called CentER Data, supplied detailed data on a small group of Dutch stock owners who were questioned in six annual interview waves. A plethora of economic and psychological variables is available for this panel. The variables include the composition of assets, degree of control of expenditures, attitudes towards saving, perceived knowledge about financial matters, attitudes towards risk, and expectations about future income. Analyses of risk attitudes, asset portfolio composition, activity level, and diversification are presented. Some data from a comprehensive German survey are also presented. Judging from some US research results, it is likely that those who are moderately active and invest very carefully are the winners in the long run. Finally, some results from experimental asset markets are introduced. The research findings indicate that many investors in stocks tend to be passive, prefer to buy rather than to sell, and do not live up to the common image of the stock owner as active and steadily on the look-out for new opportunities to make a profit.

Chapter 9 elaborates on the idea that there are differences between investors and that investors can be grouped into segments with different characteristics. With some delay and with much hesitation, financial economists in the mid-1980s granted that there might be two kinds of investors: rational traders and noise traders. Later, suggestions were made for three groups: smart-money traders, passive investors, and noise traders. Recent studies have used data on individual asset portfolios or attitude data to classify clusters of investors. Generally, it is found that only a small minority are active traders even in the most active segments. On the basis of the empirical studies, a behavioral categorization is presented. It assumes that there are in the main four groups or segments of private investors, who differ in their approach to investing in stocks. Members of one group want to secure the long-term value of their assets and preferably increase it through careful investing in stocks, never taking risks they cannot afford in case of a bad outcome. A second group consists of investors with similar aspirations, but those have considerable wealth so that they can take more risks. A third group comprises those who speculate in stocks and take advanced risks. They are the really active group of investors who continually buy and sell stocks (and rarely beat the index). A fourth group might be added: naive investors who are enticed by stories of high profits. Some of them may be lured by the marketing efforts that accompany privatization sales of stocks in government-owned companies in Western Europe.

Chapter 10 is an attempt to summarize the findings and draw some conclusions about private investor behavior. It underlines the need for behavioral studies and thinking in the financial markets. With new categories of stock owners entering the markets in many countries, more and more privately owned stocks will probably be owned by quite passive stock owners who have limited means. This may have a dampening effect in bear markets if loss aversion is as strong as recent research suggests. A closer look at individual investor behavior will be necessary and should be interesting to psychological researchers. While the subject matter of the book is not aimed at being normative, some wisdom for practical use can possibly be culled from reading the book. Private investors and their advisors may find it useful to know a little more about why human characteristics such as limited cognitive capacity, emotions, and susceptibility to influence make it difficult to be rational in the economic sense. They may also find that their guesses about other people's financial behavior, called irrationality by economists, may be slightly improved and become more useful in planning investments.

1. Efficient Markets and Rational Models of Portfolio Choice

It is obvious from the statutes concerning crédit mobilier *which were enacted in November 1852 that nothing less than control over the stock exchange was intended. Louis Napoleon would have needed to be a lesser admirer and imitator of his uncle than he proved himself to be through the decrees of 1851–1852, if he had not, like the first Napoleon, paid great attention to the stock exchange. For already under Napoleon I, the Bourse had become an important cultural power which, at a time when public opinion was repressed by armed force and the newspapers were edited by the prefects, had remained the only public medium through which the Nation could announce its opinions about the actions of the Government. Napoleon I tumbled, however, into the mistake that he did not take the Bourse for the barometer that showed the weather, but held it for an institution that made the weather. When the Bourse showed bad weather, that is, when the stock rates dropped because of some event or action by the Emperor, he became very annoyed and complained over the ingratitude of the capitalists whom he had saved from the dangers of the revolution, and tried by artificial means to push the Bourse and even to intimidate the Bourse, through which he only achieved the opposite of what he aimed at, and when it succeeded for a short while, it only misrepresented the mood of the Bourse, similar to a woman who smashed the mirror that showed her first wrinkle. Instead of removing the causes, he rather deprived himself, in so far as it was at all possible, of a wise advisor.*

Wirth (1874, pp.250–51; my translation)

The purpose of the chapter is to give an overview of financial theories and sort out psychological variables that can be included in behavioral studies in finance. *Efficient-market theory* is the main economic and financial theory about what happens in financial markets. *Portfolio theory* tells investors how they should go about putting together their portfolios of assets. Behavioral studies of financial behavior can be made with no guidance from financial theories, but there are great advantages in starting with what is known in financial economics. It gives structure to the study of behavior, and in fact many findings and advanced thinking in the field provide food for thought for the psychological study of financial behavior. A fundamental assumption in financial-market theory is that the individual knows and observes the Bayesian rules for handling probabilities. Bayes' theorem is an important starting point for many theoretical discussions of uncertainty. It is normative in the sense that it prescribes how people should act. Used as a description of how people, de facto, deal with probabilities, it has shown serious deficiencies.

BAYES' THEOREM AND THE HANDLING OF PROBABILITIES

The classical probabilists of the Enlightenment, including Condorcet, Poisson, and Laplace, equated probability theory with the common sense of educated people, who were known then as 'hommes éclairés'. . . The available mathematical tools, in particular the theorems of Bayes and Bernoulli, were seen as descriptions of actual human judgment.

Gigerenzer and Hoffrage (1995, p.684)

Investing money in assets means dealing with the uncertainties of the future and taking a position in relation to them. Nobody can know exactly what will happen to stock prices and dividends in the short run and hardly in the long run. Guesses about the future can be more or less well founded. In financial economics, the main toolbox is furnished by probability theory: probabilities quantify uncertainty (Edwards, 1982). A fundamental assumption in financial theory is that people act in accordance with Bayes' theorem, that they are Bayesian. Probability is interpreted as a subjective measure of belief. As distinguished from the frequentist school, Bayesian thinking allows individuals to assign probabilities to unique events, such as the awarding of this year's Prize in Alfred Nobel's memory to a named economist. Frequentists see probability as long-run relative frequency and refuse to assign probabilities to unique events. Bayesians assume that people revise their probabilities in accordance with new information.

Bayes' theorem or law can be written as follows:

$$p(H \mid D) = \frac{p(H)p(D \mid H)}{p(H)p(D \mid H) + p(-H)p(D \mid -H)}$$

where

$p(H \mid D)$ is the *posterior* probability of hypothesis H after datum D has been observed;

$p(H)$ is the *prior* or base-rate probability of hypothesis H before D is observed;

$p(D \mid H)$ is the probability that D will be observed if H is true;

$p(H)p(D \mid H)$ is the *posterior* probability of D when H has been observed

$p(-H)p(D \mid -H)$ is the *posterior* probability of D when non-H has been observed; and

$p(D) = p(H)p(D \mid H) + p(-H)p(D \mid -H)$ is the unconditional probability of D.

An example taken from Kemeny et al. (1962, p.156) illustrates the use.

1. Ten percent of the employees of a certain company have been to business school. Of these, 70 per cent hold administrative positions.
2. Of those that have not been to business school, 30 per cent hold administrative positions.
3. An employee is selected at random from the administrative staff. What is the probability that s/he went to business school?
4. Let $p(H)$ be the probability that the person has been to business school and $p(D)$ be the probability that s/he belongs to the administrative staff.

The sought probability is $P(H \mid D)$. Using the above formula it is calculated as follows:

$$p(H) = 0.10$$
$$p(D \mid H) = 0.70$$
$$p(H)p(D \mid H) = 0.10 * 0.70$$
$$p(-H)p(D \mid -H) = 0.90 * 0.30$$

$$p(H \mid D) = \frac{p(H)p(D \mid H)}{p(H)p(D \mid H) + p(-H)p(D \mid -H)}$$
$$= \frac{0.10 * 0.70}{0.10 * 0.70 + 0.90 * 0.30} = 0.21$$

The prior probability, $p(H)$= 0.10, is the base rate for having been to business school. Without further information this would have been the best guess. When it is known that the person belongs to the administrative staff, the probability can be revised in accordance with Bayes' theorem. The new or posterior probability is 0.21, which is of course higher since new facts have been used.

A more complicated illustration is drawn from Edwards (1982, p.361). Suppose you have two bookbags, both with 1000 chips.

1. One bag contains 700 red and 300 blue chips. The other bag contains 300 red and 700 blue chips.
2. A coin is flipped to decide which bag to choose; that is, the probability of being chosen is $p = 0.5$.
3. From the chosen bag 12 random samples are drawn, with replacement of chips after each drawing.
4. The twelve samples result in 8 reds and 4 blues. What is the probability that the samples have been drawn from the bag with 700 red and 300 blue chips?

The answer is $p = 0.97$, which is much higher than what most people think. Since the calculation involves a rather complex procedure and is not done quickly, even experts hesitate when they have to give a fast answer (Edwards, 1982).

Bayes' theorem is particularly useful when updating base-rate probabilities on the basis of specific data (Hogarth, 1987). Many tests have shown that people do not revise probabilities as they should when there is new information. They tend to concentrate on the new information and forget the base rate, especially if the information is perceived as being causal. A common failure is to forget the base rates and look exclusively or primarily at the observed probability. Tversky and Kahneman (1982a, 1982d) called this neglect of base rates 'the base-rate fallacy' or 'the representativeness heuristic'. This heuristic will be treated in much more detail in Chapter 5 since it plays an important role in behavioral finance.

The calculations are no doubt difficult in many cases. Gigerenzer and Hoffrage (1995) suggest that experimental subjects do better when frequencies are used instead of probabilities and they demonstrate in their experiments evidence that confirms their view. It may be impossible to act as a Bayesian, as Dawes (1999) suggests, because probabilities cannot be combined by humans without a good story. The story must be relevant and justify the combination. In practice, problems may rarely be structured in such a way that Bayesian solutions are possible. Gigerenzer and Goldstein (1996) and Gigerenzer and Todd (1999) discuss simple heuristics that might make people rather good problem solvers. These ideas will be further explored in Chapter 5 under the section title 'Inferences about the Unknown'.

FINANCIAL MARKETS AS EFFICIENT MARKETS

> *The so-called random walk theory was born when two types of research – theoretical and empirical – zeroed in on the same idea. In papers by Moore (1962), Granger and Morgenstern (1963) and Fama (1965), the authors claimed to demonstrate empirically that stock movements are random. At the same time, two major theory papers by Samuelson (1965) and Mandelbrot (1966) proved that if (a) information-gathering is cheap, (b) buying and selling are costless, and (c) everyone interprets information in the same way, then stock market prices are martingales, and changes in prices of stocks behave as random walks. The implication of the efficient-market theory is, in Cootner's words (1964), that 'prices have no memory, and yesterday has nothing to do with tomorrow.' It follows that careful study of the history of a given stock's price is, for a profit-seeking investor, pointless.*
>
> Maital et al. (1986, p.275)

The function of a financial market is to ensure that financial resources are allocated to productive uses in the most efficient way. Economists construct an ideal model of an optimally functioning market and compare reality with the ideal model. *Efficient markets* are defined as markets where all available information is fully reflected in prices. All information is public and all traders reveal their information through their purchase or selling bids. Stock prices immediately absorb all new information. Stock prices are assumed to follow a random walk in which ups are as likely as downs. A consequence is that no prediction of future prices can be made on the basis of current prices since all information is already contained in the current prices. Changes in stock prices do not show any pattern since if there was a pattern some traders (arbitrageurs) would spot it and make profits from the identification. The pattern would disappear as a consequence of being discerned.

Investors should only look at the (future) fundamentals of stocks: dividends and earnings growth of the firm. The theory implies that one cannot consistently beat the performance of a random selection of stocks – a shocking conclusion for investors who believe in their own skills. What is rational behavior in an efficient market? According to financial theory and rational expectations theory, rationality involves gains being maximized over a period, using the best available information. Trading is triggered when the marginal income from an alternative portfolio becomes larger than the income from the current one. Deviations from the predictions of the theory are explained by random deviations from rationality that cause undue fluctuations in the market rates. Such deviations are often called psychological, and attributed to the influence of cognitive and social-psychological, sometimes purely emotional, factors. The defenders of efficient-market theory maintain that the deviations are not large enough to disconfirm the theory.

In an efficient market, stock prices are determined by expected future dividends, discounted to present value and corrected for inflation:

$$P_{it} = \sum_{k=0}^{\infty} \frac{E_t D_{t+k}}{(1+r)^{k+1}}$$

where

P_{it} is the price of stock i at time t;
$E_t\, D_{t+k}$ is the expected value of any real dividend in the time period; and
r is the discount rate.

D includes both dividends and capital gains or losses, since returns on investments comprise both dividends and changes in (real) prices ($P_{t+1} - P_t$). The price of the security is the cash flow over a number of periods, discounted to the present so as to make comparisons possible. The discount rate may vary between individuals, but is usually assumed to be a market rate. It corresponds to time preference, which can be seen as a measure of degree of impatience (Fisher, 1930). Impatient people use high discount rates when they make comparisons among future returns. All available information about future prices is used in accordance with rational expectations theory. Prices are assumed to reflect all available information. New information about factors affecting fundamentals is the only thing that counts, in accordance with rational expectations theory. Extrapolation theories of expectation formation and adaptive expectation theory should as a consequence not be able to explain expectations. Elaborations of efficient-market theory may involve the assumption that stock prices are set by a market maker or smart-money traders to be equal to the expected fundamental value of the security (Lee, 1998).

Are stock prices then unpredictable? Or can changes in prices be forecast on the basis of new information that concerns future earnings or dividends (and prices)? If you accept efficient-market theory, the answer to the latter question is 'no'. Critics of the theory who subscribe to behavioral finance theory tend to answer a hesitant 'yes' . Prices can be predicted if the systematic nature of the errors that investors make is recognized and studied. Cognitive bias can to some extent at least be predicted.

Keynes (1936) talked about time preference in two senses: (1) the propensity to consume (or save), and (2) the liquidity of the postponed consumption means. The second dimension is now often called the *portfolio choice* and relates to the question: when do savers become investors? This does not preclude the observation that some investors are not savers in most of the senses of the word. They may start their investing careers with few assets of their own and buy shares and options on borrowed money. Typically, investment models start with a situation in which an individual is equipped with some amount of money and wants to make a choice of assets in which to invest. These models do not deal with the question of why the individual wants to invest money. This is taken care of by theories of saving, in the first place the Life-Cycle Hypothesis (LCH) which focuses on future consumption needs, especially after retirement, under the assumption that people want to maintain approximately the same standard of living over their whole life (see, for example, Wärneryd, 1999).

The Challenging of Efficient-Market Theory

Efficient-market theory has been challenged on the basis of empirical data that seem hard to reconcile with the predictions of the theory. Shefrin and Statman (1994) cite a number of such incongruous findings: (1) abnormal returns due to firm size, (2) variability in earnings-to-price ratios, (3) the performance of past winners and losers, (4) turn-of-year effects, (5) excessive volatility, and (6) the equity-premium puzzle. The list is far from exhaustive. For example, the emergence of bubbles and crashes could be added. Many of these challenges will be dealt with in this and the following chapter.

Strategies for optimal individual investor behavior are derived from financial theory and actual behaviors are mostly scrutinized in the light of optimal behavior. Investors are assumed to be Bayesian, which means that they revise their subjective probabilities when they get new information that affects the prior probabilities. The private investor hardly recognizes her/himself or finds guidance for investing behavior in the theories. Comparisons with an ideal model give opportunities for improving performance on the proviso that the guidelines derived can be followed in reality. It is hard to dispute the normative superiority of models based on pure rationality despite their lack of descriptive adequacy. If better descriptive theory is arrived at from other assumptions than rationality, can a better normative theory then be achieved? It is conceivable that better advice could be given to the private investor on the basis of a better descriptive theory. To the extent that expert advice on investments in stocks is not based on efficient-market theory, it is likely to be based on observations of empirical phenomena and little on coherent theory. Fama (1998) complains that those who criticize the theory do not themselves provide any alternative theory that could be tested. He notes that the alternatives are not coherent and so vague that they cannot be pinned down and presented as real alternatives. Both underreactions and overreactions have been proposed as explanations without reconciling the two: 'An efficient market generates categories of events that individually suggest that prices overreact to information. But in an efficient market, apparent underreaction will be about as frequent as overreaction' (Fama, 1998, p.284).

While the fact that stock prices deviate from the theory is recognized by its adherents, the assumptions about rational investors are said to be valid for the representative investor who supposedly corresponds to the professional actors or arbitrageurs in the market. Professional investors who represent large funds, insurance companies, investment and other banks and who may serve as influential advisors to private investors may attempt to make rational calculation or at least strive to observe rules of rationality and partake of analysts' work. It is still likely that most investors, acting on their own or as professionals, develop their own, often simplified techniques – heuristics – as a complement to painstaking analysis when they make investing decisions. Such heuristics, many of which may not even be described in cognitive literature, are subjectively felt to be rational and may give satisfactory results, granted the realities of the financial market.

In one of his many defenses of efficient-market theory, Fama rejects cognitive and other psychological attempts to remedy the theory:

> Market efficiency survives the challenge from the literature on long-term return anomalies. Consistent with the market efficiency hypothesis that the anomalies are chance results, apparent overreaction to information is about as common as underreaction, and post-event continuation of pre-event abnormal returns is about as fre-

> quent as post-event reversal. Most important, consistent with the market efficiency prediction that apparent anomalies can be due to methodology, most long-term return anomalies tend to disappear with reasonable changes in technique (Fama, 1998, Abstract, p.283).

While Fama admits that there are deviations from efficiency, he maintains that they balance out. For example, if all information is not used by every investor, there will always be other investors making a profit on the basis of the information. Markets will be brought back towards efficiency through the trading of arbitrageurs who exploit favorable price differences.

The assumptions of the rational use of information that lie behind efficient-market theory have been challenged from several angles, among others:

1. All information may not be reflected in stock prices because of delays; all information is not public; investors may have gained experience that they do not make public through operations in the market.
2. Investors may not deal with probabilities in the way prescribed by Bayes' theorem.
3. Investors are not independent of one another; there may be herd behavior.
4. The time perspective used: long-term variations in stock prices may be closer to a random walk than short-term price movements.

Many of the presentations in the following chapters will deal with the first three points of criticism, introduce the criticisms in more detail and relate relevant findings in cognitive and social psychology. Recent research in behavioral finance has borrowed many concepts and methods from cognitive psychology in the first place and social psychology in the second.

The fourth point is illustrated by the finding of Schachter et al. (1986) that there were some periods of random walk on the New York Stock Exchange, but that other periods were far from random: 'There are prolonged periods where price change on the market is independent from day to day and prolonged periods when the market demonstrates dependence, for yesterday's price change does, to some extent, predict today's price change' (Schachter et al., 1986, pp.253–4). The authors note that whereas Fama (1965) found that the stock-price movements on the New York Stock Exchange followed a random walk in his study of four and a half years, they extended the study to 14 years. Their conclusion is that it must be recognized that stock price is a *social* fact:

> [T]he price of a stock is more than an objective, rationally determined number; it is an opinion, an aggregate opinion, the moment-to-moment resultant of the evaluation of the community of investors. As an opinion, stock price is subject to the same set of social pressures and cultural influences as any other opinion, such as the evaluation of a work of art, the preference for a political candidate, or the popularity and spread of a fad (Schachter et al., 1986, p.254).

The quotation is from one of the few studies of aggregate stock market data carried out by psychologists. Psychological theory was employed to investigate whether there were deviations from randomness in stock-price movements and trade volume and whether such deviations could be better explained by means of the psychological concept of 'dependence'. The authors found that the psychological explanation was useful, but they admitted that their scenario was speculative since they used simple, aggregate indicators of the psychological variable, that is, macropsychological concepts. It is interesting to note what they say about random walks; in another context they report more fully on the South Sea Bubble as a random walk:

> There is abundant evidence that markets are efficient in the sense that prices adjust quickly to new information and that no source of information can be consistently exploited to make profits abnormally greater than the costs of commissions. Deviations from a random walk are small even for events as extreme as the South Sea Bubble (Schachter et al., 1986, p.265).

Rationality in the sense of objectively maximizing utility is questioned by, for example, adherents of bounded rationality theory and of cognitive theories like prospect theory. Purposes of behavior and goals that people set for themselves are difficult to reconcile with formal utility theory and may thus be judged to be less than optimal. They may still be perceived by the individual as rational and they may have the good short-run or long-run consequences that the individual wants. Individual investor behavior in the financial market may be fashioned to secure the attainment of such goals as having reserves for unforeseen expenditures, financial security when one breadwinner is incapacitated or dies, after-retirement financial security with a gilt edge, the good feeling of having money to spare, and the possibility of leaving some legacy and not dying poor. Even if financial behavior is not rational compared to an ideal model, it may still give satisfaction to the individual and this is probably the superior criterion for the individual her- or himself, despite running the risk of being classified as irrational.

THE BASIC PORTFOLIO MODELS: THE CAPITAL ASSET PRICING MODEL

The Capital Asset Pricing Model (CAPM), which was originally based on the works of Sharpe (1964) and Lintner (1965), rests on the basic assumption of perfect competition rather than on market-efficiency theory. The latter primarily deals with the use of information while CAPM makes more restrictive assumptions. The CAPM shows how rational investors should combine risky assets with a given distribution of returns. The model is based on the following important assumptions (Canner et al., 1997):

1. All assets can be freely traded.
2. Investors operate over a one-period planning horizon.
3. Investors can hold long or short positions in all assets.
4. Investors are indifferent between any two portfolios with identical means and variances.
5. A riskless asset exists.

The fourth assumption can be supplemented by the assumption that asset returns are normal, so that the *mean and variance* fully characterize the distribution of returns. The mean is the expectation of the profit to be had from a stock or any other asset. The variance depicts how much up or down the rate of the stock varies and is interpreted as a measure of risk, larger variances involving higher risk. The fifth assumption is simple in theory, but may be questionable in some financial markets. It is usually assumed that cash, bank accounts, and treasury bills represent the riskless alternative.

The reward for holding a risky security as part of a well-diversified portfolio is based on its β (beta) risk, the market or systematic risk. Beta is the ratio of a change in the return on a stock to a change in the returns on all stocks in a stock market. It is the measure of the sensitivity of the asset return to market movements. For asset *i* the risk–pricing relation can be written as:

$$E(R_i) = R_0 + \beta_i * RP_m$$

where

$E(R_i)$ is the expected return on asset *i*

R_0 is the risk-free interest rate

β_i is the sensitivity of asset *i* to market movements; and

RP_m is the market risk premium equal to $E(R_m) - R_0$.

In other words, the expected value of a stock is the yield of a riskless asset and the risk premium, corrected with the sensitivity of the stock to fluctuations in the entire market, that is, the influence of prices of other stocks. Beta is a common risk measure. The risk premium is the higher rate of return that compensates for the higher risk. The riskiness of an individual portfolio is the weighted average of each component stock's beta, with the weights determined by the stock's value in relation to the value of the whole portfolio (Maital et al., 1986). The CAPM involves only that the market risk (β) should be compensated by a risk premium in an efficient market, not the specific firm risks which can be eliminated by diversification (Solnik, 1996, p.231).

Answers to two main questions are sought in this book. The first question pertains to the possibility of distinguishing or inferring any psychological concepts (constructs) in the economic models and exploring the concept using psychological theory. The second concerns to what extent the model under scrutiny serves as a model that is espoused by investors and thus is possible to use for describing investor behavior. The CAPM formula comprises two basic concepts that are studied in both economics and psychology: *expectation* and *risk*. While economists want to derive expectations from objective data and treat them as mathematical expectation, cognitive and social psychologists try to assess expectations as characteristics of individuals that can be inferred from behavior or elicited from people. In both sciences, risk is related to probabilities. Psychologists tend to note the differences between objective and subjective probabilities and entertain some doubts about people's ability to handle probabilities. This will be further commented upon in Chapters 4 and 5.

Researchers have found patterns in stock returns that are not easily explained by CAPM. These are often called anomalies by the researchers although they may rather be sources of hope for practitioners. There are many rule-of-thumb tactics for selecting portfolios, some of them with a more or less remote foundation in the idea of efficient financial markets. A few anomalies that tend to give excess returns to some investors at some times are recognized by defenders of efficient-market theory. Fama and French (1996) identify two kinds of anomalies that appear to give excess returns. One is the effect of firm size. Small firms tend to give higher returns. The other is based on book-to-market ratio. Firms with high book-to-market ratios appear to give excess returns. Fama and French found that a regression model which included these two anomalies explained the excess returns quite well and that the results were consistent with CAPM.

If investors – on average and over time – lack the relevant and necessary data on fundamentals or find them inadequate, they may try to reduce their uncertainty by looking to other investors for cues and guidance. Interviewing other investors about their expectations may in principle be feasible, but the results may not have high validity since the competition may inspire inadequate answers in the interviews. It remains then to guess the expectations, which can be done with some accuracy if the assumptions about the models used by others are plausible. There is a choice between rationality-based behavioral assumptions and a variety of psychological hypotheses about financial behavior.

THE MEAN-VARIANCE MODEL

According to Stiglitz (1990), the problem of determining the fundamental value of an asset to be held for a period of time has three parts. The first part is to estimate the returns (the dividends of stocks) that will be received over time. The second is to estimate the terminal value the asset will have at the end of the period. The third part of the problem is to decide on the discount rates to be used for translating future returns into current values.

Markowitz (1952a) introduced an efficient process for selecting portfolios. His innovation, *mean-variance optimization*, requires financial analysts to estimate expected returns, standard deviations, and correlations. Markowitz showed how analysts could use this information to combine assets optimally so that for a particular level of expected return, the resulting portfolio would offer the lowest possible level of expected risk, usually measured as standard deviation or variance. A continuum of these portfolios displayed in dimensions of expected return and standard deviation is the efficient frontier (Chow et al., 1999). Use of the model leads to *diversification*. Markowitz introduces the model as follows:

> The process of selecting a portfolio may be divided into two stages. The first stage starts with observation and experience and ends with beliefs about the future performances of available securities. The second stage starts with the relevant beliefs about future performances and ends with the choice of portfolio. This paper is concerned with the second stage. We first consider the rule that the investor does (or should) maximize discounted expected, or anticipated, returns. This rule is rejected both as a hypothesis to explain, and as a maxim to guide investment behavior. We next consider the rule that the investor does (or should) consider expected return a desirable thing *and* variance of return an undesirable thing. This rule has many sound points, both as a maxim for, and hypothesis about, investment behavior (Markowitz, 1952a, p.77).

Markowitz did not pay attention to the first stage, which involves collecting and valuing information, and concentrated on risk handling. The theory of portfolio selection uses the mean and the variance to find the optimal combination of securities. It aims at finding the efficient portfolio with minimum variance through modeling the behavior of security prices and the correlations among security returns. The objective is to find the portfolio weights that minimize the level of portfolio risk, which is indicated (proxied) by the variance, subject to a given level of expected rate of return, given by the weighted mean returns of n securities. The portfolio variance is minimized subject to two conditions: (1) the expected return on the portfolio must be maximum, given the level of risk, and (2) all securities must be included.

The implementation of portfolio theory introduces several problems, such as the estimation of the requisite parameters and the sensitivity of the resulting portfolios to small differences in those parameters. Often, the parameters are unreliable because they are estimated from small samples (Chow et al., 1999).

> Recent experience with failed hedge funds has focused attention on a serious limitation of the typical risk-estimation procedure, which is to weight a sample's observations equally in order to estimate risk parameters. Although this procedure may produce reasonable estimates for the full investment horizon, it probably misrepresents a portfolio's risk attributes during periods of turbulence or financial cri-

> sis. In turbulent markets, asset returns tend to become more volatile and more highly correlated. Thus, the diversification that characterizes the sample on average disappears when it is most needed (Chow et al., 1999, p.65).

A recently found weakness is that, in turbulent times, stock returns have a tendency to be highly correlated – all or most of them go up or down at the same time. The variances increase, which means that the risk becomes greater. The benefits of diversification dwindle when all stocks are plummeting in the same way. Remedies aimed at mastering turbulence are suggested:

> There is a certain arbitrariness to measuring returns simply as a function of units of time. In some periods, no significant events will take place to cause prices to change, so returns will essentially reflect noise. In other periods, several important events will influence returns. But the typical estimation of risk parameters assigns as much importance to the periods with no significant events as it does to the event-filled periods. A more informative alternative might be to calibrate returns as a function of events and then to estimate risk parameters from these event-measured observations. This approach might provide a better representation of a portfolio's likely performance during turbulent markets than the time-measured approach (Chow et al., 1999, p.65).

THE MUTUAL-FUNDS SEPARATION THEOREM

'. . . two hundred pound,. . . vill be inwested in your name in – wot do you call them things agin?'
'Wot things?' inquired Sam.
'Them things as is always a-goin' up and down in the city.'
'Omnibuses?' suggested Sam.
'Nonsense,' replied Mr. Weller. 'Them things as is alvays a fluctooatin' and gettin' theirselves inwolved somehow or another with the national debt, and the checquers bills, and all that.'
'Oh! The funds,' said Sam.

Charles Dickens, *The Pickwick Papers* (1836, p 796)

Brokers whose wages rise and fall with bull and bear markets should somewhat downplay common stocks in their private portfolios – unless their job gives them a (legal) edge in knowledge about future stock moves.

Samuelson (1994, p.18)

An investor can be more or less risk averse and this should be reflected in her/his portfolio of securities. The attitude towards risk should influence the composition of the portfolio. Economists like Tobin (1958) and Lintner (1965) have devoted considerable interest to the composition of portfolios with risky assets. Their work resulted in the *mutual-funds separation theorem*, which gives very definite guidance for portfolio composition and is directly related to the most basic CAPM. According to the theorem, more risk-averse investors should hold more of their portfolios in riskless assets such as cash. The composition of risky assets should be the same for all investors. For example, every investor should hold the same ratio of bonds to stocks. The desired balance between risk and return is achieved by varying the proportion invested in the riskless asset. If there is just one fund with risky assets, all who have risky assets have the same mixture of risky assets, but those who are more risk averse have less of their total assets in the fund.

It may be debated whether there actually are riskless assets. Cash suffers from the threat of inflation and may be an easy target for burglars. Treasury bills may be riskless for short periods of time, but history gives some warnings. When risky assets are discussed, a comparison between the proportions of bonds and stocks is often made. Independent of the investor's degree of risk aversion, the ratios of these should be the same in all portfolios. Surveys of investors indicate that individual investors hardly live up the stipulations of the theorem. Popular financial advisors similarly do not appear to obey it:

> When these advisers are asked to allocate portfolios among stocks, bonds, and cash, they recommend more complicated strategies than indicated by the theorem. Moreover, these strategies differ from the theorem in a systematic way. According to these advisers, more risk-averse investors should hold a higher ratio of bonds to stocks. This advice contradicts the conclusion that all investors should hold risky assets in the same proportion (Canner et al., 1997, p.181).

Canner et al. showed that portfolio advisors maintain that more risk-averse investors should hold a higher ratio of bonds to stocks and these authors believe that the advice is heeded by investors. 'A widely cited rule-of-thumb is that the stock portion of the portfolio should equal, in percent, 100 minus the investor's age' (De Bondt, 1998, p.836). A broader diversification problem arises in modern pension systems in which contributors are given the chance to decide which assets (part of) their contributions should be invested in. In the new Swedish public pension system, 2.5 percent of annual wages are left to the individual to decide on. Benartzi and Thaler (1999) reported a study of how what they called 'naive' investors chose among investment alternatives. They found that in the groups they interviewed a common tendency was to use the simple rule of dividing evenly among the asset types offered. The respondents tended to employ the '*1/n* heuristic' where *n* is the number of available funds. Read and Loewenstein (1995) called a similar tendency the 'diversification heuristic'. Shefrin (2000, p.172) says that investors do not understand diversification at all well and therefore make many mistakes in composing portfolios.

Canner et al. (1997) distinguished three types of risk takers who were clients of investment brokers: (1) conservative, (b) moderate, and (c) aggressive investors. They studied four sources of advice to the three groups of investors and found that all of those recommended falling ratios of bonds to stocks as the investor became more willing to take risk. The authors then examined a number of possible reasons for the deviations from the theorem that investment advisors' advice involved. They concluded that none of the explanations they tried were sufficient to explain the deviations from rationality.

In theory, a single mutual fund would be enough if the theorem holds. The fact that people can choose among many mutual funds could according to Canner et al. be explained by different expectations among investors: 'If different people have different subjective distributions over future returns, then they will combine risky assets in different proportions' (Canner et al., 1997, p.183). The time horizon should influence the composition, according to advisors. A possible psychological reason for varying advice to clients could be that clients have different goals and time horizons for their investments.

Canner et al. (1997) examine a number of reasons that could explain why advisors and consequently investors do not live up to the mutual-funds theorem. They focus on the problem that the ratio of bonds to stocks declines as risk aversion falls. The general recommendation for aggressive investors is, for example, that they hold much less in cash and bonds than moderate and conservative investors. The first assumption that the authors review is that, according to the theory, investors vary the riskless assets to achieve the desired balance between risk and return. The authors suggest that the fact that there is little difference in return from cash and from bonds and that bonds may be safer than cash may influence the bond/stock ratio in a portfolio, but that it hardly can explain the whole of the discrepancy between theory and practice.

Another attempt at explaining the found relations was based on the fact that there is in the mutual-funds separation theorem an assumption that all assets are traded. Human capital – the present value of future labor earnings – is probably the most important non-traded asset. Canner et al. posit that human capital has exactly the same return as stocks. In this case, human capital is just another name for stock. For all investors to hold risky assets in the same proportion, as the theorem dictates, the following ratio must then be constant for all investors:

$$\frac{BONDS}{HUMAN\ CAPITAL + STOCKS}$$

The authors reject the idea that consideration of human capital could explain the advice given for two reasons. First, human capital may not be equal to stocks and the return on human capital need not be correlated with either stocks or bonds. Secondly, if there was an effect, those who hold more human capital (young people) would have a smaller proportion of their holdings in stocks. In their seventh attempt to solve the puzzle, the authors tried the idea that debts such as mortgages and student loans should be added to the ratio:

$$\frac{BONDS - DEBTS}{STOCKS}$$

As investors became more willing to accept risk, they would proportionately increase both the numerator and denominator of this expression. Two main objections were raised to this explanation of decreasing bond/stock ratio with less risk aversion. First, it cannot explain the advice that the young hold more stock than the old. Since the young have more debt, the opposite should be true. Second, if the existence of nominal debt were important for popular advice, the advice should be different for homeowners and renters, as well as for those with fixed-rate mortgages and adjustable-rate mortgages.

Finally, the authors compare near-rationality with the rationality axiom of maximizing the objective function. They think the former is a simpler strategy and they suggest that the loss may be negligible:

> Although the asset allocations of some of the recommended portfolios look quite different from efficient portfolios, the cost of nonoptimization is small. . . . Thus, even if the portfolio recommendations of popular advisors are not fully rational, they appear nearly rational (Canner et al., 1997, p.189).

In their conclusions, the authors recognize that the investors who receive and presumably follow the advice from financial experts may not be well described by fully rational models. The portfolios with a high proportion of stocks have a small ratio of bonds to stocks. The ratio cannot be explained by using models of fully rational investors. Near-rationality does not mean great losses. The authors note that 'the understanding of investor objectives (as opposed to their ability to reach those objectives) is deficient' (Canner et al., 1997, p.190). Other authors have introduced the label 'noise traders' to designate investors who do not invest optimally in the sense of the theory.

CAN THERE BE A SINGLE, ALL-EMBRACING THEORY?

Holding stocks is a frequent phenomenon among households in some countries and a rare phenomenon in others. It is widely spread in the USA, where approximately one-half of households own stocks, while in, for example, France (7 to 14 percent) and Italy (6 to 8 percent) few households hold stocks. The percentage is somewhat higher if mutual funds are included, but still the differences among countries are considerable. In Sweden, stock holding is common among households and the proportion of households owning stocks has grown rapidly over the last few years. When the frequency and importance of household stock holding varies so much, can there be any general theory that can explain and predict stock-price movements with any success? Maybe, today there is so much dependence between stock exchanges in different countries that strong price movements in one country may easily influence stock-price movements in other countries. In particular, if something happens on the New York Stock Exchange or the Nasdaq, repercussions immediately strike stock exchanges in other countries.

Part of the answer is that there is theory which is so abstract and general that, in principle, it covers all stock holding and developments in financial markets. The objective of the macro-level theory is to give a basis for assessing the efficiency of the market in allocating financial resources to different purposes. Efficient-market theory is the only all-embracing theory and despite recognition of its descriptive weaknesses when applied to markets in reality, most financial economists see no alternative.

Serious deviations from the predictions of both market and portfolio choice theories have been observed, leading to many attempts to elaborate the theories, primarily with a focus on public versus private information and on the size of the capital investments. Efficient-market theory in its original form is based on the assumption that there are no trading costs nor information costs. Grossman and Stiglitz (1980) introduced a model in which they distinguished between arbitrageurs (informed traders) and uninformed traders. The former considered costs both of getting information and of trading, whereas the latter were guided only by observing price.

> We have argued that because information is costly, prices cannot perfectly reflect the information which is available since if it did, those who spent resources to obtain it would receive no compensation. There is a fundamental conflict between the efficiency with which markets spread information and the incentives to acquire information (Grossman and Stiglitz, 1980, p.405).

If a financial market is efficient, no one can make excess profits, except by chance, and it does not pay to make any effort to acquire information; hence the conflict. The role of information for stock-price developments is a complicated question that is not only dependent on the individual investor's costs for acquiring information, but also, at least to behavioral scientists, a matter of personal characteristics such as the cognitive capacity to deal with and evaluate the information and the social diffusion of information.

In behavioral finance, the remedial actions include the employment of thinking and methods from psychology. New components are added to the basic formulas and new contingencies are introduced, meaning that the researcher must admit that 'it all depends' and look at more specific circumstances. Most of these attempts have been made by researchers – and practitioners – in the USA and are aimed at explaining historical price developments at the New York Stock Exchange. Consequently, most of the discussion appears in US journals. There is research in many other countries, but it seems heavily influenced by US research. Behavioral finance is spreading and fascinates both researchers and practitioners in finance. The new focus on investor differences makes research move in the direction of distinguishing segments of investors with differing inclinations and propensities to react. Since the research aims at making the theories less abstract and more descriptive by taking behavioral data into consideration, the theories may lose some of their capacity to explain and predict stock-price phenomena at all times and in all countries.

The new research on financial behavior is, in my view, a promising starting point for explaining and predicting how investors deal with stocks and other securities. Efficient-market theory may still serve many useful purposes while new theories are being built up in order to create better understanding of individual investing and the roles of information.

THEORIES OF FINANCIAL MARKET VOLATILITY, BUBBLES, SHOCKS AND CRASHES

The jargon of economics and finance contains numerous colorful expressions to denote a market-determined asset price at odds with any reasonable economic explanation. Such words as 'tulip mania', 'bubble', 'chain letter', 'Ponzi scheme', 'panic', 'crash', and 'financial crisis' immediately evoke images of frenzied and probably irrational activity.

Garber (1990, p.35)

The assumption that stock-price changes follow a random walk in efficient markets has been tested on real price developments in many stock exchanges and has sometimes been corroborated and sometimes rejected. The fact that there have been industry bubbles that have burst and serious global crashes, albeit at fairly large intervals, raises problems for the random walk hypothesis. If the random walk hypothesis is on the whole true, can bubbles such as Tulipmania in Holland, the South Sea Company scandal in Great Britain and the stock exchange crash of 1929 still occur and be considered as random, though very low probability, events? Garber (1990) asserts that they can and so does Fama albeit with some qualifications, especially in his later works (Fama, 1965; 1998).

Long-Term Returns on Stocks and the Equity Premium Puzzle

If stock prices are highly correlated with dividends we might conclude that the movements in stock prices are driven by fundamentals, not fads.

Shiller (1990, p.58)

Stocks have outperformed bonds over long periods of time. Average returns on stocks have been much higher, except during shorter spells of depressed stock markets. There have been a few periods of some length in which (government) bonds have done better, but with some patience (and not too frequent trading) investors in stocks seem to do much better than investors in bonds. An example of low average returns is found in the ten-year period when the Dow Jones Industrial Average Index was read to 1 036 in December 1972 and in April 1981 amounted to 1 024. Towards the end of 1982, the index had climbed a little to reach 1 070. There were, of course, winners and losers in the stock market and some investors could gain money by outperforming the index. Samuelson (1994) challenges the established truth that stocks are the superior investment over long periods of time. Shiller (2000) is skeptical about the superiority of stocks over bonds, and notes: 'The evidence that stocks will *always* outperform bonds over long time intervals simply does not exist' (Shiller, 2000, p.195). He expresses great pessimism about the future stock returns for pension funds as well as for the majority of private investors.

The *equity premium* is the difference between the expected return on the market portfolio of common stocks and the risk-free interest rate. When comparing the returns on stocks or equities and on bonds for long periods of time, researchers have found that stocks do much better. Investing in stocks entails higher risk than putting the money in a bank account or in treasury bills and the investor must receive extra pay to be willing to make the riskier investment. The risk premium that investors seem to want from investment in stocks is, according to the researchers, much bigger than would be warranted by the actual differences in risk between stocks and riskless treasury bills.

The *equity premium puzzle* refers to the fact that the average performance of stocks is so much higher that the discrepancy is hard to explain in purely economic terms. Mehra and Prescott (1985) asked whether the large differential between yields according to the Standard and Poor Index and the yields from short-term debts could be explained by models that abstracted from transactions costs, liquidity constraints and other functions that were absent in the current models. They concluded that the models could not explain the high size of the returns (7 percent on average) and labeled the question 'the equity premium puzzle'. This study has been followed by many others with the aim of clarifying the puzzle.

Why do investors demand such high returns on stocks? Do they really have the extremely high degree of risk aversion that the size of the equity premium implies? There seems to be consensus among economists who have studied the phenomenon that such high risk aversion is not plausible, at least according to the way economists calculate risk aversion. Many attacks on the problem have been made to explain this deviation from what rational models posit, and the problem has attracted considerable attention among economic researchers. The attempts at explaining the size of the equity premium have usually not been generally accepted as successful (for an overview, see Benartzi and Thaler, 1995). Two recent studies throw some new light on the puzzle. One persevering question has been whether the equity premium was primarily connected with the long-term development of the New York Stock Exchange and not to be found elsewhere. The answer is 'no'. According to Dimson et al. (2000), who studied the whole of the last century for twelve countries, the equity premium is found in all of those countries. Sweden shows the highest annualized real percentage returns. The equity premium at the Stockholm Stock Exchange amounts to around 8 percent over the last 100 years, 1900–2000. Sweden is followed by Australia, with slightly less than 8 percent, and in the third place, the USA, with around 7 percent. Italy, France, and Japan were at the bottom, with between 4 and 5 percent.

Interestingly, the three countries with the highest equity premiums have the highest participation in the stock market, with Australia at the top, followed by Sweden. Causality is difficult to assess, but it may be that the high equity premium has contributed to increasing the proportion of the population with stocks. Ordinary people have usually entertained doubts about the wisdom of buying and holding stocks, except maybe in the USA and, more recently, in Australia and Sweden. The results of the study suggest that stock investment strategies may be profitable also in other countries, or at least that they could have been profitable in a long-term perspective.

The second study represents a different approach to the puzzle. Fama and French (2000) estimated the expected equity premium on the New York Stock Exchange for the years 1872–1999, using two models. One of the models was the usual one of average realized returns whereas the other model included the expected dividend growth rate. Up to 1950, the two models gave almost the same estimates of the equity premium – 4 percent per year. For the last 50 years, the second model gave a much lower estimate than the average realized returns estimate – 3.4 versus 8.3 percent. The expected dividend growth rate gives part of the explanation of the equity premium puzzle, but not all. The authors suggest that the differences between the results of the two models depend on unexpected capital gains, the result of a decline in discount rates. They conclude that their analysis indicates that extreme optimism about long-term dividend growth is necessary to project an expected future equity premium near historical averages. This is another gloomy prediction for the stock market by prominent researchers in the field.

Psychological answers to the equity premium puzzle have been suggested. Benartzi and Thaler (1995) propose two components in investors' demand for compensation: (1) people have loss aversion, which leads to holding on to assets rather than realizing losses, the endowment effect, and (2) the willingness to take risks increases with increasing time horizon; the longer the time perspective, the less the resistance to taking risks. Short evaluation periods give rise to higher risk aversion than longer evaluation periods. The authors found through simulations that the actual risk aversion behind the equity premium puzzle corresponded to an evaluation period of about a year and would give a reasonable explanation of why investors demanded a high compensation for investing in stocks. They note that pension funds tend to invest less in stocks than would be profitable and attribute this to the same myopic loss aversion that materializes in frequent evaluations of assets. Stephan (1999, p.131) applies the availability heuristic and points to the fact that investors feel more familiar with bonds and other less risky securities and need an extra premium to invest in stock, which they find less familiar and are more uncertain about. Another availability effect could be that people recall stock exchange crashes very easily and exaggerate the long-run risks connected with investing in stocks. They demand more compensation than what is justified by hindsight knowledge.

The Existence of Bubbles

> *Fascinated with the brilliance of grand speculative events, economists have huddled in the bubble interpretation and have neglected an examination of potential market fundamentals. The ready availability of a banal explanation of the tulipmania, compared to its dominant position in the speculative pantheon of economics, is stark evidence of how bubble and mania characterizations have served to divert economists from understanding those outlying events highest in informational content. The bubble interpretation has relegated the far more important Mississippi and South Sea episodes to a description of pathologies of group psychology.*
>
> Garber (1990, pp.52–3)

Bubbles, crashes, and booms that are met by sudden surprise from many investors belong to the characteristics of stock markets. Long periods of upward tendencies have been followed by abrupt drops in stock indexes, and the drops have sometimes turned into crashes. The vignette above rejects the idea that there have been bubbles that cannot be explained by solicitous use of rationality-based economic theory. Non-economists may still want to delve a little deeper into the psychology of financial bubbles (see, for example, Schachter et al., 1985). Efficient-market theory admits ups and downs, even large ones. Temporary booms, bubbles, and minor crashes can apparently be accommodated in the theory with only a few modifications (Fama, 1998).

The best known and most studied anomaly is the crash of 1929. October 1987 witnessed another crash, whose consequences were not as long-lasting as those of 1929. While crashes are comprehensive and concern all stocks and are international, bubbles may be limited to a certain type of stock or the stock of an individual company. Financial bubbles are known at least since Tulipmania seized Holland in the 1630s (see, for example, Garber, 1989a. 1989b). Many Dutch people who were otherwise careful in their spending speculated in future prices of tulip bulbs. Prices of bulbs climbed rapidly to enormous heights and afforded early sellers great profits, which attracted new buyers until the Dutch government fixed prices at a relatively low level.

Stiglitz (1990) defines 'bubble' in a very simple way:

> If the reason that the price is high today is *only* because investors believe that the selling price will be high tomorrow – when 'fundamental' factors do not seem to justify such a price – then a bubble exists. At least in the short run, the high price of the asset is merited, because it yields a return (capital gain plus dividend) equal to that on alternative assets (Stiglitz, 1990, p.13).

Explanations for crashes and other disturbances are sought in many types of factors. The causal relationships between the stock crash of 1929 and the Great Depression are still debated, although some believe that they have the true answer. There are many cocksure explanations of the October 1987 crisis. They cannot all be true. What is of interest here is the assortment of psychological explanations that have been added to macro- and microeconomic attempts to explain crashes, and the primarily psychological explanations that have been launched by some economists and other social scientists.

Attempts to Explain Bubbles and Crashes

The attempts to explain and predict crashes and bursting bubbles that affect large parts of the stocks listed on domestic and international stock exchanges can be roughly categorized like this:

1. examination of general economic trends, business cycles, etc.
2. search for long-term patterns in stock-price data
3. search for short-term patterns in stock-price data
4. assumptions about psychological changes, having to do either with learning (feedback) or with the diffusion and use of information
5. mass phenomena and social influences such as herd behavior.

The first three categories of explanations are of limited interest here. Much has been written about these attempts to explain. They involve looking at turning points and what precedes them in a search for indicators that could serve as predictors of stock-price developments and potential warning signs. An example of the examination of patterns is given by Schwert (1990), who suggests that the October 1987 crash was characterized by significantly increased volatility of stock prices. After the crisis, the volatility returned to more normal levels.

The causal relationships between the Great Crash of 1929 and the subsequent Great Depression that lasted for almost ten years are still being investigated. Galbraith ([1954]1987) gives a highly readable account of the factors that seemingly influenced the stock-price fall at the New York Stock Exchange in 1929. He notes that there was a complex of factors behind the developments, some of them related to the general state of the economy such as low interest rates and easy loans; some were structural factors such as the appearance of investment funds; and some had to do with human behavior such as government policy mistakes, rampant speculation, and mass reactions.

The explanations based on efficient-market and rational expectations theory focus on the emergence of new information that could trigger the bursting of a bubble or a dramatic fall in stock prices. Notable changes in information have characteristically not been found in connection with stock market crashes. This has led to the question of whether the dissemination and handling of information can occur in such a way that they may lead to a kind of explosion. Some authors have launched the idea of information cascades or information avalanches. These will be treated in the next section.

First, a few glimpses should be given of the debate concerning what makes stock prices move over time. Shiller (1981, 1989, 1990, 1995, 2000) has devoted considerable attention to this question. In an early study, he tested the efficient-market model, examining the assumption that real stock prices equal the present value of rationally expected or optimally forecast future real dividends, discounted by a constant real discount rate. He notes that, in popular discussions, it was often claimed that stock-price indexes seem too 'volatile' to be compatible with the theory. He reached the following conclusion:

> Indeed, measures of stock price volatility over the past century appear to be far too high to be attributed to new information about future real dividends if uncertainty about future dividends is measured by the sample standard deviations of real dividends from their long-run exponential growth path. One way of saving the general notion of efficient markets would be to attribute the movements in stock prices to changes in expected real interest rates. However, the movements in expected real interest rates that would justify the variability in stock prices are very large – much larger than the movements in nominal interest rates over the sample period (Shiller, 1981, p.421).

Over long periods of time, the correlation between stock prices and dividends is high. Shiller (1990) reports that R^2 amounted to 0.819 for the period 1951–1987 when a stock-price index was regressed on real annual average dividends. This looks like a good confirmation of the assumption that stock rates develop in the way efficient-market theory posits: that investors rely on so-called fundamentals when they make their investment decisions and that their expectations are on average close to later realized returns. Shiller gave two reasons why he was still convinced there was substantial room for 'fashions and fads' in stock prices. He first noted that the year-to-year change in real stock price was not explained by change in the real dividends. Dividends showed long-run swings, and prices tracked those somewhat. Considerable variations in stock prices were possible. Secondly, Shiller pointed out that dividends could themselves incorporate some of the fashions and fads that affected stock prices. Managers set dividends, and the size of dividends is at their discretion. If most managers become optimistic at the same time as the public does, they may increase dividends because fashions cause prices to increase (Shiller, 1990, p.59).

Shiller (1990, 2000) found that the standard feedback theory of bubbles intuitively could explain ups and downs in stock prices and that there was some scanty empirical support. The feedback theory of bubbles assumes that when market prices as a whole rise substantially, many success stories are created and disseminated. Such stories lead other people to invest in the hope of achieving similar success. Conversely, when stock prices fall dramatically, investors are discouraged from investing and driven out of the market. In his recent book, Shiller (2000) assesses the possible role of three sets of factors in his discussion: (1) structural factors, (2) cultural factors, among which mass media are ascribed a prominent role, and (3) psychological factors, primarily psychological anchoring effects and herd behavior.

Numerous attempts have been made to explain the international market crash of October 1987. The attempts have involved looking for deviations from efficient-market theory such as anomalies in trading strategies. Traders who behave in an irrational manner, often called 'noise traders', have been blamed for stock market turbulence, including crashes. Noise traders will be treated in the next chapter. In my view, to the extent that noise traders are passive investors, they may have a dampening effect, slow down the fall and help recovery, since they tend to hold on to their portfolios, even at the risk of further losses, if they are possessed by loss aversion (see Chapter 4).

One type of explanation has included the assumption that there was abundant portfolio insurance (setting a floor value for a portfolio with limits that release immediate selling when stock prices have dropped to the floor, or some sophisticated hedging). Stop-losses, which refer to limits for a single stock, and portfolio insurance are often carried out as part of a computer program and can thus be purely automatic. Shiller (1989), relying on interviews with investors, found little support for the effect of automatic release of portfolio insurance. Lee (1998) who provides an explanatory model of his own, also rejects the hypothesis:

> Although they succeed in generating a pattern similar to the market crash, the actual amount of portfolio insurance during the market crash of 1987 seems to suggest otherwise; after the market crash, the surprise was not that there were more portfolio insurers than expected, but that there were fewer insurers. Therefore their explanation is not consistent with the data. Also the crash was observed in countries without portfolio insurance . . . (Lee, 1998, p.754).

Other attempts at explaining market crashes also employ the concept of information and make a point of the difference between public and private information. The next section will deal with some of these attempts.

INFORMATION AND EFFICIENT MARKETS

> *One of my favorite contrasts is that when the market rises following good economic news, it is said to be responding to the news; if it falls, that is explained by saying that the good news had already been discounted.*
>
> Fischhoff (1982a, p.345)

According to efficient-market theory, stock prices move up or down as a consequence of new information on fundamentals. Expectations are assumed to change immediately, for example when a company announces changes in its earnings. With this assumption, it seems strange that stock prices may undergo substantial changes when there is no new information. It is an anomaly that prices after new information can keep going up for a long time without any further information about fundamentals. De Bondt and Thaler (1985, 1987) talked about overreactions in such cases. Observations of how markets operate have led to hypotheses about different types of information. Harry Roberts, who was professor of statistics at the University of Chicago, distinguished three levels of market efficiency (Brealey and Myers, 1996, p.329):

1. The *weak* form of efficiency: stock prices reflect all information contained in the record of past prices.
2. The *semistrong* form of efficiency: stock prices reflect past prices, but also all other published information.
3. The *strong* form of efficiency: stock prices reflect public information and, in addition, all the information that can be acquired through painstaking analysis of the company and of the economy.

These distinctions do not make clear whether it pays for an investor to acquire painstaking information and they rather intimate that investors have to rely on luck to make higher profits than the market portfolio. As mentioned before, Grossman and Stiglitz (1980) introduced the concepts of informed traders and information costs to handle the fact that some traders may make more profits. While the original theory presumes that all information is public and has immediate effect, the newer thinking presumes that there can be lagged and hidden information that remains private with a trader or investor and does not show up in public through trading actions for some time. Some explanations of crashes rest on the effects of hidden information that suddenly cascades into public view.

Models of Hidden Information and Price Movements

Quite a few theoretical attempts have been made to construct models that can generate big price movements without substantial news about changes in stock or other security fundamentals. Caplin and Leahy (1994) constructed a model in which many investors suddenly changed their investment choice. A three-stage model of market dynamics was presented. In the first stage, called *business as usual*, routine behavior tended to keep information of common interest trapped in private hands. Individual traders could change their routines and commitments only at some cost. Whenever an individual changed a trading routine, the market learned a great deal about the individual's private information. In the second stage, *market crashes*, private information reached a threshold that triggered other traders to alter their behavior. These actions released mass information to the market. 'If sufficiently many agents decide to act and their cumulative actions reveal information that is sufficiently novel, this process of action and reaction may lead to a radical change in market sentiment' (Caplin and Leahy, 1994, p.548). The final stage, *wisdom after the fact*, involved the market's response to this news as other participants reacted to the initial departure from routine behavior. While the authors presented an application to industry investment and some other areas, other economists have applied and developed these ideas further with the more particular aim of explaining financial markets. .

Lee (1998) commented that the sudden change in Caplin and Leahy's model followed from a revelation of new information that became available only when some investors had collected significant private information. Therefore the economy before the crash was not regarded as a state in which information aggregation had failed, but was in a state of waiting for the accumulation of information. In contrast, in Lee's own model, the stock market before the crash is in a boom although the true private information if it could be studied would reveal the opposite. People have private information that goes against the boom, for example from observing how people in their environment behave (or perhaps talk).

Romer (1993) distinguished between two approaches in explaining asset-price movements:

1. The efficient-market view in which asset prices are rational assessments of expected future payoffs; prices reflect external news about future interest rates and returns
2. A 'fads', 'noise', or 'bubbles' view in which there is a component of prices that is not tied to fundamentals; changes in prices can therefore reflect news about fundamentals as well as changes in factors that are not fundamental.

The second view is represented by Shiller's (1989) hypothesis about the importance of fads and fashions and by some of the noise trader theories that do not assume rationality among all traders. Many observations of financial markets have shown that price movements very often cannot be explained by news about fundamentals or about the economy. Romer (1993) cites the stock-market crash of October 1987 as evidence: stock prices on the New York Stock Exchange fell by 20 percent in a single day without any news of any importance.

Romer further argues that an important part of price movements are caused neither by external news nor by irrationality, but by the internal news that the trading process itself provides. Strong price movements can then be compatible with rational decisions. He. considers two models that explain price movements without accompanying news. One model assumes that investors are uncertain about the quality of other investors' information and rely too much on the market price. At a certain point the best available information becomes reflected more fully in stock prices and changes occur. The other model is based on widespread dispersion of information and small costs of trading. Romer assumes that immediate processing of private information for trade is more costly than delayed processing. Due to the incentive to save information-processing costs, the time of trade is uncoupled from the time of information acquisition and the price of stocks may move long after agents acquire information.

The analysis is used to suggest a possible rational explanation of the October 1987 crash. It is argued that this view – that price movements which occur without any clear news often do convey information about fundamentals – has several important advantages over the alternative view that they largely represent fads or noise. Romer's second model is similar to Lee's model, described below, in that it characterizes a security market with dispersed information and transaction costs.

Bulow and Klemperer (1994) constructed a model of frenzies and crashes based on strategic interactions of rational agents in an auction setting. They reject the notion that financial crises are caused by irrationality or other market imperfections and maintain that 'rushes to trade and large changes in price may arise as a direct result of rational and strategic behavior in efficient markets' (Bulow and Klemperer, 1994, p.2). They define a *frenzy* as multiple sales at a single price – agents rush in to buy. 'A crash occurs if, after trade takes place, it becomes common knowledge that no further purchases will be made until the price has fallen to some given strictly lower level' (Bulow and Klemperer, 1994, p.5)

The authors argue that most markets clear through a sequence of sales rather than through a Walrasian auctioneer. Because buyers can decide whether to buy now or later, their current willingness to pay (WTP) is central to the model. They further maintain that a trader's valuation of stock – which aggregated over all traders is the demand curve – may differ from the price the trader is at a certain moment willing to pay. The WTP price is based on consideration of what is reasonable to pay now for a given stock. The buyer may have a valuation of $100 for a stock, but only be willing to pay $75 right now because s/he thinks it will be possible to find a seller at this price. This means that the WTP price is much more sensitive to price changes than the demand curve is. A consequence is that markets will be extremely sensitive to new information, leading to both frenzies in which demand feeds on itself and to crashes in which prices drop discontinuously. Small changes in bidder values can dramatically change outcomes, and successive uses of such trading processes in similar environments can yield strikingly different results.

The expression that 'demand feeds on itself' implies that the first sale at a new price triggers purchases by many agents who have high valuations and lower WTP curves and now find it opportune to buy. A frenzy seems to be similar to a bubble in which demand ultimately exceeds supply.

Lee's (1998) paper provides an explanation complementary to these attempts, using a model in which agents learn from others' action choice. The model posits a setting in which information is dispersed throughout the economy in the form of private signals. A signal is presumably a knowledge or information change. Each agent makes an investment decision based on her/his own private information and the history of previous agents' decisions.

> We consider a financial market where agents have to pay transaction costs to trade and they trade sequentially. We establish that such a market could be highly volatile if it fails to aggregate information given to the agents. The failure in information aggregation takes place because traders place a disproportionate weight on the previous price history in an attempt to utilize public information in their investment decision making. For instance, observing many trading orders based on good news, a trader with bad news tends to discount his own bad news and makes an investment choice close to the one based on good news. When mildly bad news is combined with the transaction cost, the choice based on bad news may become indistinguishable from the one based on good news. It follows that the price may remain high even if there are many traders with news (Lee, 1998, p.741).

The private signals, that is, what some traders privately believe, are not disseminated through traders acting in the market which, in Lee's terms, means that there is aggregation failure. Due to information aggregation failure, hidden information accumulates in the market. A small trigger that provokes a change in action choice may reveal the information and give rise to a high volatility in the absence of an accompanying event. An example is that a trader observes many trading orders based on good news whereas her/his own bad news is discounted. S/he makes an investment choice close to the one inspired by the good news. As a consequence, prices may remain high even though many separate traders have bad news as private information. If they all come to realize the implications of the bad news, sudden and drastic changes may occur.

The sudden change follows only if there have been many traders with private information inconsistent with the current price. The result may be an *informational cascade.* An informational cascade is an event in which a sequence of agents takes identical action as they try to exploit the information available from the history of previous action choices (Lee, 1998, p.742). An *informational avalanche* is the sudden reversal of an informational cascade. It exploits the property that non-fully revealing informational cascades are fragile. Lee explains market crashes by assuming that there are four stages: (1) boom, (2) euphoria, (3) trigger, and (4) panic. Euphoria corresponds to informational cascades and panic is synonymous to the informational avalanche. A market crash is described as a procedure that corrects a public belief which is inconsistent with the current distribution of private information.

Romer's (1993) model did not provide a mechanism through which small information pieces accumulate without being revealed through trading since delay in the trade occurred uniformly. In contrast, agents in Lee's model delay their trades only when there has been a sequence of trades that has revealed substantial information, and they trade only after a trigger, so that the model is able to explain the process of price build-up and subsequent burst. The model relies on a mechanism which highlights the possibility of learning from price movements.

Lee (1998) says that his model is able to explain a variety of features of the 1987 market crash. He finds that the result accords well with the claims of many traders that they were skeptical during the price rise (Shiller, 1989). Shiller's findings may perhaps have influenced the construction of the model and thus be doubted as independent support. Lee goes on to suggest that many agents with low signals may have been induced to buy at high prices, thus ignoring their private information:

> This was at least in part due to an uninformative cascade. They regretted their purchase once the state was revealed through the October market crash. Next the fact that the price fall began in the week before the market crash in 1987 can be explained by the model. When the rare signal is revealed, the price begins to fall and subsequently crash occurs only when a substantial number of low signals are revealed to the market. Also the modest initial price drop . . . is consistent with the model because the market crash in our model is triggered by one trader whose trading order does not induce a huge price drop by itself (Lee, 1998, p.754).

Zeira (1999) employs the concept of *overshooting*, which is reminiscent of De Bondt and Thaler's (1985) concept of overreaction. It means that when prices go up, no one knows when the rise will stop and the tendency is to continue to pay higher prices until a change in expectations is triggered. He explains the phenomenon of price overshooting and crashes through a learning process and considers a learning model in which agents do not know when the increase in the fundamental stops. He suggests that the entry of new investors may have caused the two crashes of the century, in 1929 and in 1987.

According to Zeira himself, his paper was motivated by two characteristics of many booms and crashes. The first was that after the crash, stock prices were still higher than at the beginning of the episode. The fact that stock prices rose overall indicated that profitability increased during the episode. This observation did not conform with irrational speculation, nor with arbitrary realization of one equilibrium out of many. Instead, it indicated that stock prices overshoot. The second observed fact motivating the paper was that many booms and crashes have followed financial liberalizations. A financial liberalization reduces entry costs, which induces entry of new investors and thus generates a boom and a subsequent crash.

Both the 1929 and the 1987 crashes were, according to Zeira (1999), accompanied by a real expansion and by entry of many new investors to the market. Then there is the question of potential triggers for the two episodes The paper suggests two possible triggers for booms and crashes, namely rapid technical progress and reduction of entry costs to the market. There was a substantial deregulation in US financial markets in the late 1970s and early 1980s. This deregulation reduced entry costs and enabled entry of new investors, both private and institutional, into the market. Zeira further finds that a close look at other recent episodes of booms and crashes shows that they too have been preceded by financial liberalizations. Recent examples of booms and crashes that have been preceded by financial liberalizations are Indonesia, Japan and Israel. Indonesia liberalized financial markets at the end of 1988; after that the stock market boomed and then crashed in February 1990.

The Role of Information

> *Information is not a free good. Just as you must kiss many frogs to catch a prince, maybe a lot of meaningless noise trading is needed to keep markets liquid and efficient. Maybe.*
>
> Samuelson (1994, p.23)

The definition of an efficient market contains a clue to why inefficiencies may arise: information flows do not fulfill the requisites. Dissemination must be perfect so that all concerned have physical access to the news. Furthermore, humans have to be dependable automatons to be able to act in concordance with the requirements. It is no wonder, then, that financial economists focus their attention on deficiencies in information flows in attempts to redress the theory's power to handle observed inefficiencies in the market. Efficient-market theory presupposes that all traders and potential traders have the same information about fundamentals, that is, about means and variances of future stock prices, and that they use the information in the same manner and to the full. Observations of financial markets inevitably lead to the conclusion that there are incongruous phenomena such as bubbles and crashes. Attempts to explain such occurrences have as a major ingredient novel assumptions about the role of information. Most of the attempts at explanation keep the rationality postulate and try to reconcile the spread and use of information with rational actions. Knowledge is here used as a synonym for information. At least three types of assumptions exist: (1) those about the dissemination and (possible) aggregation of knowledge, (b) those admitting learning and adaptation, that is, new information as a result of the investor's own experience, (c) those about private or hidden information that is for some time suppressed for being in conflict with public knowledge.

Little recognition is paid to the fact that, in the real world, time and space differences exist in the reception of information, even if it is in principle public from a specific moment. The dissemination of information is often a slow process because all of the investors who are potentially concerned are not exposed to and do not attend to new information at the same time. Asymmetries of information are created. According to economic theory there is no way of knowing whether all investors have received the information, since they reveal their knowledge only through their actions. This implies that information that leads to refraining from action cannot be registered.

A number of authors have recognized the fact that individual investors can learn from observing their own successes and failures and from observing those of others. At the macro level, such learning is called the positive-feedback effect. In some economists' terms, investors receive private signals from events in their own environment and the private information makes for unequal knowledge. Some authors focus on the fact that traders observe one another's actions and are influenced towards acting in the same way, to display herd behavior (see, for example, Banerjee, 1992). It may also mean doing something radically different, since as long as there are transactions both buyers and sellers are in the market. Information aggregation that thus emanates from social influence implies that all traders do not react at the same time and in the same place. Individuals who watch others or receive other pieces of information may try out the information little by little and, guided by positive experience, change their behavior in more complete ways, which essentially means that there is stepwise learning from information about the market. An important question for some authors is whether trying out the new information involves new costs being accrued, that is, transaction costs. A psychologist would add other costs, such as mental and physical effort that accompanies going against public knowledge.

Unless divulged by actions in the market, the private information is hidden and has no effect in the theories discussed here. People do not talk about their experience, and information or at least private information is not assumed to affect any other traders until it is revealed in trading. 'Actions speak louder than words.' Words do in fact not speak at all in these theories! At any rate, the hidden knowledge has the power to change the market dramatically if many traders are triggered into using it at the same time. There is some similarity between the ideas of information avalanches and cascades and Katona's (1975) social learning hypothesis, which deals with how large groups of people slowly and serially through face-to-face contacts learn new attitudes. Social learning is here a macro concept. While social learning is ordinarily a slow process, such learning may sometimes occur rapidly and dramatically through the aid of the news and other mass media along with influence from peer to peer. Modern television and the use of the Internet may radically shorten the dissemination and processing of information. The complex interaction between private experience and mass media reporting is rarely touched upon in attempts at providing complementary hypotheses about the spread of information.

The idea of hidden knowledge as a consequence of private observations is intriguing. What is less convincing is the assumption that if the knowledge is not imparted through action, it cannot affect the market. It may be true that professional investors do not reveal their secrets by talking to colleagues and only reveal their preferences through trading, but undoubtedly verbal advice passes from professionals to clients and there are many discussions among peers. People, in general, do not refrain from disclosing private information about stocks to peers. Besides, with appropriate arrangements, it is possible to elicit private information from representative population groups. One interpretation of the Index of Consumer Sentiment is that it taps private knowledge (see, for example, Wärneryd, 1999). The success of the index demonstrates that subjective information can become available and aggregated in such a way that it can be used for meaningful predictions of business cycles.

SO WHAT'S THE USE OF EFFICIENT-MARKET THEORY?

There is no need for a behavioral theory in a market composed entirely of information traders.

Shefrin and Statman (1994, p.323)

Economic growth and stability presuppose that money is saved and invested in efficient ways. The financial market has a role as the final arbiter for the allocation of scarce capital resources:

> The main concern [of the architects of public policy and the scholarly community] has been to ensure and maintain conditions under which the flow of investment funds will in fact be channeled to those enterprises whose products are most in demand by the consuming public (Lease et al., 1974, p.413).

The efficient-market theory has the main purpose of explaining aggregate market outcomes and making predictions about future developments. Efficient-market theory and its complements such as CAPM and the mean-variance model of portfolio choice do not give good descriptions of investor behavior, nor do they serve as good predictors of individual stock-price developments. Even though these theories were not meant to serve such purposes, it may be meaningful to investigate how well these rationality-based models succeed in explaining and predicting market behavior.

Many studies of stock markets note that there are certainly deviations from what the theory predicts, but that on the whole financial markets tend to behave in rough accordance with the theory (Fama, 1998). No alternative theory can better explain or predict outcomes of what goes on in financial markets. Fama maintains that efficient-market theory can handle the deviations found and that the alternative formulations of theory are by far too vague. In contrast, Thaler (1999a) argues that there is now much evidence that portfolio choice theories are inadequate and that all financial theories must incorporate psychological findings. Fama (1998) recognizes a dilemma:

> A problem in developing an overall perspective on long-term return studies is that they rarely test a specific alternative to market efficiency. Instead, the alternative hypothesis is vague, market inefficiency. This is unacceptable. Like all models, market efficiency (the hypothesis that prices fully reflect available information) is a faulty description of price formation. Following the standard scientific rule, however, market efficiency can only be replaced by a better specific model of price formation, itself potentially rejectable by empirical tests (Fama, 1998, p.284).

Plott (1990) remarks that it is easy to reject theories, but that this is not a challenging research objective:

> Those who study experimental markets tend to pose the questions in different ways. Rather than inquire whether a theory is true or false, they ask if the magnitude of error in the predictions of market phenomena is acceptable; or, if no concept of degree of acceptability is readily available, the question becomes which of several competing models is the most accurate, fully realizing that the best model may still be 'poor'. When confronted with data that suggest the existence of erratic or irrational individual behavior, the implications are immediately evaluated in terms of the possible implications for a market level of analysis (Plott, 1990, p. 147).

Although Plott specifically defends the approach used by experimental economists, his reasoning suggests a generally useful way of looking at efficient-market theory and similar theories.

While Plott as an economist immediately evaluates consequences of micro-level findings at the aggregate level, psychologists tend to stay focused on micro-level behavior and to look at findings without glancing at possible consequences at the macro level. Researchers in behavioral finance are similar to other economic researchers and develop micro models which they use to explain behavior at the market level. Psychological variables have mostly been used in micro models with the aim of explaining macro-level data. For many purposes, a focus on individual financial behavior, including a search for investor segments with different properties, is highly desirable. In so doing, researchers can learn much from rationality-based theories and the discussion of those.

As stated earlier, an important objective in this book is to move towards a better descriptive and explanatory theory at the micro level, that is, the individual and household level. A beginning is to scrutinize theory developments in financial economics from the point of view of psychology. Elaborations of efficient-market theory touch on phenomena that seem close to social psychology and mass communication theory. The CAPM, like many other models, is based on two concepts that are used and studied in psychology: expectation and risk. The concepts do not mean exactly the same thing in economics and psychology. For one thing, psychological researchers are more intent on directly measuring individual expectations and variables relating to risk. Behavioral finance researchers are more inclined to make quantitative models that are plausible and look at the consequences at the market level. If they are inclined towards experimental economics, they may test the models in the laboratory.

There are two sides to descriptions and explanations of individual investor behavior. The first one, which is closest to the rationality-based models, deals with the investor's use of models, what guides her/his behavior. The use of a rational model is one alternative that is often used as a criterion when other models are evaluated. The other has to do with what variables best explain such financial behavior. Explanations at the aggregate level may be different from those at the micro or individual level. It seems obvious that explanations of individual financial behavior are improved by the inclusion of psychological variables. There still remain some doubts as to the extent to which psychological variables contribute to explaining and predicting aggregate behavior.

When writers in economics accept psychological concepts at all, they attempt to make the psychological concepts compatible with the rationality postulate. In empirical contexts, they use proxies that are usually aggregate, macro-level concepts, derived from objective data. They make use of data on individuals, that is, subjective data, only as a last resort. Financial economics has received many suggestions of psychological variables that could be used better to explain and predict financial behavior. Noise trader descriptions are based more on psychological reasoning than on economic data. Noise traders' expectations are assumed to be formed under the influence of misinterpretations of economic information, limited information-processing capacity, emotions such as overoptimism, and (lack of) self-control. In the following chapters, the psychological variables that have been suggested are investigated in more detail.

SOME DEFINITIONS

Asymmetric information means that one side possesses more information in a trading situation and therefore has an advantage. The theory of efficient markets and CAPM presume homogeneous beliefs: all investors have homogeneous prior beliefs and receive the same relevant information sets that affect market prices.

A *bear* is, according to *The American Heritage Dictionary*, one that sells securities or commodities in expectation of falling prices. A *bear market* is a market in which prices are falling.

Beta is the ratio of a change in the return on a stock to a change in the returns on all stocks in a stock market. Beta is equal to 1 if the individual stock-price changes and all other stock-price changes are perfectly correlated and the stock has the same volatility as the market. Beta is less than 1 if the stock under consideration is less volatile, that is, fluctuates less than the market index, and larger than 1 if the development is more volatile than the market index.

A *bull* is, according to The American Heritage Dictionary, a person who buys commodities or securities in anticipation of a rise in prices or who tries by speculative purchases to effect such a rise. A *bull market* is a market in which prices are rising.

Hedging involves attempts to protect against losses by counterbalancing an investment position with another transaction that encompasses, for example, futures or other derivatives. Derivatives allow investors to *hedge* when buying a certain asset. Hedging is a way to protect against a loss in value of an investment. For example, if the holder of a certain stock is concerned that the stock price will fall, s/he might purchase a type of option whose value will increase if the stock falls in price. The option thus provides a kind of insurance against loss for the stock holder.

A *margin call* is a demand from a lender for more collateral when a stock price has dropped and the investor has practiced *buying at the margin.*

The *price–earnings ratio* (p/e) is the price of a stock, divided by the earnings per stock. *Growth stocks* have high p/e ratios whereas *value stocks* have low p/e ratios.

To *sell short* means, according to *The American Heritage Dictionary* (1997), to contract for the sale of securities or commodities one expects to own at a later date and at more advantageous terms. When you sell short, you sell stocks you do not yet own, but hope to acquire at a more favorable price in the future before delivery is due.

2. Behavioral Considerations in Financial Markets

Yes, there is no alternative to human judgment in understanding human behavior.
Shiller (1989, p.41)

Deviations from the Ideal Models

Except for efficient-market theory, there is no coherent theory for explaining market behavior. If investors behave rationally, as the theory of efficient markets presupposes, there would be no need for a behavioral theory. All investors would be Bayesian and guided by probability calculations on the basis of all available information. It is interesting to look a little more closely at the behavioral implications of the CAPM. In the first place, they involve perfect competition. This means that all investors behave as if they have no market power over prices. Second, markets are frictionless, implying that there are no transaction costs, taxes, or restrictions on security trading. In addition, all assets and securities are infinitely divisible and marketable. Third, it is assumed that all investors have homogeneous prior beliefs and Bayesian expectations. Fourth, all investors simultaneously receive the same relevant news that determines market prices. Fifth, individual preferences are restricted in the sense that all investors care only about the risk and expected-return trade-off. Finally, all investors are rational-expectations utility maximizers.

In practice, of course, markets show imperfections. Studies of markets indicate that markets are not efficient in the sense of the theory (for example, Monday and January effects, weekend effects, the emergence of bubbles, and crashes) and that traders subvert the neat information flows of the efficient market in ways that diverge from the theoretically expected behavior. While the simplifying assumptions make it possible to maintain an integrated theory that can serve as a benchmark for judging actual market performance and for market-level predictions, the theory gives little guidance for the study of individual behavior. The micro model of the rational trader may serve well for macroeconomic purposes, but it falls short for understanding behavior. The idea of two types of traders has thus reached broad acceptance. One type, which presumably represents the majority of traders, is rational and uses information as the theory posits. The other type – who should according to some not be in the market – are labeled irrational since they do not use information in the right way. They are accordingly called *noise traders*. In some views, noise traders disturb the market; in other views they are responsible for the stock-price patterns that investors can make money on.

The micro model behind efficient-market theory and other finance theories is aimed at market-level explanations and predictions, but it is normative in the sense that it provides criteria or comparison norms for financial behavior. Rational behavior in the restricted sense of pure economic theory is used as a model against which actual behavior is compared and easily stamped 'irrational', a notion that irritates and puzzles many practitioners of finance because of its connotations. Many attempts to explain inefficiencies in financial markets invoke irrational behavior on the part of actors in the markets. While the prevalent assumption among financial economists is that irrationality is unpredictable, researchers in behavioral finance have embraced ideas from cognitive psychology that some deviations from rational behavior can be explained and even predicted (see, for example, Thaler, 1999a; Shefrin, 2000).

Attempts at explaining and predicting actual behavior may start with theories based on rationality (in the very restricted sense of the pure theory). When explanations and predictions then fail, more or less ad-hoc hypotheses are advanced, such as the assumed influence of noise traders. Similarly, various possible explanations are tried of why the mutual-funds separation theorem does not seem to hold. From a behavioral stance, it seems more appropriate to start with describing behaviors using sets of variables, and note deviations from typical behavior in terms of statistical dispersion around the mean, and leave the rationality issue alone.

NOISE TRADERS AND INEFFICIENT MARKETS

> *In my basic model of financial markets noise is contrasted with information. People sometimes trade on information in the usual way. They are correct in expecting to make profits from these trades. On the other hand, people sometimes trade on noise as if it were information. If they expect to make profits from noise trading, they are incorrect. However, noise trading is essential to the existence of liquid markets.*
>
> Black (1986, p.529)

Noise Trader Characteristics

The theory of market efficiency only deals with perfectly rational traders on the stock exchange. No investor neglects the information that is relevant to the formation of prices and there is no private information that can influence individual decision making in investing. Prices are assumed to reflect future profits, discounted to today's value. The theory says nothing about how information is disseminated or how individual stock prices are set. All information about a firm is public and known by every trader. Prices follow a random walk where changes occur due to circumstances that cannot be foreseen. There is no way of predicting future prices on the basis of current prices, since all information is already utilized in forming the current prices. The advice that is implied is that an investor should make sure that s/he has a big enough sample of stocks in order to do as well as the market and, for the rest, depend on luck, hoping to end up at the better end of the dispersion around the stock index mean. In contrast, most, if not all, investors seem to believe that stock prices can be foreseen and in particular that there are stocks that have the wrong value, are mispriced, given their future returns, that is, dividends and capital gains.

In a paper with the title 'Noise', Black (1986) launched the noise trader concept. By noise he meant 'what makes our observations imperfect'. He declared that noise keeps us from knowing the expected return on a stock or portfolio, but he did not produce any succinct definition. A common assumption is that noise traders disturb the efficiency of the market by their reactions to information. Debated issues are whether less than rational traders influence stock prices in such a way that prices do not follow a random walk and may even be predictable if the influential factors can be found.

De Long et al. (1990a and 1990b), Lee et al. (1991), and many others distinguish between *rational traders*, who make their investments pretty much as the theory assumes, and *noise traders*, who base their investments at least partly on irrational factors. Noise traders form incorrect expectations, chiefly about the variance of the return distribution of a particular asset. De Long et al. (1990a) begin their paper on noise traders with the statement that there is much evidence that investors do not follow the economists' advice to buy and hold market portfolios. They say that investors do not diversify and that if they diversify they invest in stock-picking funds that charge high fees and do not beat the market. They add that many investors do their own kind of research which they believe in. Earlier financial economists had coined the label of 'noise traders' for such investors. These investors mistake noise for information that could give them an edge.

In Thaler's (1992) view, noise traders are positive-feedback traders who forecast continuations of past returns. Thaler, like many others, refers to the rational type of traders as information traders. They have unbiased expectations whereas the noise traders are defined as making systematic forecasting errors.

> Put differently, noise trader sentiment shifts over time – sometimes it is excessively optimistic about the future, at other times it is excessively pessimistic. This variability in noise trader sentiment creates a new source of risk in the markets where they trade. A final assumption is that the rational traders are risk averse and have finite time horizons, two characteristics that seem to describe most investors,

even (or maybe especially) those who manage other people's money. As a result, the risk from shifting noise trader sentiment deters rational investors from attempting aggressive arbitrage strategies (Thaler, 1992, pp178–9).

Behavioral finance models often include some concept of noise traders or noisy prices. As distinguished from the first discussants of noise traders, who vaguely talked about one inclusive category which they called irrational behavior, behavioral finance writers point to findings in psychology in their descriptions of noise traders. They often rely on a description of noise traders as prone to judgment and decision-making errors (De Bondt, 1998). On the basis of survey evidence, De Bondt described the behavior of small individual investors who managed their own equity portfolios in such terms as that they discovered naive patterns in past price movements, shared popular models of value, were not properly diversified, and thus traded in suboptimal ways (De Bondt, 1998).

The descriptions of noise trader behavior still seem to vary considerably and imply that irrationality may be acted out in many different ways, which is certainly realistic. Noise traders sell when prices fall and buy when prices go up since they always expect a continuation of trends. This can, of course, not be true for whole markets since there must be both sellers and buyers at any point in time. For efficient-market analysts, an important question concerns how information buyers, also called rational or fundamental buyers, are affected by the activities of the noise traders. It is often assumed that both categories suffer from the disturbances created by the noise traders, but that information traders restore the market balance. To some theorists, it is enough of a counterbalance that there are a few arbitrageurs or market makers who react properly on new information and set the stock prices at the right level.

The behavioral CAPM proposed by Shefrin and Statman (1994), which will be treated below, specifically incorporates the noise traders' beliefs. The theory centers on a market where both information traders and noise traders participate. The theory handles both micro and macro effects.

Individual and Aggregate Effects of Noise Trading

Friedman (1953) declared that investors who make mistakes, buying high and selling low, will lose money to rational investors. Consequently, they will lose their wealth and disappear from the market. Anecdotal evidence about investors who lost all their money in the 1930s lent intuitive credence to a similar view about the fate of noise traders. Black (1986), who launched the idea that traders reacted to noise rather than fundamental information, assumed that these traders necessarily lost money on average, but that they made it possible for information traders to make profits.

In the early 1990s, a divergent view appeared, possibly as a consequence of the fact that developments in stock returns increased the wealth of many investors. Despite their misperceptions, noise traders can, not only as single individuals but as a group, earn higher returns than do rational investors and can survive and dominate the market in terms of wealth in the long run. They can enrich themselves through successful investments in stocks, notwithstanding their irrationality. 'Such long-run success of noise traders occurs despite their excessive risk taking and excessive consumption. The case against their long-run viability is by no means as clear-cut as is commonly supposed' (De Long et al., 1991, p.18). The authors proved the possibility of such a phenomenon by performing a deductive exercise, but did not carry out any empirical test

In the same vein, Palomino (1996) further explored the possibility that noise traders could make more profit than rational traders. He found that under certain circumstances, such as prevailing risk aversion in an imperfectly competitive market, noise traders may earn higher expected utility than rational investors. This happens when noise traders hurt rational investors more than themselves. He further suggests that his result reinforces the theory that noise trading may explain closed-end fund discounts and small firms' returns, since these markets are less competitive than the market for large firms' stock.

Noise traders who speculate using technical analysis, for example head-and-shoulders or other chart patterns, cause trading volume to be exceptionally high when they are active. Head-and-shoulders sales lower prices, and buying increases prices, 'effects that disappear in two weeks' (Osler, 1998). Osler declares that the trading of noise traders is unprofitable. Actually, he seems to include the lack of profit as a criterion in the definition. Other writers believe that noise traders are usually losers on the market – they must be, since they are not acting rationally and they take risks that are too high. Even if they make profits, they are making less than they would if they behaved rationally albeit the loss in profit may be small (Canner et al., 1997). Severn (1998) maintains that irrational noise traders earn high returns for bearing risk that they themselves create.

The concept of noise traders arose out of observations of defects in financial markets. The defects involved effects of apparently irrational behavior. In this sense, noise traders are clearly assumed to have effects on markets and the effects are assumed to do ill to market efficiency via many ways of misrepresenting information, including avoidance of exposure to information. This leads to the issue of how such ill effects can be offset by other influences, in the first place arbitraging by rational information traders.

Noise traders are often depicted as emotional and disposed towards overoptimism or overpessimism. Their sentiment is shifting in unpredictable ways and gives rise to unexpected stock-price changes. Because of shifts in sentiment, noise traders make systematic forecasting errors. Some authors suggest that the 1987 stock exchange crisis was, if not caused, at least enhanced, by the operations of noise traders: Siegel (1992) advanced the hypothesis that shifts in investor sentiment, perhaps induced by noise traders, were a factor in the 1987 stock decline.

In this view, rational traders run into difficulties because of noisy prices. An arbitrageur may hesitate to exploit excess returns that in a rational market would revert towards the mean because noise traders' pessimism or optimism may delay the reversion indefinitely. This creates a risk for the arbitrageur. Analyses of rational speculation usually presume that it dampens irrational fluctuations caused by noise traders. This is not necessarily the case if noise traders follow positive-feedback strategies and buy when prices rise and sell when prices fall. An increase in the number of forward-looking speculators can increase volatility about fundamentals (De Long et al., 1990b).

Noise Traders and Passive Investors

The noise trader theories are not tested against empirical data and are thus, in the first place, explorations of possibilities. Forgetting that the idea of noise trader gives a condescending name to the absolute majority of investors in stocks, one finds that the debate about noise traders provides a number of interesting hypotheses about investor behavior, many of which will be dealt with later in this book. In my view, the dichotomy that distinguishes information trader from noise trader is too simple and rather misleading since information is used in a very narrow sense that is foreign to a behavioral scientist. Money managers and other professional investors may not be information traders to the extent often assumed and there may not be any information traders in the real sense of the word. There are certainly more than just two radically different categories of traders. The economists' advice to buy and hold a market portfolio implies that investors can be passive and still do as well as the market, which is usually represented by a stock-price index. It is then interesting that Kelly (1997) distinguishes between three types of investors: (1) smart-money traders, (2) noise traders, and (3) passive investors.

While the smart-money traders behave rationally, the noise traders buy high and sell low and the passive investors do little business. Kelly assumes that an individual's probability of being a noise trader declines with income, since those with high income have greater incentives to acquire reliable information about the market. Low-income groups are consequently mostly noise traders, very high-income groups consist predominantly of smart-money traders, and passive investors are to be found in intermediate-income groups. Market participation of noise traders is assumed to have a negative effect on future stock returns and smart-money trader participation to have a positive effect. The participation of passive investors would have no effect at all.

Kelly tested his ideas on data from the I.R.S. Statistics of Income Series which is based on income tax returns. Data on individuals were not used. He concluded that the tests strongly supported the model:

> Market participation by the general population (where noise traders are assumed to predominate) was a strong negative predictor of returns. Participation by very high-income households was a strong positive predictor, and changed in direct response to noise trader participation. Changing participation by intermediate households, who were identified as predominantly passive investors, had no power to forecast returns (Kelly, 1997, p.361).

In Chapters 8 and 9, the existence of passive investors and their possible role will be discussed further. In my view, their potential importance has been neglected by both theory and practice.

STRATEGIES AND TACTICS

A rational individual is forward-looking and plans for the future by making sure that resources will be available for future consumption. In theory, there are two steps in the procedure, namely the act of postponing consumption and thus saving, and the second step of putting the savings into assets. In practice, there may not be a clear difference between the two steps. Investment guides and textbooks start, however, with portfolio choice as their subject matter. Financial theories give guidance for investor actions in the market. They suggest strategies that involve rational behavior. If you and all other agents use information rationally when trading, efficient-market theory promises that you will do as well as others, which means that you will get the average returns (with some dispersion over time). Some, maybe many, but far from all, traders want to do better than well-composed funds and average returns and to beat the stock market index.

Strategies and tactics have been developed and tried in such attempts to beat the market. Most of them can be seen as expressions of belief in the predictability of the financial market. Most strategies make use of what is called *market anomalies* in the theory. In fact, the use of most strategies and techniques implies a disbelief in the efficient-market theory. When investors build a portfolio, they probably try to obtain the best returns and minimize the risk of loss, which means that they are rational in a limited sense. They may not live up to all the abstract criteria that economic rationality postulates, but they are subjectively rational when they try their best.

The mean-variance strategy for portfolio choice suggested by Markowitz (1952a), which is most in line with CAPM, requires a lot of calculations to be implemented. Actual market behaviors apparently deviate from the ideal model and many authors have looked for strategies that take possible deviations from strict rationality into account. Behavioral assumptions about how investors act have inspired some authors to develop strategies that they hope will perform better than average.

Strategy is here used to designate long-term plans or sets of actions and *tactics* to designate short-term operational plans. *Techniques* refer to sets of instruments for implementing strategy and tactics. A large arsenal of techniques exists, probably as many techniques as there are investors. They can be subsumed under a limited number of categories if minor variations are ignored. They all aim to perform better than average or, in the worst case, as well as the average portfolio performance. How successful they actually are is another matter.

Some strategies are closer than others to financial theories, but the common feature is that they are based on the belief that stock prices can be predicted, at least to some extent, and that even if the forecast is only a slight improvement over chance, the use of it will make a difference and be profitable.

Diversification and Indexing

> *Folk wisdom says: 'Don't put all your eggs in one basket.' That nominates the canny principle of diversification. When instead of putting $40,000 into one stock, you divide it over four independent stocks, each equally risky and each with equal mean total returns, you stand to halve your riskiness while leaving your expected mean return unchanged.*
>
> Samuelson (1994, p.20)

Diversification is used in more than one sense. Usually, diversification refers to the proportion of riskless assets compared to risky assets. In a second sense, diversification refers to the spread within an asset category, for example, how many firms are represented in the portfolio of stocks. Bernoulli ([1738]1954, p.30) was an early advocate of diversification: 'Another rule which may prove useful can be derived from our theory. This is the rule that it is advisable to divide goods which are exposed to some danger into several portions rather than risk them all together.'

Shefrin (2000, p.172) says that investors do not understand the principles of diversification at all well and therefore make many mistakes in composing portfolios. Many investors prefer to invest in mutual funds although they could get higher returns from long-term investment in their own portfolios of stocks. The reasons suggested for this preference are commonly two (Schlarbaum et al., 1978). One is that mutual funds provide an easy way of diversifying even with small investments. The second is that the professional money manager has skills that are, or at least are assumed to be, superior to those of the individual investor.

As mentioned earlier, Benartzi and Thaler (1998) report a study of how what they called 'naive' investors invested. They found that in the groups that they interviewed a common tendency was to use the simple rule of dividing evenly among the asset types offered. They employed the '*1/n* heuristic' where *n* is the number of available funds. Read and Loewenstein (1995) called the tendency the 'diversification bias'. If people make combined choices of quantities of goods for future consumption, they choose more variety than if they make separate choices immediately preceding consumption. So there may be a difference in portfolio diversification depending on whether an investor considers buying one or more stocks at the same time. Considering stocks from more firms at the same time would lead to greater diversification. The authors attribute diversification bias to two mechanisms: *time contraction*, which is the tendency to compress time intervals and treat long intervals as if they were short, and *choice bracketing*, which is the tendency to treat choices that are framed together differently from those that are framed apart.

Indexing means to invest in assets in such a way that the average returns follow an index over stock-price changes during a year or another period of choice. This strategy essentially involves stock-picking a market portfolio.

Samuelson (1989) gives some sobering thoughts about beating the index:

> Those lucky money managers who happen in any period to beat the comprehensive averages in total return seem primarily to have been merely lucky. Being on the honor roll in 1974 does not make you appreciably more likely to be on the 1975 honor roll. If you can match the index by selecting a composition of securities you should consider yourself lucky enough! (Samuelson, 1989, p.1).

Contrarian and Momentum Strategies

> *Given a set of events and a sufficiently large or rich set of possible explanatory factors, one can always derive postdictions or explanations to any desired degree of tightness. In regression terms, by expanding the set of independent variables one can always find a set of predictors with any desired correlation with the independent variable. The price one pays for overfitting is, of course, shrinkage, failure of the derived rule to work on a new sample of cases . . . The price that investment analysts pay for overfitting is their long-run failure to predict any better than market averages . . . although the cynic might say that they actually make their living through the generation of hope (and commissions).*
>
> Fischhoff (1982a, pp.345–6)

Two major types of strategies have been extensively debated and investigated: (a) contrarian, and (b) momentum (Schiereck et al., 1999; Chan et al., 1999). 'Contrarian strategies buy stocks that performed poorly over the past two to five years (prior losers) and sell short stocks that performed well over the same period (prior winners) . . . Momentum (or 'relative strength') strategies entail the purchase of stocks that performed well in the past and the sale of stocks that performed poorly – the exact opposite of what contrarians recommend' (Schiereck et al., 1999, p.104).

Long ago, security analysts used to advocate purchase of stocks whose prices seemed low relative to their fundamental value (Thaler, 1992, p.157). The idea was that the prices were temporarily low and could be expected to rise after some time, say a year. The advice was to be contrarian and go against the market. Some indicators pointing out situations when such strategies were appropriate were suggested, such as a low price to earnings per share ratio (p/e), dividend yield, and price of the stock in relation to the book value per share.

Contrarian strategies are connected with expected or assumed overreactions to news about earnings, implying that the overreactions will soon be over. Momentum strategies are correspondingly related to assumptions of underreactions on news about earnings changes. Prices are assumed to adjust only slowly to earnings surprises and analysts to be slow to revise their forecasts. More will be said about over- and underreactions in Chapter 6. Contrarian strategies are similar to strategies based on expected regression towards the mean, only the expectations of changes are supported by other explanations than statistical mean-reversion. While contrarian strategies are usually motivated by beliefs or highly subjective forecasts, regression towards the mean was, at least originally, a pure statistical phenomenon.

Studies of contrarian strategies based on time-series data on stock rate developments over long periods of time indicate that contrarian strategies can yield good profits (Thaler, 1992, pp.157–8; Dreman, 1999; Schiereck et al., 1999). One of the early empirical studies, carried out by De Bondt and Thaler (1985), reported maximum annual returns from contrarian strategies when winners and losers were measured by performance in the previous three years. They found that former loser portfolios outperformed the market by, on average, 19.6 percent over the last 50 years at the New York Stock Exchange. Winner portfolios earned about 5 percent less than the market. The former losers had initially low p/e values while the former winners had high p/e values. Critics who accept the efficient-market model have objected to the authors' reasoning and suggested that the authors' model was too vague and misspecified to be a real test of the theory. The original De Bondt and Thaler study aroused much debate and inspired a number of studies with varying results.

Two lines of argument against the results, besides the methodological criticisms, developed. One explanation was based on the empirical fact that small firms tended to be early losers and to give excess returns in the long run. The other argument referred to the extra compensation for extra risk taking connected with investing in losers. In a later paper, De Bondt and Thaler (1987) demonstrated that the results were not caused by small-firm effects or differences in risk. Chan (1988), in a similar analysis, also found gains, but economically insignificant ones. He found no strong evidence for the overreaction hypothesis and concluded that the results were compatible with CAPM. Kryzanowski. and Zhang (1992), who used data for stocks listed on the Toronto Stock Exchange 1950 to 1988, did not find the same reversals as De Bondt and Thaler.

Studies of contrarian strategies involving time series of price developments over long periods, say three to five years, may also leave room for momentum strategies in the shorter run. A study of all companies on the Frankfurt Stock Exchange for the period 1961–91 gave results similar to those of De Bondt and Thaler's studies. The authors of the study conclude:

> Momentum and contrarian strategies [with 12- or 60-month holding periods] appeared to beat a passive approach that invested in the market index. We tried to reconcile the results with standard theories, as well as with known price anomalies. However, factors such as beta, risk, or firm size do not easily account for the results. Because several of the strategies require limited trading, their implementation costs are modest. We conclude, therefore, that the results are economically meaningful – that is, substantial enough to be of interest to portfolio managers (Schiereck et al., 1999, p.114).

Momentum strategies seem to hold over short periods of up to 12 months whereas contrarian strategies perform better with a three to five-year horizon. A new approach to describing strategies is found in a paper by Hong and Stein (1999). It is interesting here because it deals with the diffusion of information and recognizes that this process may be slow and gradual over a population. These authors propose two types of traders, both of them boundedly rational: newswatchers and momentum traders. Each newswatcher recognizes some private information, but fails to extract other newswatchers' information from prices. If information diffuses gradually across the population, prices underreact in the short run. The underreaction means that the momentum traders can profit by trend chasing. The gradual-information-diffusion model is tested in a later paper (Hong et al., 2000) in which three key results are reported. First, once one moves past the very smallest stocks, the profitability of momentum strategies declines sharply with firm size. Second, holding firm size fixed, momentum strategies work better among stocks with low analyst coverage. Finally, the effect of analyst coverage is greater for stocks that are past losers than for past winners.

Momentum strategies are based on the conviction that past performance is the best predictor of future returns. Studies have indicated that this holds true for cross-sections of stock returns. Seeking explanations of the apparent success of momentum strategies, Chan et al. (1999) noted:

> [O]ver an intermediate horizon of three to twelve months, past winners on average continue to outperform past losers, so that there is 'momentum' in stock prices. Investment strategies that exploit such momentum, by buying past winners and selling past losers, predate the scientific evidence and have been implemented by many professional investors. The popularity of this approach has grown to the extent that momentum investing constitutes a distinct, well-recognized style of investment in the United States and other equity markets (Chan et al., 1999, pp.101–2).

The authors examined the reactions to earnings-related information on the New York stock exchanges from 1977 to 1993. They found that changes in returns over the next six and twelve months were predictable from a stock's prior returns and from prior news about earnings. 'The bulk of the evidence thus points to a delayed reaction of stock prices to the information in past returns and in past earnings' (Chan et al., 1999, p.105).

Moskowitz and Grinblatt (1999) distinguished between individual stock momentum and industry momentum strategies. The former strategies buy past winning stocks and sell past losing stocks whereas the latter strategies buy stocks from past winning industries and sell stocks from past losing industries, They found a strong and prevalent momentum effect in industry components of stock returns. The industry momentum effect accounted for much of the individual stock momentum. Industry momentum strategies appeared highly profitable, even after controlling for firm size, book-to-market equity, individual stock momentum, the cross-sectional dispersion in mean returns, and potential microstructure influences.

The analyses of the fruitfulness of contrarian and momentum strategies have with few exceptions been *a posteriori* and have taken their data from lists of stock prices. They apparently have not tried to imitate the decision situation of the investor, who has to make a judgment as to whether a stock price will continue to drop or start going up again. An investor has to decide when to buy and when to sell, and in both momentum and contrarian strategies there is the difficulty of knowing or merely guessing when the stock-price reversals start in earnest. The studies of the strategies have selected reversal points by inspecting actual stock-price developments and probably tend to overestimate the possible gains of using the strategies in practice. After all, some stocks lose their value completely and disappear from the lists. Chan et al. (1999, p.103) do not exclude the possibility that the whole thing is a statistical fluke.

Recent Finnish research utilizing a unique data base gives support to momentum strategies. Individual stock holdings and transactions were studied by Grinblatt and Keloharju (2000a). In Finland, as in Sweden, most capitalized stocks are registered by a central body, in Finland called the Finnish Central Securities Depositary. The authors' data base includes essentially all holdings and transactions for the whole Finnish financial market from end-1994 to end-1996 and the data are highly reliable. According to the findings, most Finnish households, independent of portfolio size, pursued contrarian strategies whereas foreign investors, mostly large funds, used momentum strategies. Households as well as professional investors in Finland tended to buy losers and sell winners. The exception was Finnish finance and insurance institutions and foreign investors, whom the authors designate as more sophisticated. Momentum strategies turned out to be much more profitable. The authors note that if large investors pursue momentum strategies, it must follow that small investors use contrarian strategies since purchases and sells must match.

Technical Analysis

The art of technical analysis is to identify trend changes at an early stage and to continue to invest in accordance with the change until the weight of the evidence indicates that the trend has reversed. Some traders place great importance on chart patterns, while others only look at them, but have little faith in their relevance to the market and trading in general. Technical analysis is meaningless according to efficient-market theory. When the stock market is up, especially for a long period of time, technical analysis seems less used. When there is turbulence technical analysis comes back, as a kind of 'voodoo' in some experts' opinion. The attempts to look for certain patterns in past stock-price movements are held to contribute to the difficulties of a turbulent period if the use becomes common (De Bondt, 1998).

Seehusen (1994) lists some common patterns: (1) head-and-shoulders formations, (2) M-tops or W-bottoms, (3) triangles, (4) trading ranges and rectangles, (5) flag formations, and (6) gaps. He says that in developing a trading system that encompasses any of these chart patterns, it is important to remain consistent. He asserts that the patterns occur often enough over a wide range of markets because they are a reflection of human behavior that is driven by fear and greed. In my view, such assumptions are debatable and serve little purpose.

Head-and-shoulders analysis techniques involve looking for patterns in tops and bottoms in the development of stock prices.

> Cycle analysts study economic trends and repetitive patterns in order to isolate the time frame within which trend changes might occur. Moving average systems are time-based and attempt to signal trend changes. Most trading systems, whether fundamentally oriented or technically based, have as their goal the isolation of specific patterns, which have profit potential (Bernstein, 1993, p.105).

De Bondt (1998) commented that the use of technical analysis was similar to people's tendency to distinguish patterns in random sequences, and that many investors find patterns where there are none. There is often extrapolation bias, that is, expected continuation of past price changes. People continue to be optimistic in bull markets and pessimistic in bear markets. A recent and complete review of technical analysis is found in Lo et al. (2000). The authors note that technical analysis, also known as 'charting,' has been a part of financial practice for many decades, but has not received the same acceptance as fundamental analysis. They suggest that one of the main obstacles is the highly subjective nature of technical analysis. The observed presence of shapes and patterns in historical price charts 'is often in the eyes of the beholder'. The authors propose a systematic and automatic approach to technical pattern recognition using non-parametric kernel regression. The method was applied to a large number of US stocks from 1962 to 1996 to evaluate the effectiveness of technical analysis and it was found to have some practical value.

> By comparing the unconditional empirical distribution of daily stock returns to the conditional distribution – conditioned on specific technical indicators such as head-and-shoulders or double-bottoms – we find that over the 31-year sample period, several technical indicators do provide incremental information and may have some practical value (Lo et al., 2000, abstract).

Regression towards the Mean

> *Hotelling pointed out that 'the seeming convergence is a statistical fallacy, resulting from the method of grouping.' The author had grouped the enterprises by their size in the initial year of a period, and then traced the average size of these groups in succeeding years. These averages converged. Hotelling pointed out that grouping the enterprises by their size in the final year would produce seeming divergence.*
>
> Friedman and Friedman (1998, p.73)

> *It appears that speculative asset prices tend to show excess volatility relative to simple present value efficient markets models, and that prices are partly forecastable as tending to returning to the 'mean' appropriately defined.*
>
> Shiller (1990, p.58)

Regression towards the mean or mean reversion is the statistical fact that in a chance process extreme values are likely to be followed by less extreme values. If you have a top score in one test the only way your score can vary is down (if it is a chance process). If you praise a person for a single outstanding performance s/he will probably do worse next time and if you scold a person for a single bad performance s/he will do better next time, for purely statistical reasons (Hogarth, 1987).

Stock values are volatile and certainly fluctuate over time. Some of the volatility may be due to random influences. The stock price at a certain point in time can be seen as a random observation from a population with a dispersion around the mean value. In Figure 2.1, the price is set as a function of earnings, say, earnings per share, to make comparisons a little more meaningful. Take two earnings points, X_1 and X_2. The prices of stocks with the same earnings levels vary. The dispersion around the value is indicated by the contour of the ellipse. It is obvious from the length of the lines that for X_2 the likelihood of a lower price is larger than the likelihood of a higher price when a new observation is taken. The reverse holds for the earnings level X_1 . This tendency is called *regression towards the mean* or, in finance, usually *mean reversion.* It means that extreme values have restricted variation: a high value is more likely to vary downwards and a low value is more likely to vary upwards and in both cases the values get closer to the mean.

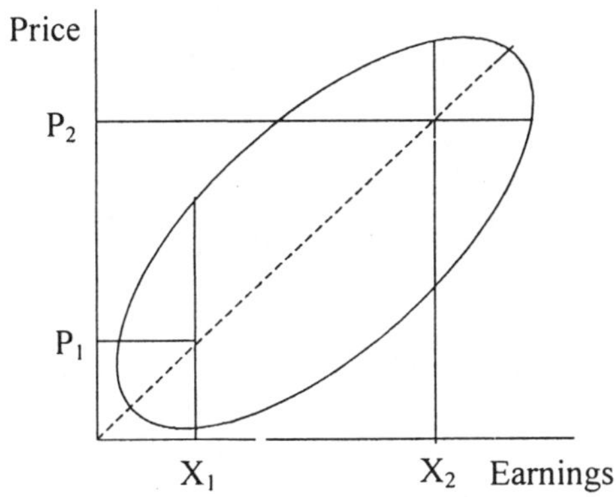

Figure 2.1 Regression towards the Mean

An investment strategy based on expected mean reversion is similar to a contrarian strategy, but it may be more short term. De Bondt and Thaler (1985) endorsed contrarian strategies on the basis of periods of three to five years. If fund managers perform well one year and performance is a random process (within limits), they cannot be expected to keep their position next year and will do less well, as Samuelson says in the vignette. Reading through many time-series studies in which groups of companies are followed over a succession of years, I am struck by the possibility that researchers may still forget to consider the possibility of the regression fallacy that Milton Friedman warned against. At least, they do not mention it or, if they have successfully handled it, say how they did so.

Stop-Loss Tactics and Portfolio Insurance

Investors may want to make sure that they do not lose too much when the prices of their stocks go down. To achieve this, they impose a limit that releases immediate selling when the stock price has dropped to that limit. This *stop-loss* may involve hedging of risks, but is often carried out as part of a computer program and can thus be fairly automatic. If a similar procedure is run for the whole portfolio rather than for a specific stock, it is called *portfolio insurance*, and may involve combinations of stocks and options so as to guarantee a minimum return. In the search for explanations of the October 1987 crash, it was suggested that portfolio insurance and stop-losses, if they did not cause anyhow enhanced the rapid fall of stock prices when a number of such programs went into effect at the same time. Shiller (1989, 2000) is rather skeptical about this explanation and suggests that there may have been some limited influence. Lee (1998) attributes only slightly more effect to portfolio insurance.

THE BEHAVIORAL CAPITAL ASSET PRICING MODEL

The gambler feels that the fairness of the coin entitles him to expect that any deviation in one direction will soon be cancelled by a corresponding deviation in the other. Even the fairest of coins, however, given the limitations of its memory and moral sense, cannot be as fair as the gambler expects it to be.

Tversky and Kahneman (1982b, p.24)

The fact that there are noise traders – and it is a fact that many traders are not rational information users in the efficient-market sense – throws doubts on the Capital Asset Pricing Model. Keeping the distinction between *information traders* and *noise traders*, Shefrin and Statman (1994) developed the Behavioral Capital Asset Pricing Model (BCAPM). Information traders are rational and follow Bayesian rules. Noise traders are non-rational because they commit cognitive errors. While the authors concur that there can be many types of cognitive errors (and other errors affecting decisions), they concentrate on two: (1) underweighting of base-rate information, and (2) probability mismapping.

Base rates are in principle derived from earlier occurrences of events and are often defined as prior probabilities (see the section 'Bayes' Theorem and the Handling of Probabilities' in Chapter 1). They play a role in intuitive predictions of values. The base-rate fallacy is the failure to take account of the prior probability when estimating a conditional probability. If people fail to take base rates into consideration when making inferences, they do not behave as Bayesians as efficient-market theories posit. This is a serious attack on these theories.

Tversky and Kahneman (1982c, 1982d) demonstrated that people tended to neglect base-rate information in favor of similarity judgments. When estimating the probability $P(H|D)$, subjects look at the similarity between some aspect of H and D. This is the representativeness heuristic. Gigerenzer and Hoffrage (1995, pp.699–700) give some reasons why base rates are neglected and point out that in many inference problems base rates are uninteresting. It is not always wrong to neglect the base rates. In Shefrin and Statman's view, noise traders are underweighters of base rates and make forecasts by overweighting recent events; they underweight more distant events. This means that noise traders neglect the base rates or prior probabilities and believe that the most recent changes will continue in the same way.

The *probability mismapping* can be compared to 'gambler's fallacy'. If a roulette player betting on black or red notices a long series of one color coming up, s/he tends to believe that the other color has a higher probability of coming up next time. If the stock price of a certain firm or the stock index has gone up continuously for a long time, it is expected to come down. What has gone up will sooner or later fall down. This cognitive error leads to the expectation that the stock price will fall whereas the base-rate underweighting involves beliefs of continued rise. If the two cognitive errors operate to the same extent, the errors may cancel out and the average effect equal zero, which means that the market can be efficient as if there were no noise traders.

The BCAPM comprises a micro model, a model of a microeconomic process and a model of what happens at the macro level. The authors propose a second type of beta, a behavioral beta to incorporate the risk involved in mispriced stock.

A BEHAVIORAL VIEW OF INFORMATION

Testing Theoretical Models against Market Behavior

The market information models that propose modifications or elaborations of efficient-market theory and that were presented in Chapter 1 are all aimed at developing micro models that might explain macro phenomena. The pertinent question concerns why price movements, also labeled market volatility, are much more extreme than justified by changes in (expectations about) the fundamentals of dividends and capital gains. The authors of the models consistently reject the idea that the market behavior is irrational. The first attempts to exploit psychological theories that may explain the irrationality assumption often involve efforts to make the theories compatible with rationality. Models of herd behavior can be taken as an example (Chapter 7).

The rules of the game do not require that assumptions be realistic. The requirement is that they serve 'as if', the famous F-twist that Milton Friedman propounded (Friedman, 1953). It asserted that the true measure of the value of economic theory was the accuracy of the predictions it made. The assumptions made could be false, but they remained valid as long as the predictions were better than those made under any other assumptions (cf. Plott,

1990; Fama, 1998). This closed the door on the psychologists' criticism of unrealistic psychological underpinnings of economic theory. Still, the authors of the models tend to argue that their assumptions at least seem plausible (unless the mathematics makes other assumptions necessary in the analysis). A model's ability to explain a broader range of phenomena is another possible criterion for choosing between models.

The micro models involve concepts that are unobservable unless subjective data are accepted. How can, for example, the difference between a willingness-to-pay (WTP) curve and a demand curve (Bulow and Klemperer, 1994) be established through behavior revealed in the market place? Even without recourse to subjective data from individual traders, there are some possibilities. The researcher can assume that the curves are different, specify crucial characteristics, and deduce consequences of the differences. If the consequences can be tested against some set of data, there may be support for the model. Sometimes the tests against empirical data are illustrations rather than tests, since the data have been selected after the fact and the selection may have been guided by a search for confirming data. Mostly, empirical tests concern the consequences of deduced consequences, and the relationships between model results and tests of consequences are distant because of the nature of the available proxies. A major concern is that many micro models may explain phenomena after the fact, but they have little predictive power and in some, not all,cases have only fair postdictive power.

Careful tests of theoretical models through laboratory experiments conducted in controlled and clean environments are another possibility that is increasingly being employed in economics. It may be feasible to design experiments in such a way that WTP and demand curves can be constructed. If subjective data are accepted, a wider range of possibilities opens up. In principle, it is feasible to ask potential traders about their valuations of a certain stock and their WTP price. It may be difficult, though, for interviewees to make fine distinctions between valuation and reservation price. Ingenious psychologists or experimental economists may be able to come up with some method for eliciting even such data in a meaningful manner.

The Diffusion and Actual Use of Information

Hidden knowledge is a central concept in the information models of financial economics. What is hidden knowledge today in a society with modern mass and other media? Hidden has the special meaning that the individual does not reveal the information through overt behavior. How the outburst of information that is labeled informational cascade actually occurs remains rather unclear, but there are two components. One of these involves somebody acting and the other the release of hidden information. The act is observed by other traders who are followed by an ever-increasing herd of others (Banerjee, 1992; Bikhchandani et al., 1992). The authors of the theories barely touch on personal influences when they stress rather mechanical imitation of others' behavior, and completely neglect the role of impersonal media. It is easy to see that the phenomena the authors ascribe to the influence of others' actions can have enhanced effects with the help of modern news media. Informational cascades and avalanches appear to happen and they are certainly affected by the prompt reporting of all kinds of company news and stock exchange events. Observation of the financial actions of others, to the individual trader usually means reports via some medium, today often the Internet and newscasts like the CNBC in the USA.

A large number of psychological experiments demonstrate that people do not use more than a fragment of the available information when they are presented with more than a few items of information. When physicians make diagnoses and have at hand a multitude of indicators, they tend to use only a few, say three or four at the most. After a certain limit, decisions tend to become worse when more indicators or information cues are given. Strangely enough, confidence in the decision increases with the number of information cues, but the quality deteriorates (Magnusson and Ekehammar, 1972).

The finding that people use only a little of the available information has been confirmed in many experiments. Jacoby et al. (1984) carried out an experiment using feedback information on securities. Two types of feedback were distinguished. Outcome feedback is information that describes the accuracy of the response, while cognitive feedback represents information about the reasons for this accuracy and thus has explanatory or predictive value. Seventeen subjects performed a realistic decision-making task using actual fundamental factor information on stock performance at the New York Stock Exchange. The subjects were professional securities analysts who worked for different investment firms. They received incentives of $500, and press coverage created an element of competition for the participants. The experiment tested the hypothesis that outcome feedback that contains neither predictive nor explanatory value would be less likely to be used by better- as compared to poorer-performing security analysts. Results supported the hypothesis in that better-performing subjects were more likely to ignore outcome-only feedback. The authors drew the conclusion that in an environment where decision makers could be selective in choosing information to consider or not to consider, not everyone chose to access feedback information (especially with outcome-only rather than predictive or explanatory value). Better decision makers were less likely to access outcome-only feedback information than poorer decision makers. In the authors' view, some important implications of the research were that more attention should be given to the diagnostic (predictive and explanatory) nature of feedback information, and that it was time for a revision of the generally accepted concept that feedback always had a positive impact on performance.

Information Overload

In consumer behavior theory, the concept of information overload was intensely debated some years ago. The basic idea was that consumers were flooded with information of varying quality and trustworthiness from many sources. Information overload was assumed to lead to worse decisions. Jacoby (1984) reviewed the research and raised and answered two questions about information overload: (1) Can consumers be overloaded? and (b) Will consumers be overloaded? While he answered the first question with 'yes, they can', he gave a qualified 'no' as answer to the second question. 'Generally speaking, no, they will not. This is because they are highly selective in how much and just which information they access, and tend to stop well short of overloading themselves' (Jacoby, 1984, p.435). Criticizing Jacoby's downplay of information overload, Malhotra (1984) contends that there is a distinct likelihood that consumers will be overloaded and that there are important consequences. If Malhotra's review of evidence is supplemented with evidence from experimental psychology, it seems clear that too much information may worsen decisions – and at the same time increase the decision maker's confidence in the decision.

Investors can, no doubt, be overloaded with information. Most likely, they use only a few of all the possible information cues in making their investment decisions. The cues used to build up the pertinent expectations are chosen on the basis of earlier experience of cues and outcomes of similar decisions. The less the experience, the more outside influences may obtain. Judging from the enormous number of newsletters and magazines selling financial advice to investors, many investors perceive a need not only for information, but for strong recommendations to buy and sell stocks and to switch between funds.

The Role of Old and New (Mass) Media

Can there be mass movements without mass media? There were certainly mass phenomena before there were mass media, only the masses were comparatively small and gathered in a geographically limited space or the process was long drawn out over time and carried by local newspapers and by personal messengers who could perhaps draw crowds in other localities after some travel time. Mass media expand the space that can be covered in a short spell of time. Shiller (2000) presumes that the history of speculative bubbles roughly begins with the advent of newspapers and proposes that the Dutch Tulipmania in the 1630s was the first bubble of any consequence to be reported on.

Modern man spends much time every day using the media. New media like the Internet provide tools that may change behaviors and give rise to new, hitherto not experienced, functions. Day-traders are products of the Internet. They apparently get most of the information on which they act from following the course of stock prices on-line and looking for patterns that they believe to be predictive. Their influence on stock-price movements is still unknown, but there are strong suspicions that they increase price volatility for some stocks during the day. Even before the Internet, prices reacted very rapidly to new information. It used to be said already in the 1980s that a stock price in the USA had stabilized ten minutes after the release of information; some even said less than two minutes.

The role of the mass media as transmitters of information and influencers is complex. Market makers and arbitrageurs presumably get information before it reaches the widespread news media. When the mass media report on the news, the first wave of reactions has already taken place and stock exchange watchers may have noticed the changes in behavior and guessed the gist of the news. Even TV newscasts that report more or less continuously during the working day may be slow to report some news events because those who were first informed hold on to the information for some time. People with inside information are a special case, with legal restrictions that limit their use and dissemination of information.

Conceivably, the mass media fulfil their role as first news transmitters to many investors who are not members of special interest circles or continuously watching stock prices to spot indications of so-called mispriced stocks that can give excess profits. Investors who are mostly passive and make few transactions may have a ritual of following stock prices through the mass media, just to keep an eye on their investments and check that they do not unexpectedly plummet or go to abnormal heights. Passive investors are long-term investors with little disposition towards rashness and panic decisions.

A few studies have looked at the effects of news on stock prices. Niederhoffer (1971) investigated the relation between world events and movements in stock prices. He noted that news of world events could reach the public in many ways and that newspaper headlines were important because they were summaries of news stories that many observed, but few read to the end, according to communication experts. The size of the headline was then an indicator of the importance of an event. Hence he defined world event as an event that got a five- to eight-column headline in the *New York Times*. The aim was to secure about 20 headlines a year, covering the period from 1950 to 1966. It turned out that world events so defined occurred on 10 percent of all days. The headlines were classified by judges into 20 categories of meaning and were rated on a seven-point good–bad scale. World event headlines tended to appear in clusters. World events occurred on only 10 percent of the days and the chance that a world headline would occur on a randomly selected day was thus 0.10. Once a world event did occur the chances of a large headline the next day were 0.19. Headlines judged as bad for the economy had a tendency to be followed by bad headlines, and headlines judged as good to be followed by good headlines. For some categories of meaning, the probability of a similar headline the next day was much lower than for others. For example, after a natural calamity the chances of a headline the next day were substantially less than after an increase in 'hot tension' in the world.

Niederhoffer (1971) found that days with world events were somewhat more likely to be followed by large changes in stock prices than randomly selected days, but the effects were not overwhelming. The particular category of the 20 into which a world event could fall did not appear to add much additional information concerning future price movements. For clusters of world events, such as those occurring during crises (defined as five or more large headlines occurring in seven days), the proportion of large changes was substantially greater than the proportion following relatively isolated world events. After extremely bad world events, there was a tendency for rises to occur on days two to five. On those occasions, the market appeared to be initially overreacting to bad news. Niederhoffer gives an example:

> On Saturday, September 24, 1955 President Eisenhower had a heart attack. On the following Monday, volume in round lots totaled 7,761,000 shares, the highest level since July 21, 1933. The market suffered the heaviest dollar loss in history up to that time with the value of stocks on the New York Stock Exchange dropping by about 14 billion. The market averages dropped from 6 to 8 percent depending on the average used. During the following days, the market seemed to respond violently to major news concerning the president's health. For example, on Monday, October 3, the price index dropped *2.5* percent on news that the president felt tired the previous night (Niederhoffer, 1971, p.204),

In all, Niederhoffer did not find important effects for world events when they were isolated. When there was a crisis the effect on the stock index became larger, but little of the stock-price movements were explained by the world events (cf. Shiller, 2000, pp.76–7).

A study by Cutler et al. (1989) did not directly concern the effects of news in the mass media, but looked at what happened to stock returns at the New York Stock Exchange following what the authors called macroeconomic events and major non-economic events. The authors used seven measures of monthly macroeconomic activity, such as industrial production, interest rates, and inflation, to represent macroeconomic news. They found that a substantial fraction of return variation could not be explained by macroeconomic news. They then studied the stock market reaction to major non-economic events such as elections, illness and death of the president, and international conflicts. Some effects were found. For example, the Standard and Poor's

Composite Stock Index declined by 6.62 percent on the Monday after President Eisenhower's heart attack in September 1955 (see also Niederhoffer's study above), but the findings indicated only a small effect for non-economic news.

In a third approach, the authors made a list of the 50 largest one-day returns on the S&P Index since 1946 and examined the account of fundamental factors that affected prices, given in the *New York Times*. On most of the sizable return days, the information that the press cited as the cause of the market move was not particularly important, according to the authors. The following idea concludes the paper: 'If many investors accept market prices as indicators of value and so do not trade on the basis of their own assessment of values, market values will be more susceptible to those who trade on the basis of their own opinions' (Cutler et al., 1989, p.11).

Mass Media as Creators of Mood

Does mood or sentiment influence stock markets and, if so, what is the role of the mass media? The causal relationships are far from clear. For one thing, stock prices seem to affect the general mood in the economy, in the first place among those who have invested in stocks, but also in other segments of the population. When stock prices plummet, even those who have no stocks or holdings in mutual funds appear to become more pessimistic and make fewer plans for consumption expenditures. When stock prices are climbing, optimism tends to spread through the population. This is indicated in studies of what determines the Index of Consumer Sentiment. Mass media effects on stock prices do not seem to be direct, but indirect, disseminating impulses that inspire and enhance mood changes (cf. Chapter Four in Shiller, 2000)

The mass media have been compared to mirrors that reflect society in its multitude of aspects. They would then be less independent instigators of change for good or evil than if they were independent sources of power and causal agents in their own right. When such assessments are made, it is of course difficult to distinguish even on a theoretical level between the effects of certain news or certain facts per se and the effects of the circumstance that the report has been given a format and disseminated to a large number of people through the mass media. The format that the mass media give to news may be even more important than the news itself.

It has been noted that even if the mass media mainly serve as mirrors, they can select, emphasize, distort, and dramatize what they mirror and thus manipulate and even delude their audiences. No doubt, contents in the mass media influence financial markets. One way is the transmitting of rumors, which may get extra effects through being spread by recognized newspapers and acclaimed trade journals. In recent years, new, apparently effective ways of spreading rumors have become available – and used – through the Internet.

'Chatting' may be an efficient way of manipulating the price of a stock and it is said that many rumors are spread this way.

People want to know what causes lie behind events. Causal attributions are furnished by the mass media. Members of the media are expected to provide explanations that are more frequent and more extreme than those that would be generated by individuals who do not expect to communicate information to others. Andreassen (1987) pictures this as an aggregate attributional process whereby one group acts on the attributions provided by others. He finds that the process is nicely illustrated in financial markets. Research shows that the financial press tends to explain recent changes in stock prices with good news after prices rise and with bad news after prices fall.

In an experimental study, Andreassen (1987) tested the hypothesis that the expectation that changes will either persist or regress to previous levels depends in large part on whether causal attributions are provided to explain recent changes. If such attributions are provided, for example by the mass media, the tendency to make predictions of reversion towards the mean is diminished. The news media do provide such attributions, according to Andreassen, and so cause aggregate-level changes in the predictions of those who receive these communications. Thereby the mass media can induce changes in receivers' subsequent behaviors. Financial news with causal attributions was shown to lead to less regressive predictions. Dawes' (1999) assertion that people cannot handle probabilities unless they are accompanied by causal information should be kept in mind. Andreassen's experimental results give interesting support to Dawes' idea.

Summing Up

Whereas Chapter 1 focused on rationality-based theories that deal with financial markets and noted the use of a few concepts related to psychology, Chapter 2 has been devoted to attempts at modifying the rationality-based theories. Such attempts have recognized the fact that segments of traders, labeled 'noise traders', may not be characterized by the rational treatment of fundamental information that the efficient-market theory postulates. The modifications involve some use of concepts that can be given psychological content. The main emphasis is still on rational behavior, but it is extended to rational use of private information which can counteract the rational use of public information. In the following chapters, the psychological view that important human differences exist and are worthwhile to consider will prevail, with the consequence that many types of irrational behavior in the economic sense will be distinguished. To some extent, certain types of irrationality may be explained and even predicted, at least when an array of specified circumstances is fulfilled.

3. Expectation Formation

The extent of human intelligence involved in problem solving should not be overestimated. The formation of new expectations is not always based on a careful consideration of all facets of a situation. Problem solving makes use of shortcuts and stereotypes; the search for reasons may be superficial and inadequate.

Katona (1972, p.554)

From Mathematical to Human Expectation

There are no real hard facts about the future, only good or bad guesses. One interpretation of uncertainty is that there is no certain knowledge about the future, only more or less well-founded guesses, which can be called *expectations*. All decisions and acts are based on expectations that are to a varying degree based on earlier facts and guesses. Still, people may feel extremely sure about certain decisions and courses of action because things have invariably turned out in a certain way. Many expectations, whether hopes or fears, never come true and people may forget that they had them. Outcomes of actual events may agree with expectations or turn out to be more or less different from what was expected, whether hoped for or feared. Consumer, business, and government decision making is based on expectations, that is, well- or ill-founded guesses about the near or distant future. Remembering that expectations remain guesses, however precisely they are calculated by financial and other experts, is a good idea for a stock investor as well as for a bettor at the race tracks.

Keynes (1936) may not have been the first economist to talk about expectations, but he was apparently for a long time the most influential. Collard (1983) noted the importance that Pigou attached to expectations; the latter was actually a precursor of rational expectations theory. Collard (1983, p.411) quoted from Pigou: 'the varying expectations of business men . . . and not anything else, constitute the immediate and direct causes or antecedents of industrial fluctuations'. With the addition of 'private investors' to business men, and 'stock exchange fluctuations' instead of industrial fluctuations, the assertion certainly holds for stock-price developments.

The use of expectations in economics arose with the discussion of how investment decisions were made and how these influenced the business cycle. Decisions on investments did not show any immediate results and they depended upon beliefs about the future which Keynes characterized as 'animal spirits'. Keynes (1936) and the so-called 'Stockholm School' of economists devoted much thought to how business decision makers formed their expectations. Keynes used the expression 'animal spirits' to designate the overoptimism that, in his view, characterized investment decisions. Consumer expectations did not matter in these discussions. Probably, Katona's (1951) work was the first to draw attention to the role of consumer expectations.

Images of the future are in economic theory expressed as mathematical expectation of subjective utility. 'The market price is the mathematical expectation of the perfect foresight price' (De Bondt, 1993, p.356). Since perfect foresight is rarely possible, mathematical expectation and human expectation do not always agree; in fact quite frequently they disagree. The problem is specified differently in the two perspectives. The calculus of probability which economics adheres to and human handling of probabilities are often very unlike, as will be shown in the next chapter. Psychologically, investing money implies some kind of confidence in the future unless the investment is made in defensive desperation. There is at least at the moment of investing a hope that something good will come out as a result or, at any rate, something better than what not investing would convey. The hope may, immediately after the act of investing has been completed, turn into fear of losing part or all of the invested money. After-decision dissonance is common, in particular when the decision involved a difficult choice between alternatives (Festinger, 1957). The possibility of what Adam Smith called 'future enjoyment' may be felt to be severely reduced through an investment failure. Or the hope may be strengthened and the prospects of large gains look more and more certain as a consequence of the reinforcement that rising stock prices confer. All of these processes can be labeled *formation of expectations*.

Macroeconomics is founded on theories that deal with the concept of expectation as an economic rather than as a psychological concept. Expectation is mathematical expectation. The main assumption is that expectations can be quantitatively derived from objective data. In behavioristic psychology, the concept is mostly replaced by 'expectancy', which means an observable tendency to perform an act. Present use of 'expectation' refers to a subjective belief about future events or objects (Feather, 1982). According to Katona (1972), expectations are routinely formed and based on past experience or, more rarely, on weighty new information that requires problem solving and restructuring of expectations. Economic psychology has adopted the view that expectations are scenarios that people have and can talk about. This view made it possible to contribute subjective measures of expectations. These are ascertained in sample surveys through sets of questions posed to consumers and business decision makers.

Expectations are formed on the basis of experience and information, they are more or less distinct, they are more or less close to action, and they may change due to new information from the environment or from thinking or from the emergence of feelings. Perception, memory, cognitive processing, and emotion cooperate in forming and changing expectations. Beautiful weather breeds more optimistic expectations and bad weather breeds more gloomy expectations, both, however, within limits which may give some comfort to the expectations researcher (Schwartz and Strack, 1985).

An expectation is an image of a future event or relationship and may resemble a scenario. There are two main types of expectations: *contingent* and *intentional*. Contingent expectations concern outcomes of events that cannot be influenced by the individual her/himself. Intentional expectations leave room for influencing future events and may be seen as beliefs in the degree of efficacy of actions undertaken by the person her/himself. Expectations may be mixtures of the two; they may, for example, encompass outcomes and actions to protect against outcomes, if those are adverse, or profit from outcomes, if favorable. Expectations can be described as views of possible futures and differ in three main dimensions; (1) good or bad outcomes, (b) controllability (can the outcomes be influenced?), and (3) temporal distance (how far in the future?) (Karniol and Ross, 1996, p.595). Expectations may also be treated as forecasts:

> People derive their forecasts from their recollections of the past, conceptions of the present, attributions of social causality, and values. Values represent criteria for defining desirable and undesirable images of the future and provide the basis for evaluating alternative possible futures (Karniol and Ross, 1996, p. 595).

Karniol and Ross do not use the word 'expectation', but they classify expectancy as one of the phenomena closely related to goals. What they say in the quotation above is highly applicable to expectation formation.

The concept of expectation is important in economic psychology. More attention has been paid to problems of measuring subjective expectations than to studying factors influencing them. Expectation is a central concept in financial economics. It should be a central concept in psychology as well, since it embodies an essential aspect of humans' relations to the future. Although psychologists, notably behaviorists, have tended to reject the concept and paid little research attention to expectation, except as a continuation of past experience, much can be found in modern psychology to complement the subjective utility concept that in many ways is analogous to expectation. A choice between alternatives or between an action and the status quo presupposes some notion about the alternatives and the outcomes they will give rise to. Such notions of future utility may be subsumed under the concept of expectation. In an economic sense, expectations, like beliefs, are probability distributions that can be described by means and variances. This reduces expectation to mathematical expectation. Expectations in a psychological sense may contain possible actions and their outcomes. They may also comprise the outcomes of future events that cannot be influenced, but may lead to actions aimed at securing or guarding against possible consequences. An expectation may be simple and focused on a single action or event or a part of complex nets of expectations, immersed in emotions.

It has been said that the old economy is based on expectations and that the new economy, which is dominated by considerations of the Internet and high-tech firms, is based on hope. What is meant is probably that calculation of fundamentals plays more of a role in the valuation of value-stock companies than high-tech stock companies, which are now the main growth companies. In my thinking, hope is also an expectation, but with a slight foundation in facts and plenty of emotional loading.

Chapter 1 dealt with theories in financial economics, and calculation and handling of expectations in the economic sense were discussed. The second chapter further developed the criticism that emanates from observations of financial markets and involves attempts to remedy efficient-market theory by paying more attention to the behavior of investors, sometimes called investor or market psychology. The role of information is one of the intricate issues that has been tackled in the attempt to create a better understanding of financial market behavior. Information from past experience, whether from one's own memory or vicarious experience through observations or the reports of others, has an important function in the formation of expectations. One of the puzzles in financial behavior is how past experience mixes with new information. This is captured in the question: When will the trend (upwards or downwards) be believed to break?

In the following three chapters, the issues will be more deeply penetrated and more details from psychological research will be given. The next chapter deals with decision making and risk. Perception of risk and attitude towards risk may be important factors in the process of forming expectations. Most of what will be said in Chapter 5 about the heuristics-and-biases approach and other cognitive phenomena can be used in the study of expectation formation. The simple rules of thumb (heuristics) that are used by people to facilitate decision making involve interpretation of past experience and taking a position in relation to new information. This is an integral part of forming expectations of the future. In addition, dynamic aspects can be added from the study of feelings and emotions, a topic that will be approached in Chapter 6.

HEDONISM OF THE PAST AND DISREGARD OF EXPECTATIONS

For many years, the concept of expectation hardly existed in scientific psychology. As a psychologist I have often found the gap between behaviorism and cognitive psychology astounding. In many ways, behaviorism in its strict sense stands for the conviction that past experience, labeled learning, dominates behavior and will govern future behavior. Cognitive psychology recognizes the import of information use, human thinking, and goal formation. It leaves room for future-orientation that is not wholly dependent on the past.

In his treatise on the history of experimental psychology, Boring (1950) distinguished between two kinds of hedonism, which is essentially the pursuit of happiness or pleasure: *hedonism of the future* or teleology or finalism, and *hedonism of the past* with a focus on learning, when behavior was reinforced through reward or punishment during or after the behavior. Mainstream experimental psychology chose the latter kind of hedonism. This choice had the sad consequence that future-orientation for many years had little place in scientific psychology. It was replaced with *expectancy*, which is essentially an extrapolation of past overt behavior; past experience became synonymous with past overt behavior. Still, 'more of the same' is an important predictor of future behavior and extrapolation of past behavior is useful for prediction when circumstances are stable (Ajzen, 1991).

Early economists like Jevons (1871) and Böhm-Bawerk (1888) emphasized that decisions concerned the future and that the future could never be known with certainty. They talked about 'anticipations' with differing degrees of probability. Böhm-Bawerk stressed the role of uncertainty about the future and the importance of having the ability to imagine the future, a property later referred to as 'prospectiveness' by Marshall (1890) and as 'foresight' by Fisher (1930) and Keynes (1936). Keynes brought 'expectations' into focus as a capstone concept of macroeconomics and used the concept to explain the role of expectations in investments during business cycles. Like the behavioral psychologists, economists tended to disregard and even reject human intention and goals. The future became tied to choice situations in which alternative actions were represented at first by expected value and later, after Bernoulli and Bentham, by expected utility Loewenstein (1992) reviews the history of what he called the Discounted Utility Model from its beginnings as anticipation up to subjective expected utility. He discusses economists' attempts at considering why people took the future into account and explains why they were not overly successful in their attempts.

Anticipations

> *Anticipation of the future has its own unique characteristics. Unlike the past, we* can *exert at least a weak influence on the future. Moreover, the future is inherently uncertain, so we have greater freedom to imagine it as we wish than is the case with memory. Our future selves are like children away at college. We can only minimally influence their behavior and can gain only a fuzzy and distorted image of their experiences; often that is all we desire.*
>
> Elster and Loewenstein (1992, pp.214–15)

Anticipation is a special kind of expectation when used in the sense given it by, for example, Jevons who, in contrast to some of his older colleagues, realized that anticipated pleasure could have present utility:

> It is certain that a very large part of what we experience in life depends not on the actual circumstances of the moment so much as on the anticipation of future events. As Mr. Bain says, 'The foretaste of pleasure is pleasure begun: every actual delight casts before it a corresponding ideal' (Jevons [1871] 1911, pp.33–4).

In this vein, anticipation means that future emotions are imagined and the imagination gives rise to feelings now. Mr Bain, who was the leading British psychologist at the time, made a very succinct statement about the utility of anticipation: 'The foretaste of pleasure is pleasure begun'. While Jevons mostly thought of feelings emanating from future pleasures, it is of course also possible to anticipate unpleasant things and be imbued with bad feelings long before the event is due, even though it may never occur. Anticipations as they were viewed by classical economists can be said to be expectations of future pleasures and pains. Judging from anecdotal evidence in the form of success and failure stories, anticipations do play an important role in investor behavior. Anticipation of future pleasures that will be possible with profits from equity investments may inspire scenarios that lead to speculation.

More recently, Elster and Loewenstein (1992) have revived the idea of deriving utility from anticipation (and memory). They propose a general framework for the study of utility that arises from contemplation of the past and the future. The focus is on the role played by comparison between past and future. Past experience shapes the upper and lower limits of the individual's range of comparisons. Something better or something worse than the past may be expected. The authors talk about *savoring* as an anticipation of pleasure and *dread* as an anticipation of something bad. This includes comparisons between expectations held at different points in time. If an investor has an expectation of a high profit which is later changed to an expectation of less profit s/he may feel disappointed on comparing the two. This relates to the problem of choice of reference point, which will be discussed in the next chapter in connection with prospect theory.

Although there was a cognitive slant in economics, economists, when discussing anticipations and finality, somehow failed to incorporate the future in their thinking, except as extrapolation of past, observable events, until rational expectations theory came along. Inspired by the good predictions made by adherents of survey data on expectations, Muth (1961) suggested that expectations were rationally formed on the basis of information, past experience being only one possible source of information. Even before him, Katona (1951) argued that past experience and new information were integrated in the formation of expectations, and he also suggested circumstances under which the role of past experience could break down in the face of new, dramatically contrasting information. His verbal formula for expectation formation could be said to reconcile hedonism of the past and hedonism of the future or at least make the distinction highly doubtful. According to Katona, most human behavior is routine behavior, characterized by repetition and habits which beget expectations based on earlier experience. Changes in expectations and genuine decision making, which Katona mostly called problem solving, occur only rarely and ensue when there is radically new information.

In rational expectations theory, there seems to be a tendency to play down the influence of past experience in favor of new information that can be handled as quantitative economic information. An intriguing question is to what extent past experience is integrated with information not based on direct experience. When does new information get the upper hand and when does past experience suppress contrary new information? The availability and the representativeness heuristics assert that recent experience is more easily attended to than older experience, a hypothesis explored by De Bondt and Thaler (1985, 1987) in their interpretation of the overreaction hypothesis. Investors who are considering whether to sell or buy stocks have notions about the future price developments of the stocks, however vague, and act in accordance with their notions. Or they may remain passive and fail to act because their expectations are not articulate enough. Even if those are articulate, some people may fail to act in accordance with the expectation through inertia or because of perceived lack of control. The more or less eternal question about trend reversals can be dealt with under this rubric.

Novel thinking in financial economics embraces the hypothesis that there may be a positive feedback from rising stock prices that reinforces price developments. Positive feedback breeds positive expectations about the future according to this thinking. It seems likely that expectation formation, interpreted as a process of construing the future, at least potentially may explain more of investor behavior than heuristics and biases if those are treated outside the context of expectation formation. After all, in financial matters the boundaries between interpretations of the past, hope, fear, and expectation are fuzzy and hard to disentangle.

Economists view expectations as determined by objective factors such as earlier developments or new information. The mainstream economist is still somewhat skeptical about measuring subjective expectations, which are now generally accepted in psychology. Expectations are subjective phenomena that can be measured in the sense that people can be asked in a more or less subtle form to state their expectations. Measurements of consumer and business expectations have turned out to be meaningful and useful.

In behavioristic psychology, expectancy, which replaces expectation, is an extrapolation of earlier performed behavior. Expectancies as well as expectations may be good predictors of behavior, but they need not be. It is perfectly conceivable that there are conflicts between behavior and expectation, since many factors besides expectations may influence behavior. Ajzen's (1991) Theory of Planned Behavior is applicable to expectations. It points out that many factors intervene between attitude and behavior, such as social influence and the individual's perception of control.

Expectations and Subjective Expected Utility

Using the concept of subjective expected utility, basic decision theory gives rules for making optimal decisions. One starts by listing all possible actions and then grades how good or bad the possible outcomes are for each action, that is, what they contribute to utility. In a simple case, all actions lead to outcomes that are certain and, if so, one just chooses the action with the most attractive set of outcomes. Future events may be described as probabilities that state the likelihood of the outcomes, that is, their future utility. If the outcomes have probabilities that deviate from 1 or 0, the decision maker must estimate and consider the probabilities. The optimal decision is reached by weighting the attractiveness of the outcomes with the corresponding probabilities and choosing the alternative with the highest expected utility.

Some psychological descriptions of how relationships to the future are formed are similar to economic utility theory. People are assumed to imagine various possible futures, to consider the advantages and disadvantages of each, select their preferred end states, and then develop plans to achieve their desired goals while avoiding negative outcomes (Karniol and Ross, 1996, p.595). If people assign probabilities to future states, they are likely to think in terms of ranks, that is, one outcome is held to be more likely than another, and they do not use precise probabilities or even probability intervals. A major problem is that there may be a correlation between preferred state and rank, since people tend to overestimate the likelihood of preferred outcomes.

Subjective assessments of both components – probability and utility or value – are necessary before a choice can be made. While it is obvious that probability has some reference to the future, it is less obvious that the utility assessment also must accommodate a prediction of future utility, which in economics usually entails the use of a discount rate to make the future outcome comparable to the current state. The future utility should be the same as the utility now and it should not change. The latter is in economics referred to as change in tastes or preferences and it is assumed that such changes rarely occur. Psychologists tend to think that preferences are rather unstable and susceptible to influences. For obvious reasons, people undoubtedly make mistakes when they assess future utility (see Kahneman and Snell, 1990). Focussing on the wrong dimension when a buyer considers the future utility of a product is rather common, according to market research on purchases of fashion clothes, shoes, and automobiles. The appearance of a product may dominate when the purchase is being made, to be followed by more substantial criteria when the product is used. Tastes tend to change as a consequence of fads and fashions. This also holds true of investment in equities. In some investor circles, it may have been highly fashionable to invest in Internet or high-tech stocks (cf. Shiller, 1989, 2000).

Kahneman and Snell (1990) distinguish *predicted utility* as one of three kinds of utility, the others being 'decision utility' and 'experience utility'. Decision utility is the mechanical formula used by decision theorists and experience or hedonic utility is what the individual gets from the outcome which s/he naturally has to predict. Experience utility refers to the fact that the consequences of a choice appear with some delay and the utility experienced may differ from the utility visualized at the moment of decision. Predicted utility is the expected experience utility, in later papers by Kahneman (1994) called *hedonic utility*. Using results from experiments with food preferences, Kahneman and Snell (1990) maintain that people often have difficulty predicting their future tastes and that they tend to underestimate the ultimate value of an object before possessing it.

People use scenarios when they form their expectations. It can also be said that expectations are scenarios in which the past and the future are bridged through processes where data from memory, available information, and imagination are employed. Explicitly imagining possible futures seems to increase estimates of the probability of the imagined event, strengthening beliefs that it will occur (Karniol and Ross, 1996).

A MODEL OF EXPECTATION FORMATION

Based on economic and psychological theories of expectations that will be explained shortly, three sets of beliefs are assumed to form expectations (Wärneryd, 1997). The sets have different importance in different contexts, indicated by weights. In its simple, individual form the model looks like this:

$$EXP_{t+1} = w_1 B_{Pt} + w_2 B_{At} + w_3 B_{It}$$

where

EXP_{t+1} is expectation about period $t + 1$ stated at time t_0

B_{Pt} is set of beliefs based on extrapolation of past experience at time t_0

B_{At} is set of beliefs due to discrepancies between expectations and outcomes (learning) at time t_0

B_{It} is set of beliefs based on new information at time t_0

w_1, w_2, w_3 are (empirical) weights which can vary from 0 to 1.

If $\Sigma w_i = 1$, the assumption is made that the components are integrated by averaging rather than summation (cf. Busemeyer, 1991). This is consistent with many findings in information integration theory (Anderson, 1991). B_{At} represents 'error-learning' (Nerlove, 1983). This set of beliefs operates primarily when the expectation is similar to a goal or plan, an *intentional* expectation (see Vanden Abeele, 1988). B_{It} is a set of beliefs that can be divided into two subsets of beliefs, one pertaining to the individual/household, the other to economy-wide information. All three sets are subjective and may be influenced by (biased) cognitive processes and emotions.

The basic idea is that expectations are formed and revised on the basis of past experience of a phenomenon (or similar phenomena, involving generalization), on the basis of learning from how successful earlier, intentional expectations were, and finally, on the basis of new information in the individual's immediate or more distant environment. If the weight of one set of beliefs equals zero, the other sets are the basis for forming an expectation. If the expectation is *contingent*, that is, the outcome cannot be affected by anything the holder of the expectation does, the weight of the error-learning beliefs is equal to zero. Many expectations are simply founded on past experience. In terms of the model, this means that the other two sets of beliefs have weights equal to zero or at least very small weights. In other cases, there is no earlier experience, but some information in the environment, which will then serve to form the expectation.

The sets of beliefs, B_{At}, can be interpreted as the theory, however modest, that the individual brings to the situation and that replaces pure extrapolation. It involves learning from earlier outcomes either as a cognitive calculation of differences between earlier expectations and outcomes as postulated by adaptive expectation theorists or as more involved cognitive processes.

A simple example illustrates the principle behind the model. Suppose you are asked to estimate how much a given stock index will rise during the next 12 months. Let us assume that for the last three years the correct figures are: 10 percent, 10 percent, and 50 percent. If you are asked for a qualitative answer, you will, for example, say 'rise very much', thinking mostly of last year's rise. If you are asked for a quantitative statement, you may believe that the rise will continue and extrapolate, say, by calculating the average rise and giving the estimate '35 percent' or you may give even more weight to the latest observation. The stated expectation is 'extrapolative'. If last year in answer to the question, you took the average, that is, estimated 10 percent, you made a wrong guess. You may then consider the error you made in last year's guess and now make a correction of what you would otherwise guess so you add the error or a fraction of it to the new estimate. This may land you at 75 percent; more subtle correction factors are, of course, possible. This is called 'adaptive expectations' formation. Suppose that you get new, trustworthy information that last year's rise was unusually high and is unlikely to be repeated, and that stock prices will probably stay at the same high level due to continued industrial growth and other circumstances. Your answer to the qualitative question will then be 'no change' and 'zero' to the quantitative question. The last estimate is an example of how information may affect expectations and illustrates 'rational expectations' theory in a highly simplified way. An important question in many contexts concerns what weight is given to past experience when there is conflicting new information.

A simple criterion for rational expectations is that the discrepancies between expectations and realizations are minimal, that is, do not deviate significantly from zero. Extrapolative as well as adaptive expectations are then compatible with rational expectations provided they give good enough predictions. The third set of beliefs in the model above involves there being new information to utilize, something that is not handled by the extrapolative and adaptive expectations theories. In some, presumably rare, cases the new information will have such dominance that other sets of beliefs get zero weights. Katona (1972) said that new and dramatic information could lead to problem-solving rather than the usual routine behavior.

Expectations Theories in Economics

In economics, three main theories of expectations exist: (1) more or less sophisticated extrapolation of earlier experience, (2) adaptive expectations, based on learning from differences between outcomes and earlier expectations, and (3) rational expectations. They were earlier often seen as mutually exclusive. (1) and (2) are actually two different ways of dealing with past experience. Past experience usually refers to objective data on earlier development rather than to subjective experience or perception of past developments. 'Extrapolative expectations' are based on past developments, which can be weighted or not weighted. In weighted models, particular weight is frequently given to the most recent developments, for example by using the geometric mean. 'Adaptive expectations' involve letting earlier discrepancies between expectation and outcome affect the new expectation. An expectation based on previous experience is corrected using some factor whose size is related to earlier expectation–outcome discrepancies.

The basic idea behind 'rational expectations' theory is that people use information about economic events when they form their expectations and, furthermore, that they do this using the best of economic knowledge (Muth, 1961). Like any other economic behavior, the formation of expectations is assumed to be rational. Some economists add a pinch of salt and think in terms of asymptotic rational expectations, that is, expectations formed through rational processing of information, given enough time. This is similar to Keynes's view that economic behavior was rational 'on average and over time'. 'Rational' is used in an economic sense and not in the way psychologists tend to think of rationality, as a process. The rational expectations theory provided a way of handling the influence of new economic information, which was apparently already accomplished by simple survey measures of expectations. The big issue for both economists and psychologists is how past experience and new information are integrated by individuals when they form expectations about the relevant future.

'Adaptive expectations' theory involves letting earlier discrepancies between expectation and outcome affect the new expectation. It means correcting an expectation based on previous experience using some factor whose size is related to earlier expectation–outcome discrepancies. Nerlove (1983) found that the adaptive expectations theory, which he called 'error-learning' theory, explained surveyed expectations quite well for business firms in Germany and France. The theory of adaptive expectations can be expected to make less sense for contingent than for intentional expectations since the latter are similar to plans that the respondent will implement.

The original rational expectations theory was explained in simple terms: 'expectations, since they are informed predictions of future events, are essentially the same as the predictions of the relevant economic theory' (Muth, 1961, p.316). The new theory referred to how businessmen formed their expectations about prices and was inspired by two conclusions from earlier studies of expectations (Muth, 1961, p. 316):

1. Averages of survey expectations in an industry were more accurate than naive models and as accurate as elaborate equation systems, although there were wide individual variations
2. Survey expectations generally underestimated the extent of changes actually taking place. There was severe criticism of adaptive expectations theory, since adaptive expectations consistently underestimated actual expectations when there was steady growth.

The theory of rational expectations is intended as a theory of how expectations of a wide range of economic variables are formed (Attfield et al., 1985, p.11). Rational expectations have been described in varying terms:

> The underlying idea is simply that economic agents behave purposefully in collecting and using information just as they do in other activities. In this general form the hypothesis is a compelling one, but in practice this idea is often translated into the requirement that expectations are, in the model at hand, formed in a way that is stochastically consistent with the behavior of the realized values of the variables in question (Nerlove, 1983 pp.1254–5).

Rational expectations involve earlier experience and new information being used in an optimal way, which means that they are treated as in economic theory. It is assumed that expectations are revised as new information, for example about income, becomes available. As Thaler (1990) noted, this can be a very demanding task requiring highly complicated calculations.

The rational expectations theory overrides the other theories of expectation formation. While the main emphasis is on the use of new information, the optimal use of information may involve pure extrapolation and sometimes an adaptive process. The reasoning around rational expectations implies that they are primarily a macro concept. On average and over time expectations will tend to be rational, when the situation is not too complex. The limited cognitive capacity of humans makes it unlikely that any human being has really rational expectations (Simon, 1984, 1990). Katona (1980) and Simon (1984) observed that one aim of rational expectations theory was to make measurement of expectations unnecessary, an ambition they did not share.

The original formulation of the rational expectations theory hardly admitted any empirical testing of its validity. While some adherents of the rational expectations theory still think that the theory cannot (and should not) be tested directly against empirical data on subjective expectations (cf. Sheffrin, 1983), there are now several formulations of the theory that invite such testing. A weak form of test means that the discrepancies between expectation and outcome should on average be equal to zero (unbiased). A stronger test demands that there is no correlation between information available when the expectation was formed and the expectation error (Attfield et al., 1985, pp.106–9).

A simple delineation of rational expectations is that expectations are rational when there is no pattern of systematic error: 'Purposeful economic agents have incentives to eliminate such errors up to a point justified by the costs of obtaining the information necessary to do so . . . The most readily available and least costly information about the future value of a variable is its past values' (Nerlove, 1983, p.1255). Extrapolation from past experience may be the only information used in many cases of expectation formation. If there is good agreement between expectation and outcome, at least one criterion for rationality is satisfied.

Tests of the rational expectations theory have been carried out using laboratory experiments and, in a somewhat different vein, interview surveys. Brown and Maital (1981) made an early test of rational expectations. They showed that economic experts in the well-known Livingston panel of economic experts underutilized available information, particularly data on monetary growth. The experts were partly, but not fully, rational. In an earlier study, Maital (1979) found that a unit change in monetary growth had the largest impact on inflation expectations of consumers. He found it unlikely, though, 'that pipefitters and stevedores furrow their brows over the latest figures on M_1, M_2, and excess reserves' (Maital, 1979, p.434). As often noted, forecasts differ in predictive accuracy. Batchelor and Dua (1991) found that individual forecasts were more likely to be rational if they were based on mainstream economic theory and included a substantial element of judgment. The latter part may be due to the importance of new information.

The primary aim of many of the tests seems to be to ascertain whether there are systematic errors when expectations and realizations are compared. The test involves there being a correspondence between expectations at time $t - 1$ for time t and the appraisals of outcomes at time t. If there is agreement, the rational expectations hypothesis is assumed to hold. This is, of course, not really a test of the rational expectations hypothesis. It is not only a very weak test of fit, it errs in presupposing that the only way to make accurate predictions, or rather to have accurate expectations, is to treat the available information in an optimal way, that is, as economic theory prescribes. Arrow (1986) has emphatically stressed that there are many plausible alternatives to the rationality assumption.

Lovell (1986) reviewed many of the tests performed so far and concluded:

> If the cumulative evidence is to be believed, we are compelled to conclude that expectations are a rich and varied phenomenon that is not adequately captured by the concept of rational expectations; while the predictions of some forecasters may be characterized as rational, in other instances the assumption of rationality is clearly violated (Lovell, 1986, p.120).

Lovell cited two reasons why the theory did not seem to be borne out. One was simply measurement error and the other the possibility that shifts in the environment might necessitate transient departures from rationality. It could be added that it is not always easy, using even the best of economic theory, to know and pursue what is rational, as Akerlof (1991) has amply demonstrated in a readable essay on procrastination and obedience.

Summing up the previous discussion of expectations as treated by economists, one arrives at the conclusion that all three theories can at times explain expectations, but under different circumstances. The discussion hints that when the economic conditions are stable and do not vary much or vary in the same way over long periods of time, for example a long spell of steady but slow growth, simple extrapolation of earlier development may do well. When there is new information, implying breakdowns of earlier patterns, both extrapolative and adaptive expectations theories fall short as single explanations of actual expectations. Adaptive expectations theory presumes that there is a correction depending on earlier discrepancies between expectations and outcomes. The theory will do normatively better than extrapolation theory in times of changing patterns similar to what is described as the 'hog-cycle', but it probably still falters as a description in such cases.

Learning from earlier misjudgments may also be rational in the sense of rational expectations theory. Most so-called tests of rational expectations theory on empirical data are compatible with this idea, since the crucial issue is the agreement between expectations as measured in surveys and actual outcomes. Depending on what periods the tests are based on, it seems possible to confirm both extrapolative and adaptive expectations theories. If the tests indicate that the expectations are unbiased, that is, the error distribution has mean zero, and that there is no relevant new information, the criteria for rationality are fulfilled.

Expectations and Goals

Thinking begins with goals and cannot move without them.
Simon (1994, p.19; cited in Karniol and Ross, 1996, p.598)

Intentional expectations are close to goals. If goals are seen as cognitive representations of states that people desire to attain, it becomes clear that expectations and goals hang together. Expectations of future events lead to the formulation of goals, but it may also be the other way round, as when goals influence expectations. This means that goals may bias the information processing that is the base of expectation formation.

Goals range from those that are waiting for immediate fulfillment to long-term goals that may involve the remainder of a long life. A distinction is usually made between *proximal* and *distal* goals. The former refer to goals to be attained in the near future and the latter to goals that are more distant in time. The time dimension of goals is important for the choice of investment strategy. Saving for retirement is ordinarily a distal goal and investments for this purpose are bound to differ from those of a proximal goal such as making large and immediate profits on stocks. Since distal goals presuppose sacrificing something now in favor of later consumption, they put more demand on self-control than proximate goals. This is a consequence of the usually prevailing positive time preference (Ainslie and Haslam, 1992).

Proximal goals have the advantage of helping to sustain motivation, since they enable people to gauge their progress. Distal goals may require them to set up proximal subgoals so as to become able to see whether they are on the right way and motivate them to continue. Proximal goals are generally assumed to be more motivating than distal goals. For a person who is pursuing long-term saving for retirement, it may be necessary to have some control stations on the way, but they should not involve too frequent checking of results when returns all the time vary up and down (Benartzi and Thaler 1995).

Conflicting information exists about the role of participatory versus externally imposed goals. Early studies indicated that goals that persons set for themselves were more highly motivating than goals that were set for them. Studies in organizations and in schools suggest that there is little difference, in particular when the people involved have high achievement motivation. Professional investment managers often have imposed on them goals that involve beating the market index. Such goals are known to affect their investment decisions (see, for example, Hellman, 2000).

The Gambler's Fallacy and Antiregressive Behavior

> *So in any world but a casino, the gambler's fallacy is rarely a fallacy. Indeed, calling our intuitive predictions fallacious because they fail on gambling devices is backwards. A gambling device is, by definition, a machine designed to defeat our intuitive predictions. It is like calling our hands badly designed because they make it hard to get out of handcuffs.*
>
> Pinker (1998, p.346)

In decision making, at least some vague notion about what might happen in the future is necessary. Commonly, the notion comprises things continuing as they always have. When expectations are being formed, past experience may imply extrapolation of earlier trends or learning from specific events. In the latter case, what is learned from past experience may be used in such a way that the person expects a broken trend. The gambler's fallacy is a case in point. After long runs of red, the roulette player is inclined to believe that black will be next. If the player is informed that there is a systematic error in the numbers of red and of black, this may instill a belief that there will be no change next time and the player may still favor the same color. Without information to the contrary, the gambler assumes that there will be reversion towards the mean. If the gambler believes that the recent trend will continue, the behavior is called *antiregressive*. Causal information is crucial to antiregressive behavior, but such information may also be necessary for continued belief in extrapolation.

The expectation that the trend will continue or be broken, which means reverting to previous levels, depends in large part on whether explanations in terms of causal attributions are provided to explain recent changes. If explanations that favor continuation are at hand, then the tendency to make regressive predictions is diminished. Andreassen (1987) argued that the news media provided such attributions in financial markets and so could cause aggregate-level changes, since those who received these attributions acted on them. Causal attributions by members of the media should be expected to be more frequent and more extreme than those that would be generated by individuals who do not expect to communicate information to others. The financial press explains recent changes in stock prices with good news after price rises and with bad news after price falls. In an experimental study carried out by Andreassen (1987), such news was shown to lead to less regressive predictions. The findings support the idea that there may be a positive-feedback effect from news about stock-price developments.

An issue for research on expectation formation is the weight given to past experience in relation to new information that diverges from past experience. When does past experience dominate and when can new information reverse expectations? Obviously, firmly based past experience which has been confirmed over time can be very hard to shake and contrary information has little influence unless it is sensational. Expectations based on past experience can be very sticky while expectations based on new information may shake more easily. Expectations that influence economic behavior do not only absorb economic or financial information. Information about social events and other people's behaviors may also contribute to the formation of financial expectations, not to forget news about world events (Niederhoffer, 1971).

The Role of Subjective Expectations in Financial Markets

From a behavioral point of view, individual financial decisions depend on subjective expectations that mostly vary among investors, but sometimes coincide for large groups, 'segments', who rightly or wrongly arrive at the same expectations. This is hard to reconcile with the prevalent theory of efficient markets, according to which all investors calculate the same expected value for a stock when new information appears. The new information is immediately absorbed in stock price. The price of a stock should reflect the present value of expected future earnings and future capital gains. Expectation is then equal to mathematical expectation. Financial markets are said to be efficient if the prices of assets reflect all available information. A consequence of this assumption is that current prices contain no information about future prices and, given a few more assumptions, stock prices follow a random walk. The economic expectations of the theory are not formed, but are calculated, are not necessarily held by any particular person, and can only be studied through revealed behavior, that is, trading activity It is assumed that (new) information is rationally used when the traders form their expectations of prices, and that the new expectations are directly translated into actions that influence stock prices.

The CAPM and the efficient-market theory assume that there is individual rationality and that all investors are rational-expectations utility maximizers, involving the rational use of (economic) information. All available information is rationally used and reflected in the prices of stocks. According to a different view, *information* traders use a proper Bayesian learning rule to form estimates of returns whereas *noise* traders commit errors because they employ non-Bayesian thinking. One may have some doubts about the pure rationality of expectations in both groups. In everyday life, expectation formation amounts to deciding to what extent learning about earlier contingencies that may seem dependable holds for the future. To what extent can past experience be a guide to future behavior, and how should new information be handled and weighed against past experience?

Subjective expectations, which according to psychological thinking can be individually assessed without being revealed in actions, are influenced by many more factors than just fundamentals. They involve perceptions of future states and vary between people and over time because of many factors besides financial information. Guesses about the future are rarely singly determined. People bring theories about contingencies to most judgment tasks. Theory is here used to designate some degree of organization of concepts: '. . . we use *theory* to mean any of a host of mental "explanations", rather than a complete, organized, scientific account' (Murphy and Medin, 1985, p.290). In consumer psychology the role of people's theories, which are often called 'prior expectations', has been much investigated (Hoch and Deighton, 1989; Baumgartner, 1995), as well as in cognitive psychology (Murphy and Medin, 1985). Prior expectations refer to the effect of previously acquired knowledge about contingencies or covariation between events, that is, about how things hang together.

Theories about expectations are essential in explanations of financial market developments. The role of expectation formation is shown by the occurrence of financial market 'bubbles' in which the price of an asset first sky-rocketed and then plummeted. Spurred by expectations of enormous profits, many people (although only a small proportion of the population), most of them ordinarily rather cautious, started investing in assets that were highly insecure unless there was continued exponential growth. Prior expectations apparently generated new and higher expectations up to the point where the grim reality behind the prior expectations was suddenly recognized. Pyramid schemes of investment, Ponzi schemes, and similar commercial strategies are based on engendering unrealistic expectations through showing initial successes. This way people, who think that they can outdo chance by being smart, are seduced to base their expectations on apparent earlier contingencies.

In an attempt to explain bubbles and crashes, Shiller (1989, p.56) propounded that stock-market operations were swayed by fads and fashions. A fad became a bubble if the contagion of the fad was spread through prices and people were attracted by observed price increases rather than by any fundamental value. As mentioned before, famous bubbles of this sort are the Tulipmania in the Netherlands (Garber, 1989a, 1989b) which took place in 1634–37, and the South-Sea bubble in England around 1720 (Schachter et al., 1985). In these bubbles, as in the real estate bubbles, that some countries have in recent years recovered from, the same pattern of expectation development seems to have occurred. Tempted by earlier sky-rocketing stock prices, many investors, including professionals who were charged with the onerous burden of beating the index, willingly paid incredible prices for stocks in firms working with the possibilities that the Internet suddenly opened up.

In a stable world, reliance on past experience is often the most rational use of information. In the case of producers, Keynes (1936) expressed it like this:

> [A] large part of the circumstances usually continue substantially unchanged from one day to the next. Accordingly it is sensible for producers to base their expectations on the assumption that the most recently realized results will continue except in so far as there are definite reasons for expecting a change (Keynes, 1936, p.51).

The expression 'definite reasons for expecting a change' is similar to what Katona (1975) referred to as radically new information. When people like something in past developments, they are even more inclined to expect it to continue and become frustrated when changes occur.

Despite the teachings of efficient-market theory, past developments may be a good guide for judgments of future developments, but many influences can change the value of past experience. Past experience is not a clear-cut concept. When does the period on which past experience is based start and when does it end? Recent events seem to have more influence than earlier events. De Bondt (1998) found that investor sentiment depended on market performance during the last 100 trading days, but somewhat longer as well as shorter influence may be possible.

The unremitting problem of continuation or reversal (or negligible changes) can be dealt with in terms of expectation formation. Observers of the financial market have, as indicated above, begun to consider private information within the realm of rational expectations theory. This brings the theory closer to what has been discussed in psychological expectation theories.

Social Influence on Expectations

> *Suppose no one believes there is a link between sunspots and stock prices. But suppose each individual thinks that every other individual believes there is such a link. The appearance of sunspots should lead each individual to buy stocks, on the grounds that other people will. Such behavior will be quite rational. As Keynes pointed out, there is nothing more disastrous than a 'rational' investment strategy in an irrational market.*
>
> Maital et al. (1986, p.281)

Influence from other people can be informative or normative, which implies that examples and rules set by others are heeded. Maital and Maital (1981) discussed social influence on consumer expectations and, using some Israeli data, found that interpersonal trust had a significant influence on inflation expectations, as had also income and age. More will be said about the social psychology of information and influence in Chapter 7.

It is commonly assumed that there are two sets of components in stock-price developments. One set has to do with expected future dividends, the other with what other traders will be willing to pay for a certain stock. In practice, it is difficult to distinguish between the effects of the two sets. Future prices are dependent not only on expected dividends, but also on how traders (presumably noise traders) will expect other traders to react.

Keynes (1936) expressed the difficulties very well:

> [P]rofessional investment may be likened to those newspaper competitions in which the competitors have to pick out the six prettiest faces from a hundred photographs, the prize being awarded to the competitor whose choice most nearly corresponds to the average preferences of the competitors as a whole; so that each competitor has to pick, not those faces which he himself finds prettiest, but those which he thinks likeliest to catch the fancy of the other competitors, all of whom are looking at the problem from the same point of view. It is not a case of choosing those which, to the best of one's judgment, are really the prettiest, nor even those which average opinion genuinely thinks the prettiest . . . we devote our intelligences to anticipating what average opinion expects average opinion to be (Keynes, 1936, p.156).

The rational investor calculates or at least imagines the future returns of stocks that s/he considers buying. What Keynes says implies that the investor forecasts socially influenced stock prices instead of company earnings. The returns depend on earnings and on guesses about what other investors will be willing to pay. It seems difficult to make any precise calculations of such values, which are at least partly formed like stamp prices. It is likely that the considerations of the private investor are often rather of the type 'continue to go up (or down)' or 'start going up (or down)' than elaborate calculations. There are, of course, professional traders and highly engaged amateurs who spend a lot of time trying to figure out the best approach. For those the following formula may be a relevant description of the decision making:

$$P_S = E_S(P_O)$$

$$E_S(P_O) = E_O(\sum_{i=1}^{T} D_t) + E_O(\sum_{i=1}^{T} PI_t)$$

where

P_s is the price the agent is willing to pay for a certain stock
P_o is the price others are willing to pay
E_s is the agent's own expectation
E_o is the agent's expectation of other agents' expectations, discounted to present value
D_t is the dividend discounted to current value
PI_t is the increase in value of company discounted to current value
T is end of time horizon.

The social influence pictured in the above formula is not direct in the sense that other people try to influence an investor or an investor tries to imitate other investors for some reason. The social influence involves outguessing other traders by foreseeing how a sizable group of fellow investors will be reasoning. For some stocks, the expectations about future earnings and dividends may be most important; for others, expectations about the future value of the company dominate. In a third case, stock value rests on the belief or expectation that other investors in sufficient numbers will be attaching a certain value to the stock. The expectations are formed on the basis of past experience and new information. The relationships between new information and stock-price developments are complex. The stock price of a certain company is seemingly influenced both by specific information about the company and by more general information at different levels of generality.

People have a tendency to explain other people's behavior as a consequence of intrinsic factors, the person's motives, rather than of environmental impact or external situation. The assumption is made that there is a closer link between actor and action than between situation and action. This type of mistake is called the *fundamental attribution error*. Other actors are ascribed motives and attitudes that are supposed to explain their behavior. Sometimes the term of fundamental attribution error is used primarily to designate one actor's attribution of her/his own motives to other actors. It is often assumed that people tend to attribute their own motives to other actors, that is, project their own motives on to others. Among traders on the stock exchange, it seems to be frequently assumed that other traders will react in the same way which may result in herd behavior (cf. De Bondt and Forbes, 1999).

Can Financial Expectations Be Manipulated?

Judging from Shefrin's (2000) case studies of financial markets, there are certainly attempts to influence expectations, for example before an initial public offering (IPO). Marketing a new product naturally means attempting to build up positive expectations about it. Previous experience with similar products may give some indication of the utility of the new product, but mostly the prospective customer has to rely on information provided by the seller. There are rules for the introduction of stocks, the strictness of which varies from country to country. The European marketing campaigns for Telecom stocks would probably not have been allowed in the USA, where information about IPOs is regulated (Shefrin, 2000). Manipulation can occur in many ways without necessarily being illegal. Starting a rumor that is supposedly based on insider information is illegal in hardly any country, unless perhaps done by an insider, while acting on insider information is. Rumors can, as will be shown in Chapter 7, certainly influence stock prices.

Experiments that involve attempts to manipulate stock prices in reality would probably raise ethical objections, but manipulating betting on horses appears to be acceptable. Camerer (1998) reports 'an unusual field experiment' in which he attempted to manipulate prices in a naturally occurring asset market: pari-mutuel betting on thoroughbred racing. He placed $500 and $1 000 bets (which he later canceled). Compared to bets on matched-pair control horses, the experimental bets moved odds on horses visibly. They had a slight tendency to draw money towards the selected horse, but the net effect was close to zero. The author concludes that some bettors saw the high bets as information while others did not.

One way of manipulating stock prices involves splitting up a sale or purchase of a large quantity in such a way that expectations of a change in demand are created. A rumor that a big buyer is planning to buy a large amount of a certain stock is bound to increase the price of the stock. Acting on such information, which may be insider information, can be profitable. In a Swedish study on ethics and finance, the following reality-based vignette of a case was presented to the sample of financial managers and auditors, among six other vignettes:

> A broker at a brokerage firm is contacted in the morning by a client who is responsible for a number of portfolios. The client places an order to buy 5 000 shares in one of the 16 most traded stocks. He is going to name the buyer later. Later the same day the client places an order to buy 225 000 shares in the same listed company. The buyer is one of the unit trusts for which he is responsible. At the same time the client names one of his smaller clients as buyer of the first block of shares. The next day the client places an order to sell the smaller block of shares. The broker carries out all orders from the client without hesitation (Bergkvist, 1995, p.44).

The case was followed by two ethical judgment questions. The first question concerned whether the respondent considered the *broker's* behavior to be unethical. The second question to be answered by the respondent was whether the behavior of the *client* was unethical. The responses were measured on a ten-point scale, with 10 as the most unethical behavior. There followed questions on the perceived frequency of the described situation in Sweden and in Western industrialized countries. The results are shown in Table 3.1.

Table 3.1 Judgments of Inappropriate Favor

	Ethics		Frequency		Percent condemning	
	Broker	Client	Sweden	West	Broker	Client
Fin. managers	4.9	7.6	6.2	6.1	31	62
Auditors	4.3	7.7	5.8	6.0	17	67

Note: 10 = 'highly unethical' and 'very frequent' respectively.
Source: Bergkvist (1995, p.45).

The behavior of the broker's client was judged to be highly unethical by both the financial managers and the auditors, most of whom were CPAs. The client did not use insider information, but had apparently disclosed information that could change expectations about the future price of the stock in question. The case, which has a background in reality, suggests ways of manipulating expectations through planned sequences of trading. According to the respondents, the situation is quite common, although it is judged unethical on the client's part. Some members of the sample also found the broker's behavior condemnable.

A Final Look at Expectation Formation

Expectation is a fundamental concept in finance as it is in economics. While in these sciences it is equal to mathematical expectation, in modern cognitive psychology, expectations are formed by individuals on the basis of available information. Both in economics and in psychology, past experience, albeit with interpretations differing in the two, long dominated the hypothesized formation of expectation, in one case the mathematical expectation based on earlier development data, in the other case an individual tendency based on observable earlier behavior. With rational expectations theory in economics and cognitive psychology replacing behaviorism, the focus is now on the role of information that is new and differs from what earlier experience attests.

Stock markets have a reputation for bringing forth decision makers who take little time to make their decisions. They seem to use *instant scenarios*, which means that new, relevant information is immediately absorbed into a scenario that strongly and unequivocally suggests a decision to act or not to act. The ability to distinguish patterns in developments, which has often been found in experts, may have a time dimension and explain some of the investor's confidence in an instant scenario (Simon, 1990).

The problem of expectation formation can be conceived of as consisting of two components, namely past experience and new information, which are given different weights depending on a number of factors. Trend reversals in stock prices can be dealt with in these terms. A reversal of a trend occurs when past experience is given a low weight for some reason, such as the emergence of dramatic news that strongly contradicts earlier experience. This does not invalidate the findings of research on trend reversals indicating that stock exchange crashes have been brought about without any real new information. From a psychological point of view, the fact that there is no news when good news was expected can bring about frustrated expectations, which may change behavior. If expectations have many components that are so interwoven that they can be called scenarios of the future, severe frustrations may occur when there is no good news for several of the components. The concluding chapter, Chapter 10, will further take up the idea of expectations as scenarios of the future.

4. Decision Making, Uncertainty, and Risk Attitudes

There are two kinds of people in the world: those who read mysteries from front to back and those who cannot resist peeking at the last page. For the latter, it is a sorrow that in life you can't peek.

Lopes (1994, p.201)

DYNAMIC DECISION MAKING

The Study of Decision Making

According to behavioristic psychology, stimuli elicited responses, and together with some observable internal conditions of the individual, stimuli or observable antecedents explained all behavior. Decision making, which is a cognitive process, was not a meaningful concept. The developments in cognitive psychology that have largely replaced behaviorism in its strict theoretical sense give a better ground for studying decision making. Cognitive psychology has a main focus on information processing and memory and tends to construe decisions as the outcome of information handling. This still leaves a gap between cognitive processes and actual behavior. Cognitive reasoning does not explain all behavior, far from it. Some reactions, especially to powerful stimuli, are preceded by very little cognitive activity (Chapter 6).

Deviations from economic rationality are often ascribed to limited cognitive capacity, as suggested by bounded rationality theory, but are also often blamed on feelings, emotions, and deep-seated driving forces over which the individual has little control. In the study of self-regulation, which essentially corresponds to the willpower and self-control concepts of earlier psychological and economic theories, the tendency is to focus rather on failure than on success in self-regulation (Metcalfe and Mischel, 1999; Baumeister and Heatherton, 1996). Many studies of decision making in practice suggest that Katona (1975) was right when he claimed that genuine decision making was extremely rare – most actions were routine or followed habit formation.

Researchers who have tried to study decisions in real-life situations have often failed to observe anything that could be called a decision at a certain point in time. A typical finding is that decisions are formed in drawn-out processes in which the action alternatives are gradually reduced through maneuvers that are not organized as structured decisions. In experimental settings, similar tendencies have been observed and characterized as 'dominance structuring' (Montgomery and Svenson, 1989). The decision process eliminates other alternatives, sometimes one and sometimes several at a time, and ends up with one alternative that is accepted or rejected. The decision process is seen as a search for a dominance structure and it is also a search for good arguments. It is studied through think-aloud instructions to subjects who are given a task which requires that only one alternative is left at the end of the process, for example, the choice of a house or a consumer product.

Despite all the talk about making (or taking) decisions in business and politics, decisions are rarely outcomes of well-structured processes and the resemblance between practice and theory is only specious. Brehmer (1992) notes that, for example, a fire chief does not think about making decisions, but sees his task as fighting fires in a fire-fighting situation. Brehmer tends to view decision making as attempts to gain control, to achieve some desired state of affairs, rather than a procedure of deliberate choice between alternatives with different outcomes.

Decision Making in Complex Systems

Most of the work on decision-making theory has been bestowed on simple isolated situations, with little consideration of repetitive decisions and cumulative effects over time. More recently, attention has been devoted to *dynamic decision making*. Dynamic decision making involves:

> decision making under conditions which require a series of decisions, where the decisions are not independent, where the state of the world changes, both automatically and as a consequence of the decision maker's actions, and where the decisions have to be made in real time (Brehmer, 1992, p.211).

Dynamic decisions are decisions in a *context* and in a *time setting* (Brehmer, 1992, p.212). Consequently, decision making by individual investors may be different from that of the professional investors, even apart from differences in knowledge and skills. While the former can usually disregard the possible influence of their purchases and sales on stock rates, the latter may have to consider the direct consequences of their actions and possible counteractions from other large operators. The professionals often face the demands of dynamic decision making. This is, of course, also true of the private investor, only to a lesser extent since the effects on the market may be neglected by the individual investor.

Modeling dynamic decision making is no easy problem, since the decision processes involve series of actions where later actions depend on effects of earlier actions. Granted that economists are interested in outcomes and changes in outcomes and psychologists are interested in processes, as Herbert Simon has suggested, the two disciplines face somewhat different problems. The former want to be able to predict outcomes without necessarily studying details in the process unless they are essential for predicting the outcome. The latter want adequate descriptions of the process so as to explain decisions. Experimental asset markets are a way for economists to study dynamic decisions and their outcomes (see, for example, Güth et al., 1997). So far psychologists have, to my knowledge, not carried out any regular simulations to study dynamic decision making in the financial area, but some of the studies reported by Brehmer (1992) could serve as a paradigm.

The real-time character of the decisions creates special problems for the decision maker. Many professional traders and speculating private investors are or feel forced to make decisions at certain moments when stock prices are moving up or down, with some latitude, and they are usually not free to make decisions when they feel ready to do so. The decisions have to be made when the environment demands decisions from them. The work is done under pressure, which involves some degree of stress.

> To cope with this stress, the decision maker must try to find a strategy that helps him or her not only to control the dynamic task, but also his or her working situation. One way to achieve this is to lower the aspiration level, and try to control the task at some lower, and less stressful level which does not require as many decisions. Thus, dynamic decisions may often be a compromise between a good strategy for controlling the decision task, and a strategy that enables the decision maker to exert some measure of control over the rate at which he has to make decisions. This kind of compromise is observed in process operators where it is often found that they do not try to run their processes close to the limits that would yield the highest output simply because this would require too much work on their part (Brehmer, 1992, p.213).

The system that the decision maker seeks to control and the means that s/he uses for control are both processes. The task facing the decision maker in dynamic decision making embodies the problem of finding a way to use one process to control another process. Another consequence is the need to consider the various time scales of the dynamic decision task and to make sure that all the relevant time scales are monitored. According to this thinking, separate individual decisions are uninteresting to study and the research focuses on tactics and strategies that are patterns of behavior or processes rather than on single acts with simple causal relationships between action and effect.

In a series of studies reviewed in Brehmer (1992), a new concept, called *heuristic competence*, was investigated. It is defined as a general competence to cope with complex systems. In a German study, psychology students, who were assumed to have low heuristic competence, were compared with managers, who were assumed to have more heuristic competence, in an economic development simulation game, essentially running a small city as mayor. The managers in the study were less activistic than the psychology students, that is, they made fewer decisions, they collected more information before they made their decisions, and they checked on the results of their decisions before making new decisions. Brehmer also stresses the importance of setting clear goals; this is in fact necessary if one wants to make evaluations afterwards. Attempts to train subjects to become more heuristically competent did not appear to be very successful (Brehmer, 1992. p.225).

It seems likely that *epistemic competence*, that is, knowledge of the area concerned, would lead to better performance. On the basis of his own studies, Brehmer (1992, p.226) concludes: 'These results suggest, then, that both epistemic and heuristic competence are needed, but if a subject were to have only one of these, heuristic competence would be more useful than epistemic competence'. In the experiments, the subjects with epistemic competence did not check on their results in any systematic way as they should have done. Heuristic competence involves setting goals and checking results.

Common Mistakes in Complex Decision Making

Unsuccessful dynamic decision making is characterized by certain pathologies, which Brehmer categorizes in two main groups. The first group encompasses failures in the goal formulation process, which is the first essential step in dynamic decision making. Unsuccessful individuals are characterized by 'thematic vagabonding', which is a tendency to shift goals, or by 'encystment', which means sticking to a specific goal that is akin to a felt special competence. If you have a special competence you are tempted to define problems and search for solutions in terms of that competence. A boy who gets a hammer will find that surprisingly many things need hammering. An expert on derivatives may believe that derivatives beat other investment alternatives. The second group of pathologies comprises refusal to learn from experience. It includes passivity or refusal to make any decisions at all. It may also mean blaming others or the system for one's own failures. Finally, it may mean delegating responsibility that cannot or should not be delegated.

In another article, Brehmer and Dörner (1993) discuss the usefulness of laboratory microworlds and further elaborate on the errors found in research on human decision making. Many of the findings come from German studies of a simulation in which the subjects have to act as mayor of a small German city and make decisions in complex systems in which economic, demographic, and socio-cultural variables interact. The systems are complex in the sense that there have to be many goals, some of which are in conflict, so that the decision maker has to make trade-offs. Many courses of action have side effects. The state at a given moment is a result of interaction between the subject and the system. The aim of the microworld simulation is to provide decision-making situations with high ecological validity and still maintain the experimenter's control over what is happening. Undoubtedly, something of use for understanding investment decisions can be learned from the observations made in such situations. Here is a brief summary of findings.

People have considerable difficulty taking into account not only the direct effects of their actions, but also the more distant effects and the side effects. They tend to adopt an ad-hoc behavior that only considers the demands of the situation at hand. Presumably because of the general problems of coping with time demands, subjects have great problems with delayed feedback concerning the results of their actions and with the delayed effects of their actions – the time constants of the system. There is a tendency – especially in crisis situations – to neglect checking the effects of the courses of actions taken. The subjects 'take a ballistic attitude, and fire the actions without checking on their effects'.

When forming hypotheses, people have a tendency to reduce the number of possibilities and to consider only one or a few causes that they believe to be of central importance. People have great difficulty integrating different courses of action, which is often necessary in the complex real world. This is clear from studies in microworlds where the subjects have to consider different subgoals. Instead of integrating courses of action, the subjects carry them out in isolation without consideration of their mutual interdependencies and the effects of one upon the other. People have difficulty understanding the regularities in the time-course of events when they receive the information about these regularities in the form of isolated events over time. Nonlinear growth is then usually seen as linear processes, and oscillating courses of events (for example, damped sinusoidal oscillations) are seen as chaotic.

In planning, the correct level of determination is necessary. Under some conditions, the subjects adopt too fine-grained a level of resolution, while under others it is not fine-grained enough. Plans with too low a level of resolution come to an end quickly because the conditions and consequences of actions are considered too superficially. If, on the other hand, the level of resolution is too high, planning never comes to an end – the planner can always say that he has not planned enough (Brehmer and Dörner, 1993, p.181).

Brehmer and Dörner (1993) explain these errors in terms of certain general characteristics of people as information-processing systems: (1) forgetting, (2) capacity limitations; the principal instrument for coping with new and uncertain systems works sequentially and slowly, and can only process rather small amounts of information, which leads to attempts at economizing, (3) protection of competence, and (4) overweighting the current motive. The last two characteristics are particularly interesting

> *Protection of competence*. To act, a person needs to be convinced that he or she can act successfully. People keep this feeling of competence by, for example, not acknowledging failures, and by not checking on the effects of their actions, thus ending up with an illusion of competence in the face of failure . . . *Overweighting the current motive*: People are concerned with the problems that they have for the moment, rather than the problems that they do not (yet) have. This leads them to ignore developments that may lead to problems in the future (Brehmer and Dörner, 1993, p.182).

Controlled experiments studying financial decisions usually deal with simple situations. Even if the decisions have consequences for developments in the experimental market, the experimental designs do not catch many of the things that have been investigated in dynamic decision making using microworlds. Dynamic decision making may involve stress and emotions that affect decisions and that may no doubt be worthy of researcher attention.

Complex decision making has also been studied in other contexts, for example, how fighter pilots perform in stressful situations. Angelborg-Thanderz (1990) developed models to describe the performance of fighter pilots. In a LISREL model, she used a number of variables to explain performance. The model started with 'challenge', which was determined by risk and difficulty of the task, and then comprised, on the one hand, 'involvement' and, on the other hand, 'effort'. A similar model could be worked out for decision makers in finance, in particular those engaged in continuous activities in financial markets, such as stock traders who are transacting via PC monitors.

RISK AND UNCERTAINTY

The Concept of Risk

The formation of expectations is the leading theme in this book. In the last chapter, a general outline of the factors influencing expectation formation was given and a model of three sets of beliefs constituting expectation was presented. The weight for each set in a given situation is decisive. With plenty of past experience in the area, the individual attaches a heavy weight to the set of beliefs associated with past experience. With little or no personal past experience, the individual has to utilize the available information to the best of her/his ability and give it the highest weight. Past experience is not a set of facts; rather, it consists of interpreted facts that give rise to beliefs, and the interpretations may vary over time. Expectations imply judgments of the future, of what is likely to happen in the future.

When interpretations of the past and of available information from various sources are made, there is room for cognitive biases and miscalculations due to limited cognitive capacity. When risk is involved, the problems become even more intricate. *Heuristics* are ways of solving problems with simpler rules than what is theoretically optimal. They can also be seen as smart ways of making surprisingly good decisions (Gigerenzer and Todd, 1999).

Like other people, investors need to have two complementary mental systems: one that sensitizes the individual to the invariant features of the environment, and a second that is responsive to the appearance of unexpected stimulus inputs.

> Knowing what to expect – and exactly where, when, and from whom to expect it – is information that renders the world a meaningful, orderly, and predictable place. On the other hand, however, to guide behavior in a truly flexible manner, minds must also be responsive to the presence of unexpected (that is novel, surprising) stimulus inputs . . . . An adaptive mind, after all, is one that enables its owner to override automated action plans and produce novel behavioral outputs as and when these responses are required (Macrae and Bodenhausen, 2000, p.94).

The step from relying on what seems invariant and stable to face in an adequate way new uncertainty is often difficult, and people evince different ability to confront unknown happenings. Life in financial markets may seem full of uncertainties as new things happen all the time. The economist Frank H. Knight (1921) made an important distinction that has influenced the discussion of uncertainty ever since. He declared that risk, which had been used to cover both measurable and unmeasurable uncertainty, should be used only about measurable uncertainty: 'a *measurable* uncertainty, or "risk" proper, . . . is so far different from an *unmeasurable* one that it is not in effect an uncertainty at all' (Knight, 1921, pp.19–20). Risks are then measured as probabilities, which is the common way of quantifying uncertainty.

The handling of probabilities is a well-researched area of study, but there is disagreement about how people actually handle probabilities as measures of risk. Researchers agree that people do not usually deal with probabilities in an optimal way, as probability theory requires. They disagree about the manner in which the deviations occur and debate whether the deviations should be considered errors. Gigerenzer (1996) opposes the idea that probabilities can be applied to single events and suggests that many studies of probability handling are misconceived. At any rate, people are as a rule not Bayesian in any complete way. The rest of the chapter will deal with different attempts at theorizing about utility and risk attitudes. How people manage in situations of uncertainty or risk will be the topic of Chapter 5.

Expected Utility

Expected utility theory, which was introduced by Bernoulli in 1738, is a theory of decision under risk. The decision maker has options which lead to outcomes whose probabilities are known. Individuals are assumed to attempt to maximize expected utility in their choices. They do so by weighting the utility of each outcome with its probability and choosing the option with the highest weighted value. Bernoulli proposed that the subjective value of money and most goods did not increase proportionally with objective amount. There was a diminishing marginal utility for money. The function showing the relationship between amount of money or wealth and utility was downward concave. Risk aversion is implied by the concavity of the utility scale because the utility of $2x$ is less than twice the utility of x. Most people were assumed to have such concave utility functions, meaning that they were *risk averse*. Risk-acceptant people had a convex curve and risk-indifferent people had a straight line. The differences can be illustrated by a simple lottery. Suppose you are offered the following gamble:

> Dfl 1 000 with certainty or Dfl 2 000 with 50 percent chance and 50 percent chance of getting nothing. Which one would you choose? [Dfl or guilder is the Dutch currency unit, worth a little less than half a US dollar]

If you are like most people – 81 percent of a representative Dutch sample (Wärneryd, 1996b) – you are risk averse and choose the certain amount of Dfl 1 000. If you are risk-acceptant (19 percent of the Dutch sample) you pick the second alternative in the hope of being lucky. A third alternative is that you are indifferent between the two alternatives. The Dutch respondents did not get the chance of selecting this answer. Interestingly, in a Dutch sample of high-income earners, 28 percent chose the 50 percent chance. Shefrin (2000) makes a point of the subjectivity of risk judgments in his examination of efficient-market theory: losing stocks are, for example, expected by investors to be more risky and to give lower returns than successful stocks. Buying such stocks clashes with the idea that higher profit is sought as a compensation for higher risk.

Regret Theories

> *Actions, or errors of commission, generate more regret in the short term; but inactions, or errors of omission, produce more regret in the long run.*
>
> Gilovich and Medvec (1995, p.379)

Selling winners too early and losers too late as well as not buying at the right moment easily create regret. Regret is one of several explanations of the disposition effect (Shefrin and Statman, 1985), which will be discussed further in Chapter 8. Regret is both cognitive, comprising the data on the action or inaction, and emotional. Regret follows the non-fulfillment of an expectation whose outcome depends on a person's own decision to do or not to do something. Regret may follow a decision by default, by inertia. Does regret mean anything for subsequent behavior? There may be a preparatory effect involving attempts to avoid actions that may be followed by regret, to minimize the probability of regretting afterwards. There may be after-the-fact regret that leads to changes in behavior, a kind of learning. Both effects seem to depend on how painful the emotional regret is. Economists' interest in regret emanates from observed violations of expected utility axioms. People may refrain from monetary gains just to escape the possibility of painful regret afterwards (Loomes, 1988). While regret may be painful and diminish subjective utility after a failed stock transaction, the issue is whether such regret will have any effect on future financial behavior. Too little is known from research on the learning effects of regret.

Two commonly cited causes of regret are purchasing stock that rapidly loses value or not selling stock when it is at its height. Kahneman and Tversky (1982) used a scenario with two investors, one of whom considered buying stocks in a company and did not, and the other of whom sold his stocks in the company. When the value of the stocks rose, both of them would have been better off by $1 200 if they had possessed the stocks. Who feels greater regret? No less than 92 percent of the respondents thought that the second person experienced more regret. Many similar studies have found that most people judge that the regret after action is more painful. Gilovich and Medvec (1995), in a thorough review of the issue, conclude that inaction gives more long-run pain. Their conclusion rests on answers to survey questions about (memories of) regret. Recent regrets tended to involve actions, whereas distant regrets tended to involve failures to act. The questions tended to elicit mostly regrets of not having done something that had to do with the respondent's destiny. This is similar to the Zeigarnic effect, which is the tendency to recall unfinished tasks better than completed tasks.

If there is learning in the case of failure to act at an earlier time, it encourages acting the next time a similar situation emerges. To me, it seems rather unlikely that investors learn from not having done something in the past even though they have suffered painful regret. They may have followed a stock price closely for some time, forecasted its price, and imagined that they bought. Such a simulation hardly gives rise to regret whatever the outcome. It seems likely that investors learn mostly from commission of error and vow not to repeat the same mistake again. Loss aversion would further strengthen such a tendency. Learning from regret is likely to make investors more passive, to shun the fire because they have been burned. The exception is when an investor is becoming desperate in efforts to succeed. Failures do not always lead to regret. Causal attribution theory notes a difference if a failure is attributed to oneself or the blame is put on somebody else, for example, an expert advisor or generally unfortunate circumstances.

PROSPECT THEORY

Studies of decision making, mostly carried out as laboratory experiments, have shown that actual risky choices deviate considerably from what maximization of expected utility presupposes (for an overview see, for example, Lopes, 1990, pp.267–70). The simple logarithmic relationship between objective value and utility obviously does not hold over a wide range of phenomena.

Reference Points, Framing, and the Value Function

Prospect theory, which was originally presented by Kahneman and Tversky in 1979 and which was later extended (Tversky and Kahneman, 1992), involves an attempt to reconcile theory and behavioral reality. It pays attention to gains and losses rather than to total wealth, assumes that subjective decision weights replace probabilities, and that *loss aversion* rather than risk aversion is an overriding concept. A *prospect* is an outcome (x_i) with a probability (p_i). It involves probable consequences and is thus another term for a risky alternative.

Choices involving risk are assumed to occur in two steps. The first step is called *editing* and consists of a preliminary analysis of the problem in which the available options are identified, the consequences of each option are valued, and the probabilities that are associated with each outcome are reviewed. An important aspect of the editing process is the *framing* in which a *reference point* (similar to level of aspiration or target) is set, marking the borderline between loss and gain. The second step is *evaluation*, in which the edited prospects are evaluated and the preferred prospect is selected.

In brief, prospect theory makes the following suggestions about risky choices.

1. The concave utility function for wealth is replaced by an *S*-shaped value function for *changes* in wealth. People think of *changes* in wealth or amounts of goods in terms of gains or losses rather than in terms of total assets after the change.
2. Choices are framed as gains or losses in terms of deviations from a reference point which can be the status quo, or for example, a level of aspiration (goal) that the person is trying to attain. Shifts in the value of the reference point are induced by the framing of the problem.
3. The value function is assumed to be concave above the reference point and convex below it. People are then risk averse with respect to gains and risk seeking with respect to losses. If they are given two positive options with equal expected value, one with certainty and the other with a probability, they tend to choose the certain option. If they are faced

with two negative options, one with certainty and the other with a probability, they tend to choose the probable option, which provides a chance of escaping the loss.

4. The value function is steeper for losses than for gains – *loss aversion*. This is the same as what Adam Smith asserted: 'We suffer more . . . when we fall from a better to a worse situation, than we ever enjoy when we rise from a worse to a better' (Smith [1759] 1982, p.213).

In prospect theory, risk aversion is no longer defined as a uniform characteristic of the utility function over wealth. 'Risk aversion is defined as a preference for a sure outcome over a prospect with an equal or greater expected value . . . Risk seeking is exhibited if a prospect is preferred to a sure outcome with equal or greater expected value' (Tversky and Fox, 1995, p.269). If a person prefers $50 for certain to a 60 percent chance of getting $100 – which has a higher expected value – s/he is risk averse. If a person prefers a 40 percent chance to get $100 to $50 for sure, s/he is risk seeking.

According to prospect theory, people are risk averse for gains with high probabilities and losses with low probabilities, risk seeking for gains with low probabilities and losses with high probabilities (Tversky and Kahneman, 1992). 'Losses loom larger than gains' is a much-cited description of this phenomenon, which is referred to as loss aversion. Loss aversion as implied by Bernoulli meant that a change in the amount of subjective (mental) fortune varied with the ratio that the change in the physical fortune had to the total fortune of its possessor. 'Thus in gambling with even stakes, one stands to lose more than one gains, for a given loss after the event bears a larger ratio to the reduced total fortune than would the same physical gain to an increased total fortune – a conclusion with a moral!' (Boring, 1950, p.284).

Prospect theory observes the strong preference for positive outcomes that are certain, the so-called *certainty effect*. The pattern is explained by the empirical weighting function for probabilities, which overestimates small probabilities and underestimates moderate and high probabilities even if the latter are close to but less than 1. This is done slightly more for gains than for losses. A non-linear transformation of the probability scale prevails. The risk attitudes found in the experiments do not agree completely with the shape of the utility function suggested by Friedman and Savage (1948), nor with that of Markowitz (1952b). All of these authors suggest functions that allow preference for gambling and for insurance at the same time. There are similarities between Markowitz's model and the value function in prospect theory, but while Markowitz recognized that the utility function is first concave and then convex, he found it necessary to have three inflexion points instead of one.

In the application of prospect theory, many interesting phenomena relate to the framing of options, whether those are framed as gains or losses, which in turn depends on the reference point or goal adopted in a particular decision situation. Some studies in behavioral finance have been devoted to the effects of framing and choice of reference points. In a survey study of large investors, Olsen (1997) found that subjective investment risk was a function of four attributes: (a) the potential for a below-target return, (b) the potential for a large loss, (c) the investor's feeling of control, and (d) the level of knowledge. Apparently, the target return is the dividing line between success and failure (see also research on the so-called disposition effect in Chapter 8).

An early study of framing effects may have interesting implications for financial markets where money managers and investors for funds are given profit targets that they are expected to attain. Payne et al. (1980) assumed that target rates of return set for managers who evaluated investment proposals tended to serve as reference points for the decisions made. If the target was set high, subjects would take more risks to avoid what they framed or perceived as losses if the returns were below the reference point. Subjects who received low set targets would tend to make less risky investments. Experiments with student subjects as well as with managers strongly supported the hypotheses and prospect theory.

In another series of experiments with similar sets of gambles, Laughhunn et al. (1980) used 237 managers as subjects and employed similar sets of gambles, but focused more specifically on below-target returns. They also investigated the effect of possible ruinous losses. In situations where only non-ruinous losses were involved, 71 percent of the managers were risk seeking for below-target returns. When information was given that ruinous losses involving bankruptcy were possible, 64 percent switched their behavior to risk-averse actions. MacCrimmon and Wehrung (1986, pp.114–23) report similar results in their comprehensive study of managers' risk taking. Their results indicated that managers were more willing to take risks when faced with threats than when faced with opportunities. Money and fund managers may correspondingly be prone to take higher risks if their goals or targets are set high, for example, to beat the stock index by some percentage. The experimental results show that the framing of the goal or target return may influence the risk taking. A return of a given size may, in the case of a below-target return, lead to more risk taking and, in another case in which the return exceeds the reference point (target), inspire more careful risk taking.

Suppose you buy a stock at $20 and it rapidly climbs to $60. Slowly, it starts going down and ends up around $30, where it remains. Do you feel satisfied with its performance? It seems likely that you feel you have lost money, although you never had it, and you regret that you did not sell when the stock price was at its height. Whether you think of it as a loss or a gain will depend on your choice of reference point. According to prospect theory, you are likely to frame it as a loss and experience feelings of having lost; losses loom larger than gains.

In prospect theory, people are assumed to know the probabilities of each outcome and to replace them with decision weights that underestimate high probabilities and overestimate low probabilities. Einhorn and Hogarth (1985; see also Hogarth, 1987, p.101f) presented an *ambiguity model* in which people are assumed to assess ambiguous probabilities by first anchoring on some value of the probability and then adjusting this figure by mentally simulating or imagining other values that the probabilities could take. According to the ambiguity model, people do not know exact probabilities. You may know the cost of your automobile insurance, but not know the exact probability that you will have an accident or that your automobile will be stolen. The implication of ambiguity is that a probability distribution should be used rather than a single value.

The tendency for people to be risk seeking for gains with low probabilities is presumably strengthened with increasing amounts of money. People will accept low probabilities to win large prizes in lotteries. The existence of large prizes with low probabilities would be more attractive than the possibilities of winning smaller prizes with much higher probabilities. The most successful lotteries are, then, those with high prizes and such low probabilities that the cost to the gambler can be held very low.

Normatively, a person should choose in such a way that the expected utility is maximized even in a single trial. This is an arguable recommendation. The argument in favor is, simply expressed, that if a person persistently pursues expected utility in risky choices over the life cycle, the gains will be highest. The trouble is that one may not get so many chances to make choices for a given category of events – or should small and big events be treated under one hat? The reality-oriented opposition against the view points to the fact that people make a clear discrimination between cases of single and repeated gambles (Lopes, 1994). Intuitively, it certainly makes a difference if one is faced with a choice of a large gain with probability $p = 1$ and a much larger gain with a probability of less than 1, whether one knows that there will be many more choice occasions of the same kind and amounts or that the choice is the only chance in a lifetime. This intuition disregards the fact that Samuelson (1963) argued and showed that if you accepted the bet when repeated 100 times, you should also accept it when offered only once.

If somebody gets a gift of a certain value, there is a tendency to ask a higher price than the value of the gift when it was received. This tendency has been called the *endowment effect* (Thaler, 1980). The effect is attributed to loss aversion; people are unwilling to part with something they have and prospective gains have to be (often two to three times) larger to outweigh losses. It seems likely that some kinds of savings can be explained by the endowment effect. Katona (1975) noted that people rather borrowed than touched their buffer capital in temporarily difficult situations. Amateur investors tend to keep their losing stocks too long and buy winning shares too late. Benartzi and

Thaler (1995) used 'myopic loss aversion' (and short evaluation periods) to explain why people in general invested in bonds rather than in stocks, even though stocks were much more profitable over a longer period.

In both economics and cognitive psychology, the assumptions are formulated as general laws that are presumed to hold for everybody with some dispersion around the mean. The decision weights in prospect theory are subjective, but assumed to be the same or at least highly similar for all individuals. Individual differences cannot be explained by these theories, except as dispersion around the mean. In economic psychology, the interest is often focused on individual differences with a view to looking for *segments* within the population, that is, for groups of people who are similar within groups and different between groups. A distinction is sometimes made between risk averters and risk takers, implying that individuals are permanently one or the other. It may not pay to look for segments whose members are consistently risk taking or risk averting over all situations, but rather to think of risk propensities as contingent also upon situations (MacCrimmon and Wehrung, 1986, pp.34–6).

Prospect theory has aroused criticism, in particular from economists. Critics have suggested that when choices are repeated and people are given time to learn or adapt, their choices become more similar to expected-utility theory (Smith, 1991). Experimental economists criticize the use of hypothetical choices with little or no monetary incentives, no chance of learning over time, and without influence from other agents in the market. Smith (1991) maintains that experimental markets tend to become more and more consonant with economic theory as the markets develop and agents become familiar with choices and their consequences which, through appropriate monetary rewards, become meaningful.

RISK ATTITUDES

Risk is a social construct invented to cope with the dangers and uncertainties of life.
Mellers et al. (1998, p.451)

Definitions of Risk Attitudes

Risk aversion is defined by the shape of the economic utility function and can be applied to an individual to the extent that a utility function can be attributed to her/him. A few attempts have been made to assess individual utility functions, but none seems very convincing. In psychological thinking, a risk attitude is a property of an individual and can in principle be elicited from the individual. An attitude measure is generally obtained from patterns in responses to questions or in actions, and indicates a disposition to act in a certain manner towards an object or a person or a collectivity. Risk attitudes can be defined and elicited in many ways.

Kahneman and Tversky (1979) and Tversky and Kahneman (1992) talk about risk attitudes as defined by how hypothetical risky choices are made. In prospect theory, which was described above, they summarize some important conclusions. Other investigators have used actual choices between risky alternatives, in particular outcomes of actual choices such as holdings of risky assets, to define risk attitudes. Finally, there is a variety of attitude scales for measuring risk attitudes (MacCrimmon and Wehrung, 1986). Financial advisors often distinguish between their clients by referring them to categories that correspond to the level of risk the clients are willing to take in their investments (see, for example, LeBaron et al., 1989; Canner et al., 1997). Judging from the literature (LeBaron et al. 1989; Roszkowski et al., 1989), some brokerage firms and financial advisors submit their customers to regular psychological tests so as to find out their level of risk taking as adequately as possible. What methods can they use?

Methods Used to Assess Risk Attitudes

Many economists view outcomes of actual choices, such as portfolios of assets, as the proper way of studying utility or preferences for assets. The composition of the asset portfolios reveals the true risk preferences. Pålsson (1996) demonstrated a way of analyzing risky wealth components using data from Swedish income tax returns. She distinguished between household portfolios on the basis of the proportion of risky assets. Bank deposits were defined as less risky assets than stock, especially if the stock was financed through loans. Real estate was also judged more risky than bank deposits. It was usually – at least to some extent – financed through mortgages and loans. Pålsson found that the degree of risky investment was negatively correlated with age: older people tended to have more of their assets as bank deposits.

In the wake of game theory, ways of assessing subjective expected utility through choices were developed. For reviews, see, for example, Farquhar (1984), and Hogarth (1987). Hypothetical risky choices are the most common method of studying risk and utility, both in economics and psychology. As a rule, economists are more insistent than psychologists that the choices should not be purely hypothetical, but have some monetary consequences for the subjects. Psychologists point to experimental comparisons of the effects of different incentives on choices and tend to draw the conclusion that subjects can be sufficiently motivated by incentives not directly related to the outcomes of the choices. They get only little support from the findings of Kachelmeier and Shehata (1992; see below). Attempts to assess risk aversion and risk seeking in economic behavior, including that of investor clients, are usually based on choices between lotteries. There are several ways of eliciting the risk attitudes.

1. Choice between a certain alternative and a probable alternative
2. Choice between two probable alternatives with the same or unequal expected value
3. Request for a certain value equivalent to a probable value (certainty-equivalent technique)
4. Request for a probability statement that makes the subject/respondent indifferent between two alternatives, one of which is certain (lottery-equivalent technique)
5. Request for a probability that makes the subject indifferent between two alternatives, one of which has a known probability (cf. MacCrimmon and Wehrung, 1986, pp.58–9; Hogarth, 1987).

In the first case, the subject/respondent is presented a lottery with a choice between a reward with $p = 1$ and a reward with $p < 1$, having the same or unequal expected value as the certain option. The second case is the same as the first, except that both options are probable. The last three cases are different forms of the equivalent technique, which asks the subject/respondent for a probability or amount. In the third type, the subject is offered a reward (loss) with a probability p and asked to state how much s/he would want to receive (pay) with certainty to be indifferent between the lottery and the other alternative. This is also formulated as the minimum selling price (maximum buying price). In case (4), the subject is asked to state the probability that makes her/him indifferent between the two options. Case (5) is a further development of (4) and involves an attempt to avoid the certainty effect. It is often recommended to use $p = ½$ rather than $p = 1$ in order to avoid the certainty effect. The task, although it may still be difficult for many respondents, is somewhat easier with a *certain* alternative (McCord and de Neufville, 1986).

The risk attitudes elicited through the different techniques are seldom the same. This is demonstrated by the so-called *preference reversal phenomenon* (see Tversky et al., 1990; Lopes, 1994, p.203f.). When asked to choose between two options, one of which has a high probability of winning a small sum (A) and another that has a low probability of winning a large sum (B), people tend to choose (A). When asked how much they would be willing to pay for each option, people tend to pay more for (B). Such reversals of preferences were even observed in an experiment carried out in a Las Vegas casino.

Most experiments that have embraced choices with probabilities have been carried out among college students and other sophisticated subjects. There are a few examples of studies with other subjects. Binswanger (1981) carried out an experiment with Indian farmers. He used pay-offs that were real and large in relation to the financial situation of the subjects. The choices comprised options in which a certain prize was offered together with a probable prize with the same expected value or two probable options with the same expected value, but varying spreads. The risk aversion measures used were validated against actual farm decisions. The farm decisions were more conservative for the more risk-averse farmers. Risk aversion increased with the amounts at stake in the risky choices.

Kachelmeier and Shehata (1992) carried out another series of experiments with high pay-offs. They used a certainty-equivalent task to get individual risk preferences. The task comprised a dichotomous lottery with a probable prize and a request to state the lowest amount that the subject would be willing to accept in exchange for the offered prize. In the second step, a card was drawn from a stack of 100. If the amount on the card exceeded the minimum amount, the amount on the card was immediately paid. If it was lower, the subject proceeded to play a lottery with the probability to win the prize stated in the first option. The size of the monetary incentives influenced the risk taking. The subjects in this study were less risk seeking (more risk averse) for the high pay-offs. The authors also found a high, non-linear sensitivity to win-probabilities that agreed with the predictions of the revised prospect theory (Tversky and Kahneman, 1992). The procedure differed in two ways from what is usually characteristic of the certainty-equivalent method: (1) there was no absolutely certain prize, and (2) the subject knew that there were repeated trials. The procedure, however, guards against the certainty effect, which is usually considered to be a problem in these measurements.

There is some tendency to avoid asking subjects to handle probabilities directly and to use easier ways (such as scales) that are simple to understand. Many investigations of businessmen's risk attitudes have employed verbal descriptions of situations in which the options have been couched. The descriptions make the situation more interesting to the respondents, but they may give rise to associations that obscure the risk propensity measure and rather reveal risk-modifying attempts. The respondents may feel a strong urge to make qualifying statements rather than choices (MacCrimmon and Wehrung, 1986, Ch. 3). Psychological tests intended to measure risk propensity have not been very successful and the agreement between different tests is often disappointingly low (MacCrimmon and Wehrung, 1986). While general tests for risk propensity do not seem to work well, tests of risk taking in specific areas do better. In psychology, it is common to use measures based on self-descriptions such as subjective reports on earlier acts of a certain type and on inferred or stated propensities to act in specified situations. Successful tests of this kind have, for example, been constructed for the area of financial investments (MacCrimmon and Wehrung, 1986; LeBaron et al., 1989; Roszkowski et al., 1989; see also Chapter 8).

5. Cognitive Bias, (Simple) Heuristics, and Mental Accounts

HUMAN INFORMATION PROCESSING

The chapter deals with selected problems in human information processing which is an essential part of cognitive psychology. The research area began to develop in the late 1950s and has shown enormous growth since then. Herbert Simon has had a great influence on the research and can be said to have made it legitimate to study human thinking in an era dominated by behaviorism, according to which no mental concepts were accepted. Using the computer as a model of the human mind, Simon produced important findings on information processing and memory (see Simon, 1979, for an overview).

Human information processing is subject to many influences that make the outcome of the process biased in comparison to the information input. In the first place, attention is selective and leaves out potentially relevant information. With modern mass media and active social environments, competition for attention is intensive. Black (1986), who coined the concept of noise trader, rightly pointed out that investors were surrounded by permanent noise which made it difficult for them to act rationally. Attending to the wrong information and missing the important information may be consequences. The treatment of information that is attended to is open to, among other things, controlling by memory and coloring by emotional states. *Cognitive bias* can arise at all steps in the process. It is often referred to as limited cognitive capacity, meaning that only a little of all available information can be handled at the same time. The bias also includes active interference from memories and emotions. Cognitive psychology does not offer a totally pessimistic view of cognitive deficiencies. On the contrary, the research finds that humans often overcome their insufficiencies and end up with satisfactory outcomes.

The chapter begins with some research findings on the role of expertise and also deals with tendencies towards pattern recognition, which may be a useful characteristic in some situations, but a flaw in others where developments follow random courses. A major part of the chapter is occupied with the heuristics-and-biases approach of Kahneman and Tversky. Many applications can already be found in behavioral finance, such as the use of the representativeness heuristic. An emerging alternative approach is then presented. It is opposed to the idea that cognitive behavior can be described as biases with a focus on human limitations rather than on 'fast and frugal' heuristics that often grant the individual satisfactory results. The chapter ends with a review of the concept of mental account, a kind of subjective accounting system with categories that control some economic behavior.

THE SIGNIFICANCE OF EXPERT KNOWLEDGE

Given that humans are far from perfect information processors, as cognitive theory suggests, the question arises: are there people who consistently do better than others and, if so, under what circumstances? Research has shown that experts may not do too well on a task although they are seen as experts and believe in themselves as experts on the basis of their knowledge and experience. While psychologists as a rule distrust the notion of overall experts, they usually concede that people may be categorized as having different degrees of expertise in domains, and that higher expertise may be important for achievements in a domain. The study of expertise 'seeks to understand and account for what distinguishes outstanding individuals in a domain from less outstanding individuals in that domain, as well as from people in general' (Ericsson and Smith, 1991, p.2). In addition to being superior, the expert should display stable characteristics over a variety of situations, according to the authors. This implies that expertise can be displayed on demand: 'One of the marks of expert performers is that they can display their superior performance reliably upon demand' (Ericsson and Lehmann, 1996, p.277).

Talent, instruction, and practice are traditionally held to be important for developing expertise. Research has focused on factors leading to expertise, such as inherited general or specific abilities, general learning and experience, and, finally, domain-specific training and practice. Findings about the role of experience indicate that experience in itself is less worth than *deliberate practice*, which is synonymous with systematic and structured training (Ericsson and Lehmann, 1996, p.278).

A number of characteristics in which people with expertise differ from novices in a domain have been listed, but contradictory findings can be cited on most points. Two of the most-cited characteristics of experts are that they have superior memory for information related to their domains and that they are better at perceiving patterns among task-related cues. They structure their knowledge better than others. A somewhat ironic finding is that experts are better at gathering and handling information and have more knowledge and often do better than novices, but their performance is rarely better than that of statistical models with simple linear combinations of cues (Camerer and

Johnson, 1991). The research-based understanding of expertise that emerged during the 1970s and 1980s led to the design of artificial intelligence systems with an effectiveness resembling that of human experts in many areas (Glaser, 1994). Such systems have been used with varying success in finance as well.

A possible reason for diverging findings is that there is certainly more than one type of expert. A distinction has, for example, been made between *routine* and *adaptive* experts. The former are assumed to be primarily able to solve familiar types of problems quickly and accurately and may have only modest capabilities in dealing with new types of problems. The adaptive experts may be able to invent new procedures derived from their expert knowledge. They have a deeper conceptual understanding of the target domain (Holyoak, 1991). Experts in the real sense are helped by their knowledge to structure stimuli and memories. The findings are robust, but there are alternative hypotheses explaining them which I need not go into (see Ericsson et al., 2000; Simon and Gobet, 2000).

A central hypothesis has been that structured knowledge is the source of power in expert thinking. While expert thinking appears highly qualified, according to the research, the general superiority of expert performance to that of novices is open to many doubts. Financial experts do not consistently make better predictions or outperform ordinary investors according to studies that will be described in later chapters. The advantages of structured knowledge that leads to superior pattern recognition may not be obvious in efficient financial markets with prices performing random walks. There may be greater advantages due to structured knowledge and other characteristics of expertise and room for experts in markets that are affected by noise trading, that is, in ordinary financial markets. Perhaps something about expertise in financial markets can be learned from the following study.

Ceci and Liker (1986) studied and tested 30 middle-aged and older men who were avid racetrack patrons and observed them over a three-year period. Of these, 14 were classified as experts and the remaining as non-experts based on their ability to predict post-time odds on the basis of factual information about horses. The important background characteristics of experts and non-experts were equivalent. Intelligence, which was measured through a conventional intelligence test, and cognitive complexity were the main personality characteristics in the study. Cognitive complexity was measured by the extent to which the subjects used a sophisticated multiplicative model to handicap races, as opposed to a simpler additive model. They were asked to handicap 10 actual races and 50 experimenter-contrived races. The analyses revealed that the task was a cognitively complex enterprise, in which the experts used a mental model that contained multiple interaction effects and nonlinearity. The findings suggested that intelligence was unrelated to skilled performance at the racetrack. 'Consistent with other types of expert performance, their superior predictions of races were mediated by a complex mental representation. This representation enabled them to reason about many interesting factors in order to extract relevant information about a specific horse from its performance in previous races' (Ericsson and Lehmann, 1996, p.286).

Pattern Recognition

> *Many people: 1. discover naive patterns in past price movements, 2. share popular models of value, 3. are not properly diversified, and 4. trade in suboptimal ways.*
> De Bondt (1998, p.831)

Expert knowledge can be viewed in terms of recognition processes and especially the recognition of patterns. Simon (1990) points out that the ability to find patterns in sequences of numbers, letters, or geometric figures is an important component of human intelligence. Tasks of this kind are often included in intelligence tests. About recognition processes, he has the following to say:

> *We now know that experts make extensive use of recognition processes, based on stored knowledge, to handle their everyday tasks.* This recognition capability, based (by rough estimate) on 50,000 or more stored cues and associated knowledge, allow them to solve many problems 'intuitively' – that is, in a few seconds, and without conscious analysis. Recognizing key cues allows experts to retrieve directly from memory information for dealing with the situation that the cues identify (Simon, 1990, pp.8–9).

An important aspect of cognitive bias has to do with perception or judgment of randomness, a research area that has attracted considerable interest (for an overview, see Falk and Konold, 1997). When people are presented with randomly generated sequences of numbers, they tend to look for and find patterns. If people are asked to produce random sequences of numbers, they are sure to make fewer runs than are ordinarily found in randomly generated sequences. The meaning of randomness is that there is no characteristic pattern. This may be accepted in principle by people, but they will still look for patterns. 'Judging a situation as more or less random is often the key to important cognitions and behaviors. Perceiving a situation as nonchance calls for explanations, and it marks the onset of inductive inference' (Lopes, 1982; cited in Falk and Konold, 1997, p.301). Random events have no explanation and need no explanation, except that they may be subjectively explained as good or bad luck. People may see runs in random sequences as indicators of imminent change: the gambler's fallacy. If they see a long series of roulette outcomes of red, they tend to guess that black will come up next time. If they see a sequence of soccer game wins and a single loss by a team, they tend to predict a win for the next game because there is an assumed causal relationship between that team and wins, such as good management of the team (DiFonzo and Bordia, 1997; cf. Dawes, 1999).

Even if stock prices truly follow a random walk, people will be able to convince themselves that there are patterns that have predictive value. Some roulette players spend hours observing the wheel to detect patterns that could be used to profit. In laboratory experiments, subjects are often reported to have been searching for patterns in purely random sequences of stock prices (Kroll et al., 1988a; 1988b; De Bondt, 1993). De Bondt (1998) noted that technical analysis was similar to the fact that many investors see patterns where there are none. Often an *extrapolation bias* is found, that is, the price changes of the past are expected to continue. People are steadily optimistic in bull markets and pessimistic in bear markets. Technical analysis comprises attempts to identify trend changes at an early stage and then to persist until the weight of the evidence indicates that the trend has reversed. Some traders place great importance on chart patterns, while others are aware of them but have little faith in their relevance to trading. Most trading systems aim to isolate specific patterns that have profit potential (Bernstein, 1993, p.105).

Pattern recognition of particular interest in financial markets involves quick identification of trends for building instant scenarios. If a trend is teased out through some more or less sophisticated procedure, the next question is whether the trend will continue or be replaced by a reversal. Predictions of continuations when reversals occur, and vice versa can, lead to serious losses or forfeited chances of profits. This problem is closely related to how expectations are formed and to the way forecasts are made. De Bondt (1993) reported a study of nearly 38 000 forecasts of stock prices and exchange rates. He found that non-experts expected the continuation of apparent past 'trends' in prices, were optimistic in bull markets, and were pessimistic in bear markets. These subjects hedged their forecasts, meaning that their subjective probability distributions were skewed in the opposite direction. As a result, expectations of risk also depended on prior performance. The author notes that the results are of considerable interest from the perspective of intuitive judgment. The subjects' price predictions conflict with the gambler's fallacy or a more universal belief that 'what goes up must come down'. The interval estimates made by the subjects did not recognize the chances of reversal. According to De Bondt, the subjects may have predicted the near future with an eye to recent price changes, but past price levels anchored their long-term forecasts of the range of possible prices and explained the asymmetry in confidence intervals.

Reasoning that contains a plausible causal explanation is often behind a belief in winning stocks and a basis for antiregressive (momentum) strategies. This is not to say that there never can be true causal relationships, only that true causes may be difficult to spot and clarify. This explains why people tend to look for patterns even where there are no patterns. If people speculating on the stock market interpret development of stock prices as random, they may not perceive patterns that can direct their investment decisions. Having a strategy presupposes recognition of some pattern or at least traces that can be interpreted.

The representativeness heuristic, which will be dealt with later in more detail, is based on similarity between a cognitive sample and some population and involves disregard of prior probabilities. People are induced to believe that they can distinguish patterns in truly random sequences, especially if they think that they find some causal explanation (Dawes, 1999). Barberis et al. (1998) give an example from finance:

> When a company has a consistent history of earnings growth over several years, accompanied as it may be by salient and enthusiastic descriptions of its products and management, investors might conclude that the past history is representative of an underlying earnings growth potential. While a consistent pattern of high growth may be nothing more than a random draw for a few lucky firms, investors see 'order among chaos' and infer from the in-sample growth path that the firm belongs to a small and distinct population of firms whose earnings just keep growing. As a consequence, investors using the representativeness heuristic might disregard the reality that a history of high earnings growth is unlikely to repeat itself; they will overvalue the company, and be disappointed in the future when the forecasted earnings growth fails to materialize (Barberis et al., 1998, p.316).

The effects of noise traders appear to be double. First, due to their misinterpretation of information, they see patterns where there are none. Second, their behavior creates disturbances in the financial market that may appear as patterns. Here is one indictment of them:

> These agents [noise traders], who speculate using the 'head-and-shoulders' chart pattern, are shown to qualify as noise traders because: 1. trading volume is exceptionally high when they are active, and 2. their trading is unprofitable. Head-and-shoulders sales lower prices and vice versa, effects that disappear in two weeks (Osler, 1998).

A sudden, drastic trend reversal may mean that earlier cues of a change in the trend have been neglected. In this vein, it is worth noting that financial economists have developed theory on how cues or signals can be ignored. Applications of rational expectations theory now take into account the possibility that individual actors possess private information which they may use or not use in forming their expectations (Lee, 1998).

Pattern recognition is an important dimension in human intelligence, and the ability to recognize early cues and patterns seems to be an essential characteristic of expertise. At the same time, research clearly suggests that experts far from always perform better than novices and that they may be prone to distinguish patterns where there are none. De Bondt's (1991) studies of financial forecasters lend support to this finding in research on expertise.

INFERENCES ABOUT THE UNKNOWN

> *Male toads, roaming through swamps at night, use the pitch of a rival's croak to infer its size when deciding whether to fight . . . Stock brokers must make fast decisions about which of several stocks to trade or invest when only limited information is available. The list goes on. Inductive inferences are typically based on uncertain cues. The eyes can deceive, and so can a tiny toad with a deep croak in the darkness.*
>
> Gigerenzer and Goldstein (1996, p.650)

Gigerenzer and Goldstein (1996) distinguished three approaches to the way organisms make inferences about unknown aspects of the environment:

1. The laws of human inference are the laws of probability and statistics
2. Heuristics and biases
3. Bounded rationality (in Simon's dual sense).

In the first approach, people are assumed to use the best of probability and statistical theory when trying to form a belief about something uncertain or unknown. Bayes' theorem, which postulates revision of probabilities as the process goes along, is a favorite assumption. The assumption does not necessarily mean that a person employs such sophisticated procedures in every decision, but rather that people on average and over time perform in such a way that this result is accomplished. This is similar to the view that assumptions only involve people behaving 'as if' they used probability theory and statistics (Friedman, 1953).

Observations of reality, in particular single observations at single points in time, have cast much doubt on the assumption that people behave rationally, even in the restricted sense of 'as if'. Alternative theory has been proposed so as to make theory of behavior come closer to reality. The *heuristics-and-biases approach* involves simplified decision making, using simple rules of thumb and simple procedures, but is more complex than the rationality assumption, which at least simplifies the theorist's life. It is closer to reality in the sense that the approach can be used directly for explanations and (some gross) predictions of individual behavior. While many decision makers have to face situations in which information is unstructured and conflicting, with no probabilities given, decision-making experiments in both the statistical and the heuristics approaches mostly deal with 'givens'. Subjects are presented with probabilities and are instructed to focus on those, paying no attention to environmental structure. The main heuristics in this approach have been labeled. They will be described in the next section of the chapter. Kahneman and Riepe (1998) give a good account of such heuristics and recommend many applications in the world of finance. McFadden (1999) reviews findings and pleads for consideration by economists.

Gigerenzer and Goldstein (1996) are critical of this approach, which they describe as using rationality theory as a norm and basis for comparison. In their view, the heuristics-and-biases approach fails to recognize the behaviors as appropriate and adaptive to the environment at a certain point in time. A major criticism of the approach is that it is said to focus on human errors, defined as deviations from an unrealistic model of rationality, and to overlook the smart tricks used by humans to produce good outcomes. In a journal discussion with Gigerenzer (1996), Kahneman and Tversky (1996) noted that the critique was based on misrepresentation of their models and repeated the ideas behind their work. Gigerenzer's response further underlined what he saw as differences between the heuristics-and-biases approach and the approach proposed and pursued by his research group. Gigerenzer (1996) uses very strong words in his critique:

> It is understandable that when heuristics were first proposed as the underlying cognitive processes in the early 1970s they were only loosely characterized. Yet, 25 years and many experiments later, explanatory notions such as representativeness remain vague, undefined, and unspecified with respect both to the antecedent conditions that elicit (or suppress) them and also to the cognitive processes that underlie them. My fear is that in another 25 years researchers will still be stuck with plausible yet nebulous proposals of the same type: that judgments of probability or frequency are sometimes influenced by what is similar (representativeness), comes easily to mind (availability), and comes first (anchoring) Gigerenzer (1996, p.592).

This line of criticism misses many of the details in the careful discussion of heuristics and biases that Kahneman and Tversky and many others have presented, and the new developments in research on many of the heuristics. While the applications of the approach in many areas, for example finance, suggest that the main emphasis of the approach is on human errors, Kahneman and Tversky have always stressed that these heuristics often are useful, but that they sometimes lead to characteristic errors or biases and that their studies have mostly focused on those. The critics have attacked Kahneman and Tversky's approach among other things for its presumed utilization of economic rationality theory as a norm for behavior:

> [T]he heuristics-and-biases view of human rationality would lead us to believe that humans are hopelessly lost in the face of real-world complexity, given their supposed inability to reason according to the canon of classical rationality, even in simple laboratory experiments (Gigerenzer and Goldstein, 1996, p.651).

It is true that there is a kind of normative or ideal model behind many of the heuristics studied and that comparisons are made between the ideal and the heuristic behavior, but this does not imply that the use of the heuristic leads to unsatisfactory results for the individual. On the contrary, Kahneman and Tversky emphasize that their approach is not meant to be a critical evaluation of actual behavior and that the use of heuristics may be a smart way of overcoming the complexities of reality. It could be added that the bias in cognitive bias refers to the selections that are needed at all steps in the information process and is not related to rationality. Nor does it stand for error.

The opposition to the heuristics-and-biases approach is part of the third approach, which begins with bounded rationality, a theory of limited cognitive capacity that was launched by Herbert Simon (1955). Incidentally, Kahneman et al. (1982, Preface) also acknowledge the great influence that Simon's work had on them. The third approach is new and there is much less research behind the hypotheses than is the case for the heuristics-and-biases approach.

The approach of Gigerenzer and his collaborators is of interest here, in the first place because it claims to describe and explain behavior without evaluating it against an unattainable ideal behavior deduced from a model that overlooks the complexity of real-life situations. In contrast to, for example, Herrnstein (1990), who designates the rationality theory of choice as the best normative theory, Gigerenzer and Todd (1999) see the possibility that economic rationality may do worse than smart heuristics due to the complexities of the situation. Their thinking is in line with traditional differential psychology in which comparisons of effects are not made with ideal models, but with other people who do not use the same heuristic, or with situations in which no heuristic was used. Secondly, the approach involves interesting research that provides alternative explanations to some robust judgment and decision phenomena. Thirdly, the approach proposes hypotheses that involve algorithms, that is, procedures that are said to guarantee solutions in contrast to heuristics that only indicate a direction towards a solution with no guarantee of a solution. While the third approach is no full-fledged alternative to the heuristics-and-biases approach, in my view it provides some intriguing ideas for research also in the financial area.

THE HEURISTICS-AND-BIASES APPROACH

When people face tasks that involve judgments of frequencies or probabilities, they employ heuristics to make the judgments easier:

> The term *judgmental heuristic* refers to a strategy – whether deliberate or not – that relies on a natural assessment to produce an estimation or a prediction. One of the manifestations of a heuristic is the relative neglect of other considerations (Tversky and Kahneman, 1983, p.294).

A *heuristic* is essentially a procedure for problem solving that functions by reducing the number of possible alternatives and solutions and thereby increases the chance of a solution. Many authors in the field of finance use the concept of *cognitive bias* to explain decisions in financial markets. While cognitive bias generally refers to limited cognitive capacity, the use in behavioral finance often concentrates on the fact that people utilize heuristics to facilitate their decision making. Since financial economists, even those with an inclination towards behavioral finance, tend to relate their hypotheses to the rationality postulate, they see the utilization of such heuristics as deviations from rationality and they call those 'cognitive errors' rather than using the psychologists' more positive word, 'heuristics'.

The Base-Rate Fallacy and Representativeness

Tversky and Kahneman (1982a) propose that people tend to simplify their judgments and decisions through the use of a few simple heuristics that help them avoid difficulties. The first observations of failures to consider base rates were made in medicine. It was found that when sets of symptoms pointed towards the presence of a disease, base-rate data such as the frequency of a diagnosis in a population and the specific information on the case at hand were not properly weighted in accordance with Bayesian theory. There were grounds for suspecting that, in some cases at least, too much attention was paid to the specific symptoms and too little to the statistical frequency of the disease. While the neglected use of base-rate data has been amply studied and discussed, less attention has been bestowed on the likely case that, when the base-rate probability is high, there could be a tendency to overlook the specific symptoms. Judging from newspaper stories, a patient with indistinct symptoms of pneumonia may sometimes be misclassified as having the flu at times when almost everyone else seems to be affected by it.

Kahneman and Tversky (1973) devised experimental tests of the first type of case. They demonstrated that, in contrast to what economic theory posited, people had a tendency to neglect base-rate information in favor of similarity judgments (Tversky and Kahneman, 1982c, 1982d). In a typical study, the subjects were asked to predict the field of study of a graduate student or the profession of somebody on the basis of a brief description. The description contained some personality traits that were similar to the stereotype of a profession, for example, of lawyers or engineers. The subjects' judgments turned out to be determined by the degree of similarity between the description and the stereotype of the profession. This happened even when the subjects were made familiar with the base rates (H), that is, the frequencies of law and engineering students and professionals in the population.

When estimating the probability $P(H|D)$, the subjects looked at the similarity between D and the stereotype of the profession rather than at the prior probabilities (H). This is the *base-rate fallacy*. It is often accompanied by the use of the heuristic of *representativeness*: an event is judged probable to the extent that it represents the essential features of its parent population or of its generating process. It means, among other things, that people in situations of uncertainty tend to look for familiar patterns and are apt to believe that the pattern will repeat itself. The neglect of base rates is more general than representativeness and cannot always be explained by this heuristic (see, for example, the problem in Table 5.1).

In intuitive forecasting, which should be distinguished from statistical forecasting, people tend to use what Kahneman and Lovallo (1993) call an *inside view*. With the inside view, the forecaster overvalues the specific details that s/he knows and disregards or downplays statistical facts that are relevant to the problem and that are used in more objective forecasts, based on the *outside view*. This may be seen as use of the representativeness heuristic.

Gigerenzer and Hoffrage (1995, pp.699–700) suggest some reasons why base rates are neglected and point out that in many inference problems base rates are uninteresting. It is not always wrong to neglect the base rates. They state that people find it more natural to handle frequencies than probabilities. Their subjects were asked what the probability was that a woman with a positive mammogram actually had breast cancer. The subjects did better with data on mammograms and breast cancer presented as frequencies than presented as probabilities. Despite the frequencies and the fact that all necessary information was offered in the tasks, only slightly less than half of the algorithms used by the subjects were classified as being Bayesian reasoning.

Cosmides and Tooby (1996) investigated whether inductive reasoning performance changed depending on whether the subjects, 75 college students, were asked to judge a frequency or the probability of an event. The subjects completed a frequentist medical diagnosis problem. The authors found that high levels of correct Bayesian reasoning were elicited by frequentist versions of the problem. They found that crucial elements of the frequentist presentation were asking for the answer as a frequency rather than as a single-event probability, and presenting the problem information as frequencies. The results are interpreted as indicating that frequentist representations cause various cognitive biases to disappear, including overconfidence, the conjunction fallacy, and base-rate neglect.

Fiedler et al. (2000) also find that frequencies are handled better in some situations. They explain the problem in terms of the *sampling hypothesis*. When making a judgment, people sample information from memory and from the environment and then make inferences on the basis of the information represented in the sample, using rather simple methods. The requested probability is referred to as the 'criterion' and the conditional as the 'predictor'. According to the results, a sample that is focused on the criterion leads to more neglect of base rates than a sample focused on the predictor. Table

5.1 is an example of the problems that were used. The subjects were asked to state the probability that a woman who had a positive mammogram had breast cancer. The figures in the Table are frequencies in a sample of 1 000 women and are the same as those used by Gigerenzer and Hoffrage (1995). The correct estimate of the hit rate is 7.8 percent, given by [8/(8+95)x100]. If percentages rather than frequencies are used, the number of correct estimates decreases significantly. Other characteristics of the samples used by the judges were also studied. The authors stress that the neglect of base rates is primarily associated with low base-rate probabilities, such as in Table 5.1. They also find that in addition to focusing on criterion or predictor, the size of the cognitive sample is important.

Table 5.1 Problem Used in the Study of the Base-Rate Fallacy

	y (breast cancer)	~y (no breast cancer)	N
x (mammography +)	8	95	
~x (mammography –)	2	895	
			1 000

Source: Fiedler et al. (2000).

The base-rate fallacy exists, but may be less common than has been assumed in behavioral finance. It is true that some findings of the fallacy may have suffered from methodological lack of clarity. Now more is known about the circumstances under which the neglect of base rates tends to occur, which may inspire a more proper – and restricted – use in applied contexts (see Fiedler, 2000; Fiedler et al., 2000). Investors, like most other people, may not construe situations in the way the experimental designs presume. Gigerenzer and Hoffrage (1995) as well as Fiedler et al. (2000) talk of natural rather than probabilistic situations and assert that people are not inclined towards logical inference and deductive reasoning, which actually concurs with the heuristics-and-biases approach of Kahneman and Tversky.

In finance, undue attention to the base rate may occur when the majority of stocks go up. Details about a specific firm are neglected and investors may believe in its stock without grounds. When, say, hi-tech stocks fall, other stocks, including those for which there is good news, tend to join. When the majority of stocks go up, a positive effect spreads to stocks that may not deserve it because of bad news. The sudden cascades of information that some economists have propounded may be cases of undue attention given to base rates: investors at first do not heed the information from their own experience and immediate environment, but concentrate on earlier developments, that is, on the base rates of stock prices. This may be seen as the reverse of the base-rate fallacy. The base rate dominates the specifics.

The phenomenon is well known in the psychology of learning and is called 'generalization' or in experimental psychology often 'stimulus generalization'. Generalization is a kind of inference about the unknown and normally means that what is known to be true about all known members of a class of objects is true of all members including those not yet observed. Observations that emanate from a large group or a majority in a population are extended to include all. The converse is 'discrimination', which means that differences, especially minor ones, are attended to. An interesting finding is that when people are anxious they tend to generalize more, that is, include more stimuli and discriminate less. Exuberance may have similar effects. Irrational exuberance may thus be explained as being caused by failures to discriminate due to strong positive or negative emotions.

Shefrin and Statman (1994, 1995) ascribe two cognitive characteristics to noise traders in their Behavioral CAPM. One is the base-rate fallacy, which they treat as synonymous with representativeness. Noise traders are assumed to underweight base-rate information. They make forecasts by overweighting recent events and by underweighting more distant events that form the base rate. Noise traders look at the most recent patterns and believe that they will be repeated in the future. This may be true for some situations, but too much attention to base rates seems more likely in many situations, in particular when investors are carried away by strong emotions. News about a single company may have some generalization effect; news about a group of companies will probably have more effect, to some extent depending on the status of the group; and when a majority is covered by some sensational news, the generalization effects will certainly spread over all or almost all company stocks.

The representativeness heuristic comprises the idea that people judge samples on the basis of similarity between the criterion and some information about properties that corresponds to what is often only a stereotype of a population. Tversky and Kahneman (1983) give the following definition:

> Representativeness is an assessment of the degree of correspondence between a sample and a population, an instance and a category, an act and an actor or, more generally, between an outcome and a model. The model may refer to a person, a coin, or the world economy, and the respective outcomes could be marital status, a sequence of heads and tails, or the current price of gold. Representativeness can be investigated empirically by asking people, for example, which of two sequences of heads and tails is more representative of a fair coin or which of two professions is more representative of a given personality (Tversky and Kahneman, 1983, pp.295–6).

The heuristic of representativeness has been widely studied and used as an explanation of many types of relationships. It was one of the first cognitive concepts to be used in attempts to explain stock-price developments (De Bondt and Thaler, 1985). It is reasonable to assume that judgments of the (future) value of a stock may be susceptible to such influence. In times of high volatility of stock prices, the interpretation of the change in the price of a certain stock may be disturbed by some information that is similar to or seems to explain the change for a particular company. In fact, stock exchanges are surrounded by such items of information, which even if they were true would have a very low probability of having any influence on fundamentals. They are overweighted. De Bondt and Thaler (1985) launched the use of the heuristic in finance when they suggested that investors were overoptimistic and overreacted in favor of winners and undervalued losers because of the representativeness heuristic. The investors allowed recent experiences to dominate. The authors advocated contrarian strategies involving selling past winners and buying past losers.

Here is an example illustrating the way a heuristic is often used in behavioral finance. Solt and Statman (1989) found, in a study covering the years 1960 to 1977, that growth companies did not give the highest returns, which implied that growth stocks and growth companies were not the same. One reason could be that the returns of growth companies were highly risky and thus low after risk adjustment. While there is some doubt as to the extent to which their results could have been the effect of regression towards the mean, the authors pose the question of why the common belief in growth companies, except when contrarian strategies were followed, could be so persistent.

> [W]e suggest that the hypothesis that investors overestimate the probability that the stock of a growth company is a growth stock because they rely on the representativeness heuristic. Specifically, they overestimate the probability that a growth stock is a stock of a growth company because a growth stock is similar to a growth company (Solt and Statman, 1989, p.42).

Why do investors favor growth stocks even though they apparently give lower long-term returns than more ordinary stocks? Apart from possible errors in the analysis, such as the operational definition of a growth company and regression towards the mean, the answer is deemed to be psychological and there is then a choice between cognitive and emotional factors. The authors chose cognitive factors and suggest the representativeness heuristic without really making clear how it could work in this case. The returns and the growth companies are assumed similar in such a way that both stock prices and firms will grow, but, without questioning investors, there is no real evidence that investors make such comparisons. The heuristic may serve as an ad-hoc explanation rather than make predictions feasible.

Shefrin and Statman have also utilized the cognitive theories proposed by Kahneman and Tversky in many other contexts and developed models in which prospect theory, mental accounting, and simple heuristics are integral parts. In an article, Shefrin and Statman (1993) discuss options as financial products and base their discussion on valuations as those are viewed in prospect theory, influenced by framing, mental accounts, and cognitive bias. The article gives an overview of call options and explores the uses of cognitive psychology at the same time. It provides another example of how the representativeness concept is employed to explain financial behavior.

> It is a common observation that many investors overweight recent performance as they evaluate financial products. Flocking to mutual funds that have done well during the previous year is one example. The tendency to overweight recent performance is a manifestation of representativeness, a class of cognitive errors. (Shefrin and Statman 1993, p.132).

It is sometimes difficult to distinguish between representativeness and the following heuristic 'availability'. Representativeness is best conceptualized in terms of Bayesian probability. Availability is not specifically associated with any well-known probability theorem (or seen as deviating from it).

Availability

The *availability* heuristic is an often cited heuristic, perhaps because it apparently covers a large number of everyday experiences. A person is said to employ the availability heuristic whenever s/he estimates probability or frequency by the ease with which instances or associations can be brought to mind. Instances of large classes are recalled better and faster than instances of less frequent classes, likely occurrences are easier to imagine than unlikely ones, and associative connections are strengthened when two events frequently co-occur (Tversky and Kahneman, 1982e, pp.163–4; Rothman and Hardin, 1997).

Stephan (1999, p.108) distinguishes between (1) experience-based, (2) memory-based, and (3) imagination-based availability. *Experience-based* availability means that people rely on what they have seen or heard. They neglect the fact that their samples probably have been small and biased. If unemployed workers answer a question about how many workers are unemployed, or social workers about how many families need social relief, they tend to overestimate the numbers according to the availability heuristic. They derive their estimates from their own experience, which involves frequent contacts with the relevant groups, and they are likely to exaggerate the actual number. Ask a stock owner how many households own stocks and you can expect that the answer will be an overstatement or at least be higher than what a non-owner of stocks would estimate.

Memory-based availability depends on the ease with which memories are available and can be brought to mind. It is related to well-known memory factors such as: (a) how intense the attention was, (b) the salience of the impression, (c) the vivacity of the impression, (d) the familiarity of the object or event, and (e) spatial and temporal propinquity. The higher the values on these factors, the stronger the memory trace and the higher the availability is. Stephan (1999) discusses how the advertising for stocks in the privatization of the German Telekom played on these factors to create availability among private investors, who were the prime target group for the campaign. He notes that the average German had earlier been very skeptical about investing money in stocks, but that many of the purchasers were persuaded to believe in the value of the company and its future development.

Stephan (1999) also demonstrates the effect of the availability heuristic in an experiment that dealt with German companies. Subjects were given a stock report of gains and losses for 51 companies of which 25, according to a pre-test were well known by the subjects and 26 less well known. When the well-known companies were reported to have more winners (stock price rose) than the less well-known companies and there was a slight majority of losers (stock price went down) in the selection, there was a strong tendency to report that there were more winners than losers. When the well-known companies had a majority of losers and the less well-known companies had a majority of winners, there was a clear tendency to report that there were more losers, despite the fact that there were (slightly) more winners. The results of the well-known companies were more available and tended to dominate the impression.

The *imagination-based* availability arises as a consequence of how easy it is to imagine something. If it is easier to imagine a certain situation than another, the former will tend to dominate the thinking. Tversky and Kahneman (1982e, pp.169–70) carried out a series of experiments in which subjects were asked to estimate the number of combinations of size *r* that could be made out of ten. They gave tasks similar to this one: 'Suppose you have to make a portfolio of two stocks out of a selection of ten stocks. How many different portfolios of two stocks could you choose between? How many different portfolios of eight stocks could you select out of the ten?' While the median answer was 70 in the first case, it was only 20 in the second case, in spite of the fact that the answer should be the same (45) in both cases. Sets of two stocks necessarily define unique sets of eight. The explanation given by the authors is that it is much easier to imagine pairs of two than sets of eight.

Stephan (1999) cites as an example of the availability heuristic a person who works for a company or who buys its new product, becomes convinced of its high quality, and decides to buy stocks in it. Stock prices seem, for example, apt to go up when a new sales contract is announced, even though the value of the contract is insignificant in relation to total sales volume.

In a study of diversification and investment in foreign equity, French and Poterba (1991) found that investors seemed to avoid foreign stocks and that there was probably a psychological reason for this – own-country bias. They refer to a paper by Tversky and Heath (1991), who found that households behaved as though unfamiliar gambles were riskier than familiar gambles.

> Investors may not evaluate the risk of different investments based solely on the historical standard deviation of returns. They may impute extra 'risk' to foreign investments because they know less about foreign markets, institutions, and firms (French and Poterba, 1991, p.225).

Tversky and Kahneman (1983) explain the *conjunction fallacy* as being caused by, among other things, the use of the representativeness or availability heuristics. The fallacy means breaking against the conjunction rule – $P(A \,\&\, B) \leq P(B)$ – in probability theory. The rule states that the probability of stock B being a winner is larger than or equal to the probability of stocks A and B being winners. The fallacy implies that the probability of stock B being a winner increases if the probability of stock A being a winner is considered at the same time. A person may see the addition of something familiar to an uncertain event as raising the probability when it actually decreases it. Experiments show that a scenario that includes a possible cause and an outcome could appear more probable than the outcome on its own (Tversky and Kahneman, 1983, p.307). Such techniques have, for example, been exploited in publicity about an event that is favorable to a company.

Here is an example from a simple experiment, carried out both as a paper-and-pencil test and with actual dice throwing.

> Consider a regular six-sided die with four green faces and two red faces. The die will be rolled 20 times and the sequence of greens (G) and reds (R) will be recorded. You are asked to select one sequence, from a set of three, and you will win $25 if the sequence you chose appears on successive rolls of the die. Please check the sequence of greens and reds on which you prefer to bet. 1. RGRRR, 2. GRGRRR, 3. GRRRRR (Tversky and Kahneman, 1983, p.303).

Sequence 1 can be obtained from sequence 2 by deleting the first G. By the conjunction rule, sequence 1 is then more probable than sequence 2. In the study, 88 percent chose sequence 2 as having a higher probability than sequence 1. The authors attribute this result to the representativeness heuristic. The second sequence was judged to be more similar to the distribution of faces of the dice. It should be noted that the conjunction fallacy occurred when the alternatives were presented one by one to different groups, so-called between-groups design. When the subjects have a chance to compare the alternatives the error is reduced and even disappears (Gigerenzer, 1996; Kahneman and Tversky, 1996, p. 587). It should be noted that the use of the availability heuristic does not always lead to incorrect estimates of frequencies (Stephan, 1999, p. 119). Some correct data may be easy to recollect.

Anchoring and Adjustment

> *If a client asks his advisor in the currency department of his bank, for example, whether the *dDollar exchange rate will be over or under DM 1.95 after six months, the following exact forecast of the exchange rate should be independent of the first given gross estimation. The exact forecast should not differ from a forecast where the client had asked whether the dollar exchange rate would be over or under DM 1.70 (or if the advisor had had a nice weekend).*
>
> Stephan (1999, p.109; my translation)

Anchoring bias means that people make estimates by starting from an initial value that is subjected to *adjustment* before the final answer is arrived at. The initial value may be given by the formulation of the problem or partial calculation. When investors make forecasts of future values, their forecasts may be affected by the value that they use as a starting point even if they do not believe in it and make adjustments. Studies show that when investors are asked to give confidence intervals for probability estimates, the intervals are often too narrow, which is ascribed to the effect of anchoring. The important thing is that due to the anchoring in the first place, the later adjustments are usually insufficient. Consequently, different starting points yield different estimates that are biased towards the initial values. A simple experiment illustrates the anchoring effect. A group of subjects asked to estimate the product 1x2x3x4x5x6x7x8 (8!) within five seconds, gave much lower estimates than a group who made an estimate of 8x7x6x5x4x3x2x1. The estimates were 512 and 2 250 and the right answer is 40 320 (Tversky and Kahneman, 1982a, pp.14–15). The first figure apparently served as an anchor and later adjustments were insufficient, more so when the anchor was low.

If there are anchoring effects, financial analysts could be expected to stick too much to their former estimates when there are surprise changes in firm earnings. In particular, they are assumed to be slow to upgrade their evaluations when there are sudden increases in earnings. An American investment fund is said to be based on the idea that the stocks of a firm may be mispriced because of anchoring effects (*Newsday, Money & Careers*, Dec. 19, 1999, p.F7). The effects may be equally well explained if they are attributed to the heuristic of conservatism (see below).

Tversky and Kahneman (1982a) also discuss how the subjective estimate of some quantity will vary depending on how the estimate is performed. For example, estimates of the Dow-Jones on a particular day will vary depending on the procedure used in the estimations. The estimates can be obtained in two ways: (1) the person is asked to select values of the Dow-Jones that correspond to specified percentiles of the probability distribution, and (2) the person is asked to assess the probabilities that the true value of the Dow-

Jones will exceed some specified value. Since the methods suggest different modes of adjustment from different anchors the results will vary.

In a German experiment with professional investors as subjects, Stephan and Kiell (2000) investigated the use of some heuristics, including the anchoring and adjustment process. They actually tested the hypothesis mentioned in the previous passage. The subjects were first shown a graph of the German DAX stock market index over the last 21 months and were then asked to indicate whether the DAX in 12 months would be below 4 500 points, in one group and, in the second group, above 6 500 points. The subjects were then asked to present more exact forecasts for the same period of time. The forecasts were significantly different in the predicted direction, with mean amounting to 5 765 in the first, low group and to 5 930 points in the second, high group.

Stephan (1999), who makes a systematic review of the anchoring heuristic, suggests that this heuristic can create overconfidence, meaning that investors have a tendency to believe too much in their well-considered estimates. The mere fact that the judgments are anchored and then adjusted inspires confidence. He demonstrates clear anchoring effects in experiments carried out by himself and co-authors. Subjects were given the task of making a seven-week forecast of the dollar exchange rate, the German DAX, and the gold price. For each estimation the subjects got graphic information about developments over the last six months. Before making the exact forecasts, the subjects had to make gross estimations, telling whether the dollar exchange rate would be over or under DM 1.50 (low anchoring value) versus over or under DM 1.70 (high anchoring value). In a corresponding way, the values for the DAX were DM 1 600 and 1 800 and for the gold price DM 16 000 and 18 000.

Table 5.2 Anchoring Effects

	High anchoring	Low anchoring	Control group
Dollar rate (DM)	1.58	1.53	1.54
DAX	1 764	1 719	1 748
Gold price	17 082	16 670	16 795

Source: Stephan (1999, pp. 109–10).

Table 5.2 shows the results from one of the studies. Obviously, there was an effect that can be called anchoring: with the higher gross estimations in the practice session, the following estimates were higher, and with the lower gross estimations, the estimates were lower. The control groups who had made no gross estimations were somewhere in between the high and low experimental groups. This experiment and others with larger variations between high and low gross estimations lead the author to conclude that the farther away the anchor (the gross estimation) is from the uninfluenced estimates of the control group, the more the forecast is drawn in the direction of the anchor. One of the experiments was made with traders working for a German brokerage firm and it gave essentially the same results as the experiments with students of business and economics as subjects.

Stephan (1999) also found that there were anchoring effects from tasks that were unrelated to the crucial forecasts. Subjects who had worked on discriminating a certain number in a series of numbers flashed on a screen showed anchoring effects when they, under a different experimenter and in a different setting, were asked to forecast a future DAX value. These studies show that anchoring and adjustment may be an important influence in forecasting values. Stephan warns that overestimation of the probability of favorable environmental conditions may lie behind many individual failures in financial markets. The anchors have in such cases been too high, especially for young investors who grew up in a predominant bull market.

Knowledge about anchoring effects may protect an investor from too easily accepting an offer to buy stocks. It happens that a less serious broker offers a client stocks that the broker knows are above the financial capacity of the client. When the client says 'no', an offer of a more reasonably priced bundle of stocks is made. In relation to the anchor that the first offer established, the second offer will appear favorable. There will also, according to Cialdini (1988), be a strong pressure on the client to accept the new offer because of the demands of reciprocity. The broker has made a concession when dropping the first offer in favor of the second, lower-price offer and this calls for an appropriate concession on the part of the client, who is more likely to buy than if there had been no high-price offer.

Conservatism

Delays in reactions to information have been attributed to various factors, some of which were mentioned in the first two chapters. In behavioral finance, the concept of *conservatism* has been used to explain slow reactions to new information. The concept was suggested by the psychologist Ward Edwards (1968, 1982) and involved slow updating of models in the face of new evidence. People's behavior is not Bayesian, but may get closer to it by more attempts. Edwards points to 'human misaggregation of data' as the major cause of conservatism. He reported that the subjects' guesses were much lower than the Bayesian value in the example with the bookbags presented at the beginning of Chapter 1. Other experimenters have shown that the subjective estimates of low objective probabilities tend to be higher, say 0.25 when the objective probability is 0.10 (Erev et al., 1994)

The use of the concept in finance has been discussed by, among others, Fama (1998), who is critical of it (and the use of other psychological concepts) in finance. Other authors apply conservatism to explain underreaction to economic news. Shefrin (2000) suggests that financial analysts face tasks that are similar to Edwards' bookbags problem and have to revise probabilities when new information appears. Like the subjects in Edwards' experiments on revision of Bayesian probabilities, financial analysts are, according to Shefrin, inclined to make only partial adjustments at first and are slow to arrive at the correct estimation of the new probabilities. Barberis et al. (1998) and Shleifer (2000) suggest that the presence of both under- and overreactions of stock prices can be explained by conservatism and representativeness. The typical investor thinks that the securities market moves between two states and that different models govern earnings in each state. Their Model 1 determines earnings in state 1 and Model 2 earnings in state 2.

Under Model 1, earnings shocks are likely to be reversed in the following period (reversion towards the mean), so that a positive shock to earnings is more likely to be followed in the next period by a negative shock than by another positive shock. The decisions tend to be conservative and involve underreaction to news. Under Model 2, shocks are more likely to be followed by another shock of the same sign and earnings trend. Investor decisions are based on the assumption of similarity of patterns, which is predicted by the representativeness heuristic. The models are based on some simplifying assumptions which there is no need to go into here, except to note that in the models, stock prices are based on the earnings streams, not on earnings plus other value-influencing factors. The main question is how investors decide which model to believe in. The authors assume that switches between models are rare for the typical investor. Here the authors rely on Griffin and Tversky (1992) and suggest that investors pay too much attention to the strength of the evidence and too little to its statistical weight. The switch from belief in one model to belief in the other may then, for example, be elicited by dramatic front-page news (cf. Niederhoffer, 1971; Schachter et al., 1986).

The representativeness heuristic has been held to be inconsistent with conservatism. Griffin and Tversky (1992) tried to reconcile overconfidence, which is close to representativeness, and underconfidence, which is similar to conservatism. The hypothesis they tested was that people focus on the strength or extremeness of the available evidence with insufficient regard for its weight or credence. This mode of judgment yields overconfidence when strength is high and weight is low, and underconfidence when strength is low and weight is high. The assumption is that people update their beliefs depending on the strength and weight of new evidence. The strength of the evidence is inferred from aspects like salience and extremity whereas weight has to do with such factors as sample size. Five experiments using 451 students demonstrated this phenomenon, beginning with a chance setup where strength is defined by sample proportion and weight is defined by sample size. These experiments are crucial to the models of over- and underreactions. Overconfidence and conservatism (which is sometimes also labeled underconfidence) are apparently not compatible in the sense that they cannot occur at the same time for one individual. The question then concerns under what circumstances overconfidence arises and under what circumstances conservatism arises (see Chapter 6).

Hindsight Bias

> *A critical aspect of any responsible job is learning from experience.*
>
> Fischhoff (1982b, p.427)

> *While the past entertains, ennobles, and expands quite readily, it enlightens only with delicate coaxing.*
>
> (Fischhoff, 1982a, p.335)

It may not be too easy to learn from experience since *hindsight bias* is a possible threat. Hindsight bias is described as follows:

> In hindsight, people consistently exaggerate what could have been anticipated in foresight. They not only tend to view what has happened as having been inevitable, but also to view it as having appeared 'relatively inevitable' before it happened. People believe that others should have been able to anticipate events much better than was actually the case. They even misremember their own predictions so as to exaggerate in hindsight what they knew in foresight (Fischhoff, 1982b, p.428).

Hindsight depends on memory and memory is fallible. Retrieving memories is a constructive process. Memory traces are deficient because of errors in impressions, limitations in storage capacity, and interference in recall processes. While this does not mean that memories are always incorrect, it points to the need to be somewhat cautious in using one's memories. Looking back, one tends to find patterns in random events, clear trends, and explanations that may seem useful for future use.

> [E]vents that the best-informed experts did not anticipate often appear almost inevitable after they occur. Financial punditry provides an unending source of examples. Within an hour of the market closing every day, experts can be heard on the radio explaining with high confidence why the market acted as it did. A listener could well draw the incorrect inference that the behavior of the market is so reasonable that it could have been predicted earlier in the day (Kahneman and Riepe, 1998, p.55).

It is not easy to protect oneself against hindsight bias. It may be good to have a notebook showing your actual expectations about the other stocks you had considered when you bought the highly successful stocks in company X and, preferably, also the probability you attributed to each possible outcome.

Recent research has focused on the relationship between confidence and hindsight, the 'knew-it-all-along effect'. Hoffrage and Hertwig (1999), who belong to Gigerenzer's research team, argue that hindsight should not be seen as an error in information processing. It is 'a by-product of two generally adaptive processes: first, updating knowledge after receiving new information; and second, drawing fast and frugal inferences from this updated knowledge.' (Hoffrage and Hertwig, 1999, pp.191–2). Three views of hindsight bias are reviewed. The first, in the literature the most common view, focuses on the potential harmful effects. A second view stresses the adaptive aspects since hindsight bias may contribute to the esteem we enjoy from others and from ourselves. The third view, which is the main point, maintains that memory must be selective and that recall when memory has sorted out certain traces is a constructive, adaptive process. The process is the updating of information, which as a by-product may have hindsight bias.

> The adaptive process of knowledge updating relieves us of the need to store everything we have thought, said, or experienced in the past. Updating makes us smart by preventing us from using information that may be outdated due to changes in the environment . . . Adaptive updating has an uninvited by-product: hindsight bias. But this by-product may be a relatively low price to pay for a memory that works fast and frugally (Hoffrage and Hertwig, 1999, p.208).

Hindsight bias emerges during the reconstruction of an outcome. The authors (see Azar, 2000) have developed a model, called RAFT (Reconstruction After Feedback with Take the Best), with the basic idea that any feedback or correct information people receive after they have conducted their initial analysis changes the knowledge base underlying the original judgment and causes a bias toward the new information. The RAFT model predicts that hindsight bias should be stronger in hypothetical situations because people must always reconstruct the outcome. The RAFT model assumes:

1. If people cannot remember the original judgment they will reconstruct the judgment based on what they know about the situation.
2. Feedback about an event's outcome automatically updates a person's knowledge about the situation.
3. People will reconstruct their original judgment using the updated knowledge rather than the knowledge they originally had. While feedback does not directly affect a person's memory for the original response, it indirectly affects the memory by updating the knowledge used to reconstruct the response.

Despite the fact that unsatisfactory outcomes may occur, the hindsight bias, like other heuristics, implies adaptive behavior that should not be classified as flaws or errors, in this view. Hindsight may be useful to the individual or it may be harmful depending upon the circumstances. Even hindsight bias may serve some purpose for the individual, such as useful self-confidence.

Hindsight is cognitive in its present use and its relation to behavior is largely unknown. Forming memories of earlier decision situations may involve leaving out trivial details and pulling out the essential factors in the situation, which can then be used for future decision making Like any other type of learning, hindsight can lead to better preparation for the future. Hindsight is necessary since 'perception of a surprise-free past may portend a surpriseful future' (Fischhoff, 1982b, p.428).

Hindsight usually outperforms foresight, since events tend to become clear and causal structures appear disentangled when one is looking back. Part of the superiority may be specious due to hindsight bias. In retrospect, decision situations that were confused may be construed as rational and the hindsight bias may prevent learning from earlier experience. Incidentally, ostensibly successful decisions in the past may lead an investor to believe in her/his own ability and serve as a guide for future decisions It should not surprise anyone that stories about how successes were achieved or failures avoided in the stock market may be far from objective accounts, even with no intention to lie on the part of the story teller. Hindsight bias is rarely fully conscious. Hindsight, with or without bias, may give rise to strong feelings such as pride or regret. Such emotional hindsight, though often biased, may influence the disposition to act in future situations and, if inducing pride, perhaps lead to buying or, if producing regret, to selling at the wrong moment.

Anecdotal evidence, with some support from survey studies (psychonomics & Capital, 1998; De Bondt, 1998), suggests that stock holders and would-be stock holders make simulations in which they mentally make transactions with stocks without turning them into practical actions. Such simulations of purchases and sales may lead to useful learning, experienced as insights, if they are properly managed. An important finding in research on expertness is that experience in itself is worth less than deliberate practice. If the mental operations are carefully written down and compared with the outcomes after the appropriate time has passed, it should be tantamount to deliberate practice. If the whole process is not written down as it goes on, the risk of hindsight bias is great and the gained insights may be grossly misleading. Hindsight bias would in such cases be likely to involve the concealing of simulation results that involved losses and the exaggeration of successful mental simulation of transactions.

The Role of Heuristics and Biases

In all experiments on the various heuristics, there are always subjects or respondents who do not perform in accordance with the heuristic (without necessarily being closer to rationality). If the deviants are few, the tendency is to accept the evidence of the heuristic and view the heuristic as a general psychological law. This means that a certain dispersion around the 'true' value is granted for a general law. If the deviants are numerous, the researcher tends to look for additional variables so as to be able to explain the individual differences. The desired further explanatory variables may be economic, sociodemographic or psychological and they may give rise to the idea that there are segments that behave differently.

Economists have objected to the experimental results relating to heuristics and to prospect theory suggesting, for example, that learning and adaptation factors have been neglected in such studies; the subjects have been given no time to gain experience or learn from others as is characteristic of a market (see, for example, Smith, 1991). In an experimental study, Camerer (1987) showed that a financial asset market developed in such a way that the prices approached what Bayes' theorem predicted. Towards the end of the game, there were few traces of the representativeness heuristic at the market level. The results suggested that with the subjects' increasing experience the market developed in a Bayesian direction. This does not disprove the representativeness heuristic. It rather confirms that there are groups of, maybe inexperienced people who use the heuristic. This indicates that financial markets may be segmented in groups of varying experience. Camerer (1987, p.996) hints that if economic theory used evidence of systematic irrationality that operated like the representativeness heuristic, it might make better predictions.

Criticisms have, as noted earlier, also been raised by psychologists such as Gigerenzer (1996). One of Gigerenzer's criticisms was that heuristics had not been studied in natural environments, but in laboratory experiments with low ecological validity. Psychologists, in the first place Kahneman and Tversky (1996), have replied to the criticisms and pointed to the robustness and stability of the findings which make predictions of behavior possible in many contexts outside laboratories. Defenders of the heuristics-and-biases approach and its application in finance, such as Stephan and Kiell (1997, 2000), have found strong support for the approach in what they call a natural environment. Evidence is accumulating that ordinary as well as professional investors use heuristics of the kinds described.

In sum, there are substantial amounts of research on heuristics such as representativeness, availability, and anchoring to support the estimation of the heuristics-and-biases approach within and outside psychology, and which has led to many unexpected applications, such as in situations of international conflict (see Farnham, 1994). Dawes (1999) presents an elegant defense for the availability heuristic, in an economic journal at that. He cites evidence from different contexts and notes some circumstances that affect the effect.

Why learn about the use of heuristics? Most of the applications of the approach in behavioral finance have emanated from the search for suitable micro models to fit aggregate data. Stephan and Kiell (2000) also make this point and advocate more studies aimed at elucidating individual financial behavior. There are at least three reasons for devoting efforts to a deepened knowledge of the approach. First, financial theory does not explain or predict a number of phenomena in the market place and hypotheses derived from observations of actual market behavior can promote understanding of individual behavior in financial markets. Second, those operating in the financial markets, professionals as well as private investors, may utilize or already be utilizing knowledge about heuristics to their advantage. Investment management firms have, in fact, been founded to exploit the ideas of heuristics, apparently on the notion that financial behavior can be better predicted if people's use of heuristics in trading with stocks is considered. Third, it may be a good idea for investors to examine financial advice from professional advisors and scrutinize their own decision making, always noting the possibility of mistakes due to the use of overly simplifying heuristics rather than proper analysis. This is the theme of a readable overview of cognitive biases written by Kahneman and Riepe (1998). These authors provide a checklist for financial advisors based on the heuristics-and-biases approach.

In finance, the findings on heuristics have inspired attempts to squeeze in the apparently deviant phenomena under efficient-market theory. Many studies of stock markets still maintain that stock prices follow a random walk and that deviations can be explained by the theory with some slight modifications, for example factors suggested by Fama and French (1996) such as firm size and book-to-market value. While authors in behavioral finance and practitioners in financial markets are paying increasing attention to the possible utilization of existing heuristics so as to beat the market, there is now an emerging alternative to the approach, also based on experimental research. More will be said about this research in the next section.

THE USE OF FAST AND FRUGAL HEURISTICS

A bit of trust in the abilities of the mind and the rich structure of the environment may help us to see how thought processes that forgo the baggage of the laws of logic and probability can solve real-world adaptive problems quickly and well.

Todd and Gigerenzer (1999, p.365)

Gerd Gigerenzer, who is professor and research director at the Max Planck Institute in Berlin, is the leading representative of a new line of thinking in cognitive psychology. The thinking is presented in a number of authored and co-authored papers and in a recent volume with the title *Simple Heuristics That Make Us Smart*. Whereas 'heuristics and biases' or 'cognitive errors', the concept preferred in behavioral finance, suggest, according to Gigerenzer, that rational decisions, though not practicable, are the norm with which actions should be compared, Gigerenzer's approach focuses on the results, good or bad, that can be achieved with simple heuristics. In his view, people are often quite smart. People use simple heuristics when they face uncertainty and these heuristics tend, according to this approach, to be adjusted to the environment and the situation at hand. 'Ecological rationality' is a concept that is often used in these contexts. Researchers should then look for the heuristics or algorithms used by people in natural choice situations. While economic rationality builds on abstraction, ecological rationality attends to the complex details of reality.

Bounded Rationality and Simple Algorithms

On the basis of everyday observation, one may easily suspect that probabilities are not the most common form of expressions of uncertainty about the future. Possible exceptions are probabilities attached to events that may have disastrous consequences; in such cases, probabilities seem to become certainties, at least for some people. Probabilities are usually replaced by vague expressions like 'most of the time', 'few people', 'often', which can be translated into probabilities, albeit with large ambiguity zones, but which are not represented in everyday parlance. Mostly, people do not deal with probabilities as quantities and when they do they tend to distort them. The heuristics-and-biases approach has demonstrated that people tend to misinterpret probabilities, and has shown some rules for distortions such as the use of decision weights instead of probabilities. How can people then maximize subjective expected utility?

An alternative to maximizing utility is to search and decide on the first acceptable alternative, Simon's (1955) satisficing principle, which is known as 'bounded rationality' theory. The following updated definition of bounded rationality is given in a psychological dictionary (Reber, 1985):

> 1. A particular characteristic of human decision-making under conditions of extreme complexity. 2. A theory of cognitive processes as they are displayed under such conditions. In either usage, the reference is to the notion that in the face of complexity one cannot behave in a totally rational manner, simply because one's information-processing capacities are too limited to encompass all the knowledge required for such ideal decision-making. The theory of bounded rationality describes man as a decision-maker who circumscribes the situation by limiting (or 'bounding') the amount of information to be dealt with – often in creative and imaginative ways – and then behaving in a rational fashion with this limited knowledge base (Reber, 1985, p.611).

The definition above is exclusively based on cognitive information-handling processes, which is in line with Simon's more recent writings about cognitive science. In its early shape, the theory was more distinctly tied to searching and stopping at the first alternative with satisfactory properties rather than maximizing utility. In his original statement of the theory, Simon set himself a task with three main components: (1) he wanted to replace the global rationality of economic man with a kind of rational behavior, (2) that is compatible with the access to information and the computational capacities that are actually possessed by organisms, including man, (3) in the kinds of environments in which such organisms exist (Simon, 1955, p.99). The focus was on less abstraction, on the role of information employing the limited capacity given to humans, and on including the demands of the environment. The theory of bounded rationality has been found useful in many research contexts and an enormous literature is around (for an overview, see Conlisk, 1996).

Gigerenzer and Goldstein (1996) point out that in Simon's discussion of bounded rationality two aspects prevail. One is the cognitive aspect that signifies limited capacity and is often seen as synonymous with heuristics and biases. The other, mostly neglected, aspect has to do with ecology or the environment. 'Simon's insight that the minds of living systems should be understood relative to the environment in which they evolved, rather than to the tenets of classical rationality, has had little impact so far in research on human inference' (Gigerenzer and Goldstein, 1996, p.651). The authors develop a set of simple algorithms that exhibit bounded rationality in both of Simon's senses. The algorithms are satisficing, not maximizing, and operate with simple psychological principles 'that satisfy the constraints of limited time, knowledge, and computational might, rather than those of classical rationality' (Gigerenzer and Goldstein, 1996, p.651). The main tenet is that inference is best described by a Probabilistic Mental Model (PMM).

The Probabilistic Mental Model (PMM)

Anxious old lady to Captain at dinner on board a deluxe cruising ship: 'How often does a ship of this type go down?'
Captain's answer: 'Only once, dear lady'.
Statistician's joke about subjective probabilities

'PMMs perform intelligent guesses about unknown features of the world, based on uncertain indicators' (Gigerenzer and Goldstein, 1996, p.652). The decision maker follows one of a set of simple algorithms, essentially using available probability cues. In the absence of discriminating cues, a search process is started. In some cases the decision maker is limited to using only cues from memory, in other cases s/he is offered environmental cues. Typically, the decision rests on only a few cues. One such simple algorithm is 'take the best'. The algorithm implies that the search stops when there are relevant cues that discriminate among alternative actions. There are five steps in the process: (1) recognition principle, (2) search for cue values, (3) discrimination rule, (4) cue-substitution principle, and (5) maximizing rule for choice.

In some cases, the mere *recognition* of an object suffices for the prediction of a target variable and constitutes the end of the process of inference. The recognition principle says that if one of two objects is recognized, the recognized object is chosen. If neither object is recognized, the choice between them is random. If both objects are recognized, a search for (further) cues starts. Transferred to financial behavior, this implies that if an investor chooses between two stocks, one of which is familiar and the other one unfamiliar, the investor chooses the familiar one. If both are recognized, a search process for discriminating cues is released.

Potential cues may be ranked from highest to lowest value and the individual looks for the highest-ranking cue in *the search for cue values*. The next step is to see whether the cue discriminates between the objects – *the discrimination rule*. The cue discriminates if one object has a positive cue value and the other does not. If the cue does not discriminate, the search starts anew and a new, potentially discriminating cue is searched for – *the cue substitution principle*. With the 'take the best' algorithm, the *maximizing rule for choice* states that the object with the positive cue value is chosen or, if no cue discriminates, the choice will be random. The 'take the last' algorithm implies that the cue that discriminated last time is tried first. If this cue does not discriminate, the cue that discriminated the time before last is tried and so on.

The presentation of the PMM seems to have both descriptive and normative aims. The tests reported indicate that the method is quick and efficient in comparison with classical inference methods. Intuitively, and with some support from research in other contexts, the method appears to give a reasonably accurate description of how inferences are made in many practical situations such as investment decisions. It is hard, though, to carry out any strict regular tests of the descriptive power of PMM. Gigerenzer and Goldstein (1996) propound that the PMM algorithms can be subsumed under the concept of *one-reason decision making*, which they see as a specific form of satisficing in Simon's sense. The inference is based on a single good reason (cue) and there is no compensation or interaction between cues.

.The PMM family of algorithms is aimed at enhancing fast inferences in situations where there is time pressure and limited cognitive capacity. An interesting question is how much of decision making in investing has such characteristics. It is conceivable that those who follow stock-price developments and trade often, using the telephone or the Internet to place their orders, may experience time pressure and rely on a few cues to guide their decisions. Those investors who trade seldom and prefer long-term investments may not feel time pressure. They may still in their decisions rely on one-reason decision making. Which cues do they use? Little is known about portfolio choice.

The Recognition Heuristic and the Stock Market

> *We propose replacing the image of an omniscient mind computing intricate probabilities and utilities with that of a bounded mind reaching into an adaptive toolbox filled with fast and frugal heuristics.*
>
> Gigerenzer and Todd (1999, p.5)

Many people seem to be doing well in the stock market without seeing themselves as experts and without consulting experts. With little knowledge of stocks and even less knowledge of efficient-market rules, they invest in stocks they believe in and stick to their investments over long periods of time, rarely sell, and, maybe, add to their portfolios once in a while (see Chapters 8 and 9). According to Goldstein and Gigerenzer (1999), such investors may use simple, fast, and frugal heuristics. A research group, with Gigerenzer in it, carried out a stock-investing experiment in which one simple heuristic called the *recognition heuristic* was used.

The main argument behind the usefulness of simple heuristics is that ignorance may facilitate the right decisions if it necessitates simple rules for reaching the right decision. One such ignorance-based heuristic is the *recognition heuristic*. In a selection task with two objects, the heuristic is stated thus: 'If one of two objects is recognized and the other is not, then infer that the recognized object has the higher value' (Gigerenzer and Todd, 1999, p.41). When recognition correlates negatively with the criterion, 'higher' would be replaced with 'lower' in the definition. The heuristic implies that one must be ignorant enough to apply the recognition heuristic. Ignorance may also mean that lack of recognition can be beneficial since the person has to be constructive in handling certain problems.

An example is given in a study of guesses about which English soccer team would win the F.A. Cup third-round soccer matches. Turkish students did almost as well as English students, 63 percent versus 66 percent right. The success of the Turkish students was explained by the fact that they used city recognition as a cue for soccer team performance. Cities with successful soccer teams are likely to be large, and large cities are likely to be recognized. City names served as mediators that guided the solution of the task. The authors concluded that partial ignorance could be turned into reasonable inferences. Ignorance is beneficial if it is correlated with what one wishes to infer. The authors warn that the recognition heuristic is not a general-purpose strategy because the correlation holds in some situations but not in others (Goldstein and Gigerenzer, 1999, pp.43–4). The students would probably have done worse if city size and team performance had not been correlated.

The availability heuristic which, was treated earlier, and the recognition heuristic show some resemblance. Goldstein and Gigerenzer (1999) maintain that there are two important differences: (1) the recognition is binary – either you recognize or you do not recognize –, and (2) how often one has been exposed is inconsequential – no further knowledge matters. Availability is about recall, which demands more effort, not about recognition.

Now to the stock market experiment. Is it possible to make money on ignorance, that is, your own partial ignorance, not that of others? Borges et al. (1999) answer this question in the affirmative and report a puzzling study of experimental investments in the stock market. Putting together a portfolio of stocks is more complicated than making choices between two objects at a time, which is an integral part of the definition of the recognition heuristic just given. The heuristic now runs as follows: 'When choosing a subset of objects from a larger set, choose the subset of recognized objects' (Borges et al., 1999, p. 61). While an individual may choose a subset of stocks s/he recognizes, the yardstick for successful investing must rather be what others recognize. The criterion is then a percentage stating how many in the population group recognize a stock. The authors suggest 90 percent. It should be noted that the success of the recognition heuristic presupposes that there is neither recognition of all stocks nor complete ignorance of all stocks. Partial ignorance is a requisite and it should be systematic. It is assumed that a large contingent of people display a 'beneficial degree of ignorance' in the stock market.

The experiment was carried out in the following way:

1. German and American subjects were asked to indicate which companies they recognized from those listed on the New York Stock Exchange and several German stock exchanges.
2. The subjects were grouped into one of four groups: American lay people, American experts, German lay people, and German experts. The lay people were pedestrians interviewed in the street in Chicago or Munich and the experts were graduate students in finance or economics.
3. Two investment portfolios were constructed for each group. They consisted of highly recognized companies for each of the four groups. One portfolio had highly recognized companies (recognized by at least 90 percent of the group) from the group's home country. The other portfolio contained the 10 companies that each group recognized most often from the other country.
4. The performance of each of the eight portfolios was calculated for a period of six months after the portfolios were assembled. The returns were compared with the returns of (a) the unrecognized stocks (recognized by less than 10 percent), (b) market indexes, (c) mutual funds, (d) chance portfolios, and (e) individuals' investment choices

(two of the experimenters actually invested in stocks recognized by Munich pedestrians).

5. The lay people portfolio of highly recognized stocks in Germany performed better than the portfolio of unrecognized stocks (47 percent vs. 13 percent gain). The performance was better in each of the four groups, suggesting that the effect was larger in the most ignorant groups.
6. The German lay people portfolio outperformed the German DAX Index (34 percent gain) and so did the expert portfolio. The American portfolios did not beat the Dow Jones Index.
7. In tests of international recognition, the recognition heuristic performed above the market indexes for each of the four conditions. The recognition heuristic beat the relevant market index.
8. The recognition heuristic beat the mutual funds and randomly composed portfolios.
9. The German lay people and experts had been asked to pick stocks in which to invest. Portfolios of the ten most often selected stocks were composed. The lay people selected highly recognized stocks whereas the experts chose less recognized stocks. The former made a large gain and the latter actually lost money.

Borges et al. (1999, p. 71) conclude: ‘The superiority of international over domestic recognition and the superiority of laypeople over experts in stock picking supports the notion that a certain degree of ignorance can be a virtue’. They discuss why the recognition effects may arise in a stock market. For example, companies with dominant market shares are likely to be both highly recognized and profitable. There may be a firm size effect, but the authors believe that there is more to the recognition effect than just size. The name of a company, the goodwill, is considered a valuable asset among companies and many companies are willing to pay much to acquire a good corporate image. It occurs to me that, perhaps, the best way to select new stocks for a portfolio is to consult the Consumer Satisfaction Barometer (Fornell, 1992), which measures the *quality* of the marketing of goods and services and captures (1) general satisfaction, (2) confirmation of expectations about the properties of goods and services, and (3) the distance from the customer’s hypothetical ideal product.

The hypothesis about the recognition effect and its counterpart, ignorance, is new and certainly needs further testing before it can be recommended as a sure way to beat the market. It may give part of the explanation of stock buyers’ success, but have low predictive value if the market is not stable or is moving downwards. The test was run in a strong bull market and the authors propose further studies in downturns. They expect that highly recognized companies will do better than the less recognized in a bearish market as well.

These results from using the recognition heuristic may cast some light on home equity effects that have puzzled financial economists. The home equity puzzle means that investors show a strong bias towards investing in domestic stocks rather than in foreign and in local stocks rather than national. Judging from their behavior, investors apparently are willing to pay more for stocks from companies in their home country or county (Grinblatt and Keloharju, 2000c). French and Poterba (1991) called the effect 'own-country bias' and suggested that unfamiliarity as suggested by Tversky and Heath (1991) made choices look riskier when dealing with unknown values. The effect is similar to a recognition heuristic effect. Against this speaks the fact that the home equity effect also has been found among fund managers who may not have the same degree of ignorance as ordinary investors (Strong and Xu, 1999).

MENTAL ACCOUNTING

Behavioral investors build portfolios as pyramids of assets, layer by layer. The layers are associated with particular goals and particular attitudes toward risk. Some money is in the downside-protection layer, designed to avoid poverty; other money is in the upside-potential layer, designed for a shot at being rich.

Statman (1999, p.23)

What do investors do with money they get from dividends and from realizing capital gains? According to the hypothesis about *mental accounting*, revenues from different sources may be treated differently. Money is not completely fungible as economic theory postulates. Shefrin and Thaler (1988) treat mental accounts as one of the building blocks of their Behavioral Life-Cycle Hypothesis (BLCH). Shefrin and Statman (1985) were the first to employ the concept in behavioral finance. They noted that people tended to vary in their risk taking depending on which mental account they were dealing in. 'Easy come, easy go' is a pertinent expression in this context.

When the concept of mental accounting was introduced by Thaler (1980) and Kahneman and Tversky (1984), no attempt was made to explain the phenomenon. There is a clear resemblance between mental accounting assumptions and the assumptions behind psychological *categorization theory* (Henderson and Peterson, 1992). Categorization is a fundamental process and involves how information that is being processed or stored in memory is organized. This is a classical philosophical problem and psychological research on categorization has been much influenced by the philosophical discussion. While there are several theories, using concepts like script or schema rather than category, there is some agreement about the characteristics of categorization. The following is mostly based on Henderson and Peterson (1992). They noted that the only difference between mental accounting and categorization seemed to be that the former specifically dealt with money and categorization could encompass all sorts of concept formation. They distinguished the following seven principles for categorization:

1. Knowledge of elements, which can be objects, people, or events, is organized into groups
2. The grouping of elements is spontaneous and can occur very quickly with minimal thought and effort. This is due to prior learning or frequent repetition
3. Cognitive efficiency is improved through categorization. This is true for all kinds of cognitive processes, such as recall and evaluation of new elements, and it leads to rapid formation of expectations
4. The groupings provide expectations about the nature of an element. In a category or class there are members that are more characteristic (prototypical) than others and they serve as a reference
5. The elements activated in a category are often context-dependent
6. An element may be a member of more than one category. This is referred to as 'graded membership'
7. Categories are ordered in hierarchies and they therefore differ in their degree of inclusion or abstraction.

Some of the principles, in particular number (3), may serve as a warning not to put objects or events into narrow categories that restrict further thinking even if such categorization is tempting and comfortable. Despite intensive research, the theories of categorization do not explain in a wholly satisfactory way how categories emerge and are changed and how new objects, people, and events are compared with existing categories. They provide a number of interesting ideas that make it possible to understand how mental accounting may function and give a stimulus for new research on mental accounting.

There is as yet little research on how mental accounts are formed and used in practice. The present support for mental accounting derives from anecdotal evidence, a few tests on propensity to consume different types of income using aggregate data, and hypothetical questions about what experimental subjects would do with incomes from different sources. It can also be said that there is supporting evidence from studies of categories used by consumers. Having expertise seems to presume that the expert forms categories and mental accounts that may differ from those of lay people. The evidence regarding experts is a little conflicting. On one hand, they are able to make finer discriminations and distinctions; on the other hand, they are also supposed to be able to pull out main factors better than non-experts.

The idea that people tend to sort changes in wealth into different categories and that different categories mean different propensities to consume is in clear contrast to the Life-Cycle Hypothesis and economic theory. When the BLCH was presented by Shefrin and Thaler (1988), they emphasized the role of framing and mental accounts. In the terms of the theory, income from different sources is framed into different mental accounts and is not fungible as economic theory implies. The individual has rules for how the income may be used. The propensity to consume or to save is assumed to depend on the source of the income and how this source is perceived by the person her/himself. Three sources of wealth and corresponding mental accounts are distinguished in BLCH: (a) current spendable income, (b) current assets, and (c) future income. The temptation to spend a marginal dollar is assumed to vary for the three types of mental accounts. Current income is the most tempting to spend, that is, it is characterized by the highest propensity to consume. Current assets and then future wealth follow it. The propensity to spend wealth from dividends should then be lower than the propensity to spend current income.

The propensity to consume additions to wealth is also assumed to depend on the form in which the wealth is received. If windfall money, say, a bonus, is paid in monthly payments, it is likely to be treated as current income and more of it will be consumed. If it is paid as a lump sum, it is likely to be treated as belonging to the assets account and less of it is consumed. The authors cited support from a study in which subjects were asked how much they would spend out of wealth derived from different sources, which were assumed to represent different mental accounts. They also found support in Japanese studies that showed the propensity of the Japanese to save out of lump-sum bonuses.

To what extent do the categories actually used by consumers correspond to the three categories proposed by Shefrin and Thaler (1988)? The ideas are provocative, and should be explored further before they inspire policy makers to plan wealth changes (payments as lump sums or distributed over time) in such a way that investment is stimulated (if that is wanted) or discouraged. It seems clear that consumers have different propensities to consume wealth changes deriving from different sources, but there is little detailed, empirical knowledge. Consumers may use other mental accounts of potential interest to researchers and policy makers than those suggested so far. An interesting question is how people react to changes in wealth components, not just to income changes. Keynes (1930, p.197) was sure that the paper losses when shares dropped in value made people inclined to save while gains in paper value could instigate increased spending on consumption. Shefrin and Thaler's (1988) hypothesis of mental accounts, combined with the loss aversion hypothesis of prospect theory, implies that unrealized gains and losses may be treated differently from what Keynes assumed. Is there really an analogous wealth effect on consumption arising from non-realized capital gains or losses on stock holdings? Recent studies of the stock-market wealth effect at the aggregate level will be dealt with in the final chapter. Such effects should be studied at the household level, not just at the aggregate level, and with the aim to find possible differences between bull and bear markets.

The concept of mental account involves the consumer putting distinct labels on amounts relating to different sources. It has been supplemented with the concept of 'mental budgets', under the assumption that separate mental budgets are made for different expenditures. Heath and Soll (1996) describe two steps in the mental budgeting process.

> We suggest that people generate two kinds of labels that affect their decisions as consumers. First, people label money as relevant for a certain class of goods, and second, they label the goods as relevant for a certain pool of money. We refer to these processes, respectively, as the budget-setting and the expense-tracking processes (Heath and Soll, 1996, p.41).

Heath and Soll suggested that putting expenses into different budget categories involved different tendencies to over- or underconsume:

> [B]udget setting leads people to overconsume some goods and underconsume others. Because budgets are set before consumption opportunities arise, they sometimes overestimate or underestimate the money required for a particular account . . . [E]xpense tracking implies that some expenses are more likely to produce over- or underconsumption. As people track their expenses, expenses that are relatively easy to categorize – those that are more typical examples of their categories – will be the most subject to the rigors of budgeting (Heath and Soll, 1996, p.40).

The authors' hypothesis that those items that are most typical for a category of expenditure are most controlled through a budget is interesting. It was supported by their data. It may amount to 'penny-wise, pound-foolish'.

Other studies and anecdotal evidence indicate that many consumers practice a special kind of budgeting procedure which makes sure that there is money for different expenditures and also provides a check on expenditures. Such budgeting can be illustrated by some anecdotal evidence. Many years ago an economist friend of mine told me that when he received his monthly salary, which was always paid in cash, the money was split up in expenditure categories and for each category a special envelope was used. Limited borrowing between envelopes was permitted. This was a way for a young family to control and keep track of expenditures. Later, informal interviews carried out by researchers in my research group revealed that some respondents practiced similar techniques for making sure that money was available and used for the right purposes. Some researchers have more recently included in their questionnaires questions about pigeonholing money for different purposes and this led to the inclusion of such questions in the CentER Data (VSB Panel) saving study.

Rainwater et al. (1959) found that working-class wives performed 'tin can accounting'. The women kept monies apart for different expenses, in tin cans or labeled envelopes. One can was for paying mortgages, another for food and groceries, and a third for entertainment. Zelizer (1993, p.199) noted: 'The wives in Bakke's landmark study of unemployed workers in the 1930's . . . used china pitchers to segregate different types of income earmarked for particular expenses: the rent of an extra room, for instance, might serve to pay off the mortgage, while a child's earnings were designated to purchase school clothes'. Hussein (1985, cited in Webley and Lea, 1993, p.470) reported 'a variety of practical ways in which people partition their money between different budget headings: some kept it in jam-jars, some distributed it around a variety of pockets while one carried it around in plastic bags'.

Money received from social welfare is not the same as money received from wages (Zelizer, 1993)

> To further support official notions of proper spending, charity organizations sponsored a large number of thrift institutions, ranging from stamps savings to fuel clubs and vacation savings clubs, all designed to earmark dependents' money into 'proper' expenses . . . How successful were they? My preliminary evidence suggests a sort of contest between official and private earmarks as people found strategies to subvert bureaucratic restrictions on the uses of their money, often spending in ways that outraged middle-class observers, paying, for instance, for burial insurance with money allocated for food purchase (Zelizer, 1993, p.206).

A dollar is not always a dollar! The examples above show that prescriptive mental accounts may not coincide with those of the consumer. It should be a task for researchers to investigate which mental accounts people have and whether and how those mental accounts affect saving and investing.

In a recent summary of the current state of knowledge about how people engage in mental accounting, Thaler (1999b) notes that three components of mental accounting have received the most attention. The first component reflects how outcomes are perceived and experienced, and how decisions are made and subsequently evaluated. It serves as a kind of subjective accounting system. A second component of mental accounting involves the assignment of activities to specific accounts. Expenditures are grouped into categories (housing, food, etc.) and spending is sometimes constrained by implicit or explicit budget rules. The third component of mental accounting concerns the frequency with which accounts are evaluated and 'choice bracketing'. Accounts can be balanced daily, weekly, yearly, and so on, and can be defined narrowly or broadly. Thaler (1999b) concludes that mental accounting influences choice, that is, it matters, and that each of the components of mental accounting violates the economic principle of fungibility.

A few more studies of mental accounting should be mentioned to show the spreading use of the idea. Prelec and Loewenstein (1998) compare the standard economic account of consumer behavior with what they call the reality of consumer hedonics. According to the economic account, the cost of a purchase takes the form of a reduction in future utility when expenditures that otherwise could have been made are forgone. The opportunity cost should be considered. When people in reality make purchases, they often experience an immediate pain of paying, which can undermine the pleasure derived from consumption. A 'double-entry' mental-accounting theory is proposed. The model implies that, in a hedonic perspective, payments should be tightly coupled to ideas of the benefits of consumption, and consumption should be decoupled from payments so that consumption does not evoke thoughts of costs.

Following up a series of studies of mental accounts that Kahneman and Tversky (1984) had inspired, Moon et al. (1999) further explored how relative savings are judged within different frames or mental accounts. The typical finding is that people hesitate to make a trip to save five dollars on an automobile, but gladly do it to save five dollars on a $20 jacket. The potential monetary saving on an item is viewed relative to the original expected cost of that item. In a number of contexts, the relative saving to be made has been found to be more important than the absolute saving. The reported experiment sought to discover whether this mental-accounting characteristic applied more widely. It was found that the effect failed to appear as the level of absolute saving to be gained increased. The authors suggest that some mental accounts are less important when the absolute amount to be saved increases over a certain threshold (Moon et al., 1999).

Finally, one test of mental accounts in the context of finance has been conducted. Winnett and Lewis (1995) hypothesized that the propensity to consume would be lower for a non-realized increase in share value, that is, a wealth effect, than for an increase in dividend. Testing the idea on data from the CentER Data (VSB Panel), they found that all income from capital tended to be seen as non-spendable, irrespective of the form in which it accrued. In the same article, these authors reported an analysis of qualitative data from informal interviews with Dutch consumers. They found that 'accounts have labels and purposes and there is evidence of non-fungibility'.

Are Cognitive Biases Systematic Enough to Be Predictable?

In the chapter, I have reviewed what is often seen as the psychological substance of behavioral finance, namely the heuristics-and-biases approach inspired by Kahneman and Tversky. In addition, a new approach which is critical of the heuristics-and-biases approach is reviewed. Some of the attention bestowed on the heuristics-and-biases approach is probably caused by the hope that deviations from rationality and other norms for behavior may be systematic and even lawful so that they can be used for making predictions and not only for after-the-fact explanations. The hope still seems a bit far-fetched, except for the fact that some qualitative predictions may be feasible. It is well established that people have cognitive biases and employ heuristics, but each heuristic is surrounded by many 'if's'. Then it should be noted that in financial markets, even a minor improvement in the educated guesses may mean a lot of money. Knowledge about heuristics may be useful if judiciously utilized.

A number of heuristics have been described in the literature on investing and there are also examples of attempts to relate the approach to economic theory (McFadden, 1999). The first heuristic to be reviewed was the base-rate fallacy, which is similar to the representativeness heuristic. When symptoms are at hand in a diagnosis and, at the same time, actual or potentially retrievable data on the occurrence of the event (the base rate) exist, people tend to neglect the base rate. They are likely to concentrate on some characteristics of the diagnosis and the similarity of those to some part of the base-rate characteristics. The heuristic has implications for valuations of stocks. When judging information on a stock, for example, investors may overlook the historical trends of sales growth (the base rate) and concentrate too much on the details of the stock.

In my view, too much attention is paid in finance to the neglect of base rates. While the neglect of base rates may certainly be a problem, undoubtedly the overuse of base rates may equally be a problem. This means forgetting the specifics of the situation and making valuations and predictions on the sole basis of historical trends. For the individual investor, it may be profitable to look for exceptions when almost all stocks are plummeting.

While there is now substantial evidence of the robustness of the findings in the heuristics-and-biases approach, some of the heuristics are admittedly vague and are better used for after-the-fact descriptions and explanations than for predictions. An emerging approach was also presented. It gives alternative interpretations of some robust findings and it makes some powerful claims which could inspire new research in behavioral finance. The approach focuses on the ecological study of cognitive processes and on elucidating how these processes are affected by situation and environment.

The concept of mental account has not yet been explored in financial research, although it has an important role in the Behavioral Life-Cycle Hypothesis of saving (Shefrin and Thaler, 1988). It seems to open ways of grappling with such problems as what people do with non-realized losses and gains on securities. Knowledge about what mental accounts people in different segments use in dealing with their stocks may promote understanding of actions and improve some predictions about future trading.

6. Emotionality, Motivation, Self-Control, and Investment

The only way in which the economist can keep his studies from duplicating the psychologist's work is by taking his psychology from those who have specialized in that field. To rely on the mere fact of choice, regardless of the kind of motives behind it, might seem to take economics out of all dependence on psychology, but it does not really do so, save at the cost of becoming utterly meaningless.

Clark (1918, p.4)

THE AIM AND SCOPE OF THE CHAPTER

The chapter covers a broad topic which can be called *emotionality*, and elucidates among other things the role of what Keynes called 'animal spirits', that is, feelings of optimism and self-confidence that made investors believe in the future success of their investments. In finance, descriptions and explanations of stock-price developments often encompass concepts such as overreaction and optimism, underreaction and pessimism. Even though the concepts used seemingly refer to human beings, the truth is that stock prices rather than traders are assumed to overreact or underreact or show signs of optimism or pessimism. In fact, characteristics of aggregate curves are labeled in this manner. Financial economists have looked for psychological concepts that refer to individuals and developed models of individual behavior that are used to explain aggregate events. Psychological research shows that the models can be tested on individual financial behavior, and experimental economists are beginning to include more of those concepts in their work.

The preceding chapter presented a number of cognitive concepts and hypotheses about relationships between the concepts and actions. The micro models applying cognitive findings have been much more common than loans from the research on emotions. This does not exclude the frequent use of emotional labels on phenomena in financial markets. It only means that such use is rarely based on psychological research on feelings and emotions. Practitioners and writers of popular guides for private investors have, however, often disregarded cognitive psychology in favor of what is called dynamic psychology, which is heavily influenced by psychoanalytic thinking (see, for example, Lifson and Geist, 1999).

In attitude theory, affect is used to designate the appreciation of value. This dimension can embody emotion, but it need not do so. It may be the cognitive representation of feelings and it can be positive or negative. It is assumed to be conscious and available in such a way that it can be communicated by the individual. While affect can be destructive under certain circumstances, it can often be a positive component of cognition, adding important dimensions to decision making and to the satisfaction with the outcome of the action undertaken. The important questions are:

1. When do affects and emotions lead to individual investment decisions that are destructive in the sense that they yield losses?
2. When do affects and emotions improve investment decisions?
3. When do market-level stock-price developments, which can usually be interpreted in many ways, actually reflect affects and emotions among investors?

In this chapter, I shall present some analytical tools that can be used to seek answers to these questions. The chapter begins with some macro-level labels that are often used in behavioral finance. To some extent, the developments that they describe can be accounted for by psychological factors such as self-confidence and overconfidence, which are also considered in the chapter. After a discussion of the characteristics of emotionality, the broad question of investor motivation is approached. Finally, the role of self-control and its converse, impulsiveness, in investment behavior is touched upon.

As a general background, the chapter is introduced by some comments on the relationships between market-level affects and individual affects and emotions. It then proceeds to the much-debated theory of over- and underreactions and confronts it with psychological research on confidence and overconfidence. Next, some distinctions between mood, affects, and emotions, and pertinent theory are presented. Affects and emotions are part of motivation for financial behavior. As a complement, the more cognitively oriented achievement motivation theory is reviewed. The final part of the chapter is devoted to a discussion of the role of self-control and the revival of volitional concepts in psychology (and in behavioral finance). The chapter ends with some ideas on speculation and speculators in finance.

MARKET-LEVEL AND INDIVIDUAL AFFECTS AND EMOTIONS

When financial commentators are faced with requests to explain plummeting stock prices, their answers commonly bring forth what they call 'psychological factors'. By such factors, they apparently mean emotions that are hard to explain and only possible to understand in part. The presumption is that there is no rationality in emotions. Both critics and adherents of efficient-market theory have described financial market events in psychological terms that are close to emotions: optimism–pessimism, overreaction and underreaction, the mood of the market. These labels are attached to phenomena at the market level and based on aggregate stock-price data. They do not directly pertain to individual behavior. They can be seen as macropsychological labels, that is, psychological labels that are placed on aggregate phenomena (Katona, 1979). Typically, it is assumed that the emotions behind such events cannot be measured. This assumption holds some truth, since psychological knowledge about emotions is far from wellstructured and too few attempts have been made to develop the macropsychology of emotions. There is still something to be learned from what is known about emotions and individual behavior.

The assumed relationships between macro and micro levels vary. The macropsychological concepts may be restricted to descriptions and explanations at the aggregate level and have no correspondence with microlevel events at the individual/household level. Pessimism can be defined as a sudden and drastic drop in a stock market index without any single individual being necessarily pessimistic. In some cases, the assumption is made that exactly the same psychological model and the same concept labels can be applied at both macro and micro levels. Psychological research on, for example, overconfidence can then perhaps provide some interesting relationships that can enrich the discussion of an aggregate phenomenon, for example, the relationship between overconfidence and information. In a third type of cases, economists develop a micro model that, for their purposes, can explain – make plausible – the macro model. In the latter cases, input of ideas from psychology is used in the search for explanations of developments that cannot be explained with the aid of current economic theory.

In macroeconomics, with a few exceptions (see Lucas, 1986), there is a quest for supporting micro models of individual/household behavior that, when aggregated, adds up to and thus explains the macro phenomenon. Similar attempts are made in behavioral finance, and many loans of concepts and research findings from the psychology of individuals are applied to market events without recourse to observations of individual investors or any marked interest in individual behavior. When concepts are borrowed from psychology they, as a rule, represent hypotheses about individuals. The question arises as to what extent such hypotheses are useful and really valid at the aggregate level. Can the relationships between the macropsychological variables and other macro variables be the same as those between the corresponding variables at the individual level? There is often reason for some doubt.

Laws of behavior can sometimes differ depending on whether the macro or the micro level is studied. Neglecting the differences between micro and macro is in economic texts referred to as 'the fallacy of composition'. In other social science contexts, it is called 'the ecological fallacy' (Langbein and Lichtman, 1978). According to Samuelson and Nordhaus (1992, p.6), the fallacy is the misconception that what is true for a part is therefore true for the whole. One of the examples they gave had to do with savings and suggests that attempts of individuals to save more in a depression may reduce a community's total savings. There is some contradiction in pointing out the composition fallacy and at the same time claiming that the macroeconomic assumptions should rest on a solid foundation of microeconomics. The fallacy concepts are signs of the awareness that micro and macro relationships may differ. Still, when a relationship is discovered at the macroeconomic level, there typically begins a quest for a micro model that is compatible with the macro findings.

Everything that deviates from rational economic behavior is sometimes blamed as being due to affect or emotions. Irrational and emotional are seen as the same thing. This neglects the possibility that emotions may accompany rational behavior and that irrational behavior may be generated by many factors such as insufficient information. The idea that limitations in cognitive capacity rather than emotions could lead to irrational behavior is found in the works of classical economists like Jevons ([1871]1911) and Böhm-Bawerk ([1888]1912). The idea was later forgotten when economic theorists became engrossed in the complex calculations that rationality presupposes and makes feasible. It was brought to new attention by economists primarily through Herbert Simon's (1955) work when he propounded a theory of bounded rationality (see previous chapter). Behaviorism found room for a few basic feelings that were based on physiological symptoms, but rejected any notion of subjective feelings. In recent years, more understanding of the possible role of affect has emerged as a consequence of research on information processing and memory. Cognitive psychology is beginning to recognize the importance of feelings for behavior and is devoting some, so far sparse, interest to cognitive representations of feelings and emotions (see Simon, 1990).

OVER- AND UNDERREACTIONS

In finance, security prices and not investors over- or underreact. Interestingly, the curves over stock-price developments have the dual purpose of providing descriptions of events and serving as explanations. A certain curve has a shape that is classified as overreaction to new information and this is interpreted as indicating investor overreaction. The explanation may stop there, but often underlying factors are sought in investor characteristics, such as optimism or overconfidence. Over- and underreactions are macro concepts; they refer to characteristics of aggregated data on developments in a financial market as a whole or in important sectors of it. In more rare cases, there is talk about the stock price of a single firm.

Barberis et al. (1998), whose micro models are inspired by psychological thinking, summarize what they call two pervasive regularities in financial markets, to wit, underreaction and overreaction.

> The underreaction evidence shows that over horizons of perhaps 1–12 months, security prices underreact to news . . . As a consequence, news is incorporated only slowly into prices, which tend to exhibit positive autocorrelations over these horizons. A related way to make this point is to say that current good news has power in predicting positive returns in the future. The overreaction evidence shows that over longer horizons of perhaps 3–5 years, security prices overreact to consistent patterns of news pointing in the same direction. That is, securities that have had a long record of good news tend to become overpriced and have low average returns afterwards (Barberis et al. 1998, pp.307–8).

The curves studied as a basis for the classification of the reactions to news reflect the behavior of all active agents in the market, not the actions of any single individual, except perhaps when a manager of a large fund makes a transaction. The aggregate reactions can be explained either by relating them to other aggregate phenomena or by treating them as the sum of individual actions and explaining them by models of individual household behavior.

Many kinds of overreactions have been distinguished and they all clash with theory which posits that stock prices immediately absorb all information. One kind involves lasting effects of (higher) earnings information. Effects up to six months after an announcement have been observed (Chan et al., 1999). The overreaction is attributed by some observers to positive-feedback trading strategies. Investors who look for trends reinforce movements in stock prices since they buy when prices go up and sell when prices fall. Another kind of over- or underreaction is long term and means that prices do not change in accordance with the information for periods of several years. The discussion of unexpected reactions has drawn attention to several dimensions that must be noted. The effects may be short term or long term, they may be cumulative over time or corrected immediately. In some cases, a reaction is not classified as being 'over' or 'under' unless it is later corrected and thus proven to be mistaken. Negative news may not have the same effect as positive news, but is usually assumed to have similar effects with a reversed sign. This suggests that both types of reaction can be classified in eight groups, depending on type of news and the appearance of correction afterwards in the short run or later. The resulting types of reaction are displayed in Table 6.1. For each type, an attempt at a brief description of symptoms is presented.

Table 6.1 Types of Under- and Overreaction

	Underreaction		Overreaction	
	negative news	positive news	negative news	positive news
Cumulative effect	Price consistently drops less than expected	Price increases less than expected	Price keeps decreasing more than expected	Price keeps increasing more than expected
With day-after correction	Price drops second day to expected value	Price increases second day to expected value	Price drops more than expected, with next-day recovery	Price increases more than expected, with drop next day
With short-run correction, within two months	Price keeps dropping until expected value is reached	Price keeps increasing until expected value is reached	Price keeps going down, then increases to expected value	Price keeps going up, then drops to expected value
No or long-run correction, after two months	Price follows earlier trend, up or down	Price follows earlier trend, up or down	Price keeps going down more than expected	Price keeps going up more than expected

With so many possible meanings associated with over- and underreactions, it is obvious that a single explanation of causal relationships will not suffice. Many attempts have been made to explain the phenomena, including through recourse to cognitive and social psychology. In the discussion of reasons for them, note should be taken of how expectations are formed according to economic theories and the simple model shown in Chapter 3. Extrapolation and probably also adaptive expectation formation lead to overreaction to originally good news and favor momentum strategies. If expectations are rationally formed, trustworthy new information may lead to different reactions that imply contrarian strategies if the information points in the direction of reversal of trend. Expectation of mean reversion is a special case of new information; the non-appearance of causal information that goes against mean reversion may lead to mean-reversion expectation.

Overreaction, optimism, and overconfidence are often used to cover the same phenomena. The latter two concepts may be used as synonyms for the first one or they may serve as explanations of it. Overreaction is not a very meaningful concept at the individual level and when investor behavior is in focus it is replaced with terms that are ordinarily more closely associated with personal characteristics such as overconfidence and optimism. Some individual investor behavior may all the same be labeled overreaction to a certain stimulus. The concept rather describes than explains. Optimism can be both a macro label applied to patterns in a series of data and an individual mood characteristic. What appears as overreaction on the stock market may, for example, be traced to trading behavior inspired by overconfidence among investors. While overconfidence, like optimism, can be a temporary or maybe more permanent, personality trait, overreaction and underreaction are tied to the aggregate effects of information events.

When stock prices do not change in an expected way, overreactions or underreactions to information on returns are frequently invoked. De Bondt and Thaler (1985) were apparently the first to use the two reaction concepts in a financial research context. They alleged that investors behaved irrationally in placing too much weight on recent information, and therefore failed to make proper Bayesian forecasts with probabilities revised after new information had emerged. They found overreactions which they ascribed to the use of the representativeness heuristic. This involves an overreliance on the most recent information or experience and lack of interest in earlier long-term trends, the so-called base rates. The findings showed that prior losers among stocks became winners in later periods and prior winners became losers given a time perspective of three to five years. As a consequence, these authors recommended more use of contrarian strategies.

The paper led to a debate over the method used, the periods studied, and the conclusions drawn. The discussant Peter Bernstein (1985) asserted that most of De Bondt and Thaler's arguments about market efficiency were badly specified. The stock market in particular was highly efficient in rapidly incorporating information that would affect prices in the short run, even if it failed to process more complex and longer-run information in an efficient manner. In later studies, the same authors have provided more evidence and defended their views (De Bondt and Thaler, 1987, 1990).

Atkins and Dyl (1993) questioned De Bondt and Thaler's arguments, citing their own results. They used a sample of all stocks that traded on the New York Stock Exchange from January 1975 to December 1984. Six stocks on each of the 300 randomly selected trading days were identified – the three stocks that had the largest percentage increase in price and the three stocks that had the largest percentage decrease in price. Large price changes that occurred on a single day were followed by price reversals on subsequent days. This was evidence that stock prices appeared to overreact to new information. Abnormal returns based on the market model were measured, which considered both differences in risk among common stocks and the effect of market fluctuations. The price reversals were usually well within the bid–ask spread and, therefore, ruled out profitable trading strategies. The authors concluded that the price developments were compatible with market efficiency.

Relying on psychological research findings, Daniel et al. (1998a) propose a theory of securities market under- and overreactions which assumes that these are based on two well-known psychological biases: (a) investor overconfidence about the precision of private information, and (b) biased self-attribution that causes asymmetric shifts in investors' confidence as a function of their investment outcomes. In the theory, investors place too much trust in their own knowledge and skill. Success is supposed to follow success owing to estimates of one's own ability whereas failures may be blamed on others or on unfavorable circumstances. Biased self-attribution implies that future success depends on one's ability and gives rise to positive short-lag autocorrelations (momentum), short-run earnings drift, but negative correlation between future returns and long-term past stock-market and accounting performance. When managerial action is correlated with stock mispricing, it further enhances public-event-based return predictability. The gist of the theory is that investors will overreact to private information signals and underreact to public information signals. Short-run overreactions are followed by long-run correction and short-run positive autocorrelations are compatible with long-run negative autocorrelations (Daniel et al., 1998b, p.24).

Next is, for a change, a non-American study reporting overreactions to news. It investigated models of investor decision making to determine whether New Zealand investors were economically rational. The authors studied a model of rationality, founded in psychology rather than economics. This model, again based on the representativeness heuristic, proposes that investors will overreact to small pieces of more recent information, hence stock prices will temporarily overshoot their true value. All New Zealand Stock Exchange companies were examined for a 12-month period. On each of 50 randomly selected trading days, the top and bottom three performing companies were analyzed. Overreaction was measured as the market-adjusted returns on these companies' stocks. Results show strong support for the overreaction hypothesis. Investors overreacted to the good or bad news, which led to abnormal returns on the selected days, suggesting that small amounts of information can cause unrealistic optimism (Swallow and Fox, 1996).

While De Bondt and Thaler (1985) cited the representativeness heuristic to explain their findings without having recourse to data on individuals, they were able to make a more direct check in a later study. Investigating security analysts, they found that those professionals could enhance over- and underreactions (De Bondt and Thaler, 1990). They had the tendency to make forecasts that were too extreme, given the predictive value of the information available to the forecaster. The authors based their results on analysts' earnings forecasts obtained from the Institutional-Brokers-Estimate-System (I/B/E/S) tapes for the period 1976–1984. They noted the same pattern of overreaction found in the predictions of naive students in Kahneman and

Tversky's (1973) study: 'People's intuitive forecasts have a tendency to overweight salient information such as recent news, and underweight less salient data such as long-term averages' (De Bondt and Thaler, 1990, p.52). Long-term trends are forgotten in the face of dramatic news with supposedly causal information, all of which points to the representativeness heuristic and the base-rate fallacy. Forecasted changes were too extreme to be considered rational.

In another study, De Bondt (1991) investigated what he described as the behavior of smart money. As in the previous study, the idea was that if those who were generally supposed to be rational traders behaved in the same way as naive subjects in cognitive experiments, the arguments for market rationality would lose force. Data from the Livingston surveys were used to examine about 5 400 individual forecasts of the Standard & Poor's index of 425 industrial companies for the period 1952 to 1986. The forecasts thus made by expert economic forecasters were for horizons of 7 and 13 months. Three main findings emerged: (1) the average forecast had no predictive power and was useless for investment strategy; (2) the experts overreacted, their forecast errors were systematic, and the errors were related to the market price–earnings ratio and to expected inflation; (3) the predictions were strongly mean-reverting. The Livingston survey evidence confirms the idea that expected returns varied through time. The author concluded that the economists had little faith in the random walk theory during the 35 years that he had investigated.

De Bondt and Forbes (1999) investigated the accuracy and dispersion of the earnings forecasts that financial analysts in the UK made for a ten-year period from 1986 to 1997. The authors found strong evidence of excessive optimism and overreaction bias in the forecasts, which were characterized by high consensus. They reported weaker, but suggestive, evidence of herding behavior among analysts. Avoidance of future regret was an important motivator, which is in line with regret theory (see preceding chapter).

Psychologically, reactions to events appear to be reasonably adequate when people face news on developments that does not deviate from past experience and from expectations based on past events. When unexpected events occur, both over- and underreactions may ensue. On one hand, past experience has a sticky influence on behavior and reliance on past experience leads to slow, inadequate reactions to news events. People underreact. Brehmer (1992) found that when his subjects in a simulation study had to plan fire brigade operations to combat forest fires, they tended to grossly underestimate exponential development of the fires. On the other hand, there may be overreactions. The weight of an event or a series of events is overestimated. Little is known about the circumstances under which the types of reactions come to pass. The main thing to remember is that past experience is extrapolated and dominates expectation formation until and unless there is dramatic news to the contrary. Mood changes and other personal characteristics may explain individual investor reactions, but it then remains to explain how the reactions spread enough to become visible in stock-price developments. It is assumed that social influence and social support may be essential.

In sum, there is evidence that the effects of news can lead both to short-run underreaction, which means delayed effect, and to overreaction of some duration. Inveterate efficient-market-theory advocates reject the psychological hypotheses and prefer explanations in such terms as firm-size effects, January effects and chance variations. Researchers with an orientation towards behavioral science seek the reasons for overreactions in psychological factors such as the representativeness heuristic and self-serving bias. Given the variety of the phenomena called under- or overreactions, it seems likely that many factors may play a role and that these factors must be better disentangled than has hitherto been the case.

THE INFLUENCE OF MOOD

Stock-Market Mood and Individual Mood

Deviations from rationality can be explained by external factors such as restricted access to information and limitations in cognitive capacity. Mood and emotions may influence cognitive capacity and cognitive functions, but they may also be modeled as special, direct influences on decision making, notably on information processing. When affects and emotions are utilized in explanations of financial behavior, it is usually for their presumed negative effects. This is in contrast to modern research on emotions, which suggests that emotions may play a positive role. The same holds for mood, but the possible positive role of mood has been better recognized, in particular the positive effects of optimism in financial markets. Both optimism and pessimism can have positive effects for a person if they stay within limits.

The concept of mood is used to characterize both the developments at a stock exchange and the behavior of investors. Stock markets are often depicted as being in a certain mood, optimistic or pessimistic, as in the headline 'Yesterday the Stock Exchange was in a pessimistic mood'. Mood is then described through observations of aggregate behavior and attempts are made to find reasonable explanations for the change in mood. Schachter et al. (1986, p.266ff) formulated some hypotheses on the effects of mood. If bull markets inspire optimism, people will talk more about the stock market, boast about their successes, and be more willing to trade than when there is a bear market. They applied their thinking to the Monday doldrums: 'On the assumption that thinking and talking are goads to action, it should be expected that the Monday doldrums will be more characteristic of bear and stable marketthan of bull markets'. Their results confirmed that the day of the week had significantly less effect on volume of sales in bull markets than in either bear or stable markets.

Mood at the market level, described as patterns in stock-price movements, may affect future trader behavior in two ways. It may be contagious and give rise to corresponding mood states in a growing number of individual investors and produce effects that appear in subsequent behavior. Or the mood label may suggest to observers that the mood may spread to large numbers of investors who will act in accordance with the mood. A pessimistic mood may turn into panic actions whereas an optimistic mood may inspire exuberance and less well-considered actions.

An individual's mood is described in various ways. In one context, it is a relatively short-lived emotional state, usually of low intensity. In another context, mood is a temporary disposition to feel and behave in a certain way, such as being in a bad mood for doing something. In a third context, mood refers to persistent mood states that are characteristic of a person. Bagozzi et al. (1999), who make serious attempts to define vague emotional concepts, note that mood is usually longer lasting than emotion and lower in intensity. Both temporary and persistent mood states have indeterminate connections to particular events. The main characteristic of mood is that it is not directly coupled with action tendencies and explicit actions, as are many emotions.

An individual mood state is likely to have some influence on a person's interpretation of past events and of new information. Such influence is stronger when the events are vaguely sketched or complex and there are conflicting sets of data that can be interpreted differently. The influence is likely to be less when the mood is temporary than when it is a persistent characteristic of the person.

Optimism and Overoptimism

> *Imagine that you are attending a convention in Las Vegas, and you walk into a casino. While passing the slot machines, you put a quarter into one machine and, surprisingly, you win $100. Now what? Will your gambling behavior for the rest of the evening be altered? Might you make a few more serious wagers, even if you usually abstain?*
>
> Thaler and Johnson (1990, p.643)

Optimism and pessimism are usually seen as moods which may rapidly change due to external and internal circumstances and are usually not considered a personality trait that is stable over long periods of time. There may still be moods that at least to spectators seem characteristic of a person, such as the eternal optimism of Voltaire's Candide. Psychologists talk about habitual optimism or pessimism, but this does not mean that switches between the two extremes are unlikely or infrequent. Those who are characterized by a deep-rooted pessimism that is similar to a personality trait probably do not participate in stock markets, and those who are constantly (over)optimistic are likely to fall out fairly soon after having consumed too much or speculated too optimistically. *Defensive* pessimists are more inclined than optimists to construct possible futures. This apparently helps them to channel anxiety about the future into plans for effective behavior (Karniol and Ross, 1996). Habitual optimists avoid thinking about negative possibilities and are less inclined to think through the future in any detail.

Mood has been shown to affect processing of information. Positive moods such as a feeling of optimism tend to lead to less processing of arguments and consequently higher proneness to being convinced. When people process information messages closely, mood seems to bias the processing. Sad or neutral (versus happy) moods lead to more effortful information processing, which may bias the processing:

> Positive affect usually denotes a benign environment that does not require any action. On the other hand, negative affective states act as information signaling that the environment poses a problem and may motivate people to engage in systematic processing, which is usually better suited to handling threatening situations . . . (Bagozzi et al., 1999, p.198).

It is a well-established truth that when people are optimistic they tend to spend money rather than save. When people are concerned about the future, they try to put something aside for future use if they possibly can. This finding also holds at the macro level, for whole national economies. The Index of Consumer Sentiment has a good reputation for revealing changes in optimism–pessimism. Many studies, in different countries, show a negative correlation between the index and total savings (Katona, 1975; van Raaij and Gianotten, 1990; Carroll et al., 1994; Berg and Bergström, 1996).

In attempting to explain at an early stage the stock market crash of 1929, Keynes (1930) wrote:

> The pessimism and the atmosphere of disappointment which the stock-market collapse engendered reduced enterprise and lowered the natural rate of interest; whilst the 'psychological' poverty which the collapse of paper values brought with it probably increased saving. – The last point is important, and we may pause upon it for a moment. It may suggest a generalization of permanent value. A country is no richer when, for purposes of swopping titles to prospective gain between one of its citizens and another, people choose to value the prospects at twenty years' purchase, than when these are valued at ten years' purchase; but the citizens, beyond question, *feel* richer. Who can doubt that a man is more likely to buy a new motor-car if his investments have doubled in money-value during the past year than if they have been halved? He feels far less necessity or obligation to save out of his

> normal income, and his whole standard of expenditure is raised. For their paper profits and their savings out of current income are not kept by most men (as perhaps they should be) in entirely separate compartments of the mind (Keynes, 1930, p.197).

Keynes, whose expression 'in separate compartments' foreshadows the much later concept of mental accounts, drew the conclusion that owners of shares and bonds were more likely to 'save' when they were losing 'paper value' than when the paper value was rising, were more likely to refrain from new extravagances and to pay off debts. This is a hypothesis of high current interest and is now discussed as the *stock-market wealth effect* on consumption (see Poterba, 2000; Lettau and Ludvigson, 1999; see Chapter 10). As far as I know, it has not yet been fully tested using behavioral data. In times of rising stock prices, and in particular when there are rapid increases, part of Keynes' argument can serve to explain increased optimism and lavish expenditures.

Keynes (1936) talked about the unreasonable optimism that entrepreneurs had about their new investments in firms and referred to it as 'animal spirits'. He defined it as a kind of spontaneous optimism that made entrepreneurs optimistically invest money in their own ideas. He referred to 'our rational selves choosing between the alternatives as best we are able, calculating where we can, but often falling back for our motive on whim or sentiment or chance' (Keynes, 1936, p.163).

One consequence of rising stock exchange indexes may be a freer, less well-considered choice of new investment objects. Investors may feel that they have money to spare and be willing to take greater risks or omit to calculate risks in the same way as before. Schachter et al. (1986) hypothesized that when investors made profits through a general rise in stock prices, they would become more independent and make freer choices of stocks. When they lost money through falling prices, they would become more dependent and susceptible to social influence. These authors found support in observations made over time at the New York Stock Exchange. A German interview survey found that those who won in the stock market felt more competent than those who lost (psychonomics & Capital, 1998, p.94).

The optimism hypothesis finds experimental support in Thaler's work (Thaler, 1992). In Thaler and Johnson's (1990) paper, 'the house money effect' is a central concept. They found that, under some circumstances, prior gains could increase subjects' willingness to accept gambles that the players would otherwise not have accepted. In contrast to economic theory, which holds that prior gains or losses should have no influence on decisions, the authors launch the hypothesis that prior gains and losses (and costs) do influence decisions. In a newspaper interview with Thaler, the latter says that the house money effect may be one reason for the previous year's development of stock prices (*Newsday, Money & Careers*, Sunday, December 19, 1999).

It seems likely that part of the high valuation of Internet firm stocks lies in an increased willingness to gamble as a consequence of earlier gains accrued from general stock-price increases. Another part may be that stock owners who have been spoiled by earlier rises in prices of ordinary stock look for higher returns when the prices of ordinary stock have stagnated or move very slowly. This seems to have been the case at the New York Stock Exchange and at some European stock exchanges during the first months of the year 2000. Then the fall in technology stocks set in.

With the exception of studies investigating factors influencing changes in the Index of Consumer Sentiment, there are few, if any, studies of factors influencing optimism–pessimism moods that affect stock-price movements. The common hypothesis is that events in the stock market, notably changes in fundamentals, are the major causes of changes in optimism or pessimism. In ad-hoc explanations offered by experts in the trade media, the focus is on events related to the stocks, but also on more general conditions (such as changes in unemployment or inflation) that influence interest rates. There is room for studies and speculative theory about how events directly influence optimism or pessimism. The purpose would be to improve predictions of behavior completing the chain: events → mood change → financial behavior → mood change. This gives rise to the question of whether an optimistic mood leads to optimistic expectations or optimistic expectations lead to optimistic moods. The best answer is probably that habitual optimism can affect expectations and expectations of favorable outcomes can inspire optimism. The same is likely to hold for pessimism.

People use different strategies to cope with situations that are risky in the sense that they present threats to self-esteem through possible failure. Anxiety and expectations that are explicitly set low may lead to performance deficits in these situations. With a strategy called *defensive pessimism*, individuals may use low expectations to cope with their anxiety so that it does not become totally debilitating. Low expectations may help individuals manage in risky situations, and research shows that interference with the defensive-pessimism strategy may impair performance. In a study conducted by Norem and Illingworth (1993), optimists demonstrated self-attribution bias in claiming significantly more control over their performance in the success condition than in the failure condition. Pessimists did not show this pattern. The data provided evidence of post-hoc cushioning efforts among optimists, whereas defensive pessimists seemed to be cushioned by their initial structuring of the situation. Individuals using the cognitive strategy of defensive pessimism will perform better and feel better when allowed to play through possible outcomes and reflect on their progress in advance. In contrast, optimists will perform more poorly and feel worse when they are encouraged or required to reflect on themselves and their goals in advance, but they cope afterwards.

Measurement of Optimism

If optimism or pessimism is used to explain over- or underreactions or other phenomena at the stock exchange it is necessary to find measures that do not depend on stock-price developments. It has already been noted that the Index of Consumer Sentiment (ICS) reflects optimism or pessimism at the macro level. The ICS is correlated with stock-price developments, but the causal direction is unclear. In explanations of changes in the ICS, stock index changes have been found important (see, for example, Shapiro, 1972). It may then be questionable to use the ICS as an independent variable to explain stock-price developments, except maybe as a confirmation of a trend reversal.

In psychology, many attempts have been made to assess an individual's degree of optimism or pessimism as a personality trait or as a more temporary characteristic related to specific situations. Typically, people are asked to answer questions in questionnaires about how they view the future and about what they expect of their life, often referred to as their life orientation. Although the tests do not seem to have been applied in financial research, they may reveal something of interest for this purpose. According to the Belief in Good Luck Scale, some people do indeed believe that their life is influenced by good luck and individuals do show differences with respect to their beliefs about luck (Darke and Freedman, 1997). Some people maintain an irrational view of luck as a rather stable force that tends to influence events in their own favor. Others hold the more rational belief that luck is random and unreliable. These beliefs show a considerable amount of stability over time, according to these studies.

A person's degree of optimism is mostly investigated through batteries of questions about the past, the present, and the future. There are some difficulties involved in this, as the following quotation shows:

> Facing this task, people use a simple heuristic: They assume that their well-being at the time of the judgment is a reasonable and parsimonious indicator of their well-being in general. Therefore, they evaluate their life as a whole on the basis of their mood at the time of judgment – unless their current mood is not considered informative (Schwartz and Strack, 1985, p.440).

The present mood seems to influence evaluations of states that comprise much more than the mood at the moment. The exception is when the current mood is not considered representative of the state that is in focus. Schwartz and Strack (1985) make the assumption that affective state is not considered relevant information in evaluating many domains where comparisons with other data can be made, for example, with data from other persons. They give an example: 'According to this reasoning, the outcome of the 1982 championship games of the German national soccer team was found to affect respondents' general life satisfaction but not satisfaction with work and income'. Subjects who were placed in an unpleasant environment and asked about their well-being were less satisfied with life than subjects who were asked the same question in a pleasant environment. The studies show that estimates of long-term, complex phenomena may be influenced by temporary mood states if there is some correspondence between present mood and total well-being. When private investors make forecasts of, say, future developments for stocks of interest, they may be influenced by their present mood. After a successful transaction, they will tend to be overoptimistic, after a failure they will tend towards overpessimism. There may still be some protection. In a study of the role of mood for expectation formation, one of the findings was that expectations of focal outcome was rather weakly related to mood, while expectations of some non-focal aspects, such as anticipated experiences, were more strongly related to mood (Sjöberg, 1989, p.342).

CONFIDENCE AND SELF-CONFIDENCE

It would be foolish, in forming our expectations, to attach great weight to matters which are very uncertain.

Keynes (1936, p.148)

Confidence in Judgments and Decisions

Keynes (1936) very carefully discussed the concept of confidence. Long-term forecasts which serve as the basis for investment are expectations with different probabilities. The investor chooses the most probable forecast, but the expectation does not only depend on the forecast: 'It also depends on the *confidence* with which we make this forecast – on how highly we rate the likelihood of our best forecast turning out quite wrong' (Keynes, 1936, p.148). Keynes argued that profit expectations, and the state or degree of confidence – also referred to as *weight* – that investors placed in their profit forecasts, determined investment.

In testing Keynes's hypothesis, Anderson and Goldsmith (1997) used business forecasts of profits for the next six months as profit expectations and a proxy for confidence or weight in Keynes's sense. This proxy was a measure of earlier accuracy in forecasts. They found a very high explanatory power for investments with the two variables, profit forecast and confidence, at the industry level for all of 14 industries in their selection.

In many studies of judgments and decision making, subjects are asked about their confidence for each judgment or decision made. A multitude of factors have been found to influence confidence in this sense (see, for example, Hogarth, 1987; Mellers et al. 1998). More recently, researchers' efforts have turned to the study of overconfidence, since confidence assessments show definite signs of more confidence than reality vindicates.

Individuals differ in how much confidence they have in their judgments and decisions, but, on average, they tend to overestimate their own ability. In situations of uncertainty such as investment decisions, high confidence in one's judgment may facilitate decision making and lead to success if the feeling of confidence is realistic. It may be disastrous if there is overconfidence with a low degree of realism. Overconfidence among investors, both professionals and private individuals, is used to explain upward stock-price movements and labeled feedback effect. It should be noted that a person can also have high confidence in a judgment that involves negative developments in stock prices. Some outstanding financial economists have, for example, predicted impending stock crashes and, according to reports in the mass media, sold all their stocks during the last few years. They get support from Fama and French (2000), Shefrin (2000), and Shiller (2000), who make rather gloomy predictions of the stock market future.

Overconfidence According to Psychology

Confidence and overconfidence, and increasingly also the related concept of illusion of control, have been used to explain reactions on the stock market (Stephan, 1999, pp.116–8). Overconfidence is related to the person's perception of her/his ability in relation to a task. It may also include the fact that people commit the error of not searching for evidence that could disconfirm the beliefs (Cosmides and Tooby, 1996; Shefrin and Statman, 1994, p.331).

The relationship between availability of information and confidence is surprising. Intuitively, it is assumed that more information leads to better decisions and more confidence in judgments and decisions. Only the second part is confirmed by research. More information inspires more confidence, but the quality of decisions tends to increase only up to a point and then deteriorate. Maximum decision quality is often reached after use of only a few, say three or four, available information cues. In a series of studies, Swedish psychologists found that confidence in judgments grew with increasing information, but that the accuracy began decreasing after a few items had been utilized (Magnusson and Ekehammar, 1972). The results were obtained, among other things, in experiments with physicians, who were presented with information cues from a variety of tests of relevance to the diagnosis. Similar results have been found in research on consumer information processing (see below) and on stock market behavior (Jacoby et al., 1984)

Researchers in cognitive psychology have been busy investigating the realism of confidence in judgments. The results may not be directly applicable to judgments and decisions in investing, but they are suggestive. When subjects make judgments it is common to ask them how confident they are about the correctness of their judgment. The confidence assessment is then checked against the objective outcome value and the degree of realism of the confidence assessment established. A common finding in cognitive psychology is that the subjects tend to be overconfident (Juslin and Olsson, 1997). A large number of studies has shown that both experts and non-experts often lack the ability to make accurate judgments, but they still have great confidence in their fallible judgments. This does not preclude the possibility that many everyday decisions are right and lead to the desired results. Everyday situations contain less uncertainty than the situations used in laboratory studies. Gigerenzer et al. (1991) found that overconfidence bias disappeared when subjects estimated frequencies that were more familiar to them rather than single-event probabilities. Overconfidence is here narrowly associated with the intriguing question of how people handle probabilities and frequencies which may not represent the whole truth about overconfidence.

Assessments of respondents' confidence in answer to questions about income and other expectations are made in many surveys. Respondents are asked how confident or certain they are that their judgments, expectations, or decisions are true or correct. Questions about income expectations seem to be regularly followed by such questions. While psychologists favor subjective measures of confidence, economists mostly prefer objective data that serve as proxies, often the variance of a distribution of earlier income outcomes. A smaller variance is interpreted as more confidence or less uncertainty. Typically, confidence or uncertainty are introduced as parameters in specified models and consequences for behavior are deduced. The predicted consequences are then tested against a set of data. Assessments of confidence in the stock-investing area tend to be of a more casual nature, being after-the-fact attempts at explanation. The assumptions about investor confidence that are made in behavioral finance models seem to rely heavily on theory developed in psychological laboratory work.

Using employees who worked in a German bank with trading and sales of securities and foreign currencies, Stephan and Kiell (1997) studied overconfidence in financial judgments. They defined overconfidence in terms of the size of confidence intervals used in estimates and judgments. The subjects were asked to provide 90 percent confidence intervals for forecasts of some selected stock and currency prices, that is, they had to give a lower and an upper limit between which they thought that the correct answer lay. The subjects were experts in these areas. As a comparison they were also asked questions about items of general knowledge, such as the weight of an empty Boeing 747 and the diameter of the moon. The authors computed the ratio between the upper and lower limits and defined overconfidence as setting the confidence intervals too closely. The smallest intervals were found for the forecasts in areas in which the subjects were experts. The confidence intervals were in fact so narrow that the correct value mostly occurred outside the interval: 17 percent hits for stock prices, 29 percent hits for currencies, and 21 percent hits for general knowledge questions. The overconfidence was thus highest for (the selected) stocks. The authors suggest that this may mean that overconfidence is more likely when there is halfway knowledge, when people believe that they know more than they actually do.

Empirical studies show a high rate of new-business failure. Camerer and Lovallo (1999) hypothesized that overconfidence could explain why people entered into a risky business. Using an experimental asset market game, they tested the hypothesis that individuals with overconfidence, defined as exaggerated belief in one's own ability, were likely to choose risky undertakings and to suffer business failures. In the experimental entry games, entrants' payoffs depended on their skill. The subjects tended to overestimate their chances of relative success and entered more frequently, compared to a control group in which payoffs did not depend on skill. The overconfidence was even stronger when subjects actively selected an experimental session, knowing that their success in it would be related to their skill. They knew that others also had self-selected. In the sessions, so much entry occurred that the average subject lost money in 34 out of 48 periods, and earned money in only four periods. Overconfidence and risk taking seemed highly correlated.

It has often been found that people tend to point to themselves as better than average in certain skills such as automobile driving. Another observation on a kind of self-confidence emanates from surveys of risk perception in which people tend to see risks to themselves as lower than risks to the population in general. Many people are more optimistic about their own prospects than about other people's prospects. Weinstein (1980) carried out two experiments. In the first study, over 200 college students estimated how much their own chance of experiencing 42 events differed from the chances of their classmates. Overall, the subjects rated their own chances to be significantly above average for positive events and below average for negative events. Cognitive and motivational considerations led to predictions that degree of desirability, perceived probability, personal experience, perceived controllability, and stereotype salience would influence the amount of optimistic bias evoked by different events. The predictions about differences between self and others were supported, although the pattern of effects differed for positive and negative events. In the second study, 120 female undergraduates from the first study participated. It tested the idea that people are unrealistically optimistic because they focus on factors that improve their own chances of achieving desirable outcomes and fail to realize that other outcomes may have just as many factors in their favor. These subjects listed the factors that they thought influenced their own chances of experiencing eight future events. When such lists were read by a new group of subjects, the amount of unrealistic optimism shown by this second group for the same eight events decreased significantly, although it was not eliminated (Weinstein, 1980).

Sjöberg (1998) reports on a survey with questions about unemployment, housing, nutrition, and health-care risks. In all four areas, general risks were regarded as higher than personal risks. This is an indication of overconfidence, apparently depending on a feeling that one can control the risk to some extent, presumably by behaving well and taking care of oneself.

The Overconfidence Concept in Behavioral Finance

Overconfidence is in behavioral finance often defined in a restricted sense. An example is: an *overconfident* investor is an investor who overestimates the precision of his private information signal, but not of information signals publicly received by all (Daniel et al., 1998b). This is another way of saying that the individual investor has drawn wrong conclusions from her/his own experience or from information received from outside sources. Such private information may have effects on stock prices, 'noise', but, according to theory, the effects tend to be balanced as more public information arrives. In Daniel et al.'s. (1998b) model, securities prices are affected by fundamentals and by misperceptions of firms' prospects. Basing their reasoning on psychological evidence, the authors assume that individuals are overconfident about their ability to evaluate securities, and hence overestimate the precision of their private information signals. Overconfidence is explained by biased self-attribution, which causes asymmetric shifts in investors' confidence as a function of their investment outcomes. This is tantamount to saying that people believe too much in what they think they have learned from their own experience. Hindsight bias may serve to reinforce overconfidence.

To some extent, overconfidence can also be learned from observing others, directly or via mass media. Such overconfidence can be even more disastrous than overconfidence based on self-attributed achievements, as the Dutch Tulipmania and the South-Sea bubble suggest. Under some circumstances, the recently divulged tendency in business circles to disregard consideration of reference groups possessing information breeds overconfidence that would not have been there if information from reference groups had been heeded (Camerer and Lovallo, 1999; see also Chapter 7).

Overconfidence is frequently used as an explanation of a high level of activity in trading. Overconfident people are assumed to trade more and to take more risks. It is often assumed that the stock market attracts overconfident people, who either become traders or active investors on their own. Odean (1998, 1999) studied the transactions in a discount brokerage firm. He examined returns patterns before and after transactions and suggests that overconfidence was one possible cause of excessive trading: Overconfident investors, who were defined by their trading activities and not by an independent measure, tended to trade too frequently, that is, the gains that overconfident investors realized through trading were less than they anticipated and did not even offset the costs of trading. The stocks that the most active investors purchased did not outperform those that they sold by enough to cover the costs of trading. On average, the stocks they purchased actually underperformed those that they sold. This was the case even when trading was not apparently motivated by liquidity demands, tax-loss selling, portfolio rebalancing, or a move to lower-risk securities.

Barber and Odean (2000b) warn against the consequences of too frequent trading, which they see as a consequence of overconfidence, and report findings from another extensive study of accounts. Here is their summary:

> Individual investors who hold common stocks directly pay a tremendous performance penalty for active trading. Of 66,465 households with accounts at a large discount broker during 1991 to 1996, those that traded most earned an annual return of 11.4 percent, while the market returned 17.9 percent. The average household earned an annual return of 16.4 percent, tilted its common stock investment toward high-beta, small, value stocks, and turned over 75 percent of its portfolio annually. Overconfidence can explain high trading levels and the resulting poor performance of individual investors. Our central message is that trading is hazardous to your wealth (Barber and Odean, 2000b, p.773).

Overconfidence is assumed to underlie frequent trading operations, but there may be other causes as well, in my view. The whole concept of investing in stocks is associated with notions of being active in the market, buying and selling at the right moment. These notions are probably encouraged by stock brokers, who mostly make money on transactions and not on passivity. Barber and Odean in fact suggest that investors should pay annual fees rather than commission based on transactions. De Bondt (1998) found that private investors in his Fox Valley study tended to be overoptimistic about the developments of their own stock and more pessimistic about average developments according to the Dow Jones Index.

While the economists in behavioral finance usually do not try to measure overconfidence directly, they develop micro models covering how overconfidence can be learned.

> We develop a multi-period market model describing both the process by which traders learn about their ability and how a bias in this learning can create overconfident traders. A trader in our model initially does not know his own ability, that is, the probability that he is receiving a valid signal. He infers this ability from his successes and failures. In assessing his ability the trader takes too much credit for his successes, that is he weights his successes more heavily than would a true Bayesian. This leads him to become overconfident. A trader's expected level of over-

confidence increases in the early stages of his career. Then, with more experience, he comes to better recognize his own ability (Gervais and Odean, 1999, Abstract).

This is an interesting way of outlining a learning process which encompasses self-attribution and a growing belief in the trader's own skill when things go well. With growing experience the tendency to be overconfident decreases, since disappointments lead to more realistic appreciation of the trader's own skill. This reasoning agrees with the success part of level-of-aspiration theory. Level of aspiration is a kind of goal that an individual sets for her/his performance in a certain respect. If the level is reached, most people are inclined to raise the future level somewhat. If the level is not reached, the individual becomes frustrated and lowers the level the next time, to make it more realistic. If this is compared to what Barber and Odean said above, the successes need not involve doing better than the market portfolio. Making satisfactory profits in relation to the expectation would be a major condition for becoming overconfident. The consequence of overconfidence may then be that the trader trades too aggressively and thereby increases trading volume and market volatility, at the same time lowering her/his own expected profits. The ability of an overconfident trader may be higher, but the expected profits in the next period may be lower than for a less successful trader because of the number of transactions. Since overconfidence in the model is generated by success, overconfident traders are not the poorest traders. Their survival in the market is not threatened. Overconfidence does not make traders wealthier, but the process of becoming wealthy can make traders overconfident (Gervais and Odean, 1999). Overconfidence is certainly far from always a bad thing for the individual and the national economy. It may inspire entrepreneurship, openness to innovation, and financial risk taking.

Overconfidence and the Use of Confirmatory Information

Use of information is a way of increasing confidence. If a person receives more information, the confidence in the judgment or decision also increases even though much of the information is not used. Searching for confirming information is a way of making sure that the judgment or decision is right and confirmatory information is another reason for confidence in one's own judgments. In cognitive psychology, a long tradition of studies shows that people try to avoid disconfirming and search for confirming information. Dissonance theory (Festinger, 1957), which has found many applications in economics (for example Akerlof and Dickens, 1982), was probably first.

Wason (1966) was inspired by Popper's idea of building up knowledge by rejecting rather than confirming hypotheses. He thus investigated in a simple experiment how people chose information. Many followers have used similar approaches. The subjects are typically shown four cards and are told that each card has a number on one side and a letter on the other. The subjects are instructed to decide which cards should be turned over to determine whether a stated hypothesis (such as the first hypothesis in Figure 6.1) is correct. The *confirmation bias* consists in the fact that most people decide to turn cards E and 4. The figure 4 can confirm the hypothesis, but this does not prove that the hypothesis is valid for other cards. It takes only one observation to reject the hypothesis. This can be done if 7 is chosen instead of 4. Many repetitions of the experiment have given the same result: people tend to choose confirming rather than disconfirming information.

E	**K**	**4**	**7**
Beer	**Coke**	**22**	**16**

Upper Row: If a card has a vowel on one side, then it has an even number on the other side.
Lower Row: If a person is drinking beer, then that person is at least 18 years old.

Source: Davidsson and Wahlund (1992,p. 347)

Figure 6.1 Hypothesis for the Subject to Test

These findings do not always hold, however. Davidsson and Wahlund (1992) tested a hypothesis that had found some confirmation in earlier experiments, namely that increasing concreteness in the task would weaken the tendency to look for confirming evidence. Two of their tasks are presented in Figure 6.1. They found that concreteness reduced the confirmation bias and that prior knowledge or experience was even more effective in reducing it. Still, a majority of the subjects showed a confirmation bias. When the experiment was carried out with real people in a bar, most people correctly selected the beer drinker and the 16-year-old (Pinker, 1998). Familiarity rather than concreteness seems to make a difference.

Cosmides and Tooby (1994), in a vein similar to Gigerenzer's (1996) attack on the heuristics-and-biases approach, accuse experimenters who have pursued confirmation-bias experiments in the same way as Wason of using artificial situations: 'the artificial nature of the experiments usually conducted might not be triggering latent competencies' (Cosmides and Tooby, 1994, p.330). These authors also found that under certain, more realistic conditions the confirmation bias tended to disappear. Friedrich (1993) maintains that a pragmatic approach shows that the confirmation bias may be useful for the individual in some situations, a point also made by Davidsson and Wahlund (1992). It is sometimes useful to be overoptimistic so as to overcome resistance to change.

Despite the challenges to the confirmation bias paradigm, many facts speak in favor of the existence of confirmation search, at any rate under certain circumstances whose characteristics are insufficiently known. Whether confirmation bias to the extent it exists in financial markets is useful or detrimental will then depend on a number of circumstances. Shefrin (2000) warns against the dangers of confirmation bias in building up expectations that may lead to overoptimistic trading. If the results that indicate less confirmation bias when there is concreteness and earlier experience are applicable, the occurrence of confirmation bias may be less of a problem than is often believed in behavioral finance. Hellman (2000) talks about 'confirming events' after decisions have been made; earnings announcements may confirm the correctness of the decision to buy or sell. If a preparatory analysis points in a certain direction, new information may, however, be too readily accepted as confirmatory if it points in the same direction.

Information and Moderated Confidence

In a paper-and-pencil test, Bloomfield et al. (1998a) divided their subjects into two groups with different amounts of information. The tasks consisted of estimating the value of securities and making a decision on how many stocks to buy at a price slightly lower than the estimated value. The subjects in the less informed group were provided with only one item of information explaining 16 percent of the variance in security value whereas the informed subjects were given three items of information, together explaining 61 percent of the variance. While the idea was that, if well calibrated, the less informed subjects would be less confident in their estimates, these subjects turned out often to be more overconfident than the better informed subjects. When the former were given guidance about the inadequacy of their information, the confidence was reduced with less trading as a consequence. The results from the paper-and-pencil test were confirmed in a laboratory financial market. Wealth was transferred from less informed investors to informed investors because the former tended to buy high and sell low. The conclusion was that if professional investors were given inside information which was unknown to the less informed, the welfare of the latter could be harmed unless they were made aware of their informational disadvantage.

In an attempt to reconcile findings that there could be both over- and underreactions following news and to sort out conditions under which one or the other type of reaction occurred, Bloomfield et al. (1998b) proposed that the reliability of the news and the rule for composing the portfolio of stocks were decisive. The more reliable information would lead to underreaction whereas the less reliable information was expected to lead to overreaction. Why? The authors assumed that the reliability of less reliable information was overestimated. It is unclear how earlier experience of such information worked in the authors' opinion. The expected underreaction to reliable information followed from underestimation of the reliability. In both cases, the investors' confidence is moderated towards an average level that is insufficiently high or low. The phenomenon was labeled *moderated confidence* and the authors found research support in a paper by Griffin and Tversky (1992).

Two types of portfolio formation rules were distinguished. The information-based rule involved selling and buying depending on the favorability of value-relevant information that was independent of the market price. In a price-based portfolio, buying and selling are determined by changes in the market price following the information release. The authors predicted that price-based portfolios would give higher overreactions or smaller underreactions than information-based portfolios 'because market prices typically include an element of random error that is subsequently reversed' (p.2). Bloomfield et al. (1998b) tested their hypotheses in two experiments run in laboratory financial markets and found support for their ideas. They claim that the hypothesis of moderated confidence helps researchers predict whether a given research study is likely to reveal over- or underreactions.

Perceived Control and Illusion of Control

Perceived control is an important factor in Ajzen's Theory of Planned Behavior (Ajzen, 1991) and it can be seen as a form of confidence. If a person perceives that there is no control of means to achieve a desired purpose, a positive attitude towards the act does not produce the commensurate behavior. Perceived control may be an illusion, as is evidenced by Langer's (1982) experiments on *illusion of control*. Illusion of control is defined as an expectancy of a personal success probability inappropriately higher than the objective probability would warrant. People behave as though chance events are subject to control. The illusion may have some basis in fact, but generally the label is used when there is some form of more or less obvious superstition behind a certain act. Why is it that people who are ordinarily reasonably rational in their decision making hesitate to make bets after a die has been thrown, but not yet read, while they are willing to place the bets before the die is thrown?

Langer conducted a series of six studies involving 631 adults to elucidate the illusion-of-control phenomenon. She hypothesized that factors from skill situations involving competition, choice, familiarity, and involvement introduced into chance situations would cause subjects to feel inappropriately confident. She comments on some earlier studies:

> [D]ice players clearly behave as if they were controlling the outcome of the toss. They are careful to throw the dice softly if they want low numbers or to throw hard for high numbers. They believe that effort and concentration will pay off. Control can also be exerted when betting; for example, always bet with the person who looks like he has the most control. These behaviors are all quite rational if one believes that the game is a game of skill (Langer, 1982, p.231).

Langer developed a series of tests, mostly lotteries, to study illusion of control. She even asked lottery participants at a racetrack about their confidence at different times. Indicators of confidence in all six of her studies gave support to her prediction that people would not distinguish chance- from skill-determined events even if they were aware of chance factors.

Similar results were obtained in a study by Tversky and Heath (1991, pp.8–9). They let their subjects choose between two alternatives as follows:

1. A stock is selected at random from the *Wall Street Journal*. You guess whether it will go up or down tomorrow. If you're right, you win $5.
2. A stock is selected at random from the *Wall Street Journal*. You guess whether it went up or down yesterday. You cannot check the paper. If you're right, you win $5.

It turned out that 67 percent of the subjects selected the first alternative. The authors suggest that the relative ignorance was lower for this alternative since nobody could know the outcome yet. Illusion of control makes people believe that they can influence future events even if they have no such power and have to rely on some magic. Only a few private stock holders are big enough to influence stock prices of certain companies in any lasting way. Temporary influence for a single stock has been observed in financial markets of limited size. The illusion of control concerns a superstitious gut feeling of being able to influence chance rather than any reality-based sense of ability.

DIMENSIONS OF EMOTIONALITY

Recent research on emotions is almost as vast and diverse as emotional life itself.

Cacioppo and Gardner (1999, p.191)

Affects, Feelings, and Emotions

Emotions have powerful effects on decisions. Moreover, the outcomes of decisions have powerful effects on emotions.

Mellers et al. (1998, p.453)

Although some people may seem to have a passion for rationality, rational behavior is usually seen as being devoid of feeling or at least neutral in relation to feelings and emotions. The classical view of emotions in economics as well as in other social sciences has been the disruptive effects of emotions. The well-known economist Albert Hirschman (1977) has written an interesting book about the history of the battle between the passions and the interests, the conflict between emotionality and rationality that economists have debated over many centuries. Philosophers have been dealing with the same issue: 'An assumption by rationalists dating back to the ancient Greeks has been that higher forms of human existence – mentation, rationality, foresight, and decision making – can be hijacked by the pirates of emotion' (Cacioppo and Gardner, 1999, p.194).

After William James (1890), who was an expert on emotions and preferred psycho-physiological explanations of these, psychologists were for many years shy about the role of emotions. Only a few basic emotions with clear physiological connotations like fear, rage, and pain were admitted into behavioristic psychology. Cognitive psychology, which began its rapid expansion in the 1960s, was long dominated by human information processing with about as much feelings as a computer. More recently, the role of emotions in human life has become more appreciated in psychology, but the field of affects, feelings, and emotions remains a much debated, complex research domain. A tendency nowadays is to treat feelings and emotions as physiological and biological issues (Cacioppo and Gardner, 1999). James's (1890) assertion that emotions were consequences and not the causes of the accompanying bodily expressions is again of interest.

A novelty is that 'emotions are increasingly recognized for the constructive role they play in higher forms of human experience' (Cacioppo and Gardner, 1999, p.14). A new approach to the study of emotions holds that the primary function of emotions is to mobilize attention to goal-relevant features of situations. Exuberance as well as fear and anxiety may serve to focus the individual's attention on objects and events that are related to a preferred goal. The effects may be favorable or, if exaggerated, disruptive. While positive affective states may reinforce the status quo, negative affective states, held within limits, seem to lead persons towards new endeavors:

> Unlike positive affective states that reinforce the status quo, negative ones lead individuals to analyze the bases of their problems, explore possible mechanisms of change, and consider the potential outcomes of different actions . . . Happiness, anger, and sadness are apparently generated by current states; fear and hope are generated by anticipated states (Karniol and Ross, 1996, p.601).

The recent interest in hedonic utility is also evidence of the role for human utility attributed to feelings (Kahneman et al., 1999). The new field of study has the broad scope of studying what makes experiences and life pleasant or unpleasant. Hedonic psychology 'is concerned with feelings of pleasure and pain, of interest and boredom, of joy and sorrow, and of satisfaction and dissatisfaction' (Kahneman et al., 1999, Preface). Doesn't this sound eminently applicable to investor psychology for a real understanding of what goes on in the mind of the investor? Is not hope the dominant characteristic of the investor's expectations? Hope may change into fear and panic when stock prices fall drastically. It is certainly not the whole truth about investors. In my view, the majority of stock owners are rather passive and consequently less shaken by emotions than the relatively few highly active speculators.

First, a few words will be said about feelings, emotions, and affects and the related, here already treated, concept of mood. While psychologists nowadays mostly refrain from defining these concepts, except by the measuring instruments, traditionally feeling had more of an experiential tone and affect and emotion were more related to arousal, which in its turn had physiological connotations. Well-being is a feeling, but it can hardly be said to be an emotion. Arousal is a physiological condition of being more or less alert. Affective is often the same as evaluative and refers to an attitude or preference dimension that is distinguished from the cognitive dimension and sometimes also from the conative, action-oriented dimension which comprises willing, that is, volition or preference.

Mood and affect are often synonyms and the same models can be used to explain them. Attempts have been made to investigate how mood or affect influence information processing. The Affect Infusion Model (AIM) describes how affect or mood is infused into information processing. The amount of influence depends on the type of processing. Forgas (1994, 1995), who is the originator of AIM, identifies four processing strategies. The first case, labeled *direct access*, involves a pre-existing evaluation that gives no new affect. The second case, called *motivational processing*, is directed towards an existing goal. Both cases comprise highly predetermined information-search patterns and do not require any new constructive processing; affects are not expected to arise in this processing. In the third case, described as *heuristic* or simplified, affect infusion is likely since affects are experienced as information in situations where no pre-set goal or earlier evaluation exist. People tend to minimize effort and use whatever shortcuts are available to them. The fourth case, *substantive processing*, requires people to select, learn, and interpret novel information about a target and relate this information to pre-existing knowledge structures (Forgas, 1994, p.8). Like genuine decision making, which in Katona's terms is a rare event, substantive processing occurs only when the task is complex and imposes demands that cannot be fulfilled with less effortful strategies. The AIM predicts a major role for affect in such processing.

The four types of information processing seem applicable to financial behavior. Decisions to buy or sell may be routine and follow pre-set rules or well-established habits, with little affect. With increasing uncertainty because new data emerge, the room for affect grows and affect may in some situations have enormous effect on action.

Emotions are subjective and depend on internal stimulation as well as on outward stimuli. Thinking afterwards about an event that was painful may give rise to stronger emotions than the event itself when it happened. This is well illustrated by the following quotation:

> Counterfactual thinking or comparing objective outcomes with imagined outcomes that 'might have been' was shown to leave bronze medalists at the 1992 Summer Olympics apparently happier than silver medalists . . . even though, by objective standards, an Olympic Silver medal is of higher value than a bronze medal (Cacioppo and Gardner, 1999, p.196).

The silver medalists had been closer to the goal of winning and had missed it more narrowly than the bronze medalists and thinking about this hurt more.

Strangely enough, positive affects towards an object may arise as a pure consequence of repeated exposure to it. This is called 'the mere exposure effect'. It is similar to the effect of increasing familiarity, but this is not the whole explanation of the effect. Marketers make use of repetition of brand names to sell goods. In mass communication, the mere exposure effect is suspected of giving news broadcasters success among political voters. Just being seen on TV night after night may influence a newscaster's prospective political career favorably. Stocks of firms that are mentioned many times daily in the mass media, the way some Internet companies have been in recent years, may have raised their attractiveness and the prices of those stocks.

Debaters in the mass media often claim that greed is a potent force in shaping financial behavior. People are reported to speculate recklessly without regard to the fact that they may be exposed to ruinous losses. Financial bubbles are seen as a case in point, but not the only one. Even in times of less turbulence in the financial markets, ill-considered speculation may bring ruin although it seems more rare than when bubbles are building up. Fear leads to panic when prices seem to drop drastically and anxious investors try to sell as quickly as possible. There is some doubt that fear and greed are generally so important in finance. What on the surface appears to be fear and greed in connection with some stock-market events may be better explained by cognitive capacity, mass influence from others, and some less sensational emotions. Emotions are important since they have effects on expectations and actions. Hope is an expectation of a very special kind. First, it is colored by emotion. Second, there may be a tinge of will. Third, there is some notion of uncertainty and likelihood associated with it.

Emotional Arousal

Arousal theory assumes that organisms strive for optimal levels of arousal. It explains, for example, gambling behavior with the assumption of boredom. The level of arousal is felt by the individual to be below the optimal level and this starts a search for new stimuli to assuage the boredom. Gambling and stock speculation may be a way of getting more exciting experiences. This assumption has its origin in the well-known Yerkes-Dodson law of arousal. It says that the optimal arousal level is a function of task difficulty. The law originates from a study in which rats had to make discriminations of varying difficulty when given shocks of varying intensity (corresponding to different levels of arousal). With increasing difficulty of discrimination, the optimal arousal decreased. The conclusion was that there was a certain level of arousal (shock) that was optimal for performance at each difficulty level and that the optimal arousal became lower as problem difficulty increased.

Interest in this law has been renewed in connection with studies of people doing stressful work, for example fighter pilots, and may be applicable also to stock and bond market traders who have to make quick decisions in front of computer monitors (Svensson et al., 1997). For really difficult decisions, it is desirable to have a relatively relaxed posture because the optimal arousal level is lower than for an easy decision and higher than the arousal when the individual is completely at rest. The more difficult the investment decision is, the more relaxed the decision maker should be. In reality, decision makers probably fail to reach the optimal arousal level and become more tense with increasing difficulty of the task.

Kaufman (1999) argues that emotional arousal can be a source of bounded rationality. When people have very low levels of arousal, they experience depression, melancholy, or boredom. These emotional states impair quality decision making:

> [B]ecause little energy is devoted to information gathering and problem solving, attention is focused on other matters than the task at hand, memory is blocked by obsessive thoughts or used to ruminate on non-task considerations, stress is induced by the imbalance between desired and actual stimulation, and autonomic activity (for example, heart rate, muscle tone) is at a low level . . . (Kaufman, 1999, p.138).

When arousal is at a low level, an increase, such as a shift from depression toward anger or from boredom toward excitement, causes the person to increase the effort level devoted to information gathering and problem solving. At the same time, autonomic activity increases – an acceleration of heart rate, a tensing of muscles – the mental focus on the problem at hand is sharpened, and recall from short-term memory is improved. These factors increase decision-making quality (which in investment decision making probably means higher returns). This occurs up to a point, which is referred to as the optimal arousal level. Up to this point, emotions play a constructive role in human behavior by helping the person to develop an effective coping strategy for dealing with change.

If emotional intensity increases beyond the optimal arousal level, the quality of decision making increasingly deteriorates. The marginal product of arousal becomes negative. The behavior tends to be less than fully rational because emotions either make preferences no longer well ordered or disrupt the person's ability to determine optimal outcomes. The decline in performance that occurs with too high arousal levels may be caused by reductions in effort devoted to decision making. High levels of emotional intensity apparently block access to short-term memory, disorganize logical or inferential thought processes, cause loss of control of body parts and functions (for example trembling hands, nausea or headaches), block out rational considerations of benefit and cost, and promote acts of aggression and violence (Kaufman, 1999, pp.138–9).

It is easy to imagine that day traders who spend most of their waking time at the computer buying and selling stocks can operate at different levels of arousal. Frustration over loss transactions and extreme delight over easily gained profits can certainly impair judgment and decision making. Kaufman argues that bounded rationality can be decomposed into two parts, one part arising from cognitive limitations and the other from extremes of emotional arousal. Both parts involve restrictions on information processing, but for different reasons. He thinks that people can learn to handle emotional arousal so that self-control is maintained, and he points to pilots as an example. They are trained to cope with the stress that frightening situations otherwise produce. It may be the same for professional traders in securities markets.

The Peak–End Rule

Memories of past experiences of pain are influenced by the peak experience and by the end experience. This lawful phenomenon was discovered in a study of physical pain connected with colonoscopy. Kahneman et al. (1997) related this finding to subjective utility and pointed out that retrospectively assessed utility could be influenced by this peak–end rule. Stephan and Kiell (2000), who investigated a number of heuristics and biases in their study of professional German investors, included in their questionnaire a scenario which had the purpose of testing the peak–end rule. The scenario described three investors with the same total losses but different distributions of them:

A –2 000, –2 000, –1 000
B –500, –3 000, –1 500
C –1 000, –3 000, –1 000

According to the peak–end rule, B will be seen as the biggest loser and the most dissatisfied investor since both the peak and the end event were higher. The predicted rank order for judged dissatisfaction is: B > C > A. The peak–end rule was confirmed:

> Retrospective investor dissatisfaction was judged differently by 71% of the sample, although all three investors in the scenario had faced the same total losses. Moreover, the majority of the respondents (53%) ranked investor dissatisfaction according to the peak–end rule. Configuration–frequency analysis revealed that this result is highly significant (p<.0001), given the 24 possible rankings and the marginal distribution of dissatisfaction ratings (Stephan and Kiell, 2000, p.419).

Does the peak–end rule only apply to pain and other negative experiences? What happens when positive and negative events are mixed? It seems likely that if the peak event and the end event are both positive, the effects of intervening negative events may be unduly reduced in memory. Even if the research evidence is still slim, it is worthwhile to remember that memories may be biased because of the pain and reward distributions of earlier events.

INVESTOR MOTIVATION

> *Motivation reflects an interweaving of one's present into the fabric of one's past and the prospects of one's future.*
>
> Karniol and Ross (1996, p.613)

Motivation can be seen as drives that push an individual to act. It is a link between the present and the future. In behavioristic approaches, the emphasis lies on drives that operate within the individual and are linked to hunger, thirst, and a few other needs, or to strong external stimuli. The motivation leads to attempts to avoid unpleasant things and attain pleasant things. The tension of the drive will then cease or at least decline. The cognitive revolution in psychology meant a new approach to motivation. It is now meaningful to say that an individual can be pulled towards something in the future, towards some future, purely imagined, event. Goals, plans, and intentions as well as expectations become legitimate concepts. It became acceptable to assume that people are able to communicate about their motivation for actions. In economic psychology as in social psychology, it has been common to ask people about motives for saving money and buying products.

While there are probably many market research studies of investor motivation, very little is published. Reports from the Dutch CentER Savings Studies (VSB Panel; see Nyhus, 1996) and some comprehensive German studies are an exception (psychonomics & Capital, 1998, 1999). In a German study, stock owners were asked about what motivated them to invest in stocks (Müller-Peters, 1999). Table 6.2 shows the distribution of answers;

more than one answer was possible. Profit is the most important motive or reason given, followed by risk. While the interpretation of profit is rather straightforward, risk may imply different things. Some knowledgeable stock owners may think of the often assumed, sometimes fulfilled, relationship between high risk and high profit and believe that it is necessary to take risks in order to make a profit. Alternatively, it seems likely that taking certain risks appears attractive and creates excitement and thrill. It is then similar to the utility of gambling, maybe with a feeling of more control.

It is interesting to note that almost half of the respondents made investments in stocks to get proof of their competence in finance. Müller-Peters (1999) reports that some old-age pensioners in his study used trading on the stock market as a compensation for missing earlier professional activities. Anecdotal evidence from the USA and Sweden supports this observation. Following daily developments at the stock exchange is entertainment for many and imagining investing in certain stocks may give some thrill although the transaction is never carried out and the owned stocks are rarely touched.

Table 6.2 German Motives for Investing in Stocks

N=215	Percent
Profit	85
Risk	64
Proof of competence	47
Leisure occupation	25
Stock option from employer	17
Club	15
Other	28

Source: Figure 6-4 in Müller-Peters (1999, p.144).

Achievement Motivation

In his discussion of motivation behind investment in stocks, Müller-Peters (1999) suggests that the *achievement motive* could contribute to explaining financial behavior. He assumes that higher motivation for achievement leads to more willingness to take risks in investments. Atkinson's (1957, 1964) theory of success and failure motivation takes its departure from some observations in the experimental situation in class rooms that students reacted differently to success. Some, who seemed to be characterized by a high need for achievement, took a pride in being successful. Others, usually with a low need for achievement, were more concerned about avoiding failure than achieving success. Atkinson postulates that the motivation for performing a certain activity is a function of the expectancy of success and the expectancy of failure and suggests the following formulas:

$$T_S = M_S * P_S * I_S$$

where

T_S is the tendency to achieve success through an activity;
M_S is the motive to achieve success, a stable characteristic of the person;
P_S is the expectancy or probability of success;
I_S is the incentive value of success at an activity, defined as $I_S = 1 - P_S$

The lower the probability of success is, the higher the incentive value. $P_S * I_S$ reaches a maximum if $p = 0.50$. The tendency to avoid failure (T_{AF}) through the performance of an activity is defined in a similar way:

$$T_{AF} = M_{AF} * P_F * I_F$$

where the terms indicate the motive to avoid failure (M_{AF}), the probability of failure (P_F) and the 'disincentive' value of failure (I_F). In congruence with I_S, I_F is set to $I_F = - P_S$. This means that failure at an easy task, that is, one with a high probability of success, is more embarrassing than failing at a difficult task, which certainly agrees with common sense. If $T_S > T_{AF}$, the individual will perform the activity.

These formulas give rise to a number of interesting questions. Some people, for example investors, are characterized by high achievement, implying that they tend to choose tasks (activities) with moderate probabilities of success, in laboratory studies approximated as $p = 0.50$. They want to succeed and they want to be proud of their achievements, which they cannot be if the success is too easily won. If, on the other hand, the task is too difficult, they may not be able to succeed without the help of some luck. The theory implies that there is a free choice of actions, at least to some extent, so that the individual can choose among more or less risky alternatives.

An interesting question concerns what happens as a result of experiences with success or failure. Weiner (1972, pp.229–30) suggests the following generalizations after examining experimental results:

1. Motivation is enhanced following failure among individuals high in resultant achievement motivation.
2. Motivation is inhibited following failure among individuals low in resultant achievement motivation.
3. Motivation is decreased following success among individuals high in resultant achievement motivation.

4. Motivation is enhanced following success among individuals low in resultant achievement motivation.

These generalizations contain implications for learning achievement motivation and for the behavior of investors (cf. Gervais and Odean, 1999). For a person with a high need for achievement, there is a curvilinear relation between tendency to choose a task and the probability of success. The peak is at $p = 0.50$ when the success is as likely as the failure.

Müller-Peters (1999) presents the theory and notes that it seems applicable to private investment behavior. Studies indicating a relationship between achievement motivation and degree of risk taken are of particular interest. Here are some implications. An investor who has high achievement motivation is likely to avoid stocks with extremely high or extremely low probabilities of success. For a person with a low need for achievement, the curve relating probability of success and tendency to choose would in the same mode be almost flat since it makes little difference whether the probability is low, moderate, or extreme; other factors determine the choice. For a person with high fear of failure, the curve is the reverse of the high need for achievement curve. The tendency to avoid the task has a peak at moderately high probability of success and is considerably lower for either extremely low or extremely high probabilities of success. To the extent that people with fear of failure do not shun the stock exchange, they may be inclined to invest in stocks with low probabilities of success such as those issued by new technology firms. It is no shame to lose money in this manner (if you can afford it). The theory of achievement motivation has been severely criticized from many vantage points, but it has often turned out to have explanatory value.

SELF-CONTROL

Anticipation, Foresight, and Willpower

In early economics, thrift was an important concept in explanations of individual and national differences in savings and investments. Thrift was assumed to depend on two sets of factors. One set had to do with perception–cognition and was called 'anticipation' and 'foresight', what in modern theories of saving is called 'forward-looking'. The other set comprised volitional factors and was labeled 'self-control' and 'willpower' or was expressed as a set of goals that were similar to saving motives (see, for example, Fisher, 1930; Keynes, 1936).

Foresight is closely related to self-control and almost a prerequisite. According to Fisher (1930), foresight and willpower are closely connected.

They are both essential components of self-control. According to Fisher, a high degree of foresight enabled a person to give to the future such attention as it deserved. A high degree of self-control enabled a person to abstain from present enjoyment in order to increase future enjoyment. Fisher made the following distinction between foresight and self-control: 'Foresight has to do with *thinking*; self-control, with *willing*. Though a weak will usually goes with a weak intellect, this is not necessarily so, nor always. The effect of a weak will is similar to the effect of inferior foresight' (Fisher, 1930, p.83).

Volitional concepts have not been welcome in psychology after Behaviorism successfully launched its attacks on non-observable phenomena at the beginning of the twentieth century. While William James (1890) elaborated on the concept of will, it ended up disappearing from psychology as well as from economics. The latter science became more and more positivistic and mathematical and dropped all psychological concepts.

Prompt to Action and Willpower

What happens between perception–cognition and behavior or action is a debated issue. Under what conditions does cognition lead to actions that are consistent with it? More than one answer exists. Industriousness and thrift were for many centuries held to be characteristics of those who displayed the virtue of saving money. Thrift was determined by the ability to anticipate the future and by self-control which was also called 'willpower'. In his discussion of thrift, John Rae (1834) drew attention to specific personality dimensions affecting saving, or capital accumulation as he usually put it. He captured important aspects of saving in the following two sentences: 'The determination to sacrifice a certain amount of present good, to obtain another greater amount of good, at some future period, may be termed *the effective desire of accumulation*. All men may be said to have a desire of this sort, for all men prefer a greater to a less; but to be effective it must prompt to action (Rae [1834] 1905, p.53).

'All men prefer a greater to a less' is the foundation of the rationality postulate that was later formulated in similar terms and further explored by John Stuart Mill (1836) and Jevons (1871). It is worth noting that Rae, who had great influence, on later economists saw capital accumulation as a search for profit, to sacrifice now to obtain more later. This idea is also found in Adam Smith's *The Wealth of Nations* (1776).

The effective desire of accumulation that in Rae's view all men had resembles what in finance and public debate is often referred to as *human greed*. It was not meant to be derogatory. On the contrary, the desire was a prerequisite for saving and investing. The problem was that the desire was not always effective and then did not prompt to action. Two phenomena contributed to making the desire for accumulation more effective: foresight (perception–cognition) and willpower or self-control (implying genuine decision making). These served as prompts to action. In modern psychology, the discussion of cognition–behavior relationships distinguishes more possibilities. At least three interpretations of the role of 'prompt to action' seem possible:

1. Environmental stimuli or situational factors are decisive. Income level changes and changes in interest rates may be such factors that make capital accumulation feasible. Internal individual factors have no or little role in capital accumulation.
2. If a person's foresight and desire for accumulation become strong enough, that is, exceed a threshold, capital will be accumulated.
3. A link is necessary between desire for accumulation and action; some psychological mechanism such as self-control or will pushing decision making serves as the prompt to action.

Differences in personal characteristics are often in economics assumed to be unimportant and are expected to cancel out in a population or to be highly stable over long periods of time so that they can be counted out as influences on economic behavior. Keynes (1936), who specified eight saving motives, held that these had negligible influence. In his view, environmental influences and changes in economic stimuli determined choice behavior, given the stable preferences. Becker (1976) maintained that opportunity sets were decisive for consumer behavior and that individual deviations from rationality had little importance. In psychology, it is recognized that strong stimuli push people to action and do not need any intermediary linking mechanism to elicit behavior. Well-known examples are warnings of immediate danger, for example 'fire', or, in the world of finance, news of plummeting stock rates that provokes immediate reactions. Panic reactions of individuals may be triggered by headlines that yell about market-level panic. In such cases, the stimuli may lead directly to actions without requiring deeper cognitive or other processes.

The second interpretation is often implicit in classical economists' reasoning about anticipation of the future. Rae (1834), Böhm-Bawerk (1888) and Marshall (1890) pointed out that the vividness of the images of the future was significant for capital accumulation. People who could not imagine future events or concentrate their attention on future consumption possibilities spent their money on present goods. This interpretation involves the perceptions of the future or the desire for accumulation itself, or both, being able to reach such a height that they directly elicit saving behavior or stricter control of expenditure. Avarice can lead to capital accumulation without any foresight and intense greed can lead to speculation with little foresight.

The third interpretation implies that there is an internal intermediary and no direct correspondence between perception–cognition and action. The desire for capital accumulation was assumed prevalent and interest was then focused on the strength of foresight or willpower. Because of the way in which decision making is usually studied, the room for willpower and self-control is highly limited.

Hoch and Loewenstein (1991) framed self-control as a struggle between two psychological forces, desire (to spend on goods) and willpower. They distinguished two classes of self-control strategies: (a) attempts to directly reduce desire to spend, and (b) overcoming of desire through a variety of willpower tactics. Three strategies were possible: avoidance, distraction, and substitution. The authors added that precommitment and entitlement (feeling that you are entitled to a reward for working hard or 'everybody else is doing it') also affected economic cost assessment. They particularly stressed long-term goals that influenced preferences and they tried to accommodate emotional behavior (unpredictable changes in moods and tastes causing changed reference points) in their desire–willpower model of self-control. If the self-control is strong enough, or through some stratagem conquers the desire to consume now, investing for future utility becomes possible.

Cognitive psychologists have to face critical questions about the relationship between cognition and behavior. Guthrie (1935), a strict behaviorist, accused Tolman, who was for many years the leading cognitive psychologist, of leaving the organism trapped within its own knowledge structures:

> Signs, in Tolman's theory occasion in the rat *realization* or *cognition*, or *judgment*, or *hypotheses*, or *abstraction*, but *they do not occasion action.* In his concern with what goes on in the rat's mind, Tolman has neglected to predict what the rat will do. So far as the theory is concerned the rat is left buried in thought; if it gets to the food-box at the end that is his concern not the concern of the theory (Guthrie, 1935, p.172; quoted in Feather, 1982, p.3).

Similar criticisms to the effect that cognitions do not predict behavior are still directed at cognitive psychology, but with less justification. Much of cognitive psychology has a focus on choices and decisions about actions. The missing link between desire and action may well be called 'decision making', but more attention to the need for self-control to ensure action is warranted. Despite voluminous research on decision making, little is known about the part of the process that turns cognition into action (see Montgomery, 1989, for an approach to this study).

The Modern Psychology of Self-Control

> *The needs of the present make themselves felt through emotion. Those needs have a strong voice and clamor for immediate attention. In contrast, the needs of the fu-*

ture have a much weaker voice, expressing themselves more through thought. Most people feel the urge to satisfy their immediate needs, but they only think about satisfying their future needs.

Shefrin (2000, pp.141–2)

The quotation from Shefrin above illustrates the difficulties of preparing for old age by saving and investing instead of consuming immediately. Self-control means control of impulses that may otherwise involve ill-considered actions. A good reason for exercising self-control is the need to guard against undue optimism about profit chances in investing and against making investments with greater risks than the investor can afford. How can emotions best be controlled and how do they affect expectations? Self-serving attributions to one's own skill after success in the equity market readily lead investors to exaggerated expectations of future gains.

William James (1890) devoted considerable effort to a thorough discussion of 'will' and spelt out the conditions under which will operated. The concept shortly afterwards fell out of use in psychology. While self-control is a concept that is now acceptable in psychology, no real, generally accepted theory exists. Dictionary definitions call self-control the ability to inhibit impulsive or narrow goal-seeking behavior for the sake of a more inclusive goal. Self-control, which is often labeled *self-regulation*, may involve many things as is apparent in the following quotation:

> Among the terms used (often interchangeably) to denote a capacity for self-regulation are freedom, autonomy, agency, responsibility, maturity, ego-strength, willpower, self-control, choice, purposiveness, self-direction, voluntary action, self-sufficiency, morality, consciousness, free will, independence, conscientiousness, self-discipline, intentional action, self-intervention, intrinsic motivation, self-determination, and volition (Karoly, 1993, p.24, footnote).

This quotation from a review article indicates that there is no overwhelming consensus about what self-control actually amounts to. If self-control is equal to hedonic self-regulation, its purpose is to serve a person's well-being. It operates in two ways (Higgins, 1997). One way involves a focus on promotion of ends. A person wants to make sure that certain pleasant things also happen in the future. The other way means a protective focus aimed at safety and responsibilities. While some people favor the first way and look for pleasure, which is a kind of optimism about life, for others protection and safety needs prevail, which reflects a more pessimistic view of life.

With a new interest in internal processes following the rise of cognitive psychology, self-control, mostly in the guise of self-regulation, is now an important object of study. In economics, the concept is again being accepted and attempts are made to reconcile it with the rationality postulate. It can be done with some additions to the rationality concept, as is demonstrated in an article by the two economists O'Donoghue and Rabin (1999), who published their elaboration of self-control theory in the *American Economic Review.* They view the maintenance of self-control as a fight between doing things now or later.

Self-Control as Ability to Delay Satisfaction

> *Traders use a variety of rules and precommitment techniques to control emotion, for example, stop-loss orders. It seems an inevitable theme of popular investment guides that people should try 'to take an objective stance', 'to master their emotions' and 'to avoid beating themselves'. It is also frequently stated that an investment plan's principal function is 'discipline'.*
>
> De Bondt (1998, p.837)

Self-control is often seen as the ability to delay gratification. This reflects a research tradition under this label, with Walter Mischel as the most prominent researcher (for overviews of this research, see Mischel, 1984; Mischel et al., 1992). Mischel (1984) pictured self-control as the mechanisms that helped people overcome 'stimulus control' – the power of situations – and achieve increasing volitional control over their behavior even when faced with compelling situational pressures. He studied

> one fundamental human quality – the ability to purposefully defer immediate gratification for the sake of delayed, contingent but more desired future outcomes. These investigations seek to clarify the ability to defer gratification both as a psychological process and as a basic human competence. They analyze the mechanisms that allow self-control . . . both in terms of the psychology of the situation and of the person (Mischel, 1984, p.353).

Mischel and his colleagues carried out a number of studies of children's ability to delay gratification and focused on the interplay between person and situation. With preschoolers (mean age about four years), Mischel ran experiments in which the children could have a desired object, for example a marshmallow immediately or two marshmallows after a delay. When the awards were unavailable for attention by being obscured during the delay, the children waited more than ten times longer on average than when the rewards were exposed and available for attention. Thinking about the rewards when instructed to do so, the children found waiting for them just as difficult as if they were in view. The temptation of the visual presence was overcome when there was a distraction in the form of the children being told to 'think fun'.

The researchers aimed at understanding what made delay acceptable:

> [H]ow people ideate about the outcomes (rather than what they face in the situation) is crucial. The more the children focus on the arousing qualities of the blocked goals, the more frustrating and aversive the choice conflict and the delay

> seem to become and the sooner they terminate the situation. Conversely, cognitive representations of the same objects that focus on their nonconsummatory (more abstract, less arousing) qualities appear to facilitate the maintenance of goal-directed behavior, presumably by allowing the person to keep the goal in mind without becoming too aroused and frustrated to continue to wait for it (Mischel, 1984, p.353).

Is this relevant for understanding adult economic behavior? If you think it is not, you should listen to what Alfred Marshall said. He remarked that the same person's mood could vary between being impatient and greedy for present enjoyment at one moment and at another dwell on the future: 'Sometimes [a person] is in a mood to care little for anything else; sometimes he is like the children who pick the plums out of their pudding to eat them at once, sometimes like those who put them aside to be eaten last' (Marshall, 1890, p.100). One implication is that people at one moment make choices that they later regret and which they would not have made if they had devoted enough forethought to the choice. A typical feature of such choices is that the present object is disproportionately overvalued in relation to the distant one.

Hoch and Loewenstein (1991) noted that proximity and vivid representation raised problems for behavior to be consistent over time, with no intervening change of preference. Research showed that instructing subjects to think of future rewards increased their willingness to defer, but that proximity and physical presence were still dominant. The authors stressed the importance of treating a possible event of transgression (yielding to the temptation of immediate pleasure) not as a single event but as an event in a long series of transgressions. Incidentally, making events isolated is used in some marketing as a technique for reducing the customer's feeling of cost. An example is a focus on the (low) down-payment and not on the future installments.

It seems safe to conclude that self-control is at least to some degree a matter of having the right kind of ideation and maintaining it over time (cf. Elster, 1977; Schelling, 1984; Sjöberg and Johnson, 1978). Self-control means taking time to reflect on matters and not jumping to decisions that current emotions favor, and to train oneself to view certain single decisions as part of a longer series of similar decisions over time.

Self-Control as Cognition–Behavior Consistency

From a cognitive-psychological point of view, self-control is a matter of *cognition–behavior consistency* (Kuhl, 1985). The consistency is dealt with under such labels as self-regulation (Karoly, 1993), and action control (Kuhl, 1985). While these two approaches focus on *processes* that end in actions, self-control is a more static, enduring characteristic of a person. The concept of self-control implies that the characteristic is stable over time and situations. An important function for self-control is to control the prioritization of goals so that long-term goals get adequate consideration. Willpower was earlier on assumed to be necessary in the face of difficulties. Self-regulation usually refers to situations in which people have to engage in aversive activities like working on boring tasks or refraining from some pleasurable activity (Kuhl, 1985). Kuhl's own concept of action control has a somewhat broader scope and it also encompasses the enactment of seemingly simple intentions like reading a letter or opening a window. Action control is used 'to denote those processes which protect a current intention from being replaced should one of the competing tendencies increase in strength before the intended action is completed' (Kuhl, 1985, p.102).

The individual is assumed to have knowledge about her/his own strategies for managing intentions. Such strategies are: (1) selectively attending to information supporting the current intention, (2) selectively encoding goal-related features of incoming information, (3) activating positive emotions and enhancing the motivational basis of the current intention by manipulating (4) the internal or (5) the external incentive structure, and (6) avoiding overlong decision making. These strategies may be used more or less automatically. Studies of children's ability to delay gratification have confirmed that children too can use them. Children may learn to maintain an experimentally induced intention against a seducing action alternative by closing their eyes or otherwise avoiding visual contact with the source of distraction, for example, a very attractive toy. Delay-of-gratification studies have shown that the amount of attention directed to a 'tempting' stimulus is an important determinant of a child's ability to delay gratification. Strategies that limit the levels of this attention facilitate 'self-control'.

The strategies suggested by Kuhl resemble those proposed by Strotz (1956), Schelling (1984) and Elster (1977). They all discussed ways of resisting temptation and avoiding disturbing changes of taste. Similar thinking is found in Akerlof's concept of *procrastination*. 'Procrastination occurs when present costs are unduly salient in comparison with future costs, leading individuals to postpone tasks until tomorrow without foreseeing that when tomorrow comes, the required action will be delayed yet again' (Akerlof, 1991, p.1). While the main purpose of Akerlof's paper was to explain unlimited obedience, Akerlof briefly noted that procrastination could explain why people did not save enough for retirement unless there were pension plans. His emphasis on the salience of present costs can be compared to Ainslie's (1975, 1991) hypothesis about the strong preference for present utility in relation to distributed future disutility and costs.

Many psychological scales for assessing self-control exist. Kuhl (1985) presented very elaborate scales for studying action control. Another scale that has been used for similar purposes is the self-monitoring scale (Briggs and Cheek, 1988). The difficulty with using such scales is often that the statements that the respondents are asked to use to describe themselves are broad and sweeping. Kuhl's scale is tied to rather concrete actions and is preferable to many alternatives. Commonly, it is found that when self-control aspects of a certain type of behavior are investigated, the results are improved if content-specific scales rather than general scales are employed. Self-control in economic and financial matters is best measured through scales that comprise questions directly concerning these areas of behavior.

Self-Control and Other Personality Characteristics

> *Rules are good self-control tools. 'Not one drop' is a good rule for people whose self-control problems center on alcohol. 'Consume from dividends but don't dip into capital' is a good rule for investors whose self-control problems center on spending.*
>
> Statman (1999, p.20)

The increasing quest for some kind of volitional concept to fill the gap between cognition and action naturally leads to a closer look at personality theories and personality inventories. When the new cognitive psychology started developing at the end of the 1950s, the computer served as a model, but computers do not decide on and carry out any actions with a view towards the future. More psychologists are now recognizing the importance of human forward-looking for subsequent behavior. Research interest in future-orientation is coming in through the back door, as a consequence of addiction studies. The hyperbolic discount function is one of the most striking results of this psychological research (Ainslie, 1975, 1991).

Many anecdotes describing personal experiences and retold by the mass media that present financial market issues to the general public depict how stock owners are moved by strong emotions. The anecdotal evidence often intimates that investors are to a large extent constantly shaken by emotions. Before purchasing, they apparently have strong feelings that a certain stock is the right one to buy. When the newly bought stock immediately starts going down, they are disappointed, even angry, and feel hurt. When the stock rises more than expected, they feel clever and may become exuberant. If they have good self-control such feelings even if they emerge will not govern their future financial behavior. Some new stock holders may, according to news media reports, even feel so bad after some transactions that they give up buying stocks because they cannot stand the emotions. A common criticism that stock experts voice in the mass media is that many stock owners neglect the long-term aspects of stock ownership. At the same time, financial theory, stock brokers, financial advisors, and columnists in the mass media seem to encourage continual surveillance of the financial market and frequent transactions.

Good self-control and more relaxed attitudes to stock ownership may lead to less trading but more successful stock ownership. Can such self-control be a personality trait? Now that volition is on its way back into decent psychology, it is often disguised as self-regulation or action control to conceal the fact that it resembles willpower and self-control (Kuhl and Beckmann, 1985). Action control varies between people, but it is hardly a personality trait and is strongly influenced by situational circumstances. Anyhow, the developments make it possible to start looking for links between perceptions and actions and in this endeavor not to shy away from concepts like future-orientation and self-control. In psychology, personality research comes closest to concerted attacks on these issues. Personality generally stands for behavioral consistency of long duration. Personality traits or factors are essentially abstracted summaries of earlier behavior.

While psychological research on personality is very comprehensive, many psychologists, especially those in cognitive psychology, pay little attention to the concept of personality. The prevailing conception is 'more of the same', that is, that people tend to behave in new situations the way they behaved in earlier, similar situations. A popular assertion is 'past behavior is the best predictor of future behavior' (cf. Ajzen, 1991, p.202). This is similar to the prevalent idea that expectations of the future are solely or mainly based on past experience and is open to the same type of criticism.

Measurement of Future-Orientation and Self-Control

In psychological personality theories, personality traits or factors related to the concept of self-control are common. The Five-Factor model is the personality theory that has received the most attention in recent years. It includes a factor called 'conscientiousness', which seems to be close to self-control (see below in this chapter). The VSB Panel project included from the beginning a personality inventory developed by Brandstätter (1995). It's foundation is a five-factor model, based on Cattell's 16PF test. It is in the form of an adjective scale version that is easily administered. The test consists of 32 polarities of adjectives, two for each of the original 16 dimensions. The test was translated into Dutch for the purpose of the study. Some results from using the test to analyze saving behavior are reported in Wärneryd (1996a).

In the fourth wave of VSB Panel interviews, a Dutch inventory based on the Five-Factor model was used (Hendriks et al., 1995). It consists of 100 descriptive statements for which the respondent indicates on a five-point scale to what extent the statement is applicable to her or him. Each factor is represented by 20 items, half of which are positively phrased and half are negatively phrased. The statements are of the type: 'Likes to follow a regular schedule', 'Acts without planning'. Five personality dimensions are held to be fundamental. The five factors in the test are *extraversion*, *agreeableness*, *conscientiousness*, *emotional stability*, and *intellect*.

The fourth wave of the Panel project also included a scale for future-orientation (Daniel, 1997). The 11 items were of the following type: 'I think of how things might be in the future and try to influence those things with my day to day behavior', 'Often I engage in a particular behavior in order to achieve outcomes that may not result for many years', 'I only act to satisfy immediate concerns, figuring the future will take care of itself'.

Three possible roles for foresight were distinguished earlier in the chapter. The first is that foresight actually plays a minor role, not only for aggregate explanations, but also for individual explanations. Situational stimuli which, above all, include income changes — corresponding to ability to spend or save — are assumed to decide consumption. The second role involves foresight being strong enough to provoke behavior that provides for the future. The third possibility is that foresight in itself may not be enough, but there is a necessity for a link between cognition of future needs and provision for the future. Here the volitional factors such as self-control may serve.

The conscientiousness subscale was used in some analyses (Wärneryd, 2000a). Four subjective measures of saving behavior were used as dependent variables in a series of ordered-probit analyses. The measures that represented foresight (future-orientation) and self-control were significant and increased the explained variance of saving behavior. Income and wealth explained little. Although the psychological measures explained much less than the socio-economic variables, the results suggest that something can be gained by including this type of variable in the analysis. The scales used were rather abstract and did not include any direct references to economic behavior. Further analyses with three variables that specifically concerned control of economic behavior gave more significant relationships and considerably more explained variance.

The Behavioral Life-Cycle Hypothesis and Self-Control

The concept of self-control is one of the main features of the Behavioral Life-Cycle Hypothesis (BLCH) of Shefrin and Thaler (1988). In this respect, it is similar to many of the verbally formulated theories of classical and neoclassical economists. The authors included three elements in their discussion of self-control: (a) internal conflict, (b) temptation, and (c) willpower. The 'internal conflict' arises because of dual preference systems, one concerned with the long run and the other with the short run. The former is called 'the planner' and the latter is 'the doer'. The planner function in the model is essentially given the role of distributing income over the rest of the life cycle while the doer is assumed to be demanding immediate spending on consumption, that is, present enjoyment.

The authors of BLCH viewed 'temptation' as an absolutely necessary element and declared that models of saving without it were misspecified. The reason was simply that some situations, or rather opportunity sets, were more tempting than others and that this influenced saving. Experiments on delay of gratification clearly support the assumption of the importance of temptation. Children's willingness to wait for a more attractive reward decreases when only the less attractive reward is physically present (Mischel et al., 1992). Early economists like Rae (1834), Böhm-Bawerk (1888) and Marshall (1890) also had the insight that present goods are more vividly represented and tempting than future goods.

'Willpower' is said to represent the real psychic costs of resisting temptation. Exercising self-control is seen as connected with a cost. It takes some effort, sometimes a lot of effort, to postpone consumption. In this respect, the ideas are similar to those of the early political economists. The assumption makes it possible to express self-control as a behavioral cost, which can possibly be studied in the same way as other behavioral costs, experimentally through varying antecedent conditions, and through survey questions.

The authors also use 'framing' and 'mental accounting' to explain saving processes and savings. 'Framing' refers to how the individual describes an alternative to her/himself and chooses a reference point with which alternatives are compared. Wealth is framed into different 'mental accounts'. Money is assumed not to be completely fungible, which means that people distinguish between different kinds of money. The source of the money is assumed to have an influence on the propensity to consume it. A brief account of these ideas was given under the heading 'Mental Accounting' in Chapter 5.

While the BLCH in the first place attempts to explain the propensity to consume, and thereby saving, it also has implications for investments. Shefrin (2000), one of the originators, particularly stresses the role of self-control for retirement saving. An important part of self-control is to make sure that there will be money available for future needs. It may, for example, be tempting to maintain high liquidity of the assets at the expense of long-term returns. Shefrin says that people feel an urge to satisfy current needs, whereas they only think about the satisfaction of needs in the more distant future. Self-control always demands effort and imposes immediate costs on the person. It may take plenty of imagination to visualize the long-run benefits.

IMPATIENCE, TIME PREFERENCE, AND LACK OF SELF-CONTROL

It was a popular notion among classical economists that whereas some people were primarily engaged in the enjoyment of the present and cared little about the future, others were forward-looking and wanted to make sure of future enjoyment. They might indeed sacrifice present enjoyment to such an extent that life at the moment was unnecessarily poor. The first group had little self-control and were said to be impatient. Irving Fisher's (1930) book had the full title of: *The Theory of Interest. As Determined by IMPATIENCE to Spend Income and OPPORTUNITY to Invest It.* It was a thoroughly revised edition of a volume first published in 1907. The title hints that there is a clear difference between those who are impatient and spend immediately and those who are less impatient and invest.

Fisher (1930) explained impatience and proposed the alternative label of *time preference*, a concept that has been a firm anchor in economic and financial theory ever since. A major contribution was that Fisher developed ways of measuring impatience in economic matters. Time preference was simply estimated as the discount rate that a person used when comparing alternative future enjoyments at their present value. Fisher proposed a method for estimating impatience by asking individuals questions about how much they were willing to pay for future or postponed enjoyments. The methods today used to measure time preferences are still based on the same basic idea.

Impatience is assumed to be negatively correlated with saving behavior. There are research findings supporting this assumption, but the evidence is not overwhelming, maybe because the measures of impatience have turned out to be rather difficult to handle. Interpreted as time preference, impatience is usually measured through hypothetical choices, a method that has been questioned (see Wärneryd, 1999, for an overview). Impatient persons tend to save less according to Fisher (1930). He suggested that socio-demographic characteristics were important when explaining impatience. Low age, low education, and low income were such factors. In addition, personality differences influenced time preferences. It seems likely that speculators on stock exchanges have high rates of time preference, that is, they tend to use high discount rates in their choices of their investments. They are said to be greedy and to want to get rich quickly. Besides being impatient, they may be gamblers who value the gambling itself highly. As far as I know, no studies of impatience and investment behavior have been done.

Some studies of gambling involving lotteries have been reported. In a Norwegian study, 261 lottery winners (aged 18–87 years) of prizes of 1 million Norwegian kroner (US $120 000) or more in the years 1987–1991 were investigated through a postal survey (Eckblad and von der Lippe, 1994). The results indicated that the winners were very much like people in general, as should be the case if most of the population participate in lotteries and the prizes are randomly distributed. Interestingly, the winners seemed to live on quite unperturbed by their increased wealth. Emotional reactions to winning were few, aside from moderate happiness and relief. Winners emphasized caution, emotional control, and inconspicuous spending. A wish for anonymity was frequent, together with fear of envy from others. Betting was modest both before and after winning. Experiences after winning were predominantly positive, and life quality was stable or had improved. Older winners were more distinguished by a puritan subculture of caution, modesty, and emotional restraint. A slightly more impatient pattern of spending was characteristic of younger winners. The results support other findings that lottery winners are not gamblers, but may be realists with good self-control. Participation in Lotto and similar lotteries is widespread, but there are some sociodemographic and psychological differences between players and non-players (Wärneryd, 1996b).

Speculators and Speculation

Irving Fisher, an outstanding economist who contributed much to the understanding of saving and investment, became a rich man through hard work and profitable investments before the stock exchange crash in 1929. Then he lost everything and remained in debt for the rest of his life. In his 1930 book, he gives a warning to speculators:

> While savings unaided by luck will ultimately enrich the saver, the process is slow as compared with the rapid enrichment which comes from the good fortune of those who assume risks and then happen to guess right. Likewise, while millions of people lose their small properties by thriftlessness, the more rapid impoverishment comes from guessing wrong. This will often turn a rich man into a poor man within a few years and sometimes within a few days (Fisher, 1930, p.336).

As always, John Maynard Keynes (1936), who was a successful investor both for his college and for himself, provided some revealing insights about speculation: 'The game of professional investment is intolerably boring and overexacting to anyone who is entirely exempt from the gambling instinct; whilst he who has it must pay to this propensity the appropriate toll' (Keynes, 1936, p.157). Keynes believed in long-term investing, but recognized that some people had an urge to make money quickly and that those people tended to become losers. It may be noted in passing that George Katona, who was the first economic psychologist in the modern sense, was a successful investor who at his death left his university a legacy of considerable size.

Bloch (1999, p.550) defines speculation as 'simply buying at a low price in the hope of selling later at a higher one'. He concludes:

> Although, at their best, speculators serve a useful purpose in identifying gaps in the market and shortfalls in supply, all too often, their short-term profit orientation and the concomitant psychological scenarios mutate the process into one that distorts the market and leads to a protracted period of disequilibrium (Bloch, 1999, p.554).

Even if the typical investor in most stock markets, in particular in countries with widespread ownership of stocks, tends to be cautious and make few transactions, except maybe adding to the stocks, active traders and speculators are frequent and visible in financial markets. A Swedish study (Gunnarsson et al., 2000) arrived at a segment of 9 percent of the sample who were risk takers in their investments. It is likely that among those only a few were real speculators. It is naturally not easy to spot real speculators. In times of crashes, some unlucky speculators are usually brought to public attention through sensational bankruptcies while the successful ones remain invisible, except maybe to their friends and acquaintances.

It seems likely that with the increased spread of participation in the stock market, a smaller proportion of stock owners are speculators now than was the case right before the 1929 crash of the stock market. Galbraith (1954) calculated that in 1929 in the USA around one and a half million people had an active association of any sort with the stock market. This number was roughly 1 percent of the population (123 million). Galbraith estimated that approximately 600 000 and certainly less than one million of those stock holders were so-called *margin traders* who borrowed money to buy stocks and used the stocks as sole collateral. The rest were not speculators if it is assumed that those stock buyers who paid cash were not really active and speculating. Galbraith ([1954]1987, p.103) noted: 'The striking thing about the stock market speculation of 1929 was not the massiveness of the participation. Rather it was the way it became central to the culture'. Unfortunately, Galbraith did not make an estimate of how much of total stock value the speculators possessed, only of their number and relative frequency.

When stock prices plummet, those who have used stocks as collateral for loans are pressed by the brokerage firms and banks who through *margin calls* request these investors to pay off or provide more collateral. The speculator will have to sell securities or other assets unless s/he has cash. The abrupt selling activities may further reinforce the downward tendency and a crisis may develop. Stock market crashes make news media look for losing speculators, whereas those who speculated in a coming crash and did it at the right time may remain unnoticed by the public eye.

Some Further Thoughts on Emotional Reactions

'Affect has a pervasive influence on how we see the world' (Forgas, 1994, p.1). No one would deny that stock-price developments give rise to emotions, but all may not agree that emotions such as joy and fear may drive stock prices towards extremes, upwards or downwards. Expressions such as overreactions, overoptimism, pessimism, and gloominess in the stock market are more generally accepted and used as explanations. In this chapter, findings on over- and underreactions have been reviewed and the concepts which relate to the aggregate, the market level, have been examined. The labels put on reactions suggest that some kind of benchmark exists; over- and underreactions are judged against some norm, in financial economics normally the values expected on the basis of changes in earnings and dividends.

Overreaction in a bull market is often explained as investor optimism while overreaction in a bear market is explained as investor pessimism. Optimism in its turn is attributed to overconfidence, which is said to be due to self-attribution of earlier successes in the market place. An assumption is made that a causal chain exists from overconfidence and overoptimism to overreaction to good news and underreaction to bad news. If the causal chain exists it should, at least in principle, be possible to assess changes in earlier links in the chain and thereby to predict the reactions. A precondition is, of course, that (over)optimism and (over)confidence can be reliably assessed by means of independent measures that are not just an interpretation of stock-price data patterns.

Good objective indicators or proxies for overoptimism and overconfidence are mostly hard to find. The only attempts at finding such indicators usually involve content analysis of news or other media. Using the concept 'pessimistic rumination', Zullow (1991) tested media influence on consumer optimism or pessimism and on economic growth. He carried out content analyses of pessimistic themes in popular music and in *Time* magazine and found that there was a correlation with the Index of Consumer Sentiment (ICS) and the gross national product (GNP). Moreover, he traced a time sequence, with popular songs as the first step or indication of growing pessimism in the USA, followed by changes in the ICS and later the GNP.

Without approaching investors and collecting data directly from them, it is rarely possible to assess mood changes in investor segments. Of special interest are those who potentially influence the financial markets through leadership and/or through large transaction possibilities. Part of the game that constantly goes on in financial markets is probably that investors, especially fund managers and money managers, always are looking for signs that may indicate strong reinforcement of the trend or a trend reversal. When market leaders display signs of changing transaction policy, other investors tend to jump on board the train. The next chapter will have more to say on the topic of social influence.

7. Social Influence

Changes in market price are caused by changes in the consensus of active investors of what the price of a stock ought to be. This consensus is determined by thousands and thousands of institutions and individuals constantly seeking opportunities for investment profit. To find these opportunities, investors study monetary and fiscal economics and political developments in all major nation; visit hundreds and hundreds of companies; attend thousands of breakfast, lunch, and dinner meetings with corporate executives, economists, industry experts, securities analysts, and other experts; study reports and analyses produced in enormous volume by hundreds of companies and dozens of large brokerage firms; read extensively in the industry and trade press; and talk almost constantly on the telephone with people who have ideas, information, or insights with which these active investors might improve their investment performance.

Ellis (1993, p 37)

THE MANIFOLD INFLUENCES FROM OTHERS

Stock Markets as Arenas Where People Interact

Ellis (1993), a successful practitioner, suggests that stock prices are set in a process leading to consensus, which arises as a consequence of social interaction between people at the workplace and in almost any other conceivable social context. He intimates that the active investor is constantly open to impressions from the social environment. The psychologists Schachter et al. (1986) similarly call stock prices 'opinions' that like other opinions may change due to many factors, mostly having to do with influence from others. Stock markets are arenas where people interact with and influence one another.

Developments on the stock exchanges are not well explained by current financial theories, and the search for new explanatory factors has led to proposals of models of social phenomena, such as models based on information cascades and avalanches (see Chapter 1). The models are highly mechanical and pay little attention to the flexibility and variability of social behaviors. Most social influences and interactions are by definition incompatible with economic rationality and produce inefficiencies, at least viewed at the macro level. People's preferences and expectations are not independent when influenced by what others, often in the nearby environment, do and believe. Social interaction creates non-additivity, which disturbs the relationships between the micro- and the macro-level models by making aggregation difficult. Somehow, bull markets and bubbles as well as bear markets, bursts of bubbles, and crashes appear to have their origin in social influences. Social influence may mean to follow a market leader, to react simultaneously with other investors on identical information, or simply to imitate behavior, spurred directly by one's own observations or indirectly by mass media reports on what significant other people are doing. The mere presence of other people in a decision-making situation may decide which course of action is taken. The naive investor may not make the same investment decision in the presence of an expert as when s/he is in the company of a family member or friend.

Smith (1991, pp.886–7), who has carried out a large number of laboratory experiments with stock market simulation and constantly found 'bubbles', emphasizes the role of social interaction: 'On the basis of cognition alone, without the language of the market and ongoing social interaction with other agents, rational decision is frustratingly illusive' (Smith, 1991, p.894).

The purpose of the chapter is to review some ideas from social psychology on social influence in a broad sense. In my view, economists' use of social influence concepts has a tendency to be too mechanical and to overlook the importance of essential subjective judgments and emotional ties. Social psychology deals with how the individual or group is influenced by other people. From this heavily researched field some things can be learned so as to enrich the psychological perspective on investing behavior. It may be appropriate to start with an observation that has found much support from research: social influence is not only strongest when the individual feels uncertain and finds no directly applicable earlier experience of her/his own, but such situations may lead to an active search for some kind of *social support* and confirmation.

Social Influence and Critical Mass

In efficient markets, traders act on information that is public. If private information diverges from public information, it is a disturbance and social influence serves to suppress it. In mechanical economic models of information diffusion, social influence in the first stage means that investors do not act in accordance with what they privately know, presumably from their own experience. They do not reveal their views through trading in the market. They are persuaded to act as others do and refrain from listening to their own information up to a point when similar information suddenly becomes public and exerts pressure on all investors. The point at which the switch from private to public information occurs, can be compared to what in innovation studies is called *the critical mass* (see, for example, Wärneryd, 1994, pp.143–5). The acceptance of information is slow before the critical mass, a large enough group of proselytes, is reached. The number of people in the critical mass has to be large enough to convince investors that the cost–benefit of acting in accordance with the earlier private information changes from negative to positive for the investors in the system.

The information cascade models may explain certain events at the macro level, but they seem to miss important aspects of investor expectation formation and decision making which have been studied in diffusion of innovation research and which can add psychological substance to the models (see Rogers, 1983). Personal convictions about likely outcomes are in the economic models neglected in favor of mechanical imitation of other investors' behavior. It is true that mass behavior can occur as an explosion, but this is, after all, rare in financial markets. Social influence is much more and is more important than just mechanical imitation at a certain point in time. The manifold dimensions of social relations at the individual and the household level cannot be left out when explanations of ordinary investor behavior are being sought. They are also important for understanding the financial behavior of professional traders and financial managers.

Growth Stocks and Social Influence

> *. . . the belief that good stocks are stocks of good companies. . .*
>
> Shefrin and Statman (1994, p.324)

Stock prices are based on expectations and expectations of stock prices may for the wrong reasons remain stable over long periods of time or be prone to change abruptly. With little or no short-term change in fundamentals, social influence accounts for much of the abrupt changes as well as, in ocher periods, for maintaining stability. Past developments that have been highly favorable are extrapolated into the future and the expectations are shared and reinforced by many investors. They appear to be more based on what investors believe about other investors' reactions to fundamentals and their expectations with respect to other investors' expectations (cf. Keynes' notion of beauty contests, Keynes, 1936; see Chapter 3). As long as investors believe that other investors believe in growth stocks with extremely high p/e ratios, the stock prices will be high. Pyramid games, Ponzi schemes, and chain letters with money requests ultimately end with more losers than winners (as may stocks).

The prices of Internet firm stocks have reached enormous heights despite the fact that many of the companies that have been extremely successful on the stock exchange have not yielded any profits. Only in a very long-term perspective may the growth and earnings of the successful survivors live up to current expectations. Part of the explanation seems to lie in the fact that some firms like Microsoft, Cisco, and Nokia have been extremely successful in terms of sales volume and earnings. Investors have made enormous profits on such companies and information and rumors about their successes have spread in many ways. The so-called Nokia millionaires in Finland have received a lot of publicity. It is likely that they have stimulated purchases of Nokia stocks and perhaps other stocks both in their near environment and in wider circles through the fact that they have been written about in newspapers and have been interviewed on TV. Nobody interviews those who bought and sold at the wrong moment and lost money.

High-tech stock prices drove up stock price indexes to such heights in the year 2000 that beating them became increasingly difficult. Managers of funds, who often have the imposed goal of being at least as good as the index, may have been forced to buy growth stocks with little substance value. The index serves as a measure of other investors' performance (Hellman, 2000, pp.208f.) The same may have been true of private investors with high-set goals. Value stocks that have low p/e ratios and remain profitable over long periods of time perform less well than the stock-price index and are avoided, in particular by fund managers who are judged against the benchmark of the stock index. The fundamentals apparently play a minor role and return expectations are based on observations of other investors' reactions and guesses that are biased by preferred outcomes.

DIMENSIONS OF SOCIAL INFLUENCE

Types of Social Influence

Influence emanating from other people, often called *social influence*, can in financial affairs be of many types.

1. Small-group influence: direct contact person to person, between relatives and acquaintances as well as between client and (professional) advisor
2. Direct observation and interpretation of other people's behavior
3. Reports on behavior in news media: news and comments on stock-price changes, trading and transactions, reports and comments on investor behavior
4. Bandwagon effects: people feel compelled to conform to an attitude or opinion or action when it is perceived as being held or performed by a majority of people in a population segment or the whole country.

When making investment decisions, people may seem to be acting independently of others, but usually influence from other people can be noted. As said before, uncertain situations tend to generate search for advice and support from others. Social influence is largest in situations of uncertainty, when other people are assumed to possess some kind of knowledge that could be useful for arriving at the best decision. Festinger (1954) listed a number of reasons why such influence is likely to occur. People have an innate tendency to compare themselves with others. People try to evaluate their attitudes and capacity against those of other people as comparison objects, especially when there are no objective, non-social objects to compare with. The probability that a person compares her/himself with another person decreases with increasing difference between them with respect to the dimension involved.

Investors, like others, are enmeshed in personal relations that may be affected by investment decisions and the investor may feel a need to give adequate thought to such a possibility. The decisions may involve conflicting opinions in the family or impartial information and advice from colleagues. Two major types of influence from groups are: (a) information received from a person or group, and (b) norms that give rules for behavior. While the information that a group provides may be utilized or not without necessarily affecting a person's relationships to the group, adherence to the social norms of the group is mostly a sine qua non. Not following a person's advice may lead to troubled relations.

A different type of influence suffuses expectations about how the market will react to news, especially dramatic news. The expectations may be based on new information about trading and transactions, at first maybe in the shape of rumors. When the institutional investors in Hellman's Swedish study (2000) made their analyses and forecasts of company and industry future earnings, they were wondering how other investors would react to the same type of forecasts. Hellman relates how such considerations strongly affected an institutional investor's decision to buy or sell drug industry stocks.

Expectations may be formed on the basis of a single source, such as the investor's own interpretation of events or information from an outside source, or more than one source with agreeing or conflicting content. Several sources of information and influence may combine into one powerful scenario, for example, when the mass media dramatize developments in the stock market and thereby enhance the changes (see, for example, Andreassen, 1987, 1988). Many (small) investors, especially retired persons with plenty of time at their disposal, tend to follow closely developments of stock prices during the day (Müller-Peters, 1999). They are usually rather passive traders, maybe because they get conflicting information and fail to see clear trends.

Financial economists have noted that stock-price changes themselves are the primary source of information for some strategies and that investors react on such information. Whether information is private or public is, according to financial economists, an important aspect of stock market development. Common or public information is revealed through observable behavior, which means making transactions in the stock market, and the behavior is mirrored in stock prices. A more subtle question is whether the absence of trading – on the basis of public knowledge – reveals any public information.

Presumably, no change in the price of a stock communicates something, though not so distinctly as a change upwards or downwards.

A fourth type of influence which is of particular interest in the present context is what Leibenstein (1950) called the 'bandwagon effect'. It has to do with the power of sheer numbers. The fact that many people act in the same way puts pressure on other people to behave or act in the same manner. The more people who sell when stock prices plummet, the stronger the pressure is on others to sell and to ask for prices low enough to attract buyers who are willing to take the risk of not jumping on board the bandwagon. De Bondt and Forbes (1999) apply this group effect in finance:

> Bandwagon effects are plausible for several reasons, for example the homogeneity of the information signals received by the investment community; the similarity in interpretation of news items because of mental frames that are socially and professionally shared; incentive systems that encourage money managers to mimic each other's trades; and notions of prudence and fiduciary duty that depend on external validation (De Bondt and Forbes, 1999, p.146).

Social influence, social interaction and exchange, and group decision making are all areas in which *significant* others are concerned. It can be argued that most, if not all, behavior ultimately in some way depends on other people and that psychology which focuses on individual behavior takes the individuals out of their natural social habitats and studies them in artifactual isolation.

Social Learning

> *The [South Sea] Bubble was a time of hysteria, when all common sense, let alone rationality, was abandoned by the aggregate of investors. Isaac Newton, who lost £20,000 in his speculations on the company's stock, is reported to have said of the event, 'I can calculate the motions of the heavenly bodies, but not the madness of people' A conservative banker of the time, after resisting for years, finally subscribed to shares after they had risen from 100 to 500 pounds a share, with the comment, 'When the rest of the world are mad, we must imitate them in some measure.'*
>
> Schachter et al. (1986, pp. 247–8)

Social learning involves a person acquiring social behavior, that is, relations with other people, by copying the behavior of models whom s/he respects (Bandura, 1977). The learning occurs in three ways:

1. *Direct learning.* Economic behavior and other behaviors are learned because other people administer rewards and punishments that are directly related to the individual's actions.
2. *Indirect learning.* This is often called 'vicarious learning' since people learn social behavior from watching what other people are rewarded or punished for. Modern mass media seem to provide ample

opportunities for such vicarious learning among their audiences. Children may experience vicarious learning over wider fields than children used to do.

3. *Imitation.* An individual acquires new behavior and performs new acts after observing another individual's behavior.

It should be noted that in psychological laboratory experiments and in simple learning situations in real life the connections between the performance of certain acts and the ensuing consequences may be obvious and easily assessed. Real life, however, offers many situations with complex relations that have to be interpreted. Assessment of causal relations, in social psychology studied under the label of 'causal attributions', is a highly important aspect of social learning. All three forms of social learning are open to mistakes, without knowing it people may misinterpret the connections between rewards, punishments, and behavioral acts. Imitation, a concept that refers to behavior which apparently can be acquired independently of rewards, can be highly conscious as when a teenager mimics the behavior of a pop star. It can also be barely conscious as when somebody follows a stranger who crosses a street against a red light. Mechanical imitation plays an important role in economic theories of information cascades and herd behavior.

While social learning as defined above applies to the influence of others on individual behavior, the concept is used in a macropsychological sense by Katona (1975). He suggested a social learning process in which new attitudes and behavior patterns were learned and which as a rule developed slowly and serially due to interpersonal contacts. In some cases, a large number of people were reached at the same time by some important information which restructured their cognitive maps and made them react in the same way. What the mass media reported could have great influence on such social learning. The concept embodied the notion that behavior which was ordinarily characterized by habits and routines and was predictable, could suddenly and simultaneously change in large population segments following dramatic news that was inconsistent with current cognitive maps. Social learning in the last sense resembles the hypothesis of information cascades, but it lacks the gradual and serial character which is a component of many information cascade models.

Social Dependence

The degree to which a person is dependent on what other people think and do varies with a number of factors. The dependence seems to vary not only with the structure and character of the social environment, but also with the amount and direction of previous experience in the relevant field: Social influence presupposes uncertainty and diminished self-confidence:

> [O]ne should anticipate that in any domain, those who are successful are likely to pursue their individual idiosyncratic ways and, in that domain, will be relatively unaffected by outside opinions and events (Schachter et al., 1986, p.255).

> In any market, things change, new circumstances arise, unanticipated events occur. At such times. it may be necessary to form new opinions or reevaluate old ones. When such is the case, dependence should increase and tendencies arise to gather information, talk things over, attend to the actions of others, and so on (Schachter et al., 1986, pp.259–60).

The strength of the tendency will depend on the extent to which the circumstances change and how incorrect the former opinion was. According to Schachter et al.'s reasoning, dependence should increase in bear markets when many investors lose money and independence would increase in bull markets when investors make money and are satisfied with their performance. Causal attribution theory suggests that investors prefer to attribute successes in bull markets to themselves while they experience losses in bear markets as 'bad luck'. The authors formed the hypothesis that in bear markets there would be higher correlations between volume of trade and length of runs, which is a sign of dependence, than in bull markets. The hypothesis was tested on data from the New York Stock Exchange and was confirmed. They concluded that psychological factors like dependence could help explain when the stock exchange was a random walk and when it was not.

At the New York Stock Exchange, the period from 1952 to 1966 was characterized by upward-moving stock prices, making many investors rich. In the period from 1966 to 1980, the stock market was unstable and took many violent turns up and down. Schachter et al. (1986) assumed that many investors gained high self-confidence during the first period and would be less inclined to listen to other people and to react to important events. In the second period, they would have been more insecure and less self-confident, which was assumed to lead to more responsiveness to events. The authors looked at what happened at the New York Stock Exchange in the period before and the period after 1966 following elections and airline catastrophes. The hypothesis was that there would be more response after 1966. The results confirmed their hypothesis. Trading volume increased by on average 47 percent the first day after an election in the second period as against 9 percent in the first period. The effect on stock prices varied depending on the type of election, but during the second period significantly more variability in stock prices was noted. The results were similar for the effects of airline catastrophes; in this case the stocks investigated comprised only the airline and manufacturing companies involved. Niederhoffer (1971) also observed effects of airline catastrophes when the catastrophe led to big headlines in the New York Times (see Chapter 2).

It is interesting to note that Shiller (2000) like earlier Bikhchandani et al. (1992) challenge the psychological concept of conformity. They discuss

Asch's (1952) famous experiments showing that people in judging tasks were inclined to follow the example of others even when they had a feeling that the judgment was wrong. While this is referred to as conformity in social psychology texts, the economists prefer to see it as a matter of information; the subjects were informed about the judgments of the majority. In my view, conformity implies that the subjects may give conforming estimates without believing in the information. As said earlier, psychologists make a distinction between normative and informative functions when discussing group influence on individual group members. An individual may not like the information and still let it influence her/his behavior because s/he feels forced to by the norms. Labeling something as conformity means that the emphasis lies on the normative, value-transmitting function rather than on the pure transmission of information. Group pressure towards conformity can be so strong that people pay lip-service and make statements they do not believe in. In fact, the reactions and after-the-experiment comments of Asch's subjects clearly indicate that values and norm conformity were concerned.

It is possible to decrease the kind of social influence that Asch found. Hochbaum (1954) demonstrated that subjects who had been made to believe that they were very good at making certain kinds of judgments consistently resisted social influence and group pressure when their judgments were different from those of the group. Those subjects who had been made to believe that they were not very good at making such judgments had more difficulty resisting the group pressure and in a majority of cases conformed.

Influence of Group Structure and Communication with Others

In social groups, the interaction pattern and group influence on individual members naturally vary with the structure and communication lines of the group, which may also vary with member characteristics and the situation in which the group operates. Due to differences in personality traits and situational characteristics, people's responsiveness to group influence shows large variation. In stock-investing contexts, investment clubs are well-known examples of small groups where the personalities of members and their communication patterns play an essential role. Many other types of small groups may have an influence on investment decisions. The relation between financial advisor and client is a dyad and is in many respects similar to a small group with the same possibilities of agreement and clash. At places of work, informal groups with great influence on investing patterns may be formed and personal characteristics of the group members play a role in the discussions.

Here is an example of a study that reports on how group structure had an influence in a stock market experiment (Tuckman, 1964). Groups with three members participated in a stock market simulation over ten sessions. The task represents a simulation of the stock exchange where the teams buy and sell stocks in order to accumulate more profits than their competitors. Personality tests helped classify the members of the groups as *abstract*, that is, individuals who perceived a more multi-faceted world and who thought in terms of alternative interpretations and approaches, or *concrete* in their approach to problems, that is, characterized by low integration of impressions and simple and categorical information processing. It was hypothesized that more abstract individuals would adopt a group structure which was more flexible and open to diversity than homogeneous groups of concrete individuals. It was further expected that the abstract groups would display more environmental sensitivity, a more informational orientation, greater differentiation, and a more integrated strategy in dealing with the task than would concrete-oriented groups. Both hypotheses were confirmed by the data. While the work proceeded differently in the two sets of groups, with acceptance of diversity in the abstract groups and more hierarchical structure in the concrete groups, the performances of the abstract and concrete groups were not different. It was concluded that both abstract and concrete approaches could lead to the goal. The main finding was that a knowledge of the personalities of group members enabled one better to predict consequent work behaviors of the group (Tuckman, 1964).

Survey studies have shown that there is considerable social influence on individual investors and that communication with others is an important component in making investment decisions. Shiller and Pound (1989) wanted to study patterns of communication and sent questionnaires both to institutional and individual investors. The answers indicated that direct interpersonal communications were indeed important in investor decisions. The authors concluded that contagion of interest could be influential in investor behavior. Among individual investors, 28 percent in the random sample and 45 percent of those who had bought stocks that showed a rapid price increase indicated that they not only knew of someone else who had bought the stock, but were influenced by this fact in their own decision to buy the stock. The rapid-price-increase investors were more likely to have been influenced by friends and relatives and less by stockbrokers. Another interesting finding was that one-third of the institutional investors and more than 60 percent of the individual investors surveyed described themselves as unsystematic in their choice of stock.

The Social Relations of Stock-investment clubs

Stock-investment clubs are groups of people who together plan and decide on investments of their jointly contributed means. The advantages of such clubs are: (1) better possibilities of diversification, that is, spreading of risks through portfolios with more categories of stocks than when each member acts on her/his own, (2) joint expertise, that is, someone usually knows a little more about the stock market and may educate and inform the others, and (3) the group helps sustain the interest in stocks and provides the opportunity of stimulating interaction. Possible disadvantages are that conflicts may impair performance and members may for various reasons want to leave the club, which causes problems of dividing the resources, in particular after losses. Studies of what happens in small groups suggest that there may arise tensions and other disturbances that inhibit the performance of the group (see Levine and Moreland, 1990, pp.605–12; Guzzo and Dickson, 1996) If one member, for example, is more of an expert, her/his influence may become unduly strong and prevent the others from contributing their own judgments and valuations. In groups that are highly valued by all of their members, there is a strong tendency to avoid conflict and agreement may be reached after pointless discussion.

Stock-investment clubs may be highly different in the ways they invest their assets and their results vary considerably. US studies have found that they rarely beat the index and, in Statman's (1999) terms, they tend to be more value-expressive than utilitarian in their investments. Barber and Odean (2000a) used account data from a large discount brokerage firm for six years to investigate the performance of 66 investment clubs. They found that the average club tilted its common stock investment toward high-beta, small firms, that is, growth stocks, and turned over 65 percent of its portfolio annually. The average club lagged the performance of a broad-based market index and earned an annualized geometric mean return of 14.1 percent, while a market index returned 17.9 percent. In addition, 60 percent of the clubs analyzed underperformed the index. (Barber and Odean, 2000a).

It should be noted that samples of accounts from a discount brokerage firm may not be representative of the population of investment clubs. The performance of the investment club is compared with that of the market portfolio or index, which may not be justifiable. Theoretically more correct, but more difficult to materialize, is a comparison with what the members would achieve in terms of gains when acting individually.

Statman (1999, p.26) remarks that 'perhaps investment clubs are mainly social clubs, whose members care about the value-expressive features of investing more than they care about the utilitarian features of risk and returns'. Shiller (2000, p.58) describes investment clubs in the following way: 'small social groups, typically meeting at members' homes in the evening, that together invest small sums of money for fun and for the purpose of learning about investments'.

When Does It Pay to Cooperate?

Working in groups may not always improve performance. Group members may affect one another in ways that worsen individual performance. For one thing, there may be a bystander or social loafing effect, meaning that a person does not do her/his best because there are so many others who work. Latané (1981) studied the influence of the real, implied, or imagined presence of other individuals on people's physiological states, subjective feelings, cognitions, values, and behavior – the so-called *social impact*. A proposed theory of social impact is based on a principle called the Psychosocial Law, which is modeled on the marginally decreasing utility of money; the first other person in a social force field is ascribed greater impact than the hundredth. The Psychosocial Law is defined as

$$I = sN^{t}, t \leq 1$$

and for inhibiting social impact

$$I = sN^{-t}, t \leq 1$$

'When people are in a multiplicative force field, the amount of social impact, *I*, they experience, will equal some power, *t*, of the number of sources, *N*, times a scaling constant, *s*. Further, the value of exponent *t* should be less than one. Impact will increase in proportion to some root of the number of people present. . . . Thus, I suggest, there is a marginally decreasing effect of increased supplies of people as well as of money' (Latané, 1981, p.344).

The inhibition or division of social impact occurs when the tendency to do something is inversely proportional to the number of people involved. An example is the disinclination of bystanders to help in an emergency, a disinclination that grows with an increasing number present. Latané (1981) reports on a study in which the amount of tipping per person in a restaurant was investigated and found to be an inverse power function with an exponent of about 0.2. Individuals dining alone tipped almost 19 percent, while groups of five to six people tipped less than 13 percent. One of the areas of application suggested by Latané is the free-rider or social-loafing problem where individuals restrict their inputs to a common task when the number of contributors increases (cf Stroebe and Frey, 1982).

If the social-loafing effect obtains in investment clubs as Latané's theory suggests may happen, the results may no doubt be worse than if each member acted on her/his own. The positive effect of social loafing, if any, is that it may save energy, at least for some members, and that the blame for mistakes and failures to act can be shared with others. There is in social-loafing theory an intimation that investors may spare some mental and physical effort when they feel they are in good company and invest with less consideration of possible negative outcomes.

Although Ekman's (1955) work on the psychology of cooperation does not qualify as a group study in the strict sense, it does suggest an approach to the study of groups that is highly fruitful. For some reason, this work has not set the example for emulation that it in my view deserves. Ekman theoretically deduced four possible effects of cooperation. The *individual*, *summa-*

tion, *average*, and *probability* effects of cooperation are described and experimental demonstrations given of each of them. In a series of simple experiments, theoretical predictions were compared with the experimental values. The agreement between the two was unusually good.

The *individual effect* relates to how individual performance is influenced by the cooperating situation. The effect can be facilitating, deteriorating, or none at all. The *summation effect* sets in when the cooperation is of a nature such that the individual performances can be added to one another, with the resulting collective performance representing the sum total of individual performances. In some cases of cooperation, the collective performance amounts to a compromise between the individual performances, and individual mistakes can cancel out. Such an *average* or *compensation effect* comes into play when several persons take part in ratings so as to make these more accurate. The *probability effect* is a function of the number of those cooperating. It sets in when a collective problem is solved as soon as one of the participants has completed a certain performance. Part of the effect may be that when a solution is proposed, the proposal is more likely to be identified as a suitable solution when more people are around to identify it.

Let us assume that there are three types of problems that groups can tackle. The simplest case is the production of something concrete. Obviously, there can be an individual effect due to the fact that it is pleasant to work together or, in other cases, group members may feel that it is unpleasant and restrict their output. It is usually possible to add the contributions of all members of the group and get a summation effect: two people accomplish more than one. The average effect involves the idea that if some members of the group contribute less than the others, the loss may be compensated for by the superior contribution of others. The average performance tends to be better than the performances of half the group members. The probability effect is perhaps less common in group production unless it is a question of being first to reach a production goal. Then the number of people working counts.

In the second type of problem, there is problem solving where a correct solution exists. As soon as somebody has found the solution, the task of the group is over. The more people who are searching for the solution, the higher is the likelihood that it will be found – a pure probability effect. If the group members have different ability and some members compensate for gaps in other group members' knowledge and skill, the solution may be reached earlier – an average effect. And there can under some circumstances be summation effects when solutions are being built up successively.

In the third type of problem, no correct solution exists. Any solution has to be evaluated and accepted by general consensus. All four effects may obtain. Individual motivation may increase through the social facilitation effect. In some cases, groups can also prevent progress towards a solution that is acceptable to all. If group members are very much alike, agreement about a solution may be easier to reach than if they are different. An average effect may be more likely, however, than a summation effect. With a number of members rather than a single individual working, the likelihood of bright ideas for achieving a good result may increase.

Applied to financial behavior, the individual effect encompasses the fact that being in the company of one or more persons may stimulate performance, so-called social facilitation. Depending on the relations between the people, the effect may be positive or negative; some people are inhibited in the presence of certain others. The presence of an advisor or an expert may inhibit the otherwise satisfactory performance of a private investor out of respect for the presumed expertise. The fourth, the probability effect, may be important in finance for those who are looking for worthy investments. The greater the number of people who are searching, the more likely the success.

The No-Business Meeting

Groups have functions that are rarely discussed by social psychologists, maybe because they cannot easily be studied in interview surveys and controlled experiments. While group researchers have delineated work and social dimensions in group contexts, they have paid little attention to the fact that in real life the main function of a group or social gathering can be to give the impression of action or defer a difficult decision rather than to accomplish any task solution or work product. Discussing what was and was not done to alleviate the 1929 stock market crash, Galbraith ([1954]1987) says that there are many reasons for meetings to transact no business:

> Meetings are held because men seek companionship or, at a minimum, wish to escape the tedium of solitary duties. They yearn for the prestige which accrues to the man who presides over meetings, and this leads them to convoke assemblages over which they can preside. Finally, there is the meeting which is called not because there is business to be done, but because it is necessary to create the impression that business is being done. Such meetings are more than a substitute for action. They are widely regarded as action (Galbraith, [1954]1987, pp.158–9).

Galbraith implies that investors had a right to expect real actions and that they should not have let themselves be seduced by meetings that substituted for action. To my knowledge, no studies of this hypothesis have been carried out systematically, but it is supported by studies of organizational behavior and public relations. In crisis situations when unpleasant decisions are called for, companies as well as governments and government bodies seem to call meetings whose main function is to mimic action.

Another little-studied group influence problem should be mentioned. In an experimental game, Camerer and Lovallo (1999) observed what they called *reference group neglect*. It referred to the tendency to underadjust to changes in the reference group one *competes* with. The reference group neglect is said to be a byproduct of a psychological phenomenon called the 'inside view' (Kahneman and Lovallo, 1993). An inside view forecast focuses on the abilities and resources of the group itself, constructing scenarios of future progress, and extrapolating current trends. An 'outside view' ignores special details of the case at hand, constructs a class of cases similar to the current one, and guesses where the current case lies in that class. While the inside view tells a colorful story, the outside view relies on statistics. In the former, there is no special role for anticipation of the number of competitors or their abilities. In the outside view, the fact that many initial public offerings (IPOs) are issued at the same time cannot be ignored.

HERD BEHAVIOR

> *In considering lessons from psychology, it must be noted that many popular accounts of the psychology of investing are simply not credible. Investors are said to be euphoric or frenzied during booms or panic-stricken during market crashes. In both booms and crashes, investors are described as blindly following the herd like so many sheep, with no minds of their own. Belief in the rationality of markets starts to sound a lot better when the only alternatives are such pop-psychological theories.*
>
> Shiller (2000, pp.135–6)

Shiller (2000) makes a very good point in the vignette above and he utilizes good psychological research in his own discussion of psychological factors influencing financial behavior. Economists have sometimes provided examples of bad psychology being turned into good mathematics and thus made acceptable to mainstream economic thinking. Herd behavior has become a popular notion about stock markets, not always for good reasons.

Keynes drew attention to the possibility that money managers were affected by what they thought that other money managers would think of them and that they were inclined to play safe in this regard: 'Worldly wisdom teaches that it is better for reputation to fail conventionally than to succeed unconventionally' (Keynes, 1936, p.158). The essential meaning of herd behavior is that investors tend to do as other investors do, at least if they are exposed to information about others' behavior. They imitate behavior and, in the typical terms of economists, disregard their own information or private signals, which for some investors are supposedly contrary to the current information from others. The conflict is resolved at a point in time when public information abruptly changes so that it agrees with the private information, presumably when a critical mass of investors possesses the conflicting information and a trigger of some kind starts the run in the new direction. The search for explanations of abrupt changes, usually involving dramatic drops in stock prices, lies behind the label of herd behavior. The question is: how can mass reactions start and develop into panic or crashes? The assumption made by economists is that at some point someone makes a wrong decision and this action is copied by others who follow in a sequence (see, for example, Banerjee, 1992). Different authors have launched somewhat different assumptions about the process.

Classical sociologists and social psychologists were long preoccupied with what sometimes made crowds turn into furious masses or mobs that behaved like today's soccer hooligans, abusing people and ravaging everything close to them. Leadership and suggestibility became two important elements in the debate of crowd behavior (see, for example, Ogburn and Nimkoff, 1950). It took someone to start the (mis)behavior and a flock of followers who were suggestible and could be provoked. Mob behavior was different from the kind of panic that could break out if somebody cried 'fire' in a theatre. The trigger of crowd misbehavior is an overt or covert signal from the leader. The fact that others act blindly in the same way serves as an excuse for otherwise illicit behavior and exonerates each individual in her/his own view. While genuine crowd behavior and mass panic after a warning of approaching disaster are different in many ways, they are similar in that leadership and suggestibility are important factors in triggering and sustaining mass behavior with little thought and deliberation.

Before herd behavior is discussed in more detail, a few things should be noted about emotional reactions in the world of finance. First, herd behavior may be a simultaneous reaction to common stimuli rather than a chain reaction as pictured by some economic writers. Second, in finance, concepts like 'frenzy' and 'panic' are labels put on observable phenomena at the market level and may find little or no corresponding individual behavior. The labels describe what happens at one or more stock exchanges in terms of price developments and sales volumes. Plummeting prices and large sales volumes may be a sign of panic, but plummeting prices and few if any buyers may be even worse. At best, the concepts may be interpreted as macropsychological concepts, with or without anchoring in individual psychology. Used by macroeconomists, such concepts usually lead to a search for a plausible micro model as part of the game.

Third, even if many people react in the same manner, not everyone in the potential mass does. For one thing, there are no sales of stocks without buyers of the same quantity. Reactions to cries of fire do include entering one's home to save certain things, actions that may be caused by loss aversion that is strong enough to lead to high risk-taking. Some people, probably a majority of stock owners, are loss averse and hold on to their stocks, at least up to a limit.

Fourth, it is debated in psychology to what extent there can be an affective reaction that precedes cognitive evaluation of a (strong) stimulus. The question is whether an affective reaction can precede and rule out cognitive evaluation altogether or delay it. If there is a primary affective reaction, people may be much more ruled by emotions than is generally assumed in rationality discussions.

Zajonc (1980) maintains that there is a primary affective reaction that evaluates the stimulus as good or bad before the stimulus is cognitively checked. He rejected the idea of most contemporary theories that affect was post-cognitive, that it occurred only after considerable cognitive operations had been accomplished. He cited a number of experimental results on preferences, attitudes, impression formation, and decision making, as well as some clinical phenomena, which all suggested that affective judgments might be fairly independent of, and precede in time, the perceptual and cognitive operations commonly assumed to be the basis of these affective judgments.

Affective reactions to stimuli are often the very first reactions of the organism, and for lower organisms they are the dominant reactions according to Zajonc. Affective reactions can occur without extensive perceptual and cognitive encoding, are made with greater confidence than cognitive judgments, and can be made sooner. Experimental evidence demonstrates that reliable affective discriminations (like/dislike ratings) can be made in the total absence of recognition memory (old/new judgments). Zajonc points out differences between judgments based on affect and those based on perceptual and cognitive processes. He concludes that affect and cognition are under the control of separate and partially independent systems that can influence each other in a variety of ways, and that both constitute independent sources of effects in information processing.

One of the chief opponents of Zajonc's position, Lazarus (1984), argues that thought is a necessary condition of emotion. He suggests that Zajonc's reasoning reflects two widespread misunderstandings about what is meant by cognitive processes in emotion: (a) that a cognitive appraisal of the significance of an encounter for one's well-being must occur in fixed stages through the information processing of initially meaningless inputs from the environment, and (b) that such an appraisal is necessarily deliberate, rational, and conscious. These common assumptions do not give the whole truth and should be relaxed.

If the common assumptions are weakened as Lazarus suggests, the differences between Zajonc and Lazarus diminish, and the fact remains that some reactions that may be important for our survival may be guided by primary affects and little or no deliberation. This may be true for certain reactions following events in the stock market. A strongly threatening stimulus leads to attempts to distance oneself as quickly as possible without really thinking until it is too late. The economist discussion of herd behavior is reminiscent of primary affective reactions without conscious evaluation.

Citing Keynes, Scharfstein and Stein (1990) propounded a model that was based on the risk to a manager if s/he acted in a way that was contrary to other managers' behavior. The model was in the first place aimed at herd behavior in the area of corporate investment, but the authors suggested that it could at least partially explain excessive stock market volatility. They noted: 'By mimicking the behavior of others (that is buying when others are buying, and selling when others are selling) rather than responding to their private information, members of a herd will tend to amplify exogenous stock price shocks' (Scharfstein and Stein, 1990, p.477). The general assumption behind the authors' concept of herd behavior is that it is rational for decision makers to try to enhance their reputation as decision makers by making decisions similar to those of other decision makers: 'correlated prediction errors lead to the "sharing-the-blame effect" that drives managers to herd'. The authors remarked that their model concerned professional money managers who cared about their reputation rather than private investors. The latter may have a similar wish to share the blame (see below on Causal Attribution Theory).

Some other economists have advanced models of mass movements that are based on imitation without further consideration. The economic models are known as *informational cascades* models and they deal with some consequences of sequential decision making. Lee's (1998) model was presented in Chapter 1 and briefly commented on in Chapter 2. In Banerjee's (1992) model, each decision maker looks at the decisions or actions made by previous decision makers or actors. 'This is rational because these other decision makers may have some information that is important for her' (Banerjee, 1992, p.797). Banerjee then proceeds with the assumption that people will do what others are doing rather than use their own information. The use of the private information is triggered through a kind of leadership. If person A has an opinion which deviates from what all other people have and demonstrates this opinion through an action, say, selling all her/his stocks, and this is observed by the person next to make a decision, the second person will follow the example despite having a different opinion. And so will all later decision makers in the sequence. The assumption that actions are triggered by the observation that one person does not act in consonance with public information, but in line with private information, raises the question as to why this person dares to deviate.

Bikhchandani et al. (1992, p.993) pose the question of why mass behavior is 'often fragile in the sense that small shocks can frequently lead to large shifts in behavior'. Their answer is that individuals rapidly converge on one course of action on the basis of some, but very little, information suggesting that a different course of action is optimal or that underlying circumstances have changed, whether or not they really have. Their model is founded on informational cascades and the authors claim that it explains not only conformity, but also rapid and short-lived fluctuations such as fads, fashions, booms, and crashes. 'An informational cascade occurs when it is optimal for an individual, having observed the actions of those ahead of him, to follow the behavior of the preceding individual without regard to his own information' (Bikhchandani et al., 1992, p.994). The authors do not explain why the individual suddenly abandons her/his own information and heeds the information from other persons' actions when the observed action goes against previous public information. One possibility that has been hinted at is that this decreases decision costs. Another that is adopted by the authors is that 'actions speak louder than words', a saying which they interpret as meaning that the information conveyed by observable actions may be more credible than the information in current stock prices.

The last two models of mass behavior or informational cascades leading to crises in financial markets remind us of psychological studies of jaywalking against a red light under varying conditions. The idea behind these studies was to observe how people reacted when they saw somebody cross the street against a red light. One person's misbehavior is observed by other people who imitate or do not imitate the behavior. Under what circumstances are people more likely to imitate? Among the interesting findings on jaywalking was that people were more likely to follow a high-status person than a poorly dressed person across the street against a red light (Russell et al., 1976). The hypothesis was that higher status models were less likely than lower status models to incur penalties and they were hence more informative. The characteristics of the person who makes the first move appears to be important for those who decide to follow or not to follow the example.

Shiller (1995), who in earlier works launched the idea that fads and fashions governed behavior in financial markets, criticized the informational cascades models in which people acquire information by observing actions of others. He rejects the idea that there is a first mover whose example others follow without considering their own information. He notes that people who interact with one another regularly tend to think and behave similarly. For understanding herd behavior, it is helpful to consider theories of information, theories that represent each group as reacting to an information set common to that group. Shiller's recommended approach is to study the mechanisms of transmittal of information within groups, using the 'conversation analysis' of anthropologists and the studies of 'socio-cognition' of social psychologists.

Herd behavior was found by Olsen (1996), who concluded that experts' earnings predictions exhibited disappointing accuracy and positive bias due to a desire for consensus. In the study by De Bondt and Forbes (1999) already mentioned, the authors investigated forecasts of security prices made and published by professionals in the UK. The authors, who saw herding behavior as a possible explanation of financial analyst behavior, discuss several meanings of herding and suggest factors that influence herding. Possible herding mechanisms include: (1) the basic human need to create a meaningful self-image, (2) the salience of shared mental frames in ambiguous decision situations, (3) payoff externalities in information acquisition, and (4) informational cascades. In the study, herding was defined as 'excessive agreement among analyst predictions'. The authors found that there was dependence among the forecasts made by different professionals and they interpreted the result as providing support for their hypothesis that there was herd behavior among professionals and that they watched one another.

> Two results stand out. First, as the forecast horizon lengthens, the accuracy of the EPS [earnings per share] forecasts deteriorates sharply but analyst consensus is unaffected and remains strong. It appears that any individual analyst can improve his relative standing by being less optimistic. This does not happen. To the contrary, increased disagreement is, on average, associated with more optimism. Second, as more analysts produce forecasts, disagreement rises, but only up to a point. Once we have 8 predictions, additional forecasts do not add to the forecast dispersion . . . [A]mong practitioners it is widely accepted that that there are sheep and shepherds, analysts who are 'followers' and analysts who are 'opinion leaders' (De Bondt and Forbes, 1999, p.161).

It seems likely that all the analysts used much the same data and methods of analysis. They may not have added what Batchelor and Dua (1990a) found to be characteristic of the most successful predictions, namely a distinctly subjective ingredient. The behavior of forecasters is apparently explained by regret theory. Avoiding regret may be an important influence for the private investor as well (cf. achievement motivation). This includes keeping up appearances in front of family, friends, and colleagues.

SUBJECTIVE ANALYSIS OF CAUSES: CAUSAL ATTRIBUTION THEORY

The behavior of other people is often of great interest to a person, even though s/he may not be directly affected by it. It is natural that people seek explanations for the behavior of others so that they get a feeling of understanding why a certain behavior occurred, a feeling of being able to adapt better to the social world, and maybe even to attain increased control over some of it. 'In common-sense psychology (as in scientific psychology), the result of an action is felt to depend on two sets of conditions, namely factors within the person and factors within the environment' (Heider, 1958, p.82). When looking for causes that can explain a person's behavior, for example, that A has enjoyed the viewing of a certain movie, another person P may find it useful to know whether the enjoyment was a consequence of factors within the individual (A is perhaps easily pleased) or of factors relating to the quality of the movie. To Heider (1958), the founder of attribution theory, the important question concerned what made a person attribute effects to objects or events in the environment and what made her or him attribute effects to acts and dispositions of the person involved. Only in the latter case could there be talk about intentional acts and motives and blame or credit. Interpersonal relations clearly depend on how each person interprets the other's behavior.

There seem to be characteristic ways of making causal attributions regarding individuals. In some cases environmental attributions dominate; in other situations attributions referring to the individual are most frequent. 'The fundamental attribution error' mentioned in Chapter 3 is a label used to denote a human tendency to overattribute other people's behavior to personal dispositions while overlooking situational causes or transient environmental influences on behavior (Nisbett et al. 1992, p.448). Kelley (1967) has formulated some general criteria for what guides causal attributions. An attribution to an object (an entity) can be explained by the degree of covariation between the effect and the following four criteria:

1. whether there is *distinctiveness*, that is, other entities fail to elicit the response, the effect is only there when the object is there,
2. whether there is *consistency over time* and the entity always elicits the response,
3. whether there is *consensus* and other people make the same attribution or make the same response to the entity, and
4. whether there is *consistency over sense modalities* and the same response is elicited under varying interactions between the actor and the entity.

In the example given above, the observer P would attribute A's enjoyment of the movie to the properties of the movie: (a) if A usually did not like movies (high distinctiveness), (b) A saw the movie more than once (consistency over time), (c) critics praised the movie (consensus), and (d) the company varied (consistency over interactions). A's enjoyment of the movie would be attributed to personal dispositions if there were low distinctiveness, low consensus, and high consistency. In general, low consistency seems to favor situational attributions. In the world of finance, successful acting by a group of professionals is more likely to be attributed to personal qualifications than to general upturns. If they fail, it must be a consequence of an unfavorable environment since they are professionals. Such attributions, if made by clients and the general public, may secure the survival of mediocre fund and money managers.

Attribution theory also treats how people make causal attributions of effects relating to themselves. They may find reasons for their behavior or for outcomes of their behavior in their own dispositions or in environmental factors. The theory has inspired a large amount of research (reviews are made by Kelley and Michela, 1980; Crittenden, 1983; Harvey and Weary, 1984). Of special interest are effects that can be construed as successes or failures.

Attribution of Success and Failure

Even though a rising market 'lifts all boats', there is still a tendency for investors to interpret their investing success as confirmation of their own abilities, and this reinforces their interest in trading stocks.

Shiller (2000, p.59)

The attributors' goal in seeking causality is to become better able to manage themselves and their environment effectively (Kelley, 1973). It can be held that social adaptation is not possible without causal analysis: 'The warrior needs to know why he is winning battles so he can survive the next one, just as the union representative needs to explain why the industry is doing poorly in order to urge wiser actions in the future' (Weiner, l985, p.549). Much recent research interest has been devoted to how the causes of success and failure in achievement-oriented situations are attributed.

Perceived causes, however wrong, lead to expectations regarding future events. If a person analyzes his or her performance and interprets successes and failures as due to external circumstances rather than personal factors such as competence, the expectations of future performance will be founded on how these circumstances are expected to develop. If the causes are perceived as pertaining to the individual her/himself, .strategies for the future become quite different and may involve personal development.

Weiner (1985) and his colleagues have conducted a long series of studies on attributions of success and failure in achievement-oriented situations and explored the consequences in terms of feelings, self-evaluations, and social behavior. Weiner (1974) has systematized the perceived causes reported by his subjects into four categories, based on two two-valued dimensions: stability (stable, unstable) and locus of control (internal, external). Table 7.1 displays the categories used.

Table 7.1 Attributions of Causality

Stability	Internal Locus of Control	External Locus of Control
Stable	ability, skill	task difficulty
Unstable	effort	luck

When a person notices that another person is successful, s/he can attribute this to skill or ability if it is a stable phenomenon and the success is something that differentiates the person from other people. This is an internal attribution. If many people constantly succeed, the task is seen as simple, which is an external attribution. If the success occurs once and can be achieved only by a few, it will be attributed to effort on the part of the successful person which is an unstable, internal cause.

The four categories of perceived causes, based on stability and locus of control, have proved to be useful, but they leave out some significant aspects (Weiner, 1985). Ability can be unstable if there is learning; effort can be seen as a stable characteristic of some people who are considered constantly industrious; and some people are thought of as being lucky (or unlucky) as a stable characteristic. *Controllability* has thus been added as a third dimension to take care of some of the earlier inadequacies. Some internal causes are perceived to be controllable and the individual can develop strategies to cope with them. In the same way, certain external factors may be controllable, while others cannot be influenced.

In a study of consumer reactions to product failures, it was found that when product failures were attributed to stable factors such as the company having a poor reputation, consumers anticipated similar dissatisfaction in the future and demanded a cash refund. If the product failure was perceived as due to unstable causes, such as the occasional substandard shipment of goods, consumers expected full product satisfaction in the future and willingly accepted a product exchange (Folkes, 1984).

Typically, attributions are subject to four kinds of bias (Kelley, 1967; Crittenden, 1983; Harvey and Weary, 1984).

1. Observers have a tendency to underestimate the influence of situational factors on behavior and overestimate the impact of personal, dispositional factors.
2. The observer is prone to see his or her own behavior as normal and appropriate, and a different, unexpected response by somebody is thus attributed to the actor's personal disposition.
3. Affective consequences for the perceiver may bias the attribution; the actor-observer may have an ego-enhancing or ego-protective tendency to take credit for success but to attribute failure to external factors; attributions of causes with respect to one's own behavior tend to be more internal, more variable and more complex than attributions made for causes of other people's behavior.
4. A perceiver may have many illusions about causality, for example, about freedom of action and possibilities of control.

In behavioral finance, self-attribution of success is often viewed as the single or main cause of overoptimism. Psychological research on how people attribute successes to their own ability and skill supports the hypothesis. It should be investigated also in finance where, to my knowledge, no empirical studies have been conducted. German survey data suggest that people readily accept credit for successful stock investing (see Müller-Peters, 1999). Other aspects of attribution theory also deserve research attention. For example, if most investors are successful in bull markets, the task of investing in stocks may be seen as easy, even so easy that there is little credit in being successful. The achievement-motivated investor may start looking for niches where it is more difficult to have success and therefore more glory can be attained through success. If investing in stocks is seen as an easy road to success, novices in large numbers may be attracted. The way other people's successes and failures are attributed to causes is important for the developments of stock markets.

In sum, research in social psychology gives support to Keynes's and other economists' intuition that sharing the blame may be an impetus to action. Attribution theory suggests that the sharing-the-blame effect is not the only possible assessment of successes and failures and that people may judge themselves according to another schema than they use to judge others. A well-known fact is that people tend to use more elaborate explanations for their own actions than they do for the actions of others. The upshot of this is that some doubts arise as to what learning from experience actually means.

RUMOR IN THE STOCK MARKET

> *Since the future is always a puzzle, and perhaps especially so to those who frequently call upon themselves to make predictions concerning a very small segment of life, those who buy and sell stocks welcome any information which will aid in the formation of their predictions. Rumor may furnish some of this information.*
>
> Rose (1951, p.462)

Rumor is not a possible influence in an efficient market since all investors get the news about fundamentals at the same time and immediately react. If rumors have effects, those may be hard to reconcile with the theory, in particular with the following definition of rumor: 'Rumor, by definition, passes from person to person and so could not reach all persons simultaneously' (Rose, 1951, p.470). Basing themselves on earlier authors, DiFonzo and Bordia (1997) comment on three dimensions that characterize rumor. It is information that (a) is not verified, (b) is of local or current interest or importance, and (c) is intended primarily for belief. Rumors are nowadays often transmitted through mass media and may reach large audiences at the same time.

Rumor is known to be an important factor influencing stock prices. What is the difference between news and rumor? It may be essential to know and, if possible, set up criteria for judging the truthfulness of a rumor. A true rumor is news that for some reason comes out prematurely (Rose, 1951). News, for example about a scientific discovery may start a deluge of rumors that are eagerly transmitted by both persons and the mass media. The effects may be good for those who react in the right way. False rumors may be positive for some, but have highly detrimental effects for others. 'Because rumor treads a thin line between reality and illusion, deciding in a given situation whether an item of communication constitutes a rumor would depend on the context in which it was situated' (Rosnow, 1991, p.485). Rumors are more easily accepted in situations that are characterized by uncertainty, lack of personal experience, and emotion. 'Rumors flourish in an atmosphere of uncertainty because they attempt to relieve the tension of cognitive unclarity' (Rosnow, 1991, p.486).

Three steps in the transmission of rumors are studied: (1) generation, (b) spreading or transmission, and (3) effects on beliefs. Rumors are generated as people attempt to make sense of ambiguous, uncertain, or confusing situations (DiFonzo and Bordia, 1997). It should be added that rumors may be generated and spread with wily intent. Shibutani (1966) called rumors 'improvised news' and said that rumors were generated when there was no information available from regular channels. Rumors are transmitted for various reasons, such as wanting to share beliefs or liking the idea of being seen as knowledgeable. The effects are on beliefs and may lead to changes in behavior. Rumors may spread rapidly in large groups and produce surprising effects.

Psychological studies that are now considered classical devoted interest to how rumors were affected under the transmitting process. Three types of changes of the original messages were found: (a) leveling, (b) sharpening, and (c) assimilation (Allport and Postman, 1952). *Leveling* refers to the fact that, as rumor travels, it tends to grow shorter, more concise, more easily grasped and told. What is left after leveling is inevitably clearer and more focused after many details have dropped out. This is the *sharpening* function. *Assimilation* has to do with the force exerted by the recipients' habits, interests, and sentiments. It may mean that preconceived notions and strong preferences contribute to shaping the rumor. The process may turn a simple guess about a company's plans into a known fact for profit-seeking investors.

Rosnow (1991), who includes personal factors such as outcome involvement, personal anxiety, and credulity in his model of rumor, distinguishes between *wish rumors* and *dread rumors*. The former invoke hoped-for consequences, the latter invoke feared or at least disappointing consequences. It is easy to see that stock market rumors can be of both kinds. In addition to wish and dread rumors, there are *non-involvement rumors* which do not concern the recipient. Even if people are unaffected by a rumor, they may want to pass it on since they may want to seem knowledgeable or may have an interest that is promoted by the spread of the rumor. In political contexts such as presidential elections, rumors about candidates' personalities are spread, apparently under the motto: 'Even if it isn't true it is a good rumor to spread'.

It would be interesting to know whether 'dread' or 'wish' rumors are more likely to spread. There is some evidence that transmitters are more anxious than non-transmitters (Rosnow, 1991). This may mean that dread rumors find their way around more easily. The credulity of the rumor appears to have importance: the higher the credulity to a group, the more likely the rumor is to spread. The source of the rumor obviously weighs heavily when people assess the credulity of a rumor. When the source is unreliable, the rumor is less likely to be accepted and have effects.

What criteria for credibility do investors employ when they face a rumor that has potential significance for their finances? A simple answer is that the rumor must fit in with the present frame of mind and that it evokes ideas of effects. 'It is a psychological commonplace that people strive to achieve a coherent interpretation of the events that surround them, and that the organization of events by schemas of cause–effect relations serves to achieve this goal' (Tversky and Kahneman, 1982c, p.117). When causal scenarios are touched on, people pay attention to the causal assumptions and may completely neglect statistical facts. 'Specifically, when making predictions, people seek information related to causality and weight this information more heavily than non-causal information of equal (or even better) predictive validity; this is the *causality heuristic*' (Ajzen, 1977, cited in DiFonzo and Bordia, 1997, p.332). Causal information in rumors is seductive and weighs more heavily than other information, even though the latter may be more useful.

Newspapers and other mass media often transmit rumors that may affect stock prices. The difference between factual news and rumors with some basis in facts, but still highly unreliable, is fuzzy to say the least. While rumors sometimes can be true and excellent predictors of events, rumors without foundation in reality may also entail consequences in the stock market. The daily comments on developments in the stock market reveal that individual stock prices have been influenced by rumors, for example about mergers or expected changes in earnings or in earning capacity. A single rumor seems to be able to shake the price of Nokia stocks by 10 percent in one day! In spite of the fact that rules and regulations governing stock markets ban the spread of (sensational) rumors, many rumors cannot be stopped and may even be part of organized campaigns (Rose, 1951).

In an early study of rumor in the stock market, Rose (1951) first developed a statistical technique for measuring the influence of what he called 'the factor of stickiness'. This factor comprised all factors that prevented the stock market from being perfectly competitive in the very short run. It was assumed that if rumor affected stock prices, it did so by creating a trend, that is, it caused prices to move in a single direction over a period of time. The author demonstrated the existence of the stickiness factor and its operation empirically from market prices. He used data from the New York Stock Exchange for two periods (1937–1938 and 1948–1949). Theoretical analysis of seven factors that could cause 'stickiness' indicated that four could be ruled out as unlikely or unimportant. The remaining three: 'waiting a few days to see what trend the market will take,' 'reading the daily quotations,' and 'rumor' could not be separated or their individual importance assessed from available data. The author concluded that these three factors might be interrelated, and that rumor might be very important. The study thus did not deal directly with rumors, but worked from possible consequences of rumor.

Later studies have tracked actual rumors. Pound and Zeckhauser (1990) studied effects of rumors of take-overs published in the *Wall Street Journal*. They used a sample of rumors published in the journal's 'Heard on the Street' column. They examined whether excess returns – above-market performance – could be realized by buying and holding stocks in the firm that according to the rumor was targeted. The conclusion was that the market reacted efficiently to rumors since simple trading strategies based on buying or selling rumored targets' stocks yielded zero excess returns. There was a significant price run-up for rumored targets in the month before publication of the takeover rumor. Widespread takeover rumors accurately predicted imminent takeover bids less than half the time. Most takeover rumors were preceded by unusual price and volume activity in the stock of the rumored target. This may have stimulated speculation that a large block position was being accumulated. Apparently, some traders were informed earlier or became suspicious earlier than the *Wall Street Journal* and changed their market expectations on the basis of not yet public information. The publication of the rumor may even have been inspired by the unusual activities. The authors did not believe that the trading was caused by leaks of inside information about immediate deals since most of the rumors were not followed by takeover bids within the next year (Pound and Zeckhauser, 1990, p.293). They ascribed the volume and price movements to financial analysts or arbitrageurs who were steadily on the lookout for signs, for example substantial purchases of stocks in a company, by large stock holders.

In a similar vein, Zivney et al. (1996) examined 871 takeover rumors published in two columns of the *Wall Street Journal* during 1985 through 1988. The study revealed that the market reacted differently to reports on the same page of the journal. Rumors in the 'Abreast of the Market' column were associated with short-term overreactions, while those in the 'Heard on the Street' column exhibited rapid price stabilization following rumor publication. Trading on these overreactions would have resulted in annualized excess returns averaging 20 percent with 70 percent of the trades being profitable. The degree of overreaction appeared insensitive to target firm size, percentage of institutional ownership, and market (beta) risk.

DiFonzo and Bordia (1997) carried out experimental studies of the effects of rumors. As a background, they reviewed earlier studies of rumor and trading in stock markets. They found evidence of effects of rumors on short-term price rises. They proposed that, by making sense of unpredictable price movements, rumors, like news, spawned anti-regressive predictions and adversely affected trading decisions. This occurs despite investor denigration of rumors. Investors who do not get news or hear rumors are assumed to be *tracking*, which essentially means that stock prices are expected to revert towards the mean. Investors then buy when the price is low (inferring that price will go up) and sell when the price is high (inferring that the price will drop). News or rumors that imply causes for momentum strategies are assumed to make investors depart from tracking. In a bull market, anti-regressive price expectations on the basis of earlier experience and other supporting evidence are an extrapolation of a trend and imply a momentum strategy.

Two experimental stock market simulations were run to investigate these ideas. In the first study, members of the experimental group in a computerized investment game were presented with news described as coming from the *Wall Street Journal*. The control group received no news. In the second study, the subjects were presented with published and unpublished rumors or, as a control, no message. The published rumors were said to belong to *Wall Street Journal*'s 'Heard on the Street' column. The unpublished rumors came from ''brother-in-law Harry whose information is "sometimes correct sometimes incorrect"'. All manipulations caused departures from a profitable buy-low sell-high (tracking) trading strategy, despite strong differences in rated credibility between types of information source. 'In sum, subjects exposed to news, published rumors, or unpublished rumors departed from tracking *equivalently* while controls adhered strongly to tracking. Furthermore, ignorance, in addition to being blissful, continues to be profitable' (DiFonzo and Bordia, 1997, pp.345–6). The subjects claimed that rumor sources were non-credible and that they were not influenced by rumors in their trading decisions. All the same, they traded on rumors as though these contained news. The authors conclude that the results demonstrate the sense-making function of rumor in situations filled with uncertainty.

Rumors undoubtedly affect stock markets. This has been known ever since the first stock exchange opened in England in the 1770s. Manipulating the stock or commodity market by generating rumors with implications has a long history. The Count of Monte Cristo delivered faked news and spread rumors to destroy the banker Danglars' fortune on the stock market!

8. Some Behavioral Data on Investors

THE PURPOSE AND CONTENTS OF THE CHAPTER

Information use constitutes the definition of an efficient market and can be seen as a precondition for correct stock prices. The first two chapters treated primarily macro aspects of disturbances in information flows. In the following five chapters, the focus was on selected human characteristics that influence information flows in the financial markets. Expectation formation is a subjective process in which present information stimuli, memories, and hopes and fears for the future are mingled. Memories and further information processing are subject to cognitive capacity limits and to subjective selection of information. Emotions play a role, sometimes furthering, sometimes inhibiting information processing. The effects of social influence should not be forgotten. Knowledge and guesses about how significant others will react have consequences for decisions to trade or not to trade. The effects of these individual characteristics can sometimes be quantitatively predicted, but, mostly the possible effects can only be suggested. Research on the cognitive, emotional, and social characteristics that influence human information processing was reviewed and some applications to investor behavior were touched on. The purpose of the next two chapters is to report on systematic research on investor behavior in which more than one type of characteristic is studied.

Compared to the extent and intensity of the discussion of market inefficiencies, surprisingly little research has been devoted to finding out about investor economic, demographic, and psychological characteristics. While efficient-market theory leaves little room for characteristics that differentiate between investors, more knowledge about investor behavior should be a worthwhile goal in itself. Some differences among investors must be recognized. Decisions to invest in stocks are made in various manners. Some investors today use the telephone or the Internet to arrive at and carry out decisions to purchase or sell. This calls for quick reactions and decisions and may be stressful. Other investors, who are more typical of private investors, may spend a long time before they effect a decision to buy or sell. Even though a long drawn-out decision process may end in a panic decision if stress keeps amassing, the process tends to be more relaxed when given enough time. A decision made in a stressful situation that requires fast decisions and is complex is likely to require fifferent psychological explanations than those for long drawn-out decision processes. Studies of decision processes of long duration can hardly be made in a laboratory and necessitate the keeping of diaries or repeated interviews; they are too often studied through retrospective interviews. Investor behavior seems to vary in bull and bear markets due to the fact that the situational stimuli vary. Certain differences between highly active and more passive stock holders can be expected. Most published studies seem, however, to bear the mark of bull-market optimism. I know of no comprehensive investor studies in periods of global pessimism.

In the chapter, the interest is focused on studies that include psychological variables and relate to investments in stocks made by individual or household investors. Four types of research on private investment have been carried out and three of those will be reported on in the chapter:

1. Testing the theory or specific hypotheses derived from the theory against time-series data on developments of stock and bond prices.
2. Surveys with interviews in which investors have been asked questions about their transactions with stocks and bonds.
3. Samples of accounts in brokerage firms.
4. Controlled experiments in laboratory asset markets in which the subjects have to decide about purchases and selling, with outcomes depending on actual stock-price developments for firms listed on a stock exchange or on market developments arising as the game proceeds.

Results from the first type of studies were utilized in the first two chapters. Since the way the psychological variables, if there are any, are dealt with differs from the use of psychological variables in studies based on individuals, no further attention will be paid to them here. In such studies, psychological variables are, as said before, used as explanations in micro models which are then applied to aggregate data while no testing is done at the individual level.

SURVEY AND PANEL STUDIES OF INVESTORS

A Mail Questionnaire Study of Brokerage Firm Customers

Surveys in which detailed questions about stock ownership and psychological and other factors possibly influencing it have been rare. Most surveys have been directed towards special groups of investors whose names are made available by a brokerage firm. An early study was carried out by Lease et al. (1974). They drew a sample from all the accounts of a brokerage firm and sent mail questionnaires to the sampled customers. The investigators received back around 1 000 questionnaires, corresponding to a response rate of 40 percent. A comparison with 'the great mass of shareholders' showed that the sample from the brokerage firm had higher income, more education, and more often belonged to the professional and managerial ranks than the average stock holder. In a separate report which will be treated later in the chapter, the authors analyzed the transactions described in the accounts.

The questionnaire contained, among others, questions about investment strategies. The respondents were given five alternatives to choose among. The most popular alternative (42 percent of choices) was: 'Fundamental approach, i.e., analysis of such fundamental factors as general business conditions, industry outlook, earnings, quality of management, etc.'. The response alternative 'technical approach, i.e., analysis of market factors such as stock-price movements, supply vs. demand, amount of odd-lot trading, resistance levels, short interest, charts, etc.' attracted only 4 percent of the answers, maybe because the description of the approach seemed rather complex; it should perhaps have put more stress on what is usually meant by technical analysis. The second most popular response (21 percent) was 'a combination of fundamental and technical approaches'. The most important objective was long-term capital appreciation, while short-term capital gains ranked low, much lower than dividend income and intermediate-term capital appreciation. A somewhat surprising conclusion was that 'while half of all nominal share-owners may be women, something like 80 to 90 per cent of all investment decision-makers are men' (Lease et al., 1974, p.420).

With respect to the assets held by the investors in the sample, it was found that they had invested most of their financial assets in stocks: 'They invest in common stocks to the virtual exclusion of everything else, with any funds they have left after satisfying their family's core living needs' (Lease et al., 1974, p.430). The respondents were asked to agree or disagree with a number of attitude statements. The answers suggested that the respondents enjoyed participating in investment activities and thought that they could do better managing their own portfolios of stocks than putting their money in mutual funds. Most respondents agreed with the statement 'Security prices are not predictable in the short run' (mean rating 3.88 on a five-point scale).

A Panel Study of A Small Sample of Stock Owners in Wisconsin

De Bondt (1998) shows selected results from a study of 45 stock owners in Wisconsin. The participants consented to make weekly forecasts of the Dow Jones Industrial Average and of the stock price of one of their main equity holdings. They also gave answers to survey questions relating to trading behavior, perceptions of value, and familiarity with finance theories. The participants turned out to be overoptimistic about the likely performance of their own stocks, but not about the performance of the stocks covered by the Dow Jones. They also underestimated the covariation in returns between their portfolio holdings and the market index. This is similar to what Lease et al. (1974) found and lends further support to hypotheses about overconfidence.

The analysis showed that the participants were unlikely to use betas or other measures of covariation to construct optimal portfolios. The idea of the value of diversification was not prevalent among the investors in this study, judging from the answers to the following statement that 89 percent agreed with: 'I would rather have in my stock portfolio just a few companies that I know well than many companies that I know little about'. The following statement to which 70 percent subscribed emphasized the need for knowledge: 'If you do not do your homework (e.g., follow the financial news, learn about the company, etc.) I doubt that you will achieve much investment success' (De Bondt, 1998, pp.840–1). These investors apparently shared the popular notion that stock owners have to be alert and active most of the time.

Non-Stock-Owners' Feelings about Owning Stocks

In a German study of a sample of households who had wealth of over DM 10 000 and/or had invested at least DM 5 000 over the last year and had no directly owned stocks, many questions were asked to establish the respondents' attitudes to and feelings about stocks (psychonomics & Capital, 1999). Table 8.1 shows the answers to a series of questions. Each question was introduced in the same way: 'Now imagine that you have bought stocks, what would happen to you?' [Stellen Sie sich einmal vor, Sie hätten Aktien gekauft, was käme da auf Sie zu?].

While Table 8.1 shows some differences according to gender and age indicating that women and older respondents are more skeptical about owning stocks, it is more intriguing to note to what extent they agree. In a way, the table demonstrates some of the most common stereotypes about stock owners. On the one hand, the chances of making a good profit would be high if stocks were acquired. On the other hand, owning stocks would mean suspense, sleepless nights for quite a few, and a need to obtain information all the time. But if you went through all this, you would feel proud when the value of the stocks increased – you are entitled to praise your own knowledge and skill when you make a profit. The stereotype is obvious and quite well-spread: owning stocks is not a simple thing and you must be active all the time. Since many respondents participated in stock funds, such investing may be simpler and more relaxed while still demanding something of the owner. Swedish tabloid readers are constantly exposed to admonishments to keep a close watch on their funds and switch to a better one if one of their earlier choices does less well than the stock index. Most do not seem to heed the advice.

Table 8.1 Non-Stock-Owners' Attitudes towards Stocks (percent agreeing with statement)

	Men	Women	Age			
			<30	31–40	41–50	51–60
I would be proud if my stocks were to go up [1]	86	91	86	88	91	88
Then I would have sleep less nights [2]	20	30	23	24	28	28
Then I would have to inform myself every day [3]	58	66	62	60	60	66
It would be tickling my nerves [4]	50	50	55	50	49	44
If questions and problems arose I would stand alone [5]	34	31	29	34	34	35
I would have a good chance of making a high profit in the long run [6]	77	63	73	71	70	64

Notes:

1. Ich wäre stolz, wenn meine Aktien steigen würden
2. Da hätte ich schlaflose Nächte
3. Da müßte ich mich jeden Tag informieren
4. Das wäre ein spannender Nervenkitzel
5. Bei Fragen und Problemen wäre ich auf mich selbst angewiesen
6. Ich hätte gute Chancen, langfristig eine gute Rendite zu erzielen.

Source: psychonomics & Capital (1999).

Financial Goals

The survey of non-stock-owners mentioned in the previous section was preceded by a representative survey of German households consisting of 3 500 interviews (psychonomics & Capital, 1998). Some of the questions in the surveys were identical and it is interesting to make some comparisons. The respondents were asked to judge the importance of a number of financial goals for the household. Table 8.2 shows the results for men and women and for young people under 30 years of age. Sample 1 is the representative sample and Sample 2 is the sample of non-stock-owners.

In Sample 1, the most important financial goal is to get a buffer for emergencies. This goal is less important for non-stock-owners, but still rated high by most. Many earlier studies have found that having a buffer is the most important goal for saving money (Wärneryd, 1999, Ch. 5). Those who do not have a buffer or enough of a buffer also rank this goal very high. In Sample 2, 'Preparing for old age' has the highest rating, even among those under 30 years of age. This goal usually ranks much lower as a saving goal. The high rank suggests that stock returns may make retirement more comfortable than living on pensions alone would allow. The second sample, with no stock owners except investors in stock funds, appears more intent on making money than the first sample, of which around 10 percent are stock owners. Accumulating money for larger purchases like cars and vacations is most frequent among the youngest.

Table 8.2 Importance of Financial Goals (percent rating goal important)

		Men	Women	Age <30	Total
Preparing for old age [1]	Sample 1	85	87	73	86
	Sample 2	73	83	70	79
Buffer for emergencies [2]	Sample 1	87	89	81	88
	Sample 2	67	82	64	74
Build a large fortune [3]	Sample 1	40	34	50	37
	Sample 2	55	52	64	53
Enable larger buys (car) [4]	Sample 1	59	49	70	53
	Sample 2	55	61	63	58
Get highest possible gains [5]	Sample 1	59	44	65	51
	Sample 2	74	65	76	69

Notes:

1. Die Vorsorge fürs Alter treffen
2. Vorsorge für Notfälle treffen
3. Ein größeres Vermögen aufbauen
4. Größere Anschaffungen tätigen, z.B. Auto, Urlaub
5. Möglichst hohe Gewinne erzielen

Source: psychonomics & Capital (1998 and 1999).

Risk Attitudes and Risk Taking

From the shape of the subjective utility function, it follows that when somebody gets more money, the willingness to take risks increases. Many deviations from this expectation have been found. One such deviation involves the impact that the source of the money has on investing. Lupfer (1970) showed that it made a difference whether people's own money or other people's money was invested. In the study, a total of 36 three-member teams met for six sessions to play a modified version of a stock market game. Teams differed in their risk-taking disposition (either low-, moderate- or high-risk disposition). Half of the number of teams invested their own money; half were given money to invest. Teams of differing risk-taking disposition did not utilize different investment strategies. Teams investing their own money: (a) transacted fewer lots of stock, (b) requested more market information, (c) accumulated a larger profit, and (d) exhibited a less stable influence hierarchy than teams investing another's money. This is in agreement with mental accounting theory (Thaler, 1999b; see also Chapter 5).

The predictive value of psychological measures of risk attitudes seems to vary considerably depending on what measures are used (Hedborg, 1996). An example of low predictive value is found in a study by Morse (1998). He investigated risk taking in personal investments. Subjects were 59 males and 54 females (aged 30–65 years) who were employed full time. Two questionnaires were used. The first was a Risk/Investment Questionnaire. The second was a form of the Sensation Seeking Scale (Zuckerman, 1979). Results showed that individual investors could accurately judge risk level of investments for all but the riskiest categories. No relationship was found between knowledge of risk and risk level of chosen investments. Participants did not match risk level of their investments to their self-reported risk level. In contrast to Harlow and Brown (1990), but similar to Hedborg (1996), the authors found no relationship between level of sensation seeking and risk taking.

Another study of risk taking in finance and personality found that Type A subjects took greater risks than Type B subjects (Carducci and Wong, 1998). Type A persons are characterized by time urgency, high level of competitiveness, aggression, irritability, and impatience. Type B are persons who cannot be characterized as Type A. They have a relaxed, easy-going approach to life, low competitiveness, and a tendency for self-reflection. The subjects were asked to make a series of everyday financial decisions that varied in degree of risk. The authors concluded that the results provided support for the influence of personality factors in everyday financial risk-taking behavior.

Traditionally, the typical small-wealth owners have been assumed to be very risk averse and avoided or limited their investment in stocks and other risky assets. Wärneryd (1996b) found low predictive value for risk attitudes, measured through hypothetical risky choices that were included in a survey questionnaire, and the respondent's investments in risky assets. Part of the explanation was that some investors with high risk aversion had some risky investments which they could well afford to lose money on.

Müller-Peters (1999, p.137) notes that attitudes towards investing in stocks are still very negative in Germany, although there has been some change since the successful sale of Deutsche Telekom stocks in 1996. He cites evidence from German research that investors who are less risk averse and more prone to take risks are more optimistic about the future and feel more competent than those who are more risk averse. The feeling of being in control of one's investments in stocks rose with increasing risk taking displayed in the composition of the stock portfolio. Müller-Peters cautions that the causality is not clear. More optimism may be caused by earlier experience and more experience may lead to feelings of more competence and control. In contrast to Maital et al. (1986), he did not find any notable relationship between locus of control and risk taking in a group of students (Müller-Peters, 1999, p.145). There was a tendency for people to take larger risks when investing inherited money than when they invested money that they had earned themselves.

Using Neal Miller's model of conflict, Müller-Peters (1999) suggests that when people are asked about risks in surveys, they tend to overstate their willingness to take risks. According to Miller, when a person gets closer to actually making a decision, the conflict between pros and cons will be enhanced because the resistance against the goal increases more than its attractiveness. When the survey questions are asked, most respondents are far from a decision-making situation, think less of possible conflict, and consequently feel more inclined to accept risks. Although answers to survey questions about risk taking indicate that people in general are highly risk averse, there may be a tendency to underestimate actual risk aversion.

SOME DATA ON RISK AVERSION AND INVESTING IN THE NETHERLANDS AND SWEDEN

The Surveys and the Investment Risk Attitude Scale

The CentER Savings Survey (CSS), earlier called the VSB Panel, collected interview data on Dutch households from the end of 1992 (1993 survey) to the end of 1997 (1998 survey). Each year, except 1998, two samples were interviewed: a representative sample of the Dutch households and a high-income sample. Sample weights were used in the analyses reported here. The analyses focus on the financial officers of those households that had invested in stocks. The Swedish sample (SSS) was a random sample of households from a Swedish National Census database and a random sample of high-income earners (Gunnarsson et al., 2000). Usable responses were received from 1 780 households (46.8 percent). The two Swedish samples are merged here without weighting. High-income households are thus overrepresented.

Socio-economic as well as psychological variables are covered in the two studies. To some extent, the same variables were included in both the Dutch and the Swedish data sets. The analyses reported are based on Wärneryd (2000b).

In financial economics, risk aversion is commonly estimated through proxies such as proportion of risky assets versus proportion of less risky or riskless assets. The surveys gave the possibility of employing *subjective* estimates of risk aversion. The Investment Risk Attitude Scale shown in the box below was constructed for the Dutch Panel and used in all interview waves. Five of the six statements in the Dutch Investment Risk Attitude Scale were included in the Swedish survey. Principal component factor analyses yielded the same two factors in both the Dutch and the Swedish studies: risk avoidance and risk seeking. A composite score of attitude towards risk was computed. For the analyses here, the respondents were divided into three approximately equal-sized groups on the basis of their risk attitude score. Those who were most risk averse and had the lowest score were placed in group 1, those who were least risk averse formed group 3 and those in between were in group 2. The risk attitudes were significantly ($p<0.001$) different between the groups. The groups were labeled: (1) most risk averse, (2) risk averse, (3) least risk averse.

Investment Risk Attitude Scale

1. I think it is more important to have safe investments and guaranteed returns than to take a risk to have a chance to get the highest possible returns.
2. I would never consider investments in stocks, because I find this too risky.
3. If I think an investment will be profitable, I am prepared to borrow money to make this investment.
4. I want to be certain that my investments are safe.
5. I get more and more convinced that I should take greater financial risks to improve my financial position.
6. I am prepared to take the risk to lose money, when there is also a chance to gain money.
7. A 7-point scale was used (disagree completely = 1, agree completely = 7.

Determinants of Risk Aversion

Financial economics and psychology do not always lead to the same hypotheses about the determinants of risk aversion. While economics posits that risk aversion decreases with wealth and otherwise remains unexplained, psychology assumes that risk aversion measured as risk attitude varies with age, gender, and personality characteristics rather than with wealth and income. To investigate the determinants of risk aversion, multiple regression analyses were carried out with the Dutch and Swedish surveys, using risk attitude score as dependent variable (lower score = higher risk aversion).

The results are displayed in Table 8.3. Economic, socio-demographic, and psychological variables were sequentially introduced in the analyses. The explained variance (Adj. R^2) is presented for each step in the sequence. The economic variables of financial wealth (home equity excluded) and net income are based on reported data for each household and were gathered through a very detailed questionnaire in the Dutch panel and a less detailed one in the Swedish survey. The socio-demographic variables are: (1) the natural log of age in years, (2) household size, (3) a dummy for gender (0 = female, 1 = male), and (4) a dummy for education (0 = no university education, 1 = university education). The psychological variables were: (1) three motives for saving money, based on ratings of saving goals, (2) a simple measure of degree of self-control, based on a scale running from 1 (like to spend all my money immediately) to 7 (want to save as much as possible), and (3) interest in financial matters (with a response scale from 1 = disagree completely to 7 = agree completely). While the year 1997 includes both the representative sample and the high-income group (weighted), the 1998 sample includes only a representative sample.

Table 8.3 Factors Influencing Risk Attitudes (Beta Coefficients)

	CSS1997	CSS1998	SSS 1999
Financial assets	0.064	-0.013	0.115[d]
Household income	–0.035	0.075	0.108[d]
Adj. R^2	0.024	0.023	0.026
Age	–0.145[d]	–0.165[b]	–0.242[d]
Household size	0.084[a]	0.018	–0.009
University education	0.004	0.010	0.075[b]
Gender	–0.075[a]	0.072	0.139[d]
Adj. R^2	0.094	0.069	0.132
Buffer saving	–0.177[d]	–0.267[d]	–0.184[d]
Financial security	0.051	0.124[a]	0.039
Goal saving	0.187[d]	0.140[c]	0.175[d]
Self-control	–0.072[a]	.–0.070	–0.086[b]
Financial interest	0.275[d]	0.305[d]	0.156[d]
Constant	(5.223)[d]	(3.970)[d]	(3.827)[d]
Adj. R^2	0.209	0.222	0.212

Note: a: $p < 0.05$; b: $p < 0.01$; c: $p < 0.001$; d: $p < 0.0001$

According to Table 8.3, risk aversion does not primarily vary with financial wealth and income. Economic variables are significant in the Swedish sample, but explain less variance than the other two sets of variables. The socio-demographic variables and the psychological variables explain more variance than the economic variables. The socio-demographic variables show no clear pattern of relationships to risk aversion. Some of the psychological variables do. It was expected that financial security, which is a long-run saving goal, would be positively related and buffer be negatively related to risk attitude. The saving goal of long-term financial security, which may involve investment in stocks, was not significantly related to risk aversion whereas the data supported the idea that high evaluation of a buffer is related to high risk aversion. More risk acceptance and interest in financial matters go together, which may reflect more acceptance of risks with increasing information.

Risk Aversion and the Composition of Portfolios

According to the Mutual-Funds Separation Theorem (see Chapter 1), more risk-averse investors should hold more of their portfolios in riskless assets such as cash and saving accounts than investors who are more risk accepting. If the risk averse choose to invest in risky assets, the composition of their risky assets should be the same as that of risk-seeking investors. The composition of risky assets should be independent of degree of risk aversion. This implies that all investors are expected to have the same bonds to shares ratio, independent of the total amount invested in stocks. Risk-averse investors are assumed to have little invested in risky assets and to prefer to keep surplus money in supposedly riskless assets. Advice that experts appear to give and empirical studies of portfolios give reason for suspecting that practice seldom confirms the theorem (see Canner et al., 1997). Investors are commonly advised to have invested in stocks a percentage equal to (100 – age in years). Old-age pensioners should then have proportionally much less invested in stocks than middle-aged people.

Figures 8.1 and 8.2 show each risk aversion group's percentage share of the total value of four kinds of assets: total financial assets, stocks, bonds, and mutual funds. The total values of the assets have been calculated as the sum total, added over all households with the asset. 'Percent of sample' is the percentage of asset holders in each group. Figure 8.1, which refers to the Dutch sample in 1997, reveals clear differences among the groups. The most risk-averse group has on average a somewhat lower proportion of the financial assets than the other two groups. Very few members owned stocks, and the average value of the stocks is relatively low. Almost 30 percent of the least risk averse owned stocks and their share of the total value amounts to slightly less than 50 percent. The middle group lies neatly in between the other groups. Very few households owned bonds, but some differences exist among the groups, again following degree of risk aversion inversely. The percentage of households owning stocks in the Netherlands can be estimated to be around 14 percent on the basis of this survey, which is probably a little too high for the beginning of 1997 but is more correct for the situation today (2000).

The situation in Sweden is different. Sweden is said to have among the highest percentage of stock-owning households in the world, even beating the USA, albeit narrowly, but beaten by Australia. Thirty percent of the most risk-averse group owned stocks against 50 percent for the least risk-averse group. While bond ownership is common in all three groups, the more risk averse seem to have invested more money in bonds than the least risk averse. One reason may be that bonds, which are mostly government-issued bonds, are believed to be as safe as cash.

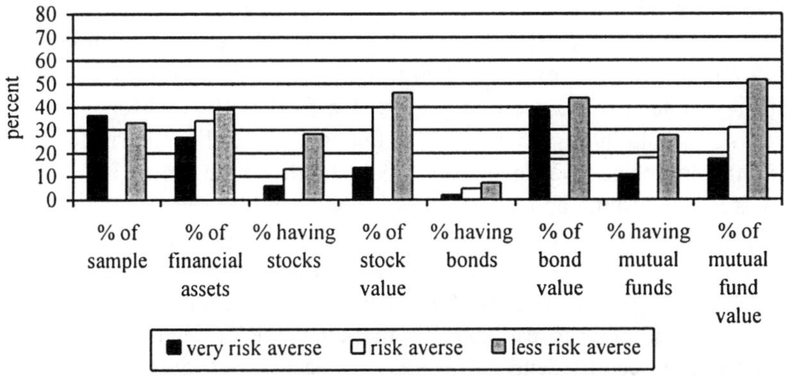

Figure 8.1 Ownership of Assets in Dutch Survey, 1997

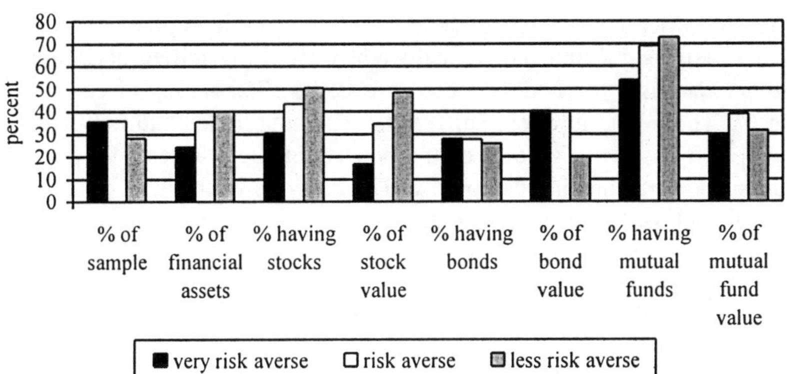

Figure 8.2 Ownership of Assets in Swedish Survey, 1999

In sum, the more risk averse in both countries are less likely to own stocks than the least risk averse. The most risk averse in Sweden hold stocks more often than the more risk accepting in the Netherlands, which shows that other factors may overcome the resistance to buying stocks that is connected with risk aversion. Most Dutch stock owners have relatively little of their total assets invested in stocks (Alessie et al., 1999).

Risk Aversion and Diversification of Portfolios

Diversification may be used in several senses: (1) it refers to the proportion of riskless assets compared to risky assets, (2) it may be the spread within an asset category, for example, how many firms are represented in the portfolio of stocks, and (3) the bond/stock ratio (see Chapter 2). While the mean-variance and other theoretical models tell investors to spread their investment over a number of stock types, preferably buying the market portfolio, investors are inclined to believe in certain stocks and invest all their funds in those that they believe in (Lease et al., 1974; De Bondt, 1998). More risk-averse investors should hold more of their financial portfolios in riskless assets while the composition of their risky assets should be the same.

A study by Blume and Friend (1975) analyzed two sets of data on household portfolios. One set was a sample of 17 000 individual income tax forms filed for the 1971 tax year. The households who had more than $100 in dividends had to report each payer of dividends and the sum received. From these data, it was possible to estimate the market value of each stock. using the appropriate price–dividend ratios. Two measures of diversification were used: (1) the number of dividend payers (the number of firms invested in), and (2) the deviation of the household portfolio share of a certain stock from the proportion in the market portfolio. Both measures indicated that there was little diversification in the household portfolios even if income level was considered. Higher-income earners had slightly more diversified portfolios. The authors also used the Federal Reserve Board's 1962 survey of consumer finances. These data gave similar results. The households had not diversified their portfolios. Fifty percent of the households held at least 90 percent of their stock portfolios in one holding. The analyses of the asset portfolios included riskless assets, various categories of risky assets, home equity, and human capital. Some effect of wealth was noted in the analysis.

.In the analyses of the Dutch and Swedish surveys, three measures were used: (1) the financial asset proportion of riskless assets such as bank accounts and the proportion of risky assets of two kinds: low risk (bonds and growth funds) and higher risk (stocks and mutual funds), (2) the number of firms invested in, and (3) the bond/stock ratio. Figures 8.3 and 8.4 show the results pf the analyses for the first type of measure. Although the Swedish frequencies for risky assets are much higher and there are some differences in diversification between the countries, the tendency is the same: the least risk averse have invested more in more risky assets like stocks than the most risk averse. While most of the Dutch stock holders seem to be quite wealthy and hold considerable riskless assets, the more risk averse appear to have more of a reserve to fall back on if they were to lose money on the more risky assets.

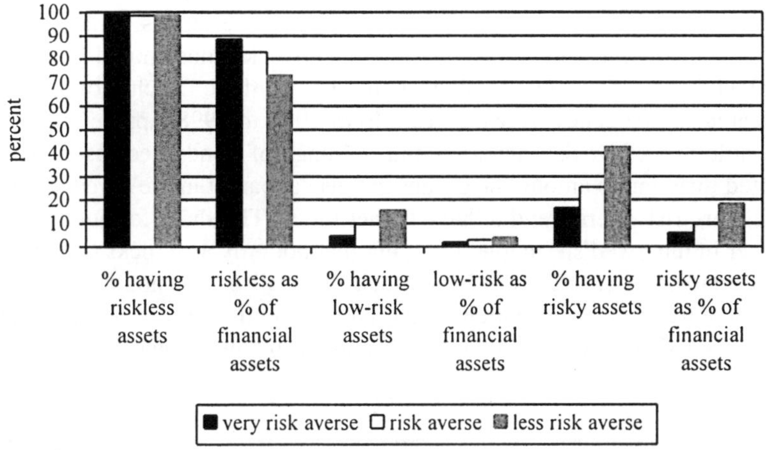

Figure 8.3 Asset Composition and Risk Attitude Groups: Dutch Sample, 1997

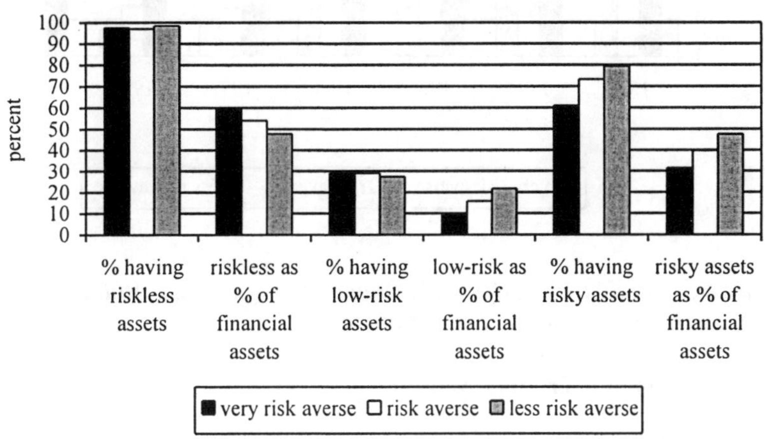

Figure 8.4 Asset Composition and Risk Attitude Groups: Swedish Sample, 1999

The Dutch risk attitude groups showed the expected differences in the number of firms invested in. The mean number of firms invested in was 2.06 for the most risk averse, 2.71 for the middle group, and 4.07 for the less risk averse. The more risk accepting thus had a little more diversification. The Swedish questionnaire did not include questions about firms invested in.

The bond/stock ratio was computed as: bond value/(stock value + bond value)*100. The ratios were expected to differ with risk attitude. Figure 8.5 shows large differences among the groups, and the results certainly do not agree with the theorem saying that the bond/stock ratios should be the same independently of degree of risk aversion. For all three Dutch groups, there is a decreasing tendency over the years from 1993 to 1998, apparently because the holdings of stocks increased and holdings of bonds decreased. The expected differences among the groups are also apparent in the Swedish survey. The more risk averse tend to have higher ratios. The share for bonds is much higher in the Swedish sample, implying that not only are stocks common, but also bonds. Many investors have stocks as well as considerable wealth in bonds. Part of the explanation is that having bonds is more frequent among the more risk averse who in the Dutch study also have higher ratios.

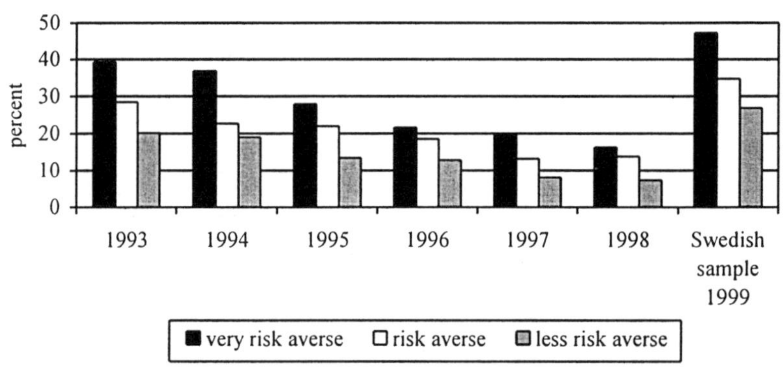

Figure 8.5 Bond/Stock Ratios and Dutch and Swedish Risk Attitude Groups (average ratios for owners of stocks and/or bonds)

Risk Aversion and Trading Activity

In the Dutch surveys, the respondent was asked to specify name, number, and value for each stock owned at the previous year's end. Since no questions were asked about stock transactions, the level of trading activity had to be measured as changes from one year to next: (a) in the number of firms in which stocks were held by the stock owner, and (b) by changes in number of stocks during one year. The percentage with no change in the number of firms was similar for all three risk aversion groups and varied between one-third and close to half of the stock owners. Typically, there were few changes from one year to the next in the number of firms invested in, but there was a slightly increased activity in all three risk attitude groups from 1993 to 1998. In 1993, even among the least risk averse, the proportion of investors with a decrease in the number of firms was larger than the proportion with an increase. Over the years, some variability in the number of firms occurred, but there was a slight tendency for fewer stock holders to reduce the number of firms invested in and rather to increase the number towards the end of the period. The groups show similar patterns, except that the most risk averse showed more variability. In 1997, more in the very risk-averse group reduced rather than increased the diversity of their holdings. Some of the variability may be due to panel attrition, with many drop-outs. At any rate, the picture seems clear: the inclination to increase the number of firms invested in and thereby diversify more was weak and the activity level was low in this sense.

For each firm invested in, a comparison was made for two consecutive years and changes in the number of stocks were recorded. This was done for the years 1993–1995. The measure is crude since changes in the number of equities owned may be caused by stock dividends and repurchases and may not be a sign of activity. The percentage who did not change varied between 11 and 34 percent and was lowest for the more risk accepting group. The data did not suggest a very high level of activity in the sense of change in number of stocks held. All in all, considering both changes in the number of firms and in the number of stocks, the stock holders did not seem very active during the years studied. The least risk averse were more active than the others. The share of total stock value was calculated for each activity level so as to give an indication of the importance. Those who were more active and changed their portfolios had a much larger share of the stocks than those who made no changes. A considerable portion of the stock capital was, all the same, owned by owners with little or no activity.

In the Swedish survey, respondents were asked whether they had made any transactions with stocks during the last year. They were also asked to classify their level of activity on a scale running from 1 (very passive) to 7 (very active). The very risk-averse group gave an average of 2.33, the risk-averse group 2.94, and the least risk-averse group 3.49. Considering that the scale had seven steps, with 7 indicating 'very active', the activity level in all three groups appears low.

The transaction frequencies are shown in Figure 8.6. Many of the respondents (43 percent) did not report any transactions at all, and when they reported activity it was often either buying or selling rather than both types of transaction. The least risk averse reported more transactions than the others and two-thirds of them had made some transactions. The middle group was somewhere in between the others.

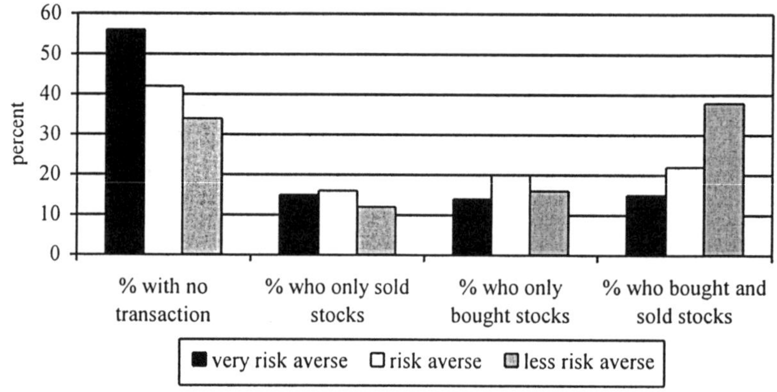

Figure 8.6 Activity Level of Swedish Sample during 1998

Interestingly, those who made no transactions at all had 14 percent of the total stock value and 24 percent of total financial assets, while those who both bought and sold stocks had 54 percent of the stock value and 45 percent of the financial asset value. In all, almost half of the stock value was either not subject to any transaction or subject only to buying or selling during the year. This gives a picture of inactivity. Passive investors who made few transactions had considerable stock holdings. This is also clear from Figure 8.7, where share of total stock value is shown for each activity level. Over 60 percent of the stock value is owned by respondents who rated their activity level as 4 or below.

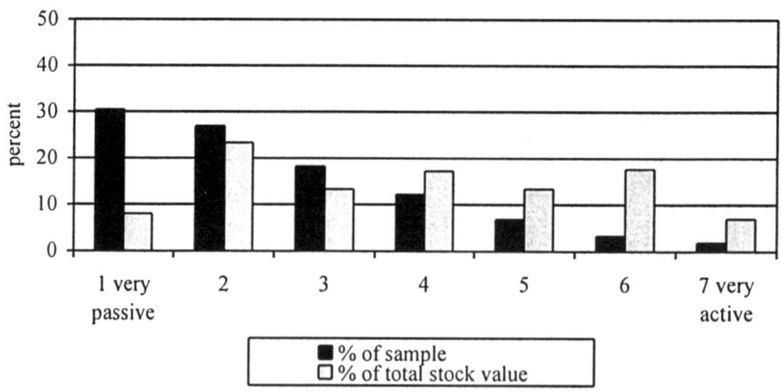

Figure 8.7 Relative Importance of Activity Groups in Swedish Sample, 1998

The analyses demonstrate that subjective assessments of risk aversion may reveal some investor differences that objective proxies fail to elucidate. Groups that differ in risk aversion behave differently in many respects, as shown by the analyses of asset composition, diversification, and activity level. The majority of stock holders are passive and make few transactions in a year. The more risk averse tend to be even less active than the less risk averse. The importance of passive investors has been neglected both by theory and practice. The majority of stock owners in each risk attitude group seem well able to afford possible losses on stocks (see Figures 8.1 and 8.2). German studies have also clearly shown the importance of risk aversion for the composition of portfolios. In a sample of non-stock-owning households who had financial wealth of over DM 10 000 or who had made investments of over DM 5 000 in the last year, the respondents were classified in two groups: risk averse and risk loving (psychonomics & Capital, 1999). It was found that among the risk averse the participation in mutual funds and willingness to buy stocks in the future were much lower than among the risk loving.

STUDIES OF TRADING RECORDS

Individual transactions can in principle be studied with the aid of records from brokerage firms. In some countries, such as Sweden and Finland, all stock transactions are registered by a central agency. In Finland, researchers have, as will be reported later, recently gained access to the data base that contains data on all stock transactions. This has opened new possibilities for testing hypotheses about investor behavior. While brokers are usually hesitant about subjecting their customers' accounts to outsiders' analysis, except for proprietary purposes, a few researchers have had access to samples from some brokers. Samples of accounts are unfortunately not representative of the whole population of stock or other security owners. It is, for example, possible that those who trade through a certain brokerage firm are more frequent and larger traders than others who do not trade through this broker.

Individual Investors Doing Better than Funds

Behind one of the few published studies of trading records lay the observation that institutional investors were increasing their share of the US financial market and individual investors were turning towards indirect participation through mutual funds and other institutional arrangements. Schlarbaum et al. (1978, p.300) suggested that there could be two reasons for this development: (1) the convenient and inexpensive diversification offered by institutional portfolios, and (2) the relative investment skills of the individual and the professional money manager.

The authors, who published a survey study in 1974 (Lease et al; see earlier in this chapter), analyzed the accounts of the survey respondents over a period of seven years (1964–70). In their main sample, Schlarbaum et al. analyzed accounts that were available for seven years. The study was aimed at elucidating the skills of the private investor. The authors noted that most studies of professional investors had not convincingly shown that they did better than a market portfolio.

The authors followed what they called 'round trips', which were complete cycles from purchase to resale, and computed the actually realized rates of return. The identified round trips yielded net returns over risk-free Treasury Bills in 52 percent of the cases, which the authors judged as suggesting 'some reasonable skill in security selection, particularly in connection with short term trading cycles' (Schlarbaum et al., 1978, p.299). The authors made a conjecture about why individual investors may have an advantage:

> It is possible that individuals are in fact able to engage in prompt trading responses to many temporary securities price disequilibria that emerge in the market, to take positions small enough not to eliminate those disequilibria immediately, and on average to turn a profit before they disappear, whereas large-bloc institutional trading pursuit of the same discrepancies would be self-defeating. This might, in many instances, give the small investor a modest competitive edge (Schlarbaum et al., 1978, p.322).

These investigators thus found that there could be some truth in the beliefs of active stock investors that they can make more profit by trading themselves than by participating in funds.

The Disposition Effect according to Trading Records

A discount brokerage firm gave a team of financial researchers access to a large number of accounts, in one case 10 000 accounts (Odean, 1999) and in another 66 465 (Barber and Odean, 2000b). While this is an impressively large number of transactions, one should note the authors' caution that the investors trading through a discount brokerage firm are not a representative sample of the whole investor population in the nation. Odean (1999) warns that the holders of the accounts may be overconfident and trade more than other investors. He says that the study should be repeated, if possible, with samples of accounts from a retail brokerage house and from institutional trading.

In one of the studies, Odean (1998) focused on the *disposition effect*, the tendency of investors to hold losing securities too long and sell winning securities too soon. The label was suggested by Shefrin and Statman (1985). It is a somewhat unfortunate abbreviation of 'disposition to sell winners and keep losers'. Disposition is in psychology a very general concept for tendency to act and is preceded or followed by a specification of the kind of behavior that the tendency is related to. When Shefrin and Statman (1985) introduced the concept, they relied heavily on prospect theory (Kahneman and Tversky, 1979). The shape and slope of the value function of this theory suggests that losses loom larger than gains and that people have loss aversion. Loss aversion involves aversion against making losses and resistance against realizing them. The authors' framework also included other elements, namely mental accounting, regret aversion, self-control, and tax considerations. Support for the framework was found in data from Schlarbaum et al. (1978) and from data on mutual funds.

Odean (1998) talks about three alternative explanations of the disposition effect: (1) investors may believe that current losers will change and do better in the future and current winners do less well, (2) winners are sold to rebalance portfolios, and (3) losers are not sold because of the higher transaction costs of trading at lower prices. An alternative formulation of the first explanation is the reversion-to-mean hypothesis which Odean also discusses and tried to test in the study.

Odean showed that the investors in the sample had a strong preference for disposing of winners rather than losers. He found that taxes had an influence and that tax-motivated selling was most evident in December. This was not enough to explain the disposition effect. For taxable investments, the behavior was suboptimal and led to lower after-tax returns. The behavior did not appear to be motivated by a desire to rebalance portfolios, or to avoid the higher trading costs of low-priced stocks. It was not justified by later performance since the kept losers tended to do worse than the sold winners.

Although the results provided support for the hypothesis about disposition effects, the competing reversion-to-mean hypothesis could not be decisively rejected. Odean (1998) discusses crucial tests to make a clearer distinction. Both hypotheses predict that investors will sell their winners too soon and keep their losers too long. Mean-reversion expectation is, of course, an expectation that extremes will become less extreme. The main difference between the two seems to be that mean reversion applies to stocks that an investor does not already own while prospect theory comprises only stocks that the investor owns. The disposition effect was found to be related to the size of the loss or gain, an unexpected finding. Neither hypothesis predicts the finding that investors tend to sell their larger gains and losses at a slower rate than their smaller gains and losses.

Odean (1998) finds some indication of investors tending to believe that big winners will continue to outperform other stocks; consequently they are not sold. A puzzle that remains to be resolved is the tendency to keep the largest winners, which has also been found in some other investigations Apparently, there may be a momentum effect that goes against the disposition and mean-reversion effects. People may devise causal schemas that incite the expectation that large winners will not revert towards the mean. As mentioned in Chapter 2, Andreassen (1987) showed the importance of the fact that causal attributions are provided to explain recent changes (see also Dawes, 1999). If these attributions are provided, for example by the news media, the tendency to make predictions of reversion towards the mean is diminished.

The problems associated with the disposition effect have also been attacked by experimental economists (see later in this chapter under 'Experimental Asset Markets'). An intriguing problem that has not been studied is what happens to stock markets when more and more stock holders with high loss aversion are recruited. They may slow down falls and dampen booms.

Frequent Trading and Investor Performance

Overconfident investors are assumed to trade more frequently than is good for them. This involves too frequent changes in the composition of their portfolios. While an individual investor may exaggerate trading without the total market falling prey to excessive trading, excessive trading assessed at the macro level involves at least some important groups dealing excessively. Odean (1999) started with the assumption that overall trading volume in equity markets was excessive and he wanted to demonstrate this by showing that trading was excessive for a particular group of investors, namely those with discount brokerage accounts. Using the same trading records as in the study on the disposition effect, he tested his hypothesis. These investors traded frequently and excessively in the sense that their returns were, on average, reduced through trading. No independent definition or measure of excessive trading was given and such measures are probably not easy to produce unless subjective assessments are possible and accepted.

The hypothesis that investors trade excessively because they are overconfident was tested on the account data. Investors may be overconfident because they take too much credit for earlier successes. Feeling confident, they may listen to information that has low predictive value and act on it in full trust of their own judgment. Odean (1999) found that overconfident investors traded even when their expected gains through trading were not enough to offset trading costs.

In fact, even when trading costs were ignored in the analysis, these investors actually lowered their returns through trading. Most trades that seemed motivated by liquidity demands, tax-loss selling, portfolio rebalancing, or a move to lower-risk securities were then eliminated, but trading still lowered returns. Overconfidence could then be seen as what remains after exclusion of a number of other factors. Odean says that his result is more extreme than is predicted by overconfidence alone. It should be noted that the excessive traders did not necessarily lose money since the investigated years 1987 through 1993 were good years, only that they did not do as well as they could have done.

'Individual investors who hold common stocks directly pay a tremendous performance penalty for active trading' (Barber and Odean, 2000b, p.773). This is a summary of another study of trading accounts, this time representing 66 465 households. The authors compare two models. One is the rational expectations model, which says that investors will trade when the marginal benefit of trading is equal to or exceeds the marginal cost of the trade. This model predicts that investors who trade more will not differ from those who trade less; they will have the same expected utility.

The alternative model is the overconfidence model propounded and tested by Odean (1999). It predicts that investors who trade more will have lower expected utility. The data demonstrated very clearly that high turnover of stock portfolios led to smaller returns, due to high trading costs. Differences were also found in the kinds of stocks preferred by very active traders. The high-turnover households had a bias towards high-beta, small-firm, and growth stocks (Barber and Odean, 2000b, p.792).

A Study of Swedish Institutional Investors' Transactions of Stocks

In a detailed study of eight Swedish institutional investors' decision making, Hellman (2000) prepared for the personal interviews by first studying available public information and by administering questionnaires that covered all transactions of the investors over a period usually of six months. Detailed interviews with analysts and portfolio managers in the investor firms were then conducted. Each interview covered one or more selected transactions. The findings indicate that the respondents used much non-public information in their valuation of the future of the company under scrutiny. Public information was defined as including all information that is equally available to the mass media (Hellman, 2000, pp.112–13). Non-public information included all other kinds of information. It turned out that work on building up expectations varied, but that expectations were in principle formed on fundamentals both of the considered company and of the whole industry.

Expectations which were short term (three to five years' horizon) were based on quantitative analysis, but were complemented by qualitative judgments that involved assessment of managers and their personalities (Hellman, 2000, p.123). In the long descriptions of the reasoning behind transactions, one type of finding is of particular interest. When the investors made their forecasts of company and industry future earnings, they were wondering how other investors would react, assuming that they made similar forecasts. Considering other investors' possible reactions to future changes in company and industry earnings strongly affected the decision to buy or sell. The respondent could say, for example: 'That's when we made the decision to lose some weight [since] we were worried that investors in general were going to move away somewhat from this type of equity and they would fare worse than the market' (Hellman, 2000, p.91). This illustrates how other investors' expected expectations may have effects on buying and selling stock.

Studies with Complete Access to Transaction Data

Grinblatt and Keloharju (2000a) analyzed individual accounts in Finland, where most capitalized stocks are registered by a central body called the Finnish Central Securities Depositary. Their data include highly reliable data on almost all holdings and transactions for the Finnish financial market from end-1994 to end-1996. The findings show that most Finnish households, independent of portfolio size, pursued contrarian strategies whereas foreign investors, that is, large funds, used momentum strategies. Households and Finnish professionals tended to buy losers and sell winners. The exception was Finnish finance and insurance institutions and foreign investors who the authors call more sophisticated.

Momentum strategies turned out to be much more profitable, maybe because of a bull market. The authors note that if large investors pursue momentum strategies, small investors must use contrarian strategies since purchases and sales have to match. In a later study using the same data set, Grinblatt and Keloharju (2001) found evidence that investors were reluctant to realize losses and tended to sell large winners as predicted by the disposition effect theory. The effect was somewhat offset by tax-loss selling, which was most apparent in December before the end of the fiscal year.

In a third paper, these authors analyze 'home bias' exploiting the demographic variables in the data base. They found (Grinblatt and Keloharju, 2000b, pp.1–2):

- Investors in various municipalities in Finland prefer to hold and trade stocks headquartered in nearby locations to those in more distant locations.
- The distance bias is piecewise linear in the log of distance, with an abrupt change in the slope of the distance bias coefficient at 100 kilometers.
- Firms that are headquartered in Helsinki, and thus are better known nationally have much less distance bias exhibited towards them.

- Investors whose native tongue is Finnish prefer to hold and trade stocks from companies that publish their annual reports in Finnish rather than Finnish companies that publish their reports in Swedish. Multilingual companies lie between the one-language companies in the preferences of both the Swedish-speaking and Finnish-speaking investors.
- Investors in Finland exhibit a cultural bias that is separate from the language bias. They prefer to hold and trade stocks of firms whose CEO is of a similar cultural origin to their own.
- The distance, language, and cultural biases are smaller for financially 'savvy' institutions than for households or less 'savvy' institutions.
- The distance and cultural biases are smaller (but still sizable) for more sophisticated household investors.

The results seem to support the idea that 'home bias' may be inspired by feelings of familiarity. Both the availability heuristic and Gigerenzer's recognition heuristic make the same predictions of home bias in uncertain situations.

EXPERIMENTAL ASSET MARKETS

An important message seems to underlie the experimental research of a small but growing number of economists and psychologists interested in economic behavior. Briefly, it states that laboratory microeconomies are real live economic systems which are behaviorally richer than the systems parameterized in most economic theories.

Kroll et al. (1988a, p.388)

The Controlled Experiment as a Tool for Financial Research

Many findings in cognitive psychology emanate from simple experiments which can be carried out also in classroom and other group sessions such as with professionals in finance. Introducing a lecture by letting the audience first participate in an experiment the results of which the lecturer can predict with some confidence is often a good opening for making the audience aware of problems. The famous Asian disease problem from prospect theory can be translated into an investment problem and convincingly demonstrate the possibility of framing effects (Stephan and Kiell, 2000). A younger colleague of mine, Dr Richard Wahlund, has conducted a number of such experiments.

Psychological research was from its beginning characterized by the use of controlled experiments that were carried out in laboratory settings. While the experiment is still the preferred approach in some branches of psychology, survey interviews and questionnaires have become important research tools in most fields of psychology, in particular in personality and social psychology. Critique of the laboratory experiment has focused on certain problems that plague experimental research. Two phenomena that may affect economic as well as psychological laboratory experiments warrant special attention: (1) demand characteristics and (2) experimenter expectancy.

The *demand characteristics* effect arises from the fact that subjects' thoughts about an experiment may affect their behavior in carrying out the experimental task. The effects are caused by the subjects' perception of the purpose of the experiment, of the settings, of the experimenter's personal characteristics, and many other things that may contribute to the subjects forming an opinion and adjusting their behavior in accordance with the opinion. A boring task may give rise to many creative guesses about the purpose of the experiment. Studies indicate that even small details may give signals that are important to subjects. The presence of a panic button in a stressful laboratory experiment may entice subjects to experience panic while subjects with no access to a panic button do not panic. If the experimenter wears a white coat (or a tie) instead of casual wear, the different demand characteristics may lead to different results. An economist as experimenter may get different findings from a psychologist running the same experiment.

While demand characteristics emanate from the subjects' hypotheses about the experiment, *experimenter expectancy* refers to the possibility that the experimenter's hypotheses are somehow conveyed to the subjects, who knowingly or unknowingly behave in accordance with them. A simple example is that the experimenter or interviewer (without necessarily knowing it) looks pleased at certain answers and sad at others. The experimenter bias arises from the fact that experimenter hypotheses may influence the treatment of subjects. Experiments in classrooms have, for example, shown that telling a teacher in advance that a class was bright and highly motivated led to better class performance than when the teacher was told that the class was average.

Some remedies for these biases are now standard procedure in experimentation with humans. Instructions are, for example, given in written or tape-recorded form to avoid personal variations. The stimuli used and the tasks or problems are presented via computers. The responses are recorded by computers. This does not exclude the risk of demand characteristics, and for this reason it is desirable to include a debriefing at the end of the experimental session. The debriefing of subjects after an experiment involves telling the subjects about the purpose of the experiment and giving a chance for questions and comments. It is usually introduced by questions that try to find out how the subjects perceived the experiment. In a simulation study of tax evasion using a supermarket game, my colleagues and I found when debriefing subjects that some did not dare to dodge taxes with a computer! It is recommended to provide an independent test of the effectiveness of the experimental treatment – a so-called 'manipulation check' (see Aronson and

Carlsmith, 1968). Some psychologists have recommended and used deception of subjects, but there are ethical objections and the rule is that there should be informed consent for participation in an experiment.

The purpose of the laboratory experiment is to develop and test theory and establish possibilities of relationships rather than to provide estimates of the external probabilities of relationships. The laboratory experiment has survived many attacks and remains an important research tool to develop theory. Furthermore, the controlled experiment is now the major research tool in a new branch of economics, *experimental economics*. There are some characteristic differences between experiments carried out by psychologists and by economists (see Hey, 1992; Smith, 1991). While psychologists nowadays tend to strive for experimental setups that are close to the complexity of reality and have ecological validity, economists want to create clean environments to have maximum control of the situation.

Hey (1992) pictured laboratory experiments as a way for economists to test abstract theory. A given economic theory is usually assumed to be valid 'with all other things remaining the same' (*ceteris paribus*). When tested against data representing reality, this condition is rarely fulfilled. Many factors are free to play a role. In a laboratory experiment, variables that should not affect the test are in principle (but not always in practice) held under control. Hey saw this as an important reason for the rapidly increasing interest in experimental economics, despite earlier resistance from mainstream economists. He suggested that experiments should also be run on more complex theories of economic behavior, since he felt that it was in the handling of complexity that economic theory failed.

Economists study economic decisions and they want to make sure that the subjects are motivated to make economic decisions. This means that they tend to insist on monetary incentives that are related to the performance of the subjects. Whereas psychologists attempt to produce subject involvement and create motivation to participate fully in the experiment through the setup and, if possible, minor rewards, the experimental economists are anxious to instill real economic motivation, which they assume to be primarily based on monetary incentives. Variations in monetary rewards, from the usual subject payments to amounts that were considerable in size for their Chinese subjects, were studied by Kachelmeier and Shehata (1992). They found that the large rewards made some difference, which both psychologists and economists have used to support their claims.

Hey (1992) indicated that economic experiments were most often tests of specified theory and that psychological experiments were primarily aimed at suggesting theory. Typically, the psychological experiments on economic behavior have been richer, with diminished control of influencing variables as a consequence. The experiments run by economists have had a tendency to be rather abstract and somewhat devoid of content. In some cases, economic experiments have been characterized as tests of the subjects' ability to make calculations rather than tests of decision making.

Financial Market Experiments

Financial markets have for some time been studied by experimental economists, who have developed special procedures for determining or following prices of securities as these are traded in laboratory settings with the aid of computers. Experimental asset markets provide the possibility of changing and isolating factors that may influence price movements. Caginalp et al. (1999) describe the typical asset market experiment and devote special interest to the booms and bubbles that have been found to be characteristic of trading in laboratory experiments. An experiment is commonly run something like this (cf. Caginalp et al., 1999):

1. A number of participants are given some combination of cash and securities at the beginning of the experimental session.
2. The value of the securities and the cash is defined and instructions given about the trading procedure (bidding and consequences).
3. Dividends and borrowing possibilities (if any) are described.
4. The subjects trade through an auction procedure using a computer network.
5. Trading usually occurs over a number of trading periods, for example fifteen.

Attempts to avoid some of the artificiality of the laboratory experiment and to enable study of complex problems have provoked psychologists to use *microworlds* that presumably have high ecological validity. The aim of the microworld simulation is to provide decision-making situations with high ecological validity and still maintain control over what is happening (Brehmer and Dörner, 1993) . They are dynamic computer-generated environments that the subjects interact with in the laboratory and that simulate conditions encountered in the field.

Microworlds have three characteristics, according to Brehmer and Dörner (1993). They are (a) complex, (b) dynamic, and (c) opaque. The first characteristic means that subjects have to consider a number of things, such as many and conflicting goals and coupled processes with side effects. The second characteristic is that microworlds have memories. Their current state is a function of the history of the interaction between the subject and the system. The subjects have to act in real time; they cannot choose when to make a decision. The opaqueness characteristic involves that not everything is visible and that some aspects of the system have to be inferred. Precise levels of experimental control and improved accuracy and efficiency of data collection procedures are characteristic of microworlds in the opinion of DiFonzo et al. (1998). They propose that these benefits are achieved along with concomitant gains in internal validity, which is produced by high levels of experimental realism, and external validity which is produced by the replication of the temporal-interactive nature of most field phenomena. In the section on 'Rumor in the Market Place', Chapter 7, some of the results of rumor studies in experimental stock markets, designed as microworlds, were presented.

A Stock-Market Game Simulation with Personality Variables

An early game simulation of stock market behavior was carried out by Maital et al. (1986; Maital, 1982). These authors combined ideas from financial portfolio theory and psychological theory. They launched the notion that investors brought something more to the stock market than just money to invest and that there were personality characteristics that influenced how money was invested. The experiment had the following design.

1. A week before the game the subjects were given a description of the game, and a 36-week price history of seven common stocks, which were labeled alpha, beta, etc. The subjects were not told that the price histories were fabricated.
2. The subjects filled out questionnaires about their socio-economic status including asset holdings, risk aversion as measured by choices between chance bets with different probabilities, and degree of internal control according to the Rotter locus-of-control scale.
3. In the experimental session, the subjects were told that they had $10 000 and that they could spend the money on buying and selling stocks in the seven companies in such a way that they had a maximum amount at the end of the game.
4. A 1 percent commission was charged on each stock transaction. It was permitted to hold cash and 5 percent interest per annum was credited.
5. When the subjects had handed in their order form for each of the six experimental rounds, they were told the (by the experimenter predetermined) prices of the stocks.

The risk aversion measure was, as expected, negatively related to risk taking and those who were more internally controlled according to the Rotter locus- of-control scale took more risks. Those who had more internal locus of control, that is, thought that they could better control their destiny, were more prone to take risks. Men made more transactions than women and ended up with an average loss of $91 whereas women traded less often and had an average profit of $228. More women than men followed a buy-and-hold strategy. This is early evidence of an effect that Odean (1998, 1999) and Barber and Odean (2000b) demonstrated much later with the aid of accounts data. Older women who trade infrequently and who are probably insightful have been achieving the best results with their portfolios.

Experiments on Information Use

It was noted in Chapter 2 that information is used in efficient-market theory in a very special sense. Prices adjust immediately to all new information and they perfectly reflect fundamental values and nothing else. It is a sign of inefficiency if people can make money on the basis of any information, except maybe arbitrageurs who act to restore temporary imbalances in prices. The information that noise traders are assumed to act on, not knowing that they had better not react, is either misinterpreted information from price changes or private information that deviates from public information. For all its sophistication, the theory gives little guidance for behavioral research on financial information. Next, a few experimental studies that test behavioral hypotheses on the use of information in financial decision making will be summarized.

A study by Davis et al. (1994) examined the effects of seemingly helpful information on forecasts of stock earnings. The subjects' task was to forecast stock earnings. MBA students from an advanced finance course served as subjects. They used a computerized information system designed to simulate systems used in practice. Three different treatments were used: (1) baseline information, (2) baseline plus redundant news information, and (3) baseline plus non-redundant news information. Disguised actual company data were presented. While the redundant information made subjects significantly more confident in their forecasts and the non-redundant information made subjects even more confident than the baseline group, the forecast accuracy was significantly diminished in both the redundant and non-redundant conditions compared to baseline. The additional news information, whether redundant or non-redundant, had the effect of degrading performance while increasing confidence. The results are similar to psychological findings on confidence in judgments reported in Chapter 6 in the section on overconfidence.

Private information in the sense of prior knowledge was investigated in another study of behavior in a laboratory market (Anderson and Sunder, 1995). The subjects were experienced commodity and stock traders who were compared with MBA student traders. Unlike previous research, subject experience was a treatment variable in the experiment. Trading experience actually made a difference. It was found to be an important determinant of how well market outcomes approximated equilibrium predictions. Markets with student traders exhibited biases consistent with what is usually found in the literature on noise traders. Bias levels in markets with experienced traders were substantially reduced and tended towards zero. The market-level results were confirmed in individual-level tests. The authors found that it could not be unambiguously determined whether the market outcomes with experienced traders were better organized through using Bayes' rule or through using a heuristic base-rate neglect.

In an efficient market, insiders may conceivably have information before others. If they use it – which is mostly illegal – the relevant stock price should adjust immediately and the market remain efficient. Insiders have information that is not as yet available to other traders and is thus asymmetric. Traders who are not insiders can receive the information only through the signals which they get from insiders' behavior in the market and as revealed by stock prices. Güth et al. (1997) report an experiment in which information and asset value and composition were varied. In contrast to the insider view that follows from efficient-market theory, the authors relied on evidence from behavioral studies and formulated hypotheses that challenge the theory.

A pilot experiment was conducted with 54 student subjects who traded in 14 rounds, a number not known in advance by the subjects. Two investment alternatives were open to the subjects. The riskless asset was cash, which gave no interest. The risky asset was called a security and its money value or payoff varied depending on the drawing of balls from an urn. At the end of each round, five balls were randomly drawn from an urn containing a mixture of white balls (worth DM 0.2) and black balls (worth DM 0.04). The sum of the balls was the fundamental value of the security. The price of the security was fixed in such a way that the lowest possible price was chosen from the set of prices that maximized the number of units traded. At the end of the experiment, the subjects were paid the real value of their portfolios. The security was valued at its fundamental value.

Two groups of subjects started trading with cash as the only asset, either DM 10 or DM 50, while two groups started trading with securities as the only asset, either 14 or 70 securities. The small portfolios corresponded to a 'poor' condition whereas the large portfolios were the 'rich' condition. The hypothesis was that there would be an endowment effect such that the cash traders would end up with less securities than the securities traders. The hypothesis was supported by the data and the alternative hypothesis that portfolio composition depended only on differences in risk aversion was rejected. Half of the subjects were informed traders, 'insiders', and were told about the fundamental value of the security at the end of each period in addition to common knowledge about the price and sales volume. The other group, 'outsiders', got the same information without the fundamental value. It turned out that uninformed traders displayed more of an endowment effect than the informed traders. Risk aversion, which was assessed through a pre-test involving risky choice with some financial consequence, did not contribute to explaining the trading behavior. The design permitted analysis of discrepancies between prices and fundamental value. The conclusion was that there was a systematic tendency for an undervaluation of the asset in relation to its fundamental value. Interestingly, the curve for the fundamental value looks like a bubble since in the ninth period a dramatic drop occurred in it.

Tests of the CAPM and Mean-Variance Model

Normative portfolio theories are used to describe financial market behavior. Kroll et al. (1988a) set out to test the use of the mean-variance model for practical decisions in experimental game situations. In the same vein, Kroll et al. (1988b) tested the CAPM separation theorem. In the first study, 15 statistically knowledgeable male and female undergraduate students took part in two self-paced sessions, each involving 20 portfolio selection problems with monetary payoff contingent on performance. The portfolio selection task: (1) included two independent risky assets with normally distributed returns, (2) provided access to information about past returns, (3) permitted borrowing and lending at a fixed interest rate, and (4) forced on each decision period a selection between two risky assets with normally distributed returns. The task was administered to each participant individually by a computer. Findings showed: (1) a high percentage of inefficient mean-variance portfolios that did not decrease with practice, (2) a high rate of requests for information concerning past returns even though the subjects had complete information about the parameters of the distributions of return (it probably meant a vain search for patterns), (3) a large frequency of switches between the two risky assets, and (4) sequential dependencies. The authors concluded that the findings were not particularly favorable to the mean-variance model.

In the second study, Kroll et al. (1988b) let the subjects, who were of the same type as in the preceding experiment, make choices between three risky assets and in part of the experiment a riskless asset was added. As predicted by CAPM, the subjects diversified their investments among the three assets, but they invested in the riskiest asset much more than predicted. When the assigned capital was increased tenfold, the subjects selected less risky portfolios and diversified more among the three assets. The introduction of the riskless asset did not change as is predicted by the mutual-funds separation theorem; all traders are expected to have the same composition of risky assets and to show their risk aversion in the balance between risky and riskless assets. The authors warn against using too trivial amounts of money in experiments. Since rewards were related to performance subjects in the second experiment were on average very well paid.

Experimental Tests of the Disposition Effect

Weber and Camerer (1998) studied the *disposition effect*, which involves investors tending to sell winners and keep losers. Two phenomena that can be investigated in laboratory experiments make up the disposition effect: (a) the choice of the reference point that decides whether something is a loss or a gain, and (b) risk seeking for losses in order to avoid losses and risk aversion guiding the striving for gains. Loss aversion makes people hesitate to realize losses. The authors assume that the initial purchase price is a first natural reference point. They note that 'for a larger number of periods each former price of the stock (or some weighted average of them) could serve as a reference point' (Weber and Camerer, 1998, p.170). Both types of reference point are used in the experiments reported. It can be argued that after some time the choice of reference point may be strongly affected by the highest price during a period. Anecdotal evidence suggests that people are very much disappointed when prices of their stocks drop from a high value. Tax advisors tell stories of people who have sold stocks at a much lower price than the top price noted and want to claim deductions for losses despite the fact that the original purchase price was much lower than the selling price.

The above authors found that both purchase price and previous prices affected framing and guided choices. The disposition effect caused the subjects, who were students familiar with probabilities and statistics, to make less money than they would otherwise have done. The effects were in accordance with prospect theory and in clear conflict with portfolio theory. The evidence was in favor of prospect theory, but the authors could not wholly exclude the alternative hypothesis that there were expectations of reversion towards the mean. The subjects may have thought that losing stocks would bounce back and that winning stocks had reached their top level and would fall.

A recent experiment on the disposition effect paid special attention to the effect of reference points (Heilmann et al., 2000). Two reference points were used, namely the price of the previous period and the fundamental value of the asset in the previous period. In these experiments, the asset prices were determined by the actions of the traders and the fundamental value followed a certain stochastic process whose parameters were known by all subjects. At the beginning of each period, the subjects received information about the expected fundamental value so that, in that sense, all were insiders (cf. Güth et al., 1997, reviewed earlier). The results indicated a clear disposition effect, independent of reference point.

The authors raise the question of how there can be trade when a large number of holders of winners want to sell. They suggest two answers on the basis of their research data. One answer is that not all individuals are subject to the disposition effect. The second answer is that stock holders do not have the same reference point and consequently are not all in the market at the same time for the same type of transaction. As Grinblatt and Keloharju (2000a) pointed out, when large investors practice momentum strategies, small investors have to be contrarian.

Experimental Studies of Bubbles

According to efficient-market and rational-expectations theory, stock prices will converge at fundamentals. Prices in experimental asset markets tend to bubble and then crash to the dividend value at the end of the asset's useful life. The experiments are usually run in 15 rounds and dividends are given with known probabilities. Explanations for the bubble and crash phenomenon are, according to Porter and Smith (1995): (1) participants cannot form reliable future price expectations, or (2) dividend risk aversion. The paper reports results of experiments to test these hypotheses. In one experimental series, a futures market was introduced so that participants could obtain information on future stock prices. In another series of experiments, the per-period dividend was known with certainty. While the futures-market treatment reduced the bubble, the certain-dividend treatment had little effect on the character of bubbles with inexperienced traders. The initial-period trading price was well below the fundamental value, but in the intermediate periods the price rose well above the fundamental value and then dropped to the fundamental value of zero at the end of the experiment.

Caginalp et al. (1999) remark that in experimental markets with dividends during a defined number of time periods and a definite end, bubbles and final crashes inevitably occur in price movements:

> The large number of variations on this experiment have included the use of short selling and margin buying, the imposition of trading costs, the removal of any uncertainty of expected dividends, the use of equal initial endowment to traders, the addition of futures markets, the imposition of price change limitations and the use of corporate executives or small business persons as the subject pool. None of these factors were found to eliminate the boom and bust (Caginalp et al., 1999, pp.216–17)

These experiments are analogous to initial public offerings (IPOs) of stocks in financial markets. Caginalp et al. (1999) note this and suggest that the discounts often found in closed-end funds can be explained with the same differential equation theory as the experimental bubbles and crashes. The explanation of the discount is that there is a saturated market at the outset and investors who would like to purchase have inadequate cash because of earlier commitments.

Some Reflections on Investment Games

Results from experimental asset markets seem to confirm many observations showing that individual investors act in ways that are highly different from the micro model that is the underpinning of efficient-market theory. Controlled experiments serve to clarify issues and provide theory that can be adapted and tested in surveys through diary-keeping, careful questioning, repeated interviews or observations, and judicious use of tests built into questionnaires. Hypotheses can also be tested through actions in practical financial-market situations, provided the actions are properly prepared and followed up. Economic and psychological experiments yield results that can give structure to attempts at understanding financial behaviors. Shefrin (2000), for example, relies on many experimental findings and applies the thinking to illuminating cases and anecdotal evidence. He finds that theories from laboratory experiments provide plausible explanations of market events.

In investment games, a term used here to cover all sorts of experiments, subjects are typically left alone with instructions in front of a computer and requested to make decisions in a number of periods with little delay. While the experimental markets are often determined by interaction among buyers and sellers, personal interaction and influence are rarely permitted. In view of the importance of social influence in its many forms, more research interest devoted to social interaction in financial management is called for.

Studies of behavior in experimental asset markets may give an exaggerated picture of investor activity, given the pressures on the subjects. Or maybe the investigators fail to report on observations of passivity in the games. In real life, many investors are rather passive, judging from their number of transactions, but may still be involved and interested in what goes on in the stock market. Perhaps psychologists could develop experimental procedures for studying passive, but large investors more closely. It is likely that their decision making is at variance with the assumptions of steady activity that underlies most theory. The passive investors have considerable portions of total stock ownership.

9. Investor Groups and Market Segments

INVESTOR DIFFERENCES AND SEGMENTS OF INVESTORS

The Need for Data on Individual Financial Behavior

Many observations and studies of financial markets suggest that individual investors, like people in general, do not display the rational behavior that efficient-market and portfolio-choice theories posit, not even if averages over long periods of time are considered. While the pursuit of rationality implies limited dispersion around the mean and suggests homogeneity and similarity among investors, non-rationality leaves room for the pursuit of many types of goals and opens up possibilities of many ways of acting. In economic psychology, the prevalent tendency is to stress the importance of individual differences and to group people into clusters or segments on the basis of differences in behavior or personal characteristics. Clusters formed on the basis of differences in one set of variables are then compared with regard to other characteristics. Data on financial and psychological characteristics of investors have in some cases been used to distinguish segments of investors in such a way that large groups of investors with great similarities within groups and significant differences between groups have been distinguished. The purpose of the chapter is to review some studies that have made such attempts at finding segments of investors, whether as a basis for financial marketing campaigns or for more basic scientific reasons.

Aggregate data rarely permit any breakdowns corresponding to individual characteristics. Data from income tax returns can sometimes be used to study broadly defined groups (Blume and Friend, 1975; Kelly, 1997) or data from accounts in brokerage firms can be employed to analyze individual trading patterns (Schlarbaum et al., 1978; Odean, 1999). On the whole, special interview surveys, which tend to be expensive and may be seen by respondents as intrusive, are necessary to provide the data desired for distinguishing segments. When survey data are gathered, the focus is usually on socio-demographic, income and wealth variables while only a few psychological variables, if any, are included. Some notable exceptions exist, such as US studies of old-age financial and health conditions (the AHEAD project; Hurd, 1999), the Dutch CentER Savings Surveys (Alessie et al., 1999), and a few, comprehensive German (psychonomics & Capital, 1998, 1999) and Swedish (Gunnarsson et al., 2000) studies. Shiller (1999, 2000) reports a number of surveys he has conducted over many years which have been based on judgment and evaluation questions as well as questions on financial expectations. In principle, financially interesting segmentation could be based on these variables, but to my knowledge this has not been done.

Marketing Use of Breakdowns into Segments

A fundamental idea in many marketing policies is that there exist groups of potential and actual consumers who have to be treated differently in achieving marketing success. Minor differences in preferences or tastes among consumers may stimulate producers to differentiate their products and to seek varying ways of reaching and communicating with the market targets. Among the ways of dividing up and serving the groups in the market, segmentation based on differences in perceived benefits have been the most talked about. Segmentation based on psychological variables other than perceived benefits is also commonly discussed in marketing texts.

Market segmentation is a well-established idea and has its place in financial marketing. A few studies have, for example, concerned the use of segments in the marketing of financial services by banks (see, for example, Ramaswamy et al., 1996). For a review of studies, see Gunnarsson (1999). Kamakura et al. (1991) make the assumption that financial services are adopted in a certain order. Classification of bank customers into different categories based on this order was used to estimate the likelihood (transition probability) that a customer who belonged to a certain category would purchase additional services.

While segmentation in marketing contexts is oriented towards decision and policy making, the study of segments can also serve other purposes. If there are significant differences in characteristics and behaviors between segments of investors, it may be possible to explain earlier developments and make forecasts of aggregate behavior in a better way. The effects of policy changes at the macro level, such as changes in interest rates or the effects of plummeting stock prices, may vary for different segments of investors. Margin buyers may react more strongly than usually passive investors. Adding the differential effects of segments may give a better picture of the total effect or at least improve the understanding of what is happening. In estimating possible effects of policy changes or of stock-price developments, it seems important to look for groups of investors who may react differently in the financial market.

Most of the segmentation studies reported on in the rest of the chapter have been done by researchers who in a broad way have had marketing applications in mind, but the segments found also have a wider application. They may, for example, serve financial analysts in their attempts to interpret and foresee market developments. Understanding of behaviors and reactions in various segments may improve forecasts of effects of policy measures and of events like political elections and political disturbances. The findings in some studies that were reviewed in earlier chapters suggest that the differences among investors may be considerable and worth serious attention. All investors very seldom react in exactly the same way to news and other mass media reports that depress stock prices. If they did, there would not be any buyers willing to buy the stocks that anxious sellers throw into the market. The effects of catastrophes and other portentous events may vary significantly between segments of active and passive investors (Niederhoffer, 1971; Schachter et al., 1986).

From One to Many Types of Investors

The debate over market efficiency has already recognized there may be more than one kind of investor and launched the concept of noise trader for a kind of non-rational investor. While some economists leave room for alternative assumptions about rational behavior, they usually assume that at least one group of information traders or arbitrageurs exists and attempts to maximize expected utility in the way the theory prescribes. Otherwise, it would be hard to calculate equilibria. Campbell and Mankiw (1989, 1990, and 1991) accepted the fact that the Life-Cycle Hypothesis (LCH) could explain only part of household savings and proposed the existence of two groups of consumers. One group consisted of those who were liquidity-constrained or rule-of-thumb consumers and who spent all of their current income. The other group comprised those who were forward-looking consumption smoothers and who behaved in accordance with the rationality-based LCH and invested their money. The two groups were assumed to have about equal sizes in the USA. The authors expected that the rich would behave more like the way that the LCH assumed and prescribed. They tested their model on aggregate data from the USA and a number of other countries and found support for it (Campbell and Mankiw, 1991, p.753). The proportion of LCH savers varied considerably among the countries studied.

In a similar vein, Browning and Lusardi (1996, p.1797) said: 'It is unlikely that a single explanation will suffice for all members of a population at any given time or even for the same person over a long stretch of time'. The distinction made by Campbell and Mankiw is analogous to the common division of investors into information and noise traders. One type lives up to the predictions of the rationality-based theories and makes close calculations; the other type simply follows the spur of the moment. Since this distinction concerns only savers, a third group should perhaps be added: the never-savers. The idea of three groups of savers was suggested by Weil (1991). His groups were: (a) non-savers, (b) forward-looking savers, and (c) the non-forward-looking savers. The very rich were likely members of the last category. Weil also recommended that more attention should be given to the value of housing. A comparatively large proportion of the elderly population in the USA owned a valuable house but few financial assets.

Shiller (1989) proposed a model with two types of traders in financial markets: smart-money investors and ordinary investors. Smart-money investors are assumed to search systematically for investments with abnormal returns and to respond quickly and appropriately to information that becomes publicly available. Ordinary investors include everyone who does not respond to expected returns optimally forecasted, but are supposed to overreact to news and be vulnerable to fads.

Kelly (1997; see Chapter 2) distinguishes between three types of investors. He appends the passive investor to the collection: (1) smart-money traders, (2) noise traders, and (3) passive investors. While the smart-money traders behave rationally, the noise traders buy high and sell low and the passive investors do little business. Kelly assumes that an individual's probability of being a noise trader declines with income since those with high income have greater incentives to acquire reliable information about the market. Low-income groups are consequently mostly noise traders – if they trade at all. Very high-income groups predominantly contain smart-money traders. Passive investors are to be found in intermediate-income groups. Market participation of noise traders is assumed to have a negative effect on future stock returns and smart-money trader participation to have a positive effect. The participation of passive investors would have no effect at all. Kelly tested his ideas through simulations performed on data from the Internal Revenue Service, Statistics of Income Series, which is based on income tax returns. He concluded that the simulation tests strongly supported the model.

The results from other financial research also give strong support to the idea of more than one category of investors. Canner et al. (1997), who examined policy recommendations to customers of leading brokerage firms, distinguished between three types of risk takers among investors: (1) conservative, (b) moderate, and (c) aggressive risk takers. They studied four sources of advice to the three groups of investors and found that all of them recommended falling ratios of bonds to stocks as the investor became more willing to take risk. The study can be seen as an example of finding categories that can be used for segmentation purposes. The brokers obviously worked with market segments to which they attributed different qualities and tried to some extent at least to adjust their recommendations.

For the categories of investors that have been proposed by the above financial economists, no direct estimates of the relative frequencies have been made by the authors, except for the estimates of Campbell and Mankiw. The latter authors did indeed suggest that about half of US consumers could be labeled rational, LCH-conforming consumers. The categories have in no case that I know of been used in attempts to assess whether the reactions to market changes differ between them so as to get a better understanding of what is happening.

A British Survey of Market Segments of Savers

In two British studies, one of which was a replication for validation purposes, Harrison (1994) reported on financial segments. She arrived at the idea of four financial segments through crossing financial knowledge and financial maturity with two values each (low and high). This gave four groups which were labeled: (1) apathetic minimalists, (2) financially confused, (3) capital accumulators, and (4) cautious investors. Cluster analysis of mail interview data from a sample of 1 400 respondents identified the expected four groups and revealed that 42 percent of the sample could be classified as apathetic minimalists, 16 percent as financially confused, 10 percent as capital accumulators, and, finally, 32 percent as cautious investors. The last two segments are of particular interest here.

The capital accumulators were married, male, aged 55–64 years, had older children or none, had higher education, had high income, and were heavy savers. They were knowledgeable and ready to to take risks in their investments. The author says that they had a bias towards equity-based investments. The cautious investors were more often single, aged 16–34 years, had finished education at age 18–25, were employed in supervisory or managerial occupations, and had very high income. They were interested in safer savings, pensions and endowments.

This British study gives the impression that a large proportion of the two investor clusters were persistent savers for long-term goals and were rather passive as investors. It is interesting to note that if the financially confused, who had low income and low education, had stocks, the stocks mostly came from privatization issues.

Studies of Saver Groups

Gunnarsson and Wahlund (1997) employed the idea of saver groups in their analysis of a 1993 sample (N = 503) of Swedish households who were interviewed in a mail survey. In a carefully executed cluster analysis, with possessions of a number of assets as clustering variables, they distinguished six groups of savers who differed in their financial strategies. The six groups were labeled as follows (Gunnarsson and Wahlund, 1997, pp.210–11):

1. *Residual savers* (45 percent of the sample). They put aside money when some money was left and preferred saving forms with high liquidity. They had a fairly high debt-to-asset ratio of 1 (the financial debts divided by financial assets).
2. *Contractual savers* (22 percent). They seemed to have borrowed freely and saved through paying off debts and had a debt-to-asset ratio of 4.2.
3. *Security savers* (14 percent). They were the heaviest investors in retirement-related financial instruments such as private pension plans and they had some investment in stocks and bonds, but mostly avoided risky investment. Their debt-to-asset ratio was 1.3.
4. *Risk hedgers* (9 percent) They had large financial wealth, invested in risky and long-term assets (stock, mutual funds, and options). Their debt-to-asset ratio was 0.52.
5. *Prudent investors* (3 percent). They had large savings and avoided risky investments, preferring bonds to stocks. Their debt-to-asset ratio was 0.28.
6. *Divergent strategies* (6 percent). They had well-diversified portfolios and invested in risky, complex, and unusual assets such as options. Their debt-to-asset ratio was 0.50.

A few things should be noted with respect to investments in stocks and mutual funds. Groups 3, 4 and 5 invested in stocks and mutual funds among other things. They thus tended to avoid high risk taking, but could afford to lose some money if need be. The last group comprised the real risk takers, who apparently were prepared to lose their own money since they had on average little debt.

The authors discussed the use of this grouping as a way of segmenting the population of households and found that there were clear implications for policy and marketing strategies. The idea behind segmentation in marketing is that consumer groups, which can be revealed, for example, through cluster analysis, are differently sensitive to marketing activities, and therefore should be treated differently through product differentiation and choice of market communication means.

Gunnarsson and Wahlund's (1997) study with data from 1993 was repeated with a new representative sample in 1999 (Gunnarsson et al., 2000). Cluster analysis was again used to sort out the same segments of savers. The segment of residual savers decreased from 45 percent in 1993 to 26 percent in 1999. The contractual savers decreased from 22 to 17 percent whereas the segments with a wider assortment of financial activities increased. The authors suggest that there had been a development towards more activity, more interest in risky assets, and more diversification among the households.

Using cluster analysis of Dutch data from CentER Savings Surveys at Tilburg University, Gunnarsson (1999) investigated the stability of segments. The segmentation variables used were similar to those used in the earlier Swedish study: liquid and transactional saving forms, savings or deposit accounts, bonds, saving certificates, mutual funds, common stocks, pension insurance, and employer-sponsored savings plans. For each segmentation variable, only two values were used in the analysis: used by respondent household or not used. A solution with five clusters gave the best fit. The clusters were labeled: (1) diversifiers (20 percent of the households in the 1996 survey), (2) liquid savers (27 percent), (3) security-focused savers (14 percent), (4) risk minimizers (32 percent), and (5) non-savers (7 percent).

Stock owning was most common among the diversifiers, of whom 10 percent owned stocks and 15 percent participated in mutual funds in 1996. The most important variables for distinguishing between the clusters (but not included in the cluster analysis) were household net income, net wealth, and being a homeowner. Two psychological variables were important: the household's attitudes to financial risk taking and the importance of safe savings. While the segments were fairly stable over time (two years), individuals showed considerable movements between segments. The major factor affecting the segmentation was the introduction of an innovation, namely employer-sponsored saving plans, which rapidly became popular.

Part of the study carried out by Gunnarsson et al. (2000) focused on a special sample of high income earners. Four clusters or segments were distinguished in this sample:

1. *Cautious diversifiers* (24 percent) had well-diversified portfolios with on average 28 percent of the financial wealth invested in stocks and 14 percent in bonds.
2. *Aggressive diversifiers* (34 percent) had broad portfolios without any bonds. The members of this segment had significantly lower risk aversion than the others.
3. *Contractual savers, with children living at home* (21 percent) had relatively simple portfolios with little (but still some) investment in stocks and bonds. They were often burdened by loans and debts which they were paying back (for example, student loans).
4. *Pension averse* (21 percent). This group had little interest in retirement saving, partly because many of them were single or already retired. They had broad portfolios with little investment in insurance and pension systems.

Table 9.1. gives some further information on the segments. The net sample size (after non-response) was 515 respondents. Nearly 90 percent of the members in both segments of diversifiers were stock owners. With respect to level of activity, the table shows that while there were clear differences compared to the other segments, the two segments of diversifiers were rather similar in being passive during 1998: 38 percent of the cautious diversifiers and 35 percent of the aggressive diversifiers did not make any transaction at all. Around 60 percent in both groups judged themselves to be passive in financial matters on the seven-point scale used. At the same time, their mean subjective ratings of interest and involvement in financial matters were very high and they similarly rated their regular information seeking as very high. Even passive investors seemed to want to be continually informed and they judged themselves to be knowledgeable. The fact that there are few transactions of stocks in certain segments should not be interpreted as lack of interest and knowledge. It could rather mean discretion and self-control.

Table 9.1 Some Characteristics of Swedish High-Income Segments

	Cautious Diversifiers	Aggressive Diversifiers	Contractual Savers	Pension Averse
Bought and sold stocks in 1998 (%)	41	38	20	8
No stock transactions in 1998 (%)	38	35	60	58
Judged themselves passive (%)	60	59	91	90
Regular information seeking *	4.9	5.1	3.7	4.4
Fin. Interest and involvement *	5.2	5.1	4.6	4.7
Subjective knowledge rating *	5.5	5.4	4.7	5.0
Average age in years	55	53	49	53
Stock owners (%)	89	90	11	34
Participating in mutual funds (%)	80	87	16	60

* Scale from 1 to 7 where 7 means highest.
Source: Gunnarsson et al. (2000).

Investor Segments in Germany

German researchers in economic psychology have carried out a number of studies of German investors (see Müller-Peters, 1999; psychonomics & Capital, 1998, 1999; see also Chapter 8). One survey comprised interviews with a sample of around 3 500 households. Questions about economic and socio-demographic characteristics were asked, but the dominant content of the interview was concentrated on various aspects of what the researchers called 'financial mentality'. Six psychological variables were used in a cluster analysis. These were: (1) the need for control of financial matters, (2) the fun found in dealing with financial matters, (3) the preparedness to take risks, (4) the preference for simplicity in investments, (5) the quest for liquidity, to have easy access to assets, and (6) the preference for personal advice from financial experts. Seven groups of private investors emerged. They were labeled and described in the following way (only brief summaries of the descriptions are given here).

1. *The professional* [Der Profi] (9.2 percent). Very familiar with finances, high income makes taking high risks possible. Returns are primary consideration. Self-confident and independent of advisors.
2. *The choosy* [Der Anspruchsvolle] (17.1 percent). Knowledgeable, but – probably for reasons of time – delegates actions to competent others without giving up control. Rather low risk taking and this person prefers real estate and fixed-income securities. Places high demands on her/himself and on others.
3. *The player* [Der Spielerische] (12.9 percent). Takes high risks without having ample resources. Usually goes ahead without advice although s/he does not have a feeling of knowing everything. Main goal is to have fun and gratifying experiences. Interested in stocks, not in real estate. This person is willing to finance life-style through credits.
4. *The holder-back* [Der Zurückhaltende] (13.4 percent). Over average income. Somewhat suspicious of everything that has to do with investing. Rejects advice and has high risk aversion. Places money in fixed-income securities and real estate, which means that the wealth remains modest.
5. *The regular saver* [Der Ansparer] (13.1 percent). This person patiently and regularly puts aside money from under-average income and accumulates considerable wealth in relation to income. Appreciates advice, but wants simple investing, preferably keeping the money in bank savings accounts (with low interest). Avoids any risk taking and is not even fond of fixed-income securities.
6. *The constrained* [Der Eingeschränkte] (17.9 percent). Does not have enough cash to invest. Liquidity considerations are very important due to permanent shortage of money. Cannot indulge in any investing, but would be interested if both hands were not tied.
7. *The resigned* [Der Resignierte] (16.4). The idea of investing money is foreign and uninteresting because of poor financial situation. Main concern is about immediate liquidity.

The frequency of stock ownership and participation in mutual funds for each segment is shown in Table 9.2, displayed as 'sample 1'.

Table 9.2 Financial Mentality in German Samples (percent in agreement with statement)

	Profes-sional.	Choosy	Player	Holder-Back	Regular Saver	Con-strained	Resigned
Risk[1]							
Sample 1	85	23	64	4	5	6	3
Sample 2	85	10	75	1	7	4	6
Returns[2]							
Sample 1	88	68	66	48	38	39	29
Sample 2	86	76	73	73	51	59	54
Liquidity[3]							
Sample 1	54	64	58	61	26	92	90
Sample 2	52	64	65	65	45	91	93
Simplicity[4]							
Sample 1	69	90	76	85	98	98	95
Sample 2	52	91	80	91	98	98	99
Stocks							
Sample 1	42	13	13	8	2	3	1
Mut. funds							
Sample 1	26	5	4	3	3	2	0
Sample 2	40	17	26	16	12	9	6

Notes:

1. I am willing to take a higher risk to achieve higher interest or return (Um eine höhere Verzinsung oder Rendite zu erzielen, nehme ich auch ein erhöhtes Risiko in Kauf).
2. When you think of the next two years, how important is your financial goal: achieving the highest possible gains? (Wenn Sie an den nächsten zwei Jahren denken: Wie wichtig sind Ihnen dann Ihre Ziele im finanziellen Bereich: Möglichst hohe Gewinne erzielen?).
3. You tie yourself up too much with long-term investment. I want to have my money at my disposal at all times (Mit langfristigen Geldanlagen bindet man sich zu stark. Ich möchte jederzeit über mein Geld verfügen können).
4. For me, investing must be as simple and uncomplicated as possible (Geldanlage muß für mich möglichst einfach und unkompliziert sein).

Source: psychonomics & Capital, (1998, 1999).

The differences in stock ownership are striking. Whereas 42 percent of the professionals own stocks, the resigned group owns stocks in less than 1 percent of cases. Participation in stock funds is much lower than direct ownership of stocks. The professionals group is also here clearly different from the others. The choosy segment and the players are similar in frequencies and at a level somewhere between the professionals and the last three groups. The segments show dramatic differences in risk aversion. The professional group is much more risk seeking than the others, followed by the players group, which is also quite risk seeking in comparison with the other groups.

In the later study (psychonomics & Capital, 1999), a sample of people who either had some wealth (over DM 10 000) or had invested over DM 5 000 in the last year, and had no direct-owned stocks, were interviewed by telephone. The purpose was again to ascertain the respondents' 'financial mentality'. The questions were similar to those used in the 1998 study and the idea was to find out about psychological resistance to buying stocks. The authors talk about the 'magic rectangle of investment decisions', according to which the decision to invest in stocks depends on: (1) risk taking (degree of risk aversion), (2) returns, (3) liquidity, and (4) simplicity Those who want high liquidity and simplicity and are highly risk averse are not attracted by the higher returns that stocks can give. In Table 9.2, the second study is referred to as 'sample 2'.

The same clusters or segments were applied to sample 2. The members of sample 2 were wealthier than those of sample 1, due to the sampling condition, and the sizes of the clusters differed from those of sample 1. The professionals were 15.3 percent, the choosy 23.9 percent, the players 11.4 percent, the holders-back 12 percent, the regular savers 11.4 percent, the constrained 18.5 percent, and the resigned 6.4 percent. The first sample had around 10 percent stock owners and 5 percent of the sample participated in mutual or other funds. The second sample contained no stock owners, but participation in mutual funds was 19 percent and thus much higher than in sample 1.

The response patterns are quite similar for the two samples. For each segment type, at least one difference is larger than the others, but the dimensions vary from segment to segment. Those who are willing to take higher risks are more frequent among the professionals and the players. The former are apparently financially more able to take losses if losses occur than the latter, who seem to be more gamblers. The differences in risk seeking between the samples are small, except for the choosy groups and the players. The players in sample 2 show a high frequency of risk seekers who probably seek their risks outside of the stock market, but one-fourth of them participate in mutual funds. Maximizing gains is highly important for the professionals and only slightly less so for the choosy. For the least affluent segments, liquidity is the most important consideration. They also value simplicity.

The major distinguishing attribute for the professionals segment in the two samples is the simplicity demanded by members of the first sample. Somehow, this difference seems to run in the wrong direction since 42 percent in this segment in sample 1 own stocks directly and stock owning is usually assumed to be rather complex than simple. Obviously, many stock owners in the professionals group must have seen stock owning as fulfilling the requirement of simplicity. Another possible interpretation may be that members of this segment who did not possess common stocks did not perceive trading with stocks as attractive for other reasons; the fact that many of them (48 percent) did not find simplicity important may not have helped them overcome their hesitation. Other data in the reports suggested, according to the authors, that many non-owners of stocks had exaggerated views of the difficulty of stock trading and ownership. Forty percent of the professionals in sample 2 had invested in stock funds, which is presumably simpler than investing in stocks, but need not always be. These may be easier to understand, tend to be more stable thanks to the diversification over companies, and may not be perceived as requiring constant attention.

While Table 9.2 contains interesting information about segments, it gives little guidance for discriminating between owners and non-owners of stocks. The two reports present a wealth of material that illustrates differences between owners and non-owners of stocks which unfortunately cannot be summarized here for lack of space.

IS THERE A COMMON THREAD?

The theoretical discussion of investor groups has concentrated on two or three groups. Consistent with efficient-market theory, a group of rational, Bayesian traders has been assumed to exist. While the assumed size of this group has varied from 100 percent in the original assumption down to doubts about whether it exists at all, the current discussion intimates that the doubts about its existence may be closest to the truth. Black (1986) asserted that noise trading was prevalent and actually a prerequisite for a functioning financial market in practice. The implication is that noise traders create new opportunities for those who are able to look through the patterns of noise trading and use the knowledge to their own advantage.

Empirical studies demonstrate that most privately owned stocks are held by people who are well-to-do and who can relatively easily (but hardly willingly) afford losses on their holdings. A small group of investors speculates actively and some of those buy at the margin, that is, they buy stock on borrowed money. They may have chosen to borrow money to buy stocks since they had few other assets. Their holdings may go up and down so that they are rich one day and poor the next. If the prices of their stocks plummet, the loan givers ask for new collateral, which may bring ruin to the borrowers. Such investors probably admit, even to themselves, that they are taking great risks and depend on luck since skill is not enough.

The survey-based studies of investors that were briefly summarized in the last two chapters show results that confirm the idea that there are important differences among investors. There are active and passive stock investors and those can be further divided into subgroups. From an individual investor perspective, it seems reasonable to distinguish at least three groups of investors:

1. Investors who invest some, but never all of their wealth in risky securities and who are not very active; they prefer to buy rather than to sell, and keep adding to their financial wealth.
2. Wealthy investors who systematically invest in securities and who often employ the services of expert traders.
3. Investors who speculate, have few other assets, and sometimes borrow money to exploit what they think of as opportunities.

A fourth group should be added:

4. Naive investors who are enticed by stories of high profits. Some of them may be lured by the marketing efforts accompanying privatization sales of stocks in government-owned companies.

These categories or segments have some similarity to Kelly's (1997) three groups in that passive investors are included. The first group is a passive group. The second group is more active. To what extent the two groups are noise traders or rational, smart-money traders may be difficult to ascertain and it may not be useful to know for segmentation purposes. They act within their limits, which means that they do not take risks that they cannot (easily) afford, but they may sometimes act on the spur of the moment and be pushed by some shifts in sentiment. Even if their retirement income may not turn out to be as high as expected, they will certainly manage. The third group may be rational, but it seems more likely that they are noise traders who act on all sorts of information and rumors.

The first group is likely to play safe, meaning that they probably choose stocks in large, well-known companies rather than put their money into developing companies with more uncertain futures but the potential for higher returns. Cautious investors tend to choose stocks that come from well-known firms that have had good results over long periods of time. The members of the first group are closer to struggling for financial survival and the third group tries hard to upgrade its wealth. The strategy of playing safe is likely to lead to some overinvestment in popular stocks with exaggerated prices as a consequence (a consequence of the use of the recognition heuristic, perhaps). The fourth group, finally, is very small, but the losses may cut deeply and cause financial difficulties. If they gain, the profits tend to be moderate over the first years – unless they happened to invest in Finnish Nokia at an early stage and kept their stocks long enough to enjoy the upward swing. There are in fact Nokia millionaires in Finland with no other stocks or assets, according to mass media reports, which are corroborated by Grinblatt and Keloharju (2000a, 2001).

10. Implications and Some Further Thoughts on Private Investing

With social science, theories change the way people think about themselves, and that changes what people are.

Lopes (1994, p. 222)

The Aims of the Chapter

Finance is an interesting and promising area for psychological research that can get much inspiration from economics and, in particular, from behavioral finance. Financial economics as well as much of behavioral finance has market-level events and outcomes as its main preoccupation, and researchers use models of individual behavior with this perspective in mind. Researchers in both disciplines help practitioners in the search for explanations of stock-price developments and they try to modify the prevalent theory so as to accommodate developments in financial markets that are foreign to it. Even in behavioral finance, the use of findings from psychology is mainly aimed at making observed market-level developments understandable and plausible. For a psychologist, it is natural to concentrate interest on individual experience and behavior, to test hypotheses about individuals, and then perhaps see if the thinking can be applied to aggregates, in the first place to broad segments in the population of investors.

The final chapter will summarize some of the ideas from earlier chapters and in some cases push those a little further to generate a more coherent picture of investors and their financial idiosyncrasies. The suggested hypotheses which do not always as yet have sufficient empirical support may stimulate researchers to new research and practitioners to do some extra pondering about individuals and segments in financial markets.

WHAT IS THE TYPICAL STOCK HOLDER LIKE?

What is the typical stock holder like? The answer that emerges from the earlier chapters, in particular from the last two chapters, is that the typical stockholder does not exist if typical refers to most stock holders. There is simply not one dominant type of investor. Investors vary in characteristics, but may be classified into categories, the number of which depends on the intended use of the categories. Certain actions or reactions in specific situations can be said to be typical in the sense that the majority of investors sometimes tend to act and react in the same way. The common stereotype of one single-minded investor should be avoided.

Are common descriptions about investor expectations anywhere near the truth? In financial economics, the economic description of the rational stock investor dominates. Although efficient-market theory needs a maximizing, Bayesian investor who handles probability distributions expertly, the theory nowadays allows for considerable individual deviations from rationality, and recognizes the existence of so-called noise trading. The disagreement is rather focused on how disturbing to the market noise trading is than on whether noise traders exist in the market. In behavioral finance, the typical stock owner or trader is characterized by cognitive limitations and the use of simplifying heuristics, commonly referred to as cognitive bias or cognitive errors. Sometimes, all or most investors are assumed to suffer from the same cognitive bias. In other cases, a variety of investor types follows from acknowledging that investors have varying cognitive and other biases. The popular image of the stock owner that is transmitted by the mass media is an active, tense, and greedy human who is constantly on the lookout for opportunities in the stock market. Few investors seem to live up to that image.

There are a few highly active stock holders who may gain less than the market portfolio because they trade too much. Their scenarios are *instant scenarios* and new information is rapidly merged with highly selective memories of successes and failures. Often, the scenario suggests higher probabilities of gains than justified by (subsequent) reality. Then, in increasing numbers, there are many passive investors who hold on to their financial assets, inspired by their mostly strong loss aversion. By forming modest and stable expectations or scenarios which they adhere to over long periods of time, they tend on average to make more money than the active investors. The upshot is that the relatively passive stock holders may hold a considerable proportion of total stock value. Their number is increasing for many reasons, such as privatization of government-owned companies, retirement saving, and judicious imitation of successful investing. In the following section, some behavioral areas that make for even more differences among investors than just level of activity will be explicated.

Expectations as Scenarios

> . . . *the past and the future are social cognitive constructions.*
>
> Karniol and Ross (1996, p.594)

The main theme of this book is that private investing depends on images of the future that investors, guided by selective memories and selective information, form, often under the influence of others. The image derives from formation of expectations, which can be assumed to give a direction to and even guide behavior. Expectations behind investing can be more or less entangled with other expectations, depending on the individual and the situation. Often, the sets of expectations relevant to a decision – investment or otherwise – are strongly intertwined and form patterns that can be called *scenarios*.

Scenarios, which often are colored by emotions, are the person's images of the future or rather possible futures. They are composed of past experiences, mixed with causal attributions, pieces of new information, and social influences from different sources, some of them also with assumptions about cause and effect, and pure fantasies about what the future will and should be like. All scenarios are related to the person's self-image, which adds affects to them. Too often, making a decision means that a few relationships are taken out of a scenario and are allowed to determine the choice of an alternative. While this may be necessary to bring about a decision, some risks are certainly involved, as shown by research on dynamic decision making (Brehmer, 1992). Kahneman and Lovallo (1993) issue strong warnings against becoming too involved in a scenario. People may find a scenario very attractive and use it as a prediction when it is actually a preference.

To what extent is it possible to understand and predict the scenarios that will determine an individual investor's behavior, or to aggregate the scenarios of different persons into something that can predict what will happen at the market level? There are a few, tentative, answers. In the preceding chapters, many possible influences on scenarios have been reported. The past and the present are treated by aid of heuristics that make life simpler. It may be arguable whether the heuristics are smart, whereas there is more agreement that they can be fast and frugal. Causal attributions tend to have a self-serving bias and involve ascribing successes too much to one's own skill and efforts and failures to bad luck or to others' misdemeanor. In rising markets, all boats are lifted as Shiller (2000) appropriately says, and no particular boast may be warranted. When potential investors see other people, apparently without any special qualifications, being successful in stock investments, the temptation to invest in earlier profitable stocks is there. Daydreaming about the use of future profits may complete an unrealistic scenario.

Little is known about how financial scenarios are constructed. What matters when professionals and other investors shape instant scenarios? Suppose that potential investors start with some sort of goal for their financial activities. The desire to accumulate wealth was held by classical economists to be a characteristic goal of all humans. This desire may take shape as some vague goal that gives a sense of direction to financial behavior. Scenarios are then made with the goal as a kind of selecting mechanism. It is often an interactive process so that the goals are in their turn influenced by what happens in the process and tend to become more specific as the process goes on. Maybe a sampling theory (Fiedler, 2000) can provide some useful insights about the making of scenarios. People base their judgments and decisions on samples from memory and from the environment. Sampling involves many types of errors, such as statistical errors due to the number of units sampled and the bias of the sample. In fact, Fiedler et al. (2000) propose that heuristics and many other cognitive phenomena, called errors, can be explained by sampling theory. Investment scenarios may be based on inadequate sampling due to the fact that memory is selective, causal attributions are self-serving or denigrating the skills of others, and external information sources are biased and reveal too little of the needed information.

Luck and Skill

> *While most people will agree that there is much overlap between skill and luck, a full understanding of how inextricably bound the two are has yet to be attained.*
>
> Langer (1982, p.231)

Future-orientation means that an individual has to create an image of some part of the future. The picture may be well structured or it may lack important details as a consequence of lack of information or lack of effort. If a contingent expectation comes true, luck and some foresight or forecasting skill may be credited. An intentional expectation that comes true is to a varying degree the outcome of a mixture of skill and luck. Most people seem to agree that with more skill, less need is felt for luck. When investments fail, a close examination of the relevant decisions can contribute hindsight ideas for reducing what may otherwise be blamed on bad luck.

.How important is skill in explaining success in stock transactions? Skill means being able to make proper forecasts and to put in mental effort behind a transaction. Investing skill is hard to measure in any adequate way since the outcomes always seem to depend on many factors besides skill. If luck is involved, it probably escapes both the investor's and the researcher's notice and is concealed in the unexplained variance. Luck is often not recognized by the person who experienced a positive outcome and had made some effort. Degree of experience with pertinent matters and knowledge of market facts have been singled out as important, but not totally decisive, factors. The fate of Long-Term Capital Management demonstrates that knowledge and skill are not enough of a protection against decisions that may turn out to have bad, even disastrous consequences. Only hindsight can always do better, or can the joint occurrence of many events, each with low probability, simply be called bad luck without any reflection on skill?

People are led by their samples of their own experience and their perceptions of their own skills. Many tests of causal attribution theory have been made and observations of stock holders have confirmed the usual patterns of attribution (see, for example, psychonomics & Capital, 1998; De Bondt, 1998). The results evince that there are important details in the manner people attribute effects to causes. If no effort was involved and the outcome is favorable and unique, luck may be credited with the success. Some investors may at least for some time think of themselves as lucky and indeed believe in continued luck. With even a minor effort expended, the tendency to claim credit for the actors themselves increases. Dependence on luck may hopefully be replaced by some amount of skill with increasing experience. Studies of expertise suggest that systematic, deliberate practice is better than unsorted experience (Ericsson and Lehmann, 1996).

It takes both luck and skill perhaps to be really successful in financial markets. In a truly efficient market, all investors have the proper skill and only chance can be credited or blamed for differences in returns. If both skill and luck count, professional traders are in for difficulties. Without luck they may not be able to beat the index because skill cannot totally replace luck or always overcome fateful combinations of events with low probabilities. The role of skill in investing in stocks has not been investigated in any systematic way, but there have been some attempts at comparing professional and private investors, as shown in the last two chapters. Knowledge and skill appear to matter and long-term dependence on intuition and luck may lead to ill consequences. Investors had better acquire some knowledge and skill to get at least moderate success in their investments, but increased knowledge and skill should not necessarily entice the investor to yield to the temptation of making more transactions or taking higher risks.

Rational investors are not inclined to take higher risks unless they are rewarded by profits that are commensurately higher than the returns on riskless assets. Skill may, in the context of high-risk investments, be defined as skill in seeing through probabilities, presumably on the basis of special causal information. Investment decisions are determined by prior risk expectations which are necessarily surrounded by large zones of uncertainty. Is it skill when the risky choice pays off and bad luck when the risky choice ends in costly failure? Or is it perhaps that the risky choice was afterwards found to be less risky than calculated in the favorable case and more risky in the unsuccessful case? Skill in the successful case implies that the investor saw through the prior probability and perhaps made an estimate that was close to the posterior, higher probability. In the second case, the prior probability of success may have been judged to be higher than the outcome justified. Skill would mean not investing or asking for higher compensation. Maybe skill in risk taking means being able to see through an entangled network of influential factors and arriving at probabilities that may deviate from general expectation, but are close enough to posterior probabilities. At any rate, the equity premium puzzle appears to be less of a puzzle if subjective risk is considered.

Trading Activity Levels and Degree of Diversification

Survey interviews and examination of account transactions provide arguments for believing that many stock holders are highly inactive. Even though they may have considerable proportions of their financial assets invested in stocks, they are not dependent on immediate returns on their stocks and they mostly have house equity of considerable size. Besides, according to some thinking and some empirical research, those who are inactive and do not trade too much do better in the long run than those who closely follow stock market ups and downs in their own trading. Remember the stories about successful elderly women that have circulated in the news media (like *The New York Times* and *The Economist*) in recent times! These winners probably follow the developments in the stock markets closely and are knowledgeable.

Diversification is a golden rule both according to Bernoullian probability theory and financial theory. Diversification seems foreign to many investors for two main reasons: (1) people want to invest in stocks of companies they think they know and believe in, which keeps down the number of firms invested in (De Bondt, 1998; psychonomics & Capital, 1998), and (2) if one has stocks in many different firms, they may develop differently and in ways that threaten the ubiquitous loss aversion. The portfolio idea involves that some stocks may do better than the market and others do worse, maybe even be real losers. The concept of a market portfolio seems to clash with the way many investors view stocks. In the first place, the investor has and wants to have feelings about her/his stocks, approaching a personal relationship with a chosen company. Composing a market portfolio implies that stocks may be included that the investor does not believe in and may not like. Second, people often avoid treating together and as one aggregate choices that are concurrent (Kahneman and Lovallo, 1993, pp.20–21). They have a tendency to isolate choices and to consider each choice as unique rather than to deal with each choice as one in a series that will involve many repetitions over time.

A simple way of diversifying and thus diminishing risks is to invest in mutual funds, in particular funds that cover a good selection of both companies and industries. There is less security in mutual funds that specialize in one or a few industries, such as Internet firms or telecom stocks. This is true even though the fund managers may invest in many companies and diversify in this sense of the word. Many stock owners hold shares in mutual funds as well as stocks in individual firms. In this case, they can invest directly in stocks from a single company or a few companies and still have some of the security that ensues from diversification. For those who believe that they can do better than funds and choose to invest most of their financial assets directly in stocks, the lack of diversification may be no problem for some time when the stock market as a whole moves upwards.

Ethical Investing and Investor Morality

Ethical investing or social investing as it is more often called in the USA means that the investor avoids investing in stocks from certain types of companies. The use of 'ethical' rather than 'social' implies that the individual's own beliefs are in focus. Social investing has more bearing on the societal consequences. An ethical investor may screen the selection of stocks to satisfy her/his own conscience or may hope and expect that there will be broader effects and that the stock market can be influenced. In the latter case, more attempts to convince other investors may be expected and asked for.

Three cases may be distinguished. An investor who invests directly in stocks may decide not to buy stocks in certain companies such as companies engaged in arms manufacturing or tobacco production or companies that are profitable but have a bad reputation for employment conditions. If s/he is or becomes the owner of such stocks through inheritance or through new acquisitions that a company makes, s/he is inclined to sell these stocks, maybe even at some loss. The second case is the investor's wish to support a cause actively by investing in companies that, for example, are outstanding in environmental protection or pursue social goals to a greater extent than other companies. It may not be easy to find and maintain long-term criteria for selecting such stocks. The third case involves participation in funds that are guided by certain ethical principles or rules. Participation in funds usually means that there is a mixture of stocks that is hard to follow in detail and new acquisitions may result in involvement in firms that manufacture or sell goods that are not ethically acceptable to the ethical individual investor.

In Canada and the USA, the social mutual funds are making the claim that their investing is subject to social considerations and in the UK ethical unit trusts are tailored in a similar way. From 1997 to 1999, the assets in socially responsible portfolios in the USA almost doubled to reach the impressive size of US$2.2 trillion (Statman, 2000). Some of the funds offering retirement pensions in the Swedish pension system claim that they are guided by ethical principles in the selection of stocks. It is possible that the US Social Security funds will be invested in stock funds and that the funds will be screened for social responsibility of companies (Statman, 2000).

It is truly difficult to set up clear-cut criteria for a selection of firms to invest in. Statman (2000) reports a number of criteria for socially responsible companies. Quantitative criteria may exclude the following types of firm:

- companies that derive 2 percent or more of their sales from military weapons systems
- companies that derive any revenues from the manufacture of alcohol or tobacco products, and
- companies that derive any revenues from providing gaming products or services.

The qualitative screens applied to company records comprise diversity, employee relations, environmental concern, and similar causes.

Alan Lewis, who is professor of economic psychology at the University of Bath, has over the last ten years or so frequently raised the question: 'Do people put their money where their morals are?' and he has in a number of research projects sought answers to this question. A sequence of studies have carefully explored investor attitudes towards ethical investing (Lewis and Webley, 1994; Lewis and Mackenzie, 2000; Winnett and Lewis, 2000). The findings in a survey of 1 146 British ethical investors indicated that they were similar to other investors: 'These individuals are neither cranks nor saints: they are commonly middle-income professionals mixing ethical investments with not so ethical ones' (Lewis and Mackenzie, 2000, p.187). Most of the respondents thought that they were taking a slight loss by investing ethically and they were prepared to take some loss, something that was not related to the proportion of assets invested ethically. The authors conclude: 'This persistence cannot easily be dismissed merely as fashionable or faddish behaviour in the market place' (Lewis and Mackenzie, 2000, p.187).

The returns of social investments compare favorably with the returns on regular investments. Typically, findings have shown that return on social or ethical investing is equal to and sometimes better than return from regular investing funds; the favorable outcome usually includes risk-adjusted returns. Unit or mutual funds, in general, do not outperform the market portfolio (Cummings, 2000; Shefrin, 2000; Statman, 2000).

THE PERFORMANCE OF PROFESSIONALS

> *Senior clairvoyants*
> *New, web-based financial journal seeks writers who, if not actually clairvoyant, are accustomed to thinking and writing about the next thing to happen in markets. Candidates should possess knowledge, imagination and writing ability. They will be expected to conceive, as well as to write, analytical articles that professional investors will pay good money to read. Our coverage will span the gamut of markets, from bonds and stocks to currencies and commodities. Although we will be situated in* [*city*], *you wouldn't have to be. Send resume and writing sample to . . .*
>
> Advertisement in *The Economist* (1999)

Luck and skill are inextricably bound together, and little is known about how they are bound, as Langer (1982) said. It holds true as far as psychological research on financial markets goes. Professionals in the field may be thought to have more skill on the basis of their experience and training. This little difference may give them a long-run advantage over investors who have less skill, but maybe are more lucky, in the short run. Professionals may be more prone to use forecasts made by financial experts, but such forecasts seem to have flaws judging from some studies made by De Bondt (1991, 1993) and others (see review in Shefrin, 2000). The cognitive biases or, more neutrally expressed, the cognitive capacity of professional investors resembles that of ordinary people (see, for example, Stephan and Kiell, 1997, 2000).

In finance, many types of experts can be distinguished. Four categories are usually mentioned: (a) newsletter writers, (b) financial analysts, (c) professional traders, who are mostly fund or money managers, and (d) financial advisors and brokers. How good are they as experts? All four categories have been subjected to research.

Many brokerage firms issue newsletters that presumably influence their clients. Newsletter writers are usually assumed to be midway between amateur individual investors and the expert financial strategists (Fisher and Statman, 2000). Recommendations made in newsletters to investors have been analyzed in a number of cases. Metrick (1999) investigated the equity-portfolio recommendations made by 153 investment newsletters. He found that overall there was no significant evidence of superior stock-picking ability for his sample of newsletters. Moreover, there was no evidence of abnormal short-run performance persistence. Jaffe and Mahoney (1999) analyzed the recommendations of common stocks made by the investment newsletters followed by a financial digest. They concluded that, taken as a whole, the securities that newsletters recommended did not outperform appropriate benchmarks. The data provided modest evidence that the future performance of a newsletter was related to its past performance when performance was measured by raw returns. Evidence of persistence vanished when performance was measured by abnormal returns. Little evidence was found of herding, that is, dependence of recommendations across newsletters. Newsletters tended to recommend securities that had performed well in the recent past. Earlier studies have reached the same conclusion that newsletter writers err considerably in their stock picking (see Shefrin, 2000, pp.60–68).

Some time ago, Batchelor and Dua (1990a, 1990b) noted that forecasts were often misleading. They studied the predictive success of US economic forecasters and found that those who made the best forecasts worked with specified econometric models based on some ideology, in the first place Keynesian theory. The authors commented that all forecasters added a lot of subjective judgment to the model: they put more weight on judgment than on any formal modeling technique. It appears likely that the same tendency may be even stronger in financial forecasts, whether done by experts or by laymen, since the forecasts concern subtler, more ego-involving material than consumption and inflation forecasts usually do. De Bondt and Forbes (1999) list three main reasons why financial analysts' forecasts are often wrong: (1) overoptimism and too extreme forecasts, (2) reluctance to deviate from the predictions of peer groups, and (3) earnings forecast revisions from companies tend to be clustered (good news from one company brings forth good news from other companies whereas bad news is deferred). Consideration of client reactions is said to be a non-negligible influence on forecasts.

On the whole, investigations seem to indicate that professionals tend to do all right and as money managers make money on investments, but that they rarely beat the market portfolio in a consistent way over the years. For one thing, they may make single mistakes that can be costly to the clients. An early study found that some private investors had 'some reasonable skill in security selection, particularly in connection with short term trading cycles' (Schlarbaum et al., 1978, p.299). These authors made a conjecture about why individual investors might have an advantage. It was, they wrote, possible that individuals could engage in prompt trading responses to many temporary securities price disequilibria that emerged in the market. They could take positions small enough not to eliminate those disequilibria immediately, and score a profit. Large-bloc institutional trading pursuit of the same discrepancies would be self-defeating. This might, in many instances, give the small investor a modest competitive edge. These investigators thus found that there could be some truth in the belief of active stock investors that they can make more profit by trading themselves than by participating in funds.

Shefrin (2000, pp.167–9) paints a rather gloomy picture of professional money managers, showing that their results are often poorer than the market portfolio performance. He notes that if skill is a factor in fund performance the winners of one year should be the winners next year. The results of the studies that he reports indicate that, although a few winners remain winners the next year, the majority become less successful. This is a sign of a non-negligible random component in fund performance and it means that the mean-reversion effect is an alternative explanation to differences in expertise and skill. To the extent that the mean-reversion effect operates, it improves the performance of losers and worsens the performers of winners. It is possible to make a little less gloomy interpretation of the results of this and some other studies. It is conceivable that the average level of professional skill may be high and raise the mean performance. The dispersion around the stock index mean may mostly be a matter of chance, but superior skill, in a very few cases, can still pay off and outperform the market portfolio.

Wermers and Moskowitz (2000) used a new data base to perform a comprehensive analysis of the mutual fund industry. Funds were found to hold stocks that outperformed the market by 1.3 percent per year whereas their net returns underperformed by 1 percent. Of the difference between these results, 0.7 percent was due to the underperformance of non-stock holdings and the rest was due to expenses and transaction costs. The authors conclude that funds picked stocks well enough to cover their costs and that active management was important. Critics who claim that individual investors can do better on their own than by participating in funds may get some support from this study. Complaints about high charges of fees and less than average performance have been raised against some mutual funds.

Financial economists often pronounce criticism on professional investors because they do not operate the way efficient-market theory stipulates and predicts. Canner et al. (1997) scrutinized the guidance given by some leading investment advisors and found that different recommendations were given to investors with differing degrees of risk aversion. It is in line with the theory that clients with varying risk aversion should get different advice with respect to what proportion of their assets to invest in risky assets. The kind of advice given diverges from theory. The mutual-funds separation theorem predicts equal bond/stock ratios independent of degree of risk aversion and the advisors certainly did not live up to this; presumably the clients followed the recommendations. The authors conclude in a rather conciliatory way:

> Financial decisions are widely viewed to be difficult to make, and advisors are experts who are trying to help people optimize. That the advice being offered does not match economic theory suggests that our understanding of investor objectives (as opposed to their ability to reach those objectives) is deficient (Canner et al., 1997, p.190).

This leaves room for assuming that client goals may differ and that advisors do mind differences in client needs.

In sum, the predictions of stock prices and recommendations made by newsletter writers do not appear overly successful, according to the findings. Financial analysts do not do too well with their forecasts which, besides the difficulty of the task, is also attributed to the special considerations they have to make because of clients. Studies of fund managers often show that, in bull markets, funds rarely do better than the market portfolio, while still being profitable. Few managers succeed in being successfully above the market index for more than one year. How fund and money managers perform in bear markets has apparently not been investigated. The performance of personal financial advisors probably varies and, to my knowledge, no studies have been carried out.

PSYCHOLOGY AND AGGREGATE EFFECTS

The Use of Psychological Micro Models

In economics, the main purpose of micro models is to explain aggregate behavior, if not for all participants in a market, at least for sizeable segments. Explanations of aggregate phenomena employ, in the first place and in line with mainstream economics, economic variables representing other aggregate phenomena. Most, but not all, of macroeconomics is based on micro models of economic behavior with the property that they can be added up to form aggregates. A basic condition is that the micro models are compatible with the rationality postulate. Macro phenomena that do not agree with existing micro models create serious difficulties. Attempts to grapple with those can proceed along different lines.

The simplest line is to regard the deviations as dispersion that is larger than really expected, but still compatible with the micro model. Another line of thought is to concentrate on the macro data and discount the importance of the micro model (see, for example, Lucas, 1986) – macroeconomics does not necessarily need microeconomics. A third line of reasoning is to extend or even twist the rationality postulate a little. Arrow (1986) noted that many micro models could fit as explanations of macro phenomena and that the models based on rationality were only one alternative. A fourth way is to find a new micro model, elaborating the rationality concept or just using rationality as a kind of benchmark. The rationality benchmark defines the kind and quantity of errors in cognition. This is what researchers in behavioral finance have done. In cognitive and social psychology, they have found competitive micro models. They have found inspiration and support for their use of concepts and models in psychological research and have themselves done little testing of individual behavior. One difficulty is that economists hope to find a few psychological laws that are generally valid with few exceptions, whereas psychologists have become used to the fact that human differences tend to invalidate claims of generality. Psychological research teems with domain-specific, contingent laws.

From a psychologist's point of view, it is then not satisfactory that the micro models are not directly tested on financial behavior. When, for example, availability or some aspect of prospect theory is evoked as explanation of a financial event, it is desirable that some test is made at the individual level showing that the selected principle operates. Tversky and Kahneman (1983), for example, noted that people could be asked questions relating to the representativeness heuristic. Two promising tendencies can be recorded in this respect. One is that behavioral finance and experimental economics have joined forces and that many experiments with a focus on individual psychological characteristics have been and are being performed (see, for example, Güth et al., 1997). The other is that psychologists also have begun to run experiments on problems related to financial markets (see, for example, Kroll et al. 1988a, 1988b; Fischer et al., 1999).

The Psychological Stock-Market Wealth Effect

People who have accumulated money are in saving theories assumed to consume more. The existence of such a wealth effect is still debated, but there is some consensus that the effect obtains at the aggregate level. When stock prices go up and stock holders become richer on paper, but do not realize their paper gains, the possibility of a wealth effect is largely unrecognized. Keynes (1930) maintained that there were such effects on consumption, working both in upward and downward markets. Lower value of stock holdings would lead to pessimism and more control of expenditure; higher value would lead to optimism and more willingness to spend.

Studies have shown that the Index of Consumer Sentiment (ICS) is influenced by stock market developments. Shapiro (1972) investigated how well total disposable income, unemployment rate, a price index, and an index of industrial common stocks explained the ICS of 1956–70. He found $R^2 = 0.83$ and could not reject the hypothesis of stability over time. The lagged ICS played an important role in the equation. Shapiro concluded that equity prices were one of several factors determining ICS.

> The results do imply, however, that a stable model of consumer attitude formation can be isolated from readily available data on income, inflation rates and equity prices, and that for some purposes (for example short-term forecasting), this information may be used in models of consumer behavior in place of survey results (Shapiro, 1972, p.378).

Poterba (2000) reviews the evidence for a wealth effect on consumption. He notes that the increase in consumption is small. He finds that in the year after a change in stock market values, consumer spending is likely to rise by between one and two cents for each dollar increase in the value of corporate stock. The effect may be due either to the fact that higher stock prices raise consumption by raising household net worth, and thereby expanding consumption opportunity sets, or to the fact that the stock market responds to news that suggests consumption will rise in the future. In the latter case, the rising prices inspire optimism that may not be confined to stock owners, but may spread as well to non-stock-holders in the way the studies of the ICS intimate. For years up to the end of the year 1999, the focus was on the positive wealth effect on consumption. After the strong drop in the value of most household portfolios during the year 2000, signs of a negative wealth effect are appearing. How strong it will be is, of course, unknown, but there is agreement that a negative wealth effect obtains. Positive and negative wealth effects are not symmetric if prospect theory is correct. Paper losses are bound to give more emotions than the corresponding paper gains if people are characterized by the strong loss aversion that prospect theory assumes. Psychologists with an orientation towards dynamic psychology would probably expect some deferring of consumption cutback as a consequence of attempts to suppress the processing of bad news at first.

Psychology and the Formation of Bubbles

A bubble arises, according to Stiglitz (1990), when a stock price is currently high *only* because investors believe that the selling price will be high tomorrow and fundamental factors do not seem to vindicate such a price. In the short run, the high price of the asset may be justified because it yields a return (capital gain plus dividend) equal to that on alternative assets.

A bubble means that there is an upward stock-price trend, usually steep, that is suddenly interrupted by a drop that is also steep. Investor expectations somehow change in relation to the steps in the formation of the bubble. Obviously, expectations about future values that are above fundamentals may lead to bubbles. The first component is the expected development of future earnings, which may well be exaggerated due to unjustified extrapolations. It will probably not lead to extreme valuations. The second component is expectation about others' expectations or what actions to expect from other investors. There may be expectations of immediate bandwagon effects that strongly enhance the upward effect or result in mass reactions that mean the burst of the bubble. If the first, the expected earnings, component dominates, there is seldom a bubble unless the extrapolation is drawn-out so long that expectations become mere speculation. The more the second component prevails, the more likely a bubble is to start forming.

The task of psychology is to try to explain how expectations can deviate so much from fundamentals that there will be bubbles. A simple answer is that people use simplified scenarios based on biased sampling and they do not calculate very much. They form their expectations on superficial, biased information and slim evidence, transmitted by peers and the news media and, for some investors, by financial advisors. Investors may closely follow the development of certain stock prices and let their observations of ups and, with plenty of lag, downs determine their actions, disregarding actual price–earnings and similar ratios. Such behavior may be (mis)labeled momentum or contrarian strategies, depending on the resulting behavior. The influence from others should not be underestimated. Bandwagon effects may occur, meaning that the mere number of people who act in a certain way puts pressure on others to do the same. It is similar to what economists prefer to call herd behavior. If investors in certain situations are led by primary affective reactions (see Chapter 6) that often inspire immediate actions without further thinking, the field seems open for overreactions on the part of some investors.

When earlier experience exists it tends to be sticky. If earlier experience is perceived by the individual as inadequate, s/he becomes inclined to depend on new information from the environment. Investors who have followed ups and downs of stock prices over long periods of time and have made money are less likely to react immediately and affectively to highly positive or negative news than those who have invested most of their wealth and are new in the market. Studies of dynamic decision making indicate that people are generally slow to respond in adequate measure to exponential developments (see Chapter 4). They underreact and hesitate to use the really drastic measures that may be necessary. If people are trained to face such situations they are more prone to do the supposedly right thing, that is, when a crash seems to be rapidly approaching, to sell as much as possible at short notice and not sell losers too late in the downfall. Maybe they are reluctant to give up momentum strategies that have richly paid off earlier and thus keep enhancing the growth of the bubble until the signs of a burst are implacably there.

New information, if dramatic, can start a serious break in the trend. This gives rise to the question of what news is really about. It has been noted about stock market crashes by economists that there has been no information about important changes before the crashes started. Financial economists use news in two main senses. The first sense is that events that will change (expectations about) fundamentals are brought to public attention (with an immediate effect on stock prices according to the theory). The second sense is the effect of changing stock prices themselves, often called the feedback effect. Some authors have explained both bubbles and crashes by pointing to feedback effects, which means that investors are influenced in such a way that they, up to a point, follow momentum strategies and then, suddenly, when they see a dramatic drop in prices, switch to getting rid of stocks at sinking prices. Apart from the fact that social-psychological studies of dissemination of information suggest much less mechanical processes, with both cognition and emotions involved, this reasoning may miss the pervasive effects of rumors. Shiller's (1989) studies strongly support the idea that a stock market crash may be, if not caused, at least enhanced by rumors among professionals and big investors.

An additional thought that is easy to overlook should be brought to attention. The fact that there is no news may communicate something important. The absence of reports on success among Internet firms, no information about substantial growth in the telecom sector, and no news of good events in the business sector of the economy may communicate pessimism and lead to pessimistic strategies. After a long spate of optimistic reports on hi-tech companies, the non-appearance of such reports may have huge consequences.

Passive Investors = Little Panic?

> *It is well known that the typical individual investor trades much less relative to the market value of his portfolio, than do institutions. Among institutional investors, the portfolios of money management firms show more turnover than do those of insurance companies.*
>
> De Bondt and Forbes (1999, pp.145–6)

If a significant portion of the stock capital is owned by investors who are characterized by loss aversion, there will be no real bursts of bubbles, at least not with long-lasting effects. Loss aversion will make investors refrain from realizing their losses and make them hope for improvement at least in the distant future. My guess is that, in 1929, there were relatively few passive investors, which enhanced the ill consequences. In October 1987 there were more passive investors, which made the recovery easier and smoother after the professionals had panicked (see Shiller, 1989). In the year 2000, there may be so many of the passive investors that global bubbles do not grow and later explode, but dissolve less dramatically. Bubbles may still arise and burst in industries whose stocks are shunned by passive investors. Allowance must always be made for the effects of those professionals, fund managers, and a few active small investors who may be more prone to panic and are pressed to reach their imposed goals of being at least as good as the market index.

Stock-price developments over the last two years (end of 1998 to seond half of 2000) have created surprises. Many stock holders now seem to fear that the whole stock market is an enormous bubble that will explode at an unknown moment in the near future. Let me try a somewhat reassuring answer which, if not wholly satisfactory, is anyhow worth looking at. The role of passive investors and long hold-outs in properly selected stocks are of primary interest in this context.

Traditionally, investing in stock listed on stock exchanges was an activity for the few. Many wealth owners, especially small ones, were reluctant to speculate with their money. Stock markets were dominated by rich people, some of whom speculated (with some notable ruins), and by pure speculators with small financial resources. Over the last decades, the investors in stocks have changed. There is a tendency for wealth owners, including small ones who are persistent savers, to invest part and far from all of their wealth in stocks. In the USA, Australia, and, strangely enough, in Sweden, the proportion of households owning stocks, directly or indirectly through funds, has increased to about half of the households. The proportion is fairly high in the UK and lower but growing in Germany and the Netherlands. In the latter countries, there is an increasing interest among wealth owners to buy stocks. Among other things, interest has increased as a consequence of intensive campaigns in connection with privatization of telecommunications monopolies. The privatization of Deutsche Telekom (Stephan, 1999) is a case in point. Similarly, in the Netherlands many people who otherwise did not invest in stocks bought KPN (Telecom) stock.

Most studies of investors are based on samples of accounts in stock brokerage firms or samples of people classified as active or large investors. This supports some misperceptions and wrong conclusions about the activity level of the typical stock holder. The tendency is to overestimate the activity and to believe that the majority of investors are gambling along with the market. Besides, most studies have been carried out in bullish markets.

Activity levels of investors have not often been studied. This is true of US investors. As reported earlier, Kelly (1997) distinguished a group of passive investors. His study suggests that the passive investors hold a considerable part of the total stock value. Survey data from other countries indicate that the majority of stockholders are rather passive and make few transactions per year. Their share of total stock owning is of considerable size (see Chapter 8). This segment is large enough to be of special interest to institutions in the financial markets. Marketing of financial services seems to be built upon the presumption that all investors are active and always eager to increase their wealth, referred to as greed. This misconception is probably enhanced by the financial theories that are dominant. In behavioral finance, there is recognition of the fact that investors deviate from the financial theory image of the typical stock holder, but little is said about the fact that important proportions of stocks are held by investors who trade sparsely. Many investors invest only in one or a few firms. It seems likely that they believe in the particular firms and are willing to trust some of their money to one or a few well-known firms for long-term investment.

For old people, the rule-of-thumb says that the percentage of stocks in less risky bonds should be (100 – age in years). At least two reasons support this. One is that old-age pensioners seem to want to supplement their retirement income with income from capital. The second reason is the risk of paying inheritance tax on a fictitious amount of money. If, for example, somebody died in early October 1987 and left a considerable stock portfolio, which lost 60 percent of its value after the stock exchange crash, the taxes would probably be calculated on the value the portfolio had on the day of death. The inheritance of bonds, which are appropriately often referred to as 'fixed income' in financial circles, appears much safer.

Can the long-term, mostly passive investors in stocks have a balancing influence on stock-price developments in such a way that the probability of expansive bubbles bursting is strongly reduced? If the passive investors keep their composure and do not sell, but rather look for opportunities to add to their portfolios, does this not mean a sobering influence on stock-price developments? Earlier, when most of the total stock value was held by very active stock holders, many of whom engaged advisors and professional money managers, panic sales were more likely than today. In 1987, the stock market recovered surprisingly quickly in accordance with my hypothesis that a sizable proportion of stock holders remained cool and, after a while, bought rather than sold stocks.

If my hypothesis is right, the passive investors who are disparagingly counted among noise traders in financial economics are in fact the stabilizing element in the financial markets. Black (1986), who invented or discovered noise traders, said somewhat mystifyingly that noise trading was essential to the existence of liquid markets. It may mean that these traders were given some credit. Those who create real noise and disturbances are the speculators and hyperactive investors.

My belief is that, in the long run, there will be some return to fundamentalism, a development that will be complemented – or corrected – by some guesses about other investors' expectations. It seems likely that when stock ownership is broadened in a country, the proportion of total stock value held by passive investors will increase and may even reach a considerable proportion. If this is the case and the hypothesis of the stabilizing influence of passive stock ownership in bubble times holds, the stock markets in countries with a low proportion of stock holders should be more sensitive to bubbles and crashes, that is, take longer to recover than countries in which there are many passive stock owners.

The dampening effect may unfortunately be small because individual stock holders own relatively little of the total stock holdings. It is said that in the USA, 80 percent of the stock holders own only roughly 4 percent of the total stock holdings (*The Economist*, August 12th, 2000). If this figure is correct, the remaining 20 percent must own a lot, since in 1996 approximately 47 percent of equity investments in the USA was held directly by households (Barber and Odean, 2000b, p.773). Pension funds owned 23 percent and 14 percent was held by mutual funds In 1998, Swedish households directly owned 15 percent of the total Swedish stock market value, a decrease from 30 percent in 1983 (Hellman, 2000, pp.3–4). The other owner groups were Swedish financial enterprises (mutual funds, insurance companies, banks etc.), which owned 29 percent, foreign owners with 35 percent, non-profit organizations with 7 percent, non-financial enterprises with 7 percent, and government, which had 8 percent.

With increasing participation in the stock market, the new phenomenon of trading through the Internet may work in the other direction and increase short-run volatility at least. Stock holders who ordinarily trade rarely and only after careful consideration may be tempted to trade more often and take more risks in the hope of gaining more. Day-traders are as yet relatively few. Their efforts to make short-run profits may not be sufficient to shake the stock markets, but may increase the volatility of single firm stocks. The day-traders are not the only ones using the Internet for trading stocks. Ordinary stock owners are also using it and their number will certainly grow. At first, an investor may be tempted to make more transactions with the convenient use of the Internet, but it is doubtful that most stock owners will in the long run increase the scope and frequency of their transactions. Such activities are taxing both financially and emotionally.

SOME IMPLICATIONS FOR THE PRIVATE INVESTOR

Folk wisdom (or was it Will Rogers?) says: 'Buy land. They ain't making any more of it.' What folk wisdom forgets is that, 'Everyone knows land is limited in supply; and what everyone already knows can't help but get already built into today's competitive bids.'

Samuelson (1994, p.20)

Si non è vero, è molto ben trovato.

Giordano Bruno

Points Worth Considering

Brief summaries of phenomena that are in themselves complicated and hard to understand and even harder to predict are popular in the news media. Whether the explanations and predictions are close to the truth seems less important than that they serve the purpose of making interesting news. People are with some right assumed to want practical advice and to believe that any complex of relationships can be summarized in one sentence and need no qualification. The reader of this book should not expect to find simple rules for making profits out of stock investments. The psychology behind the stock market is by no means simple and transparent. The role of psychology often seems to be to provide some help with ad-hoc hypotheses when elegant economic models fail to explain. While mainstream economists think that no valid scientific explanations can be found in such cases (but they feel free to guess), others look for help from psychological research. And the help from psychologists is often seen as providing doubts or statements of the type: 'it depends on many things', or 'there are no general behavioral laws, but many contingencies'. Unfortunately, there are, in addition, competing psychological answers to many questions about the development of stock prices because many determinants may lie behind any single event. Some disbelief in simple psychological explanations and predictions is well justified.

Here are some points to consider, if the theories and data analyses that have been presented in this book are stretched a little for convenience.

- Do not believe that one has to be active all the time to make money on investments in stocks, but stay reasonably informed.
- Do not pay too much attention to the stock market and do not believe that you need to pay continual attention to stock-price developments.
- If you are new to the market, begin by investing in mutual funds with a good spread of stocks over firms and industries.
- Try to diversify by buying and holding stocks that are a representative sample of the market. If this is not possible, make sure that much of your investment in stocks is in diversified mutual funds.
- Be more afraid of single-firm losses and bankruptcies than of total stock market crashes; after some time – which seems to become shorter as more people hold stocks – the stock prices on average tend to return to earlier levels.
- If you cannot afford to spread your investments over a wide assortment of stocks, close to a so-called market portfolio, be prepared to pay the charges of one or more funds that are well diversified (and that do not pretend to beat the market index, which may be costly to you).
- Do not borrow money to buy stocks unless you have a collateral that is not based on stocks.
- If you have stocks and plan to bequeath them make sure you die at the end of a bearish period. If you die at the end of a bull period when stock prices plummet, the inheritance taxes (at least in Sweden) may soak up most of the wealth.
- If you are wealthy enough, you may indulge in some recreational stock buying such as doing some high-risk investing on a small scale.
- Buy high-risk stocks only if you can well afford to lose the gamble.
- Remember that the fundamentals (and chain-letter effects) of some firms may deteriorate and the stock lose value while all other stocks go up.
- Check carefully the kind of growth and the time perspective of your investment before you invest in a so-called growth stock. What does a history of losses mean for the future?

The private investor should be aware of the real sense of 'taking a higher risk'. The expression is used by financial advisors to indicate higher future gains, usually for growth companies that do not show any current profit (or even turnover). What does a higher risk mean? It means that the pay-off is high(er), but the probability of the pay-off is low(er). The expected value of the gain should be higher than the expected value of an alternative investment; since you are entitled to be better paid for taking a risk and the probability of a loss is high. For long periods of time, investors in stocks have been overpaid for taking risks, according to the equity premium puzzle. Will that continue? Shiller (2000) is very doubtful and, like Fama and French (2000), issues a warning to pension funds and private retirement funds. In my view, there is room for some pessimism. The strong upward trend of the last years can hardly be expected to restart, but the present (January, 2001) setback is sure to stop and reverse at some point. For those who are content with less than the maximum yield and hold out, the stock market will in the long run probably turn out to be satisfactory or in Simon's (1955) term 'satisficing'.

Can Everybody Become Rich by Investing in Stocks?

The developments in the stock market are of fundamental importance to many people since the size of their future retirement pensions depends on company stocks gaining in value or at least retaining their value over a long period of time. Putting away money for retirement and investing it in stocks means that there is a chance to profit from the general, long-term growth of the private sector economy. Individuals can in many cases have some influence over the investments in their future by making choices of funds to invest in. The differences between successful funds and unsuccessful funds can be expected to be considerable. Random effects and differences in skill make for large differences.

In the Swedish public pension scheme, individuals have the chance to place 2.5 percent of their annual wages or salaries in a selection of approximately 400 funds. There is also a default alternative for those who do not wish to make an active choice. The first opportunity to choose opened up in the fall of the year 2000. Two-thirds of those who had the right to choose made an active choice and on average 3.4 funds were invested in. The latter number exceeds what Benartzi and Thaler (1998, 1999) found. Slightly more women than men made an active selection of funds. Funds that were described as high-risk funds were also chosen, especially by younger men.

Whereas under certain circumstances all can gain from stock market investments, all cannot beat the market. Winnett and Lewis (2000) point out:

> Popular beliefs typically involve an assumption that it is possible to 'beat the market', especially by drawing inferences from past patterns of, say, share price behaviour or by exploiting information about a particular share or group of shares not appreciated by other market participants, even if it was in principle available to them (Winnett and Lewis, 2000, p.323).

Hunting for mispriced stocks is popular in some investor circles and it has probably contributed to financing companies that otherwise would have had difficulties (and perhaps should have such difficulties). Transactions mean that there is at least one buyer and one seller whose valuations of a stock coincide at a certain moment: one of them is willing to sell at the price and one is willing to buy at the price. While the seller may be forced to sell at the price because s/he needs the money, the buyer is free to choose time and the price which s/he is willing to pay. Both will gain if the stock price has gone up since the seller's acquisition and continues to go up after the new transaction. Can everyone gain on stocks in the long run? It appears possible under certain conditions.

1. Stock prices are based on fundamentals (dividend and firm value).
2. Expectations about future fundamentals usually come true, that is, are realistic predictions of future values.
3. Stock prices rise as most firms grow and become more prosperous.
4. Only a minority of firms show losses and/or drop out altogether.

In practice, there are many disturbing factors, including the investor's own psychological makeup. Here are a few.

1. Stock prices may not be based on fundamentals, but on cognitive, emotional, and social factors (some of which work like chain letters or Ponzi schemes).
2. Expectations, both of ups and downs, are often exaggerated and based on extrapolations of earlier trends for lack of new information to the contrary.
3. Stock prices also move in the absence of new public information.
4. If reactions to public information are hard to predict, reactions to some kinds of missing information with potentially disastrous effects are even harder to foresee.
5. There are high intercorrelations among stock prices, implying that many firms are affected by ups and downs independent of fundamental growth factors.

The conditions for safe stock investments for everybody are rarely fulfilled. Besides that, there is the problem of personal inclinations among investors, inducing them to speculate and gamble or, at the other end, to be completely passive. The question arises as to whether it is possible to foresee and, furthermore, predict with reasonable accuracy the turning points in price movements. A succinct answer is 'No!'. It is not possible to make accurate predictions for the stock market as a whole or for individual stocks. The numerous attempts to explain booms followed by stock crashes convincingly demonstrate that even after-the-fact explanations are inadequate. And in spite of all this or, in some cases, thanks to this, a majority of stock investors may do quite well.

A FEW IDEAS FOR FURTHER RESEARCH

The psychology of private investing offers many opportunities for research. While researchers in behavioral finance have since long found a place for psychology in their basically economics-oriented research which aims at explaining market-level events, psychologists have only more recently discovered the field and carried out research directly related to finance. Earlier, a few psychologists made generative use of psychological research results, that is, they believed that their results were valid far outside the laboratory. They suggested or supported applications in the field of finance (see, for example, Kahneman et al., 1982; Kahneman and Riepe, 1998). Even if the transfer of results from basic research is still the predominant tendency, a growing number of attempts are being made to study directly behavioral problems in finance. This is shown among other things by an increasing number of such presentations at the annual meetings of IAREP, the International Association for Research in Economic Psychology.

In my view, researchers in behavioral finance certainly need to possess comprehensive knowledge of at least some fields of psychology, such as cognitive and social psychology, and many of them apparently do. Psychologists who enter the field need to know about this research and they should furthermore acquire some knowledge about financial economics. A narrow psychological perspective will not produce good research whose results can be of value also to economics and finance even if it may be satisfactory enough to be published in psychological journals.

What do we know about bubbles and crashes? Economic variables such as (news of) fundamentals or news about factors influencing fundamentals such as industrial production, inflation, unemployment, and international trade do not provide sufficient explanation. Psychological variables have been launched in ad-hoc, after-the-fact explanations by interested parties in business, economics and, more recently, in behavioral finance. Without psychological models that can be used to deduce possible consequences of entangled events and with no measurements at hand, psychological explanations may perhaps satisfy a low level of ambition for plausibility, but they are not very useful and they hardly teach something that can be used to predict the future. An essential step towards better understanding of stability, bubbles, and crashes is to combine economic, demographic, and psychological approaches in analyses of events and processes in the financial markets. A problem is that psychological models tend to suggest variables that require costly and time-consuming measurement and that rarely can be replaced by adequate, more easily available proxies. Even with this drawback, it is advisable to start with economic events as stimuli, insert demographic and socio-economic as well as psychological variables in multivariate analyses of growing bubbles and threatening crashes, and make analyses for properly selected segments of the population. When distinguishing segments, it is important to pay attention to possible reactions of investors (and non-investor groups) with varying degrees of activity in the market. How do mostly passive investors react to market developments? How much of the stocks do they hold?

Many interesting themes can be followed up by further research. In the first place, I care about passive investors. Passive investors seem to have a crucial portion of total stock investments. As the proportion of stock owners grows in a country, a larger share of them is likely to be passive. Anecdotal evidence suggests that some people who try to be what they think of as typical stock owners become bored and withdraw from the stock market altogether. They are tired of steadily harboring a feeling of having to continuously watch stock-price developments and make frequent transactions, with ensuing disappointments when purchased stocks lose value immediately after the purchase and disposed-of stocks augment in value. Studies of investors who leave the stock market after a while may be as revealing as the study of newcomers. Both categories have been neglected by theory and research.

The heuristics-and-biases approach that is the foundation of most of behavioral finance is debated. Prospect theory and the various heuristics from the heuristics-and-biases approach are mostly used in after-the-fact explanations. The proposed alternative tries to describe behaviors as they are in an ecological context and not in terms of deviations from an ideal model that can never be achieved. People are instead said to use fast and frugal heuristics that make them smart rather than deviants from economic rationality. These ideas should give food for thought and deserve to be explored in the field of the psychology of private investing. Cognitive sampling theory is another theory to explore. What are the characteristics of the samples that are the basis of investors' scenarios and how do they differ among investors?

Few if any attempts have been made to submit the use of heuristics to real testing on the financial behavior of individuals. The findings in laboratory experiments are used as theory to explain the shapes of aggregated curves after the fact and not to predict events or processes. Investment advisors and investment funds have to some extent tried to apply the ideas in actual transactions, apparently with some success. This may give some support to the validity of the models, but no tested results from such applications have been shown.

According to Friedman (1953), making good or at least better predictions than alternative theories is the only acceptable criterion for judging the value of a theory. Do postdictions count? The objection to testing theory with postdiction is that postdictions may capitalize on chance and do not exclude alternative theories that may do the same or even a better job. Under laboratory conditions, it is possible to make accurate predictions on the basis of the cognitive theories. The effects of framing in terms of survival or death in the

Asian Disease problem are robust and stable phenomena that hold over highly different populations and problems. Predictions of the framing effects can be made quite accurately. Successful applications to financial markets may have been done, but the results may be kept secret for commercial and proprietary reasons. Investment funds founded on the idea of exploiting some cognitive heuristic are reported to have been successful (see, for example, Shefrin, 2000). If there are more such successful cases the confidence in the theories augments.

There is ample room for stimulating research directed at heuristics used in financial decision making both by professional traders and private investors. Many observations suggest that professional traders also use some kinds of simple heuristics rather than penetrating analysis in their decision making. The main focus should be on individual financial decisions, which can be studied through detailed interviews, observations, and controlled experiments. A pertinent follow-up question is whether there are segments of investors characterized by different uses of heuristics.

It is true that behavioral finance theory has been developed and is being developed beyond the basic laboratory experiments, but the hypotheses derived are too often tested on existing aggregate data rather than on data describing individual investors. Apparently, more studies have been conducted on professional investors like newsletter writers and money and fund managers than on investors in households. A good overview of the former type of studies is found in Hellman (2000), who himself contributes a comprehensive analysis of how eight large Swedish institutional investors made equity-investment decisions. His work provides ideas and a framework for deep-going research on both professional and private investors. A few recent studies of household portfolios among the elderly (see Hurd, 1999) are based on interview surveys that have included some psychological questions, but so far I know of no attempt to make any behavioral analysis of these data.

A major focus should be on passive stock owners who remain owners for long periods of time. They are noise traders in the disparaging language of the financial economists, but they may, in my view, actually contribute to balancing stock markets rather than being the cause of high volatility. How do they form the expectations that make up their scenarios? Will they be inveigled to trade more through new facilities such as the Internet?

References

Ainslie, G. (1975), 'Specious rewards: A behavioral theory of impulsiveness and impulse control', *Psychological Bulletin*, **82**(4), 463–96.

Ainslie, G. (1991), 'Derivation of "rational economic behavior" from hyperbolic discount curves', *American Economic Review*, **81**, AEA Papers and Proceedings, May, 334–40.

Ainslie, G. and N. Haslam (1992), 'Self-control', in G. Loewenstein and J. Elster (eds), *Choice over Time*, New York: Russell Sage Foundation, 177–211.

Ajzen, I. (1977), 'Intuitive theories of events and the effects of base-rate information on prediction', *Journal of Personality and Social Psychology*, **35**, 303–14.

Ajzen, I. (1991), 'The theory of planned behavior', *Organizational Behavior and Human Decision Processes*, **50**, 179–211.

Akerlof, G.A. (1991), 'Procrastination and obedience', *American Economic Review*, Papers and Proceedings, **81**(2), 1–19.

Akerlof, G.A. and W.T. Dickens (1982), 'The economic consequences of cognitive dissonance', *American Economic Review*, **72**(3), 307–19.

Alessie, R., S. Hochguertel, and A. van Soest (1999), 'Household portfolios in the Netherlands', Paper presented at European University Institute Conference on 'Household Portfolios', Florence, December 17–18.

Allport, G.W. and L.J. Postman (1952), 'The basic psychology of rumor', in G.E. Swanson, T.M. Newcomb, and E.L. Hartley (eds), *Readings in Social Psychology*, New York: Henry Holt and Company, 160–71.

Anderson, M.A. and A.H. Goldsmith (1997), 'Mr. Keynes' theory of investment: Do forward looking expectations and weight really matter?' *Journal of Economic Psychology*, **18**, 547–73.

Anderson, M.J. and S. Sunder (1995), 'Professional traders as intuitive Bayesians', *Organizational Behavior and Human Decision Processes*, **64**(2), 185–202

Anderson, N.H. (ed.) (1991), *Contributions to Information Integration Theory. Volume I: Cognition*, Hillsdale, NJ: Lawrence Erlbaum Associates.

Andreassen, P.B. (1987), 'On the social psychology of the stock market: Aggregate attributional effects and the regressiveness of prediction', *Journal of Personality and Social Psychology*, **53**(3), 490–96.

Andreassen, P.B. (1988), 'Explaining the price–volume relationship: The difference between price changes and changing prices', *Organizational Behavior and Human Decision Processes*, **41**(3), 371–89.

Angelborg-Thanderz, M. (1990), *Prisvärd militär flygning med rimliga risker*, [Military Flight Training at A Reasonable Price and Risk], Doctoral dissertation, Stockholm: Stockholm School of Economics.

Aronson, E. and J.M. Carlsmith (1968), 'Experimentation in social psychology', in G. Lindzey and E. Aronson (eds), *Handbook of Social Psychology,* Vol. 2, Reading, MA: Addison-Wesley, 1–79.

Arrow, K.J. (1986), 'Rationality of self and others in an economic system', *Journal of Business*, **59** (4, Pt 2), S385–S399.

Asch, S. (1952), *Social Psychology*, Englewood Cliffs: Prentice-Hall.

Atkins, A.B. and E.A. Dyl (1993), 'Reports of the death of the efficient markets hypothesis are greatly exaggerated!', *Applied Financial Economics*, **3**(2), 95–100.

Atkinson, J.W. (1957), 'Motivational determinants of risk taking behavior', *Psychological Review*, **64**, 359–72.

Atkinson, J.W. (1964), *An Introduction to Motivation,* New York: American Book/Van Nostrand/Reinhold.

Attfield, C.L.F., D. Demery, and N.W. Duck (1985), *Rational Expectations in Macroeconomics: An Introduction to Theory and Evidence,* Oxford: Basil Blackwell.

Azar, B. (2000), 'Blinded by hindsight', *Monitor on Psychology*, **31**(5), 28–9.

Bagozzi, R.P., M. Gopinath, and P.U. Nyer (1999), 'The role of emotions in marketing', *Journal of the Academy of Marketing Science*, **27**(2), 184–206.

Bandura, A. (1977), *Social Learning Theory*, Englewood Cliffs, NJ: Prentice-Hall.

Banerjee, A. (1992), 'A simple model of herd behavior', *Quarterly Journal of Economics*, **107**, 797–817.

Barber, B. and T. Odean (2000a), 'Too many cooks spoil the profits: Investment club performance', *Financial Analysts Journal*, **56**(1), 17–25.

Barber, B. and T. Odean (2000b),'Trading is hazardous to your wealth: The common stock investment performance of individual investors', *Journal of Finance*, **55**(2), 773–806.

Barberis, N., A. Shleifer, and R. Vishny (1998), 'A model of investor sentiment', *Journal of Financial Economics*, **49**, 307–43.

Batchelor, R.A. and P. Dua (1990a), 'Forecaster ideology, forecasting technique, and the accuracy of economic forecasts', *International Journal of Forecasting*, **6**(1), 3–10.

Batchelor, R.A. and P. Dua (1990b), 'Product differentiation in the forecasting industry', *International Journal of Forecasting*, **6**(3), 311–16.

Batchelor, R.A. and P. Dua (1991), 'Blue chip rationality tests', *Journal of Money, Credit and Banking*, **23**(4), 692–705.
Baumeister, R.F. and T.F. Heatherton (1996), 'Self-regulation failure: An overview', *Psychological Inquiry*, **7**, 1–15.
Baumgartner, H. (1995), 'On the utility of consumers' theories in judgments of covariation', *Journal of Consumer Research*, **21**(4), 634–43.
Becker, G.S. (1976), *The Economic Approach to Human Behavior,* Chicago, IL: University of Chicago Press.
Benartzi, S. and R.H. Thaler (1995), 'Myopic loss aversion and the equity premium puzzle', *Quarterly Journal of Economics*, **110**, 73–92.
Benartzi, S. and R.H. Thaler (1998), 'Naïve diversification strategies in defined contribution saving plans', Working Paper, Anderson School at UCLA.
Benartzi, S. and R.H. Thaler (1999), 'Risk aversion or myopia? Choices in repeated gambles and retirement investments', *Management Science*, **45**, 364–81.
Berg, L. and R. Bergström (1996), 'Consumer confidence and consumption in Sweden', Working Paper 1996:7, Uppsala: Department of Economics, Uppsala University.
Bergkvist, L. (1995), 'Ethics and Finance: An Empirical Study of Ethical Judgments and Attitudes', Occasional Paper No 72, Stockholm: SNS, Center for Business and Policy Studies.
Bernoulli, D. ([1738]1954), 'Exposition of a new theory on the measurement of risk', *Econometrica*, **22**(1), 23–36.
Bernstein, J. (1993), *The Investor's Quotient: The Psychology of Successful Investing in Commodities & Stocks*, New York: John Wiley & Sons, Inc.
Bernstein, P.L. (1985), 'Does the stock market overreact? Discussion', *Journal of Finance*, **40**(3), 806–9.
Bikhchandani, S., D. Hirshleifer, and I. Welch (1992), 'A theory of fads, fashion, custom, and cultural change as informational cascades', *Journal of Political Economy*, **100**(5), 992–1026.
Binswanger, H.P. (1981), 'Attitudes toward risk: Theoretical implications of an experiment in rural India', *Economic Journal*, **91**, 867–90.
Black, F. (1986), 'Noise', *Journal of Finance*, **41**(3), 529–43.
Bloch, B. (1999), 'Speculation', in P.E. Earl and S. Kemp (eds), *The Elgar Companion to Consumer Research and Economic Psychology*, Cheltenham, UK and Northampton, MA, 550–55.
Bloomfield., R., R. Libby, and M.W. Nelson (1998a), 'Confidence and the welfare of less-informed investors', Working Paper, Johnson Graduate School of Management, Cornell University.
Bloomfield., R., R. Libby, and M.W. Nelson (1998b), 'Underreactions and overreactions: The influence of information reliability and portfolio formation rules', Working Paper, Johnson Graduate School of Management, Cornell University.

Blume, M.E. and I. Friend (1975), 'The asset structure of individual portfolios and some implications for utility functions', *Journal of Finance*, **30**(2), 585–603.

Böhm-Bawerk, E. von ([1888] 1912), *Positive Theorie des Kapitales*, Dritte Auflage, Zweiter Halbband, Innsbruck: Verlag der Wagner'schen Universitäts-Buchhandlung (first published in 1888).

Borges, B., D.G. Goldstein, A. Ortmann, and G. Gigerenzer (1999), 'Can ignorance beat the stock market?', in G. Gigerenzer and P.M. Todd and the ABD Research Group (eds), *Simple Heuristics that Make Us Smart*, Oxford: Oxford University Press, 59–72.

Boring, FOR EXAMPLE (1950), *A History of Experimental Psychology*, 2nd edition, Englewood Cliffs, NJ: Prentice-Hall.

Brandstätter, H. (1995), 'Saving behavior related to personality structure', in S. Troye and E. Nyhus (eds), *Frontiers in Economic Psychology*, Vol. 1, 20th IAREP Conference Bergen, Norway, August 2–5, 60–78.

Brealey, R.A. and S.C. Myers (1996), *Principles of Corporate Finance*, 5th edition, New York: Irwin/McGraw-Hill.

Brehmer, B. (1992), 'Dynamic decision making: Human control of complex systems', *Acta Psychologica*, **81**, 211–41.

Brehmer, B. and D. Dörner (1993). 'Experiments with computer-simulated microworlds: Escaping both the narrow straits of the laboratory and the deep blue sea of the field study', *Computers in Human Behavior*, **9**, 171–84.

Briggs, S.R. and J.M. Cheek (1988), 'On the nature of self-monitoring: Problems with assessment, problems with validity', *Journal of Personality and Social Psychology*, **54**(4), 663–78.

Brown, B.W. and S. Maital (1981), 'What do economists know? An empirical study of experts' expectations', *Econometrica*, **49**(2), 491–504.

Browning, M. and A. Lusardi (1996), 'Household saving: Micro theories and micro facts', *Journal of Economic Literature*, **34**, 1797–1855.

Bulow, J. and P. Klemperer (1994), 'Rational frenzies and crashes', *Journal of Political Economy*, **102**(1), 1–24.

Busemeyer, J.R. (1991), 'Intuitive statistical estimation', in N.H. Anderson (ed.), *Contributions to Information Integration Theory. Volume I: Cognition,* Hillsdale, NJ: Lawrence Erlbaum Associates, 187–215.

Cacioppo, J.T. and W.L. Gardner (1999), 'Emotion', *Annual Review of Psychology*, **50**, 191–214.

Caginalp, G., D. Porter, and V.L. Smith (1999), 'Experimental asset markets', in P.E. Earl and S. Kemp (eds), *The Elgar Companion to Consumer Research and Economic Psychology*, Cheltenham, UK and Northampton, MA, 215–22.

Camerer, C.F. (1987), 'Do biases in probability judgment matter in markets? Experimental evidence', *American Economic Review*, **77**(5), 981–97.

Camerer, C.F. (1998), 'Can asset markets be manipulated? A field experiment with race track betting', *Journal of Political Economy*, **106**(3), 457–82.

Camerer, C.F. and E. Johnson (1991), 'The process–performance paradox in expert judgment: How can experts know so much and predict so badly?', in K.A. Ericsson and J. Smith (eds), *Toward a General Theory of Expertise: Prospects and Limits*, Cambridge: Cambridge University Press, 195–217.

Camerer, C. and D. Lovallo (1999), 'Overconfidence and excess entry: An experimental approach', *American Economic Review*; **89(1)**, 306–18.

Campbell, J.Y. and N.G. Mankiw (1989), 'Consumption, income and interest rates: Reinterpreting the time series evidence', Working Paper No. 2924, Cambridge, MA: National Bureau of Economic Research.

Campbell, J.Y. and N.G. Mankiw (1990), 'Permanent income, current income, and consumption', *Journal of Business and Economic Statistics*, **8**(3), 265–79.

Campbell, J.Y. and N.G. Mankiw (1991), 'The response of consumption to income: a cross-country investigation', *European Economic Review*, **35**(4), 723–67.

Canner, N., N.G. Mankiw, and D.N. Weil (1997), 'An asset allocation puzzle', *American Economic Review*, **87**, 181–91.

Caplin, A. and J. Leahy (1994), 'Business as usual, market crashes and wisdom after the fact', *American Economic Review*, **84**(3), 548–64.

Carducci, B.J. and A.S. Wong (1998), 'Type A and risk taking in everyday money matters', *Journal of Business & Psychology*, **12**(3), 355–9.

Carroll, C.D., J.C. Fuhrer, and D.W. Wilcox (1994), 'Does consumer sentiment forecast household spending? If so, why?', *American Economic Review*, **84**(5), 1397–1408.

Ceci, J.S. and J.K. Liker (1986), 'A day at the races: A study of IQ, expertise, and cognitive complexity', *Journal of Experimental Psychology: General*, **115**, 255–66.

Chan, K.C. (1988), 'On the contrarian investment strategy', *Journal of Business*; **61**, 147–64.

Chan, L.K.C., N. Jegadeesh, and J. Lakonishok (1999), 'Momentum strategies', in L.E. Lifson and R.A. Geist (eds), *The Psychology of Investing*, New York: John Wiley & Sons, Inc., 101–46.

Chow, G., E. Jacquier, M. Kritzman, and K. Lowry (1999), 'Optimal portfolios in good times and bad', *Financial Analysts Journal*; **55**, May/June; 65–73.

Cialdini, R.B. (1988), *Influence: Science and Practice*, 2nd edition, Glenview, IL: Scott, Foresman and Co.

Clark, J.M. (1918), 'Economics and modern psychology: I', *Journal of Political Economy*, **26**(1), 1–30.

Collard, D. (1983), 'Pigou on expectations and the business cycle', *Economic Journal*, **93**, 411–14.

Conlisk, J. (1996), 'Why bounded rationality?', *Journal of Economic Literature*, **34**, 669–700.

Cosmides, L. and J. Tooby (1994), 'Better than rational: Evolutionary psychology and the invisible hand, *American Economic Review*, **84**(2), Papers and Proceedings, 327–32.

Cosmides, L. and J. Tooby (1996), 'Are humans good intuitive statisticians after all? Rethinking some conclusions from the literature on judgment under uncertainty', *Cognition*, **58**(1) 1–73.

Crittenden, K.S. (1983), 'Sociological aspects of attribution', *Annual Review of Sociology*, **9**, 425–46.

Cummings, L.S. (2000), 'The financial performance of ethical investment trusts: An Australian perspective', *Journal of Business Ethics*, **25**, 79–92.

Cutler, D.M., J.M. Poterba, and L.H. Summers (1989), 'What moves stock prices?', *Journal of Portfolio Management*, **15**(3), 4–12.

Daniel, K.D., D. Hirshleifer, and A. Subrahmanyam (1998a), 'Investor psychology and security market under- and overreactions', *Journal of Finance*; **53**(6), 1839–85.

Daniel, K.D., D. Hirshleifer, and A. Subrahmanyam (1998b), 'Investor overconfidence, covariance risk, and predictors of securities returns', Working Paper, Ann Arbor, MI: University of Michigan Business School.

Daniel, T.R. (1997), 'The economic psychology of saving: the role of individual differences associated with intertemporal choice', Valencia: PROMOLIBRO. Proceedings, IAREP 22nd Conference, University of Valencia, September, 1997, 127-155.

Darke, P.R.and J.L. Freedman (1997), 'The Belief in Good Luck Scale', *Journal of Research in Personality,* **31**(4) 486–511.

Davidsson, P. and R. Wahlund (1992), 'A note on the failure to use negative information', *Journal of Economic Psychology*, **13**(2), 343–53.

Davis, F.D.; Lohse, G.L., and Kottemann, J.E (1994), 'Harmful effects of seemingly helpful information on forecasts of stock earnings', *Journal of Economic Psychology*, **15**(2), 253–67.

Dawes, R.M. (1999), 'A message from psychologists to economists: Mere predictability doesn't matter like it should (without a good story appended to it)', *Journal of Economic Behavior and Organization*, **39**, 29–40.

De Bondt, W. F.M. (1991), 'What do economists know about the stock market?' *Journal of Portfolio Management*, **17**, Winter, 84–92.

De Bondt, W.F M (1993), 'Betting on trends: Intuitive forecasts of financial risk and return', *International Journal of Forecasting*, **9**(3), 355–71.

De Bondt, W.F.M. (1998), 'A portrait of the individual investor', *European Economic Review*; **42**, May, 831–844.

De Bondt, W.F.M. and W.P. Forbes (1999), 'Herding in analyst earnings forecasts: Evidence from the United Kingdom', *European Financial Management*, 5(2), 141–63.

De Bondt, W.F.M. and R.H. Thaler (1985), 'Does the stock market overreact?', *Journal of Finance*, **40**, 793–805.

De Bondt, W.F.M. and R.H. Thaler (1987), 'Further evidence on investor overreaction and stock market seasonality', *Journal of Finance*, **42**(3), 557–581.

De Bondt, W.F.M. and R.H. Thaler (1990), '.Do security analysis overreact?', *American Economic Review*, **80**(2), 52–57.

De Long, J.B., A. Shleifer, L.H. Summers, and R.J. Waldmann (1990a), 'Noise trader risk in financial markets', *Journal of Political Economy*, **88**(4), 703–38.

De Long, J.B., A. Shleifer, L.H. Summers, and R.J. Waldmann (1990b), 'Positive feedback investment strategies and destabilizing rational speculation', *Journal of Finance*, **45**(2), 379–95.

De Long, J.B., A. Shleifer, L.H. Summers, and R.J. Waldmann (1991), 'The survival of noise traders in financial markets, *Journal of Business*, **64**(1), 1–19.

Dickens, C. ([1836]1994), *The Pickwick Papers*, London: Penguin Books.

Dickens, C. ([1849–50]1994), *David Copperfield*, London: Penguin Books.

DiFonzo, N. and P. Bordia (1997), 'Rumor and prediction: Making sense (but losing dollars) in the stock market', *Organizational Behavior and Human Decision Processes*, **71**(3), 329–53.

DiFonzo, N., D.A. Hantula, and P. Bordia (1998), 'Microworlds for experimental research: Having your (control and collections) cake, and realism too', *Behavior Research Methods, Instruments & Computers*, **30**(2), 278–86.

Dimson, E., P.R. Marsh, and M. Staunton (2000), *The Millennium Book: A Century of Investment Returns*, London: ABN-Amro/ London School of Business.

Dreman, D. (1999), 'Investor overreaction', in L.E. Lifson and R.A. Geist (eds), *The Psychology of Investing*, New York: John Wiley & Sons, Inc., 1–9.

Eckblad, G.F. and A.L. von der Lippe (1994), 'Norwegian lottery winners: Cautious realists', *Journal of Gambling Studies*, **10**(4), 305–22.

Edwards, W. (1968), 'Conservatism in human information processing', in B. Kleinmmutz (ed.), *Formal Representation of Human Judgment*, New York: Wiley, 17–52.

Edwards, W. (1982), 'Conservatism in human information processing', in D. Kahneman, P. Slovic, and A. Tversky (eds), *Judgment under Uncertainty: Heuristics and Biases*, Cambridge: Cambridge University Press, 359–60.

Einhorn, H.J. and R.M. Hogarth (1985), 'Ambiguity and uncertainty in probabilistic inference', *Psychological Review*, **92**, 433–61.

Ekman, G. (1955), 'The four effects of cooperation', *Journal of Social Psychology*, **41**, 149–62.

Ellis, C.D. (1993), *Investment Policy: How to Win the Loser's Game*, 2nd edition, Chicago, IL: Irwin Professional Publishing.

Elster, J. (1977), 'Ulysses and the sirens: A theory of imperfect rationality', *Social Science Information*, **16**, 469–526.

Elster, J. and G. Loewenstein (1992), 'Utility from memory and anticipation', in G. Loewenstein and J. Elster (eds), *Choice over Time*, New York, NY: Russell Sage Foundation, 213–34.

Erev, I., T.S. Wallsten, and D.V. Budescu (1994), 'Simultaneous over- and underconfidence: The role of error in judgment processes', *Psychological Review*, **101**(3), 519–27.

Ericsson, K.A., W. Kintsch, and V. Patel (2000), 'How experts' adaptations to representative task demands account for the expertise effect in memory recall: Comment on Vicente and Wang (1998)', *Psychological Review*, **107**(3), 578–92.

Ericsson, K.A. and A.C. Lehmann (1996), 'Expert and exceptional performance: Evidence of maximal adaptation to task constraints', *Annual Review of Psychology*, **47**, 273–305.

Ericsson, K.A. and J. Smith (1991), 'Prospects and limits of the empirical study of expertise: An introduction', in K.A. Ericsson and J. Smith (eds), *Toward a General Theory of Expertise: Prospects and Limits*, Cambridge: Cambridge University Press, 1–38.

Falk, R. and C. Konold (1997), 'Making sense of randomness: Implicit encoding as a basis for judgment', *Psychological Review*, **104**(2), 301–318.

Fama, E.F. (1965), 'The behavior of stock market prices', *Journal of Business*, **38**, 34–105.

Fama, E.F. (1998), 'Market efficiency, long-term returns, and behavioral finance', *Journal of Financial Economics*, **49**(3), 283–306.

Fama, E.F. and K.R. French (1996), 'Multifactor explanations of asset pricing anomalies', *Journal of Finance*, **51**(1), 55–84.

Fama, E.F. and K. R. French (2000), 'The equity premium', Working Paper No. 522, Center for Research in Security Prices, University of Chicago, Graduate School of Business.

Farnham, B. (ed.)(1994), *Avoiding Losses/Taking Risks. Prospect Theory and International Conflict*, Ann Arbor, MI: The University of Michigan Press.

Farquhar, P.H. (1984), 'Utility assessment methods', *Management Science*, **30**, 1283–1300.

Feather, N.T. (1982), 'Actions in relation to expected consequences: An overview of a research program', in N.T. Feather, (ed.), *Expectations and Actions,* Hillsdale, NJ: Lawrence Erlbaum Associates, 53–90.

Festinger, L. (1954), 'A theory of social comparison processes', *Human Relations*, **7**, 117–40.

Festinger, L. (1957), *A Theory of Cognitive Dissonance*, Evanston, IL: Row, Peterson and Company.

Fiedler, K. (2000), 'Beware of samples! Cognitive-ecological sampling approach to judgment biases', *Psychological Review*, **107**(4), 659–76.

Fiedler, K., B. Brinkmann, T. Betsch, and B. Wild (2000), 'A sampling approach to biases in conditional probability judgments: Beyond baserate neglect and statistical format', *Journal of Experimental Psychology: General*, forthcoming.

Fischer, L., T. Kutsch, and E. Stephan (eds) (1999), *Finanzpsychologie*, München und Wien: R. Oldenbourg Verlag.

Fischhoff, B. (1982a), 'For those condemned to study the past: Heuristics and biases in hindsight', in D. Kahneman, P. Slovic, and A. Tversky (eds), *Judgment under Uncertainty: Heuristics and Biases*, Cambridge: Cambridge University Press, 335–351.

Fischhoff, B. (1982b), 'Debiasing', in D. Kahneman, P. Slovic, and A. Tversky (eds), *Judgment under Uncertainty: Heuristics and Biases*, Cambridge: Cambridge University Press, 422–44.

Fisher, I. (1930), *The Theory of Interest*, London: Macmillan.

Fisher, K.L. and M. Statman (2000), 'Investor sentiment and stock returns', *Financial Analysts Journal*, **56**, March/April, 16–23.

Folkes, V.S. (1984), 'Consumer reactions to product failure: An attributional approach', *Journal of Consumer Research*, **11**, 398–409.

Forgas, J.P. (1994), 'The role of emotion in social judgments: An introductory review and an affect infusion model (AIM)', *European Journal of Social Psychology*, **24**, 1–24.

Forgas, J.P. (1995), 'Mood and judgment: The affect intrusion model (AIM)', *Psychological Bulletin*, **117**, 39–66.

Fornell, C. (1992), 'A national customer satisfaction barometer: The Swedish experience', *Journal of Marketing*, **56**, 6–21.

French, K.R. and J.M. Poterba (1991), 'Investor diversification and international equity markets', *American Economic Review*, **81**(2), 222–6.

Friedman, M. (1953), *Essays in Positive Economics,* Chicago, IL: University of Chicago Press.

Friedman, M. and R.D. Friedman (1998), *Two Lucky People: Memoirs*, Chicago, IL: University of Chicago Press.

Friedman, M. and L.J. Savage (1948), 'The utility analysis of choices involving risk', *Journal of Political Economy*, **56**, 279–304.

Friedrich, J. (1993), 'Primary error detection and minimization (PEDMIN) strategies in social cognition: A reinterpretation of confirmation bias phenomena', *Psychological Review*, **100**(2), 298–319.

Galbraith, J.K. ([1954]1987), *The Great Crash 1929*, London: Penguin Books.

Garber, P.M. (1989a), 'Tulipmania', *Journal of Political Economy*, **97**(3), 535–60.

Garber, P.M. (1989b), 'Who put the mania in Tulipmania?', *Journal of Portfolio Management*, **16**(1), 53–60.
Garber, P. (1990), 'Famous first bubbles', *Journal of Economic Perspectives*, **4**, 35–54.
Gervais, S. and T. Odean (1999), 'Learning to be overconfident', Unpublished manuscript, Finance Department, Wharton School, University of Pennsylvania.
Gigerenzer, G. (1996), 'On narrow norms and vague heuristics: A reply to Kahneman and Tversky (1996)', *Psychological Review*, **103**(3), 592–6.
Gigerenzer, G. and D.G. Goldstein (1996), 'Reasoning the fast and frugal way: Models of bounded rationality', *Psychological Review*, **103**(4), 650–69 .
Gigerenzer, G. and U. Hoffrage (1995), 'How to improve Bayesian reasoning without instruction: Frequency formats', *Psychological Review*, **102**, 684–704.
Gigerenzer, G., U. Hoffrage, and H. Kleinbölting (1991), 'Probabilistic mental models: A Brunswikian theory of confidence', *Psychological Review*, **98**, 506–28.
Gigerenzer, G., Todd, P.M. and the ABC Research Group (eds) (1999), *Simple Heuristics that Make Us Smart*, Oxford: Oxford University Press.
Gilovich, T. and V.H. Medvec (1995), 'The experience of regret: What, when, and why', *Psychological Review*, **102**(2), 379–95.
Glaser, R. (1994), 'Expertise', in M.W. Eysenck (ed.), *The Blackwell Dictionary of Cognitive Psychology*, Oxford: Blackwell Publishers, 139–42.
Goldstein, D.G. and G. Gigerenzer (1999), 'The recognition heuristic: How ignorance makes us smart', in G.Gigerenzer, P.M. Todd, and the ABC Research Group (eds), *Simple Heuristics that Make Us Smart*, Oxford: Oxford University Press, 37–58.
Griffin, Dale and A. Tversky (1992), 'The weighing of evidence and the determinants of confidence', *Cognitive Psychology*, **24**(3), 411–35.
Grinblatt, M. and M. Keloharju (2000a), 'The investment behavior and performance of various investor types: A study of Finland's unique data set', *Journal of Financial Economics*, **55**(1), 43–67.
Grinblatt, M. and M. Keloharju (2000b), 'Distance, language, and culture bias', Working Paper No.00–04, Yale International Center for Finance.
Grinblatt, M. and M. Keloharju (2001), 'What makes investors trade?', *Journal of Finance*, **56**(2), 589–616.
Grossman, S.J. and J.E. Stiglitz (1980), 'On the impossibility of informationally efficient markets', *American Economic Review*, **70**(3), 393–408.
Gunnarsson, J. (1999), *Portfolio-Based Segmentation and Consumer Behavior*, Doctoral dissertation, Stockholm: Economic Research Institute, Stockholm School of Economics.
Gunnarsson, J. and R. Wahlund (1997), 'Household financial strategies in Sweden: An exploratory study', *Journal of Economic Psychology*, **18**, 201–33.

Gunnarsson, J., R. Wahlund, and H. Flink (2000), *Finansiella strategier i förändring: segment och beteenden bland svenska hushåll* [Changing Financial Strategies: Segments and Behaviors of Swedish Households], EFI Research Report, Stockholm: EFI, Stockholm School of Economics.

Güth, W., J.P. Krahnen, and C. Rieck (1997), 'Financial markets with asymmetric information: A pilot study focusing on insider advantages', *Journal of Economic Psychology*, **18**, 235–57.

Guthrie, E.R. (1935), *The Psychology of Learning*, New York: Harper.

Guzzo, R.A. and M.W. Dickson (1996), 'Teams in organizations: Recent research on performance and effectiveness', *Annual Review of Psychology*, **47**, 307–38.

Harlow, W.V. and K.C. Brown (1990), 'Understanding and assessing financial risk tolerance: A biological perspective', *Financial Analysts Journal*, **46**(6), 50–62.

Harrison, T. (1994), 'Mapping customer segments for personal financial services', *International Journal of Bank Marketing*, **12**(8), 17–25.

Harvey, J.H. and G. Weary (1984), 'Current issues in attribution theory and research', *Annual Review of Psychology*, **35**, 427–59.

Heath, C. and J.B. Soll (1996), 'Mental budgeting and consumer decisions', *Journal of Consumer Research*, **23**, 40–52.

Hedborg, A. (1996), *Studies of Framing, Judgment and Choice*, Doctoral dissertation, Stockholm: Economic Research Institute, Stockholm School of Economics.

Heider, F. (1958), *The Psychology of Interpersonal Relations*, New York: Wiley.

Heilmann,, K., V. Läger, and A. Oehler (2000), 'The disposition effect – evidence about the investors' aversion to realize losses. A contribution to behavioral finance through the use of experimental call markets', Proceedings, IAREP/SABE 2000 Conference, Vienna: WUV Universitätsverlag, 186–90.

Hellman, N. (2000), *Investor Behaviour: An Empirical Study of How Large Swedish Institutional Investors Make Equity Investment Decisions*, Doctoral dissertation, Stockholm: Economic Research Institute, Stockholm School of Economics.

Henderson, P.W. and R.A. Peterson (1992), 'Mental accounting and categorization', *Organizational Behavior and Human Decision Processes*, **51**, 92–117.

Hendriks, A.A.J., W.K.B. Hofstee, B. de Raad, and A. Angleitner (1995). 'The Five-Factor Personality Inventory', Unpublished manuscript, Heymans Institute, University of Groningen.

Herrnstein, R.J. (1990), 'Rational choice theory: Necessary but not sufficient', *American Psychologist*, **45**, 356–67.

Hey, J.D. (1992), 'Experiments in economics – and psychology', in S.E.G. Lea, P. Webley, and B.M. Young (eds), *New Directions in Economic Psychology: Theory, Experiment and Application,* Aldershot, UK and Brookfield, US: Edward Elgar, 85–98.

Higgins, E.T. (1997), 'Beyond pleasure and pain', *American Psychologist*, **52**, 1280–1300.

Hirschman, A.O. (1977), *The Passions and the Interests: Political Arguments for Capitalism before Its Triumph,* Princeton, NJ: Princeton University Press.

Hoch, S.J. and J. Deighton (1989), 'Managing what consumers learn from experience', *Journal of Marketing*, **53**, April, 1–20.

Hoch, S.J. and G.F. Loewenstein (1991), 'Time-inconsistent preferences and consumer self-control', *Journal of Consumer Research*, **17**, 492–507.

Hochbaum, G.M. (1954), 'The relation between group members' self-confidence and their reactions to group pressures to uniformity', *American Sociological Review*, **19**, 678–88.

Hoffrage, U. and R. Hertwig (1999), 'Hindsight bias: A price worth paying for fast and frugal memory', in G. Gigerenzer, P.M. Todd, and the ABC Research Group (eds), *Simple Heuristics that Make Us Smart*, Oxford: Oxford University Press, 191–208.

Hogarth, R.M. (1987), *Judgement and Choice: The Psychology of Decision*, 2nd edition, Chichester: John Wiley & Sons.

Holyoak, K.J. (1991), 'Symbolic connectionism: Toward third-generation theories of expertise', in K.A. Ericsson and J. Smith (eds), *Toward a General Theory of Expertise: Prospects and Limits*, Cambridge: Cambridge University Press, 301–35.

Hong, H., T. Lim and J.C. Stein (2000), 'Bad news travels slowly: Size, analyst coverage and the profitability of momentum strategies', *Journal of Finance*, **55**(1), 265–95.

Hong, H. and J.C. Stein (1999), 'A unified theory of underreaction, momentum trading, and overreaction in assets markets,' *Journal of Finance*, **54**(6), 2143–84.

Hurd, M.D. (1999), 'Portfolio holdings by the elderly', Paper presented at Conference on Household Portfolios, December, Florence: European University Institute.

Hussein, G. (1985), 'An examination of the psychological aspects of money', Unpublished M.Phil. thesis, University of Exeter, UK.

Jacoby, J. (1984), 'Perspectives on information overload', *Journal of Consumer Research*, **10**(4), 432–5.

Jacoby, J., D. Mazursky, T. Troutman, and A. Kuss (1984), 'When feedback is ignored: Disutility of outcome feedback', *Journal of Applied Psychology,* **69**(3), 531–45.

Jaffe, J. and F. Mahoney (1999), 'The performance of investment newsletters', *Journal of Financial Economics,* **53**(2), 289–307

James, W. ([1890]1983), *The Principles of Psychology*, Cambridge, MA: Harvard University Press. (first published in 1890).

Jevons, W.S. ([1871]1911), *The Theory of Political Economy*, 4th edition, London: Macmillan and Co. Ltd (first published in 1871).

Juslin, P. and H. Olsson (1997), 'Thurstonian and Brunswikian origins of uncertainty in judgment: A sampling model of confidence in sensory discrimination', *Psychological Review*, **104**(2), 344–66.

Kachelmeier, S.J. and M. Shehata (1992), 'Examining risk preferences under high monetary incentives: Experimental evidence from the People's Republic of China', *American Economic Review*, **82**, 1120–41.

Kahneman, D. (1994), 'New challenges to the rationality assumption', *Journal of Institutional and Theoretical Economics, JITE*, **150**, 18–36.

Kahneman, D., E. Diener, and N. Schwartz (eds) (1999), *Well-Being: The Foundations of Hedonic Psychology*, New York: Russell Sage Foundation.

Kahneman, D. and D. Lovallo (1993), 'Timid choices and bold forecasts: A cognitive perspective on risk taking', *Management Science*, **39**(1), 17–31.

Kahneman, D. and W. Riepe (1998), 'Aspects of investor psychology', *Journal of Portfolio Management*, **24**(4), Summer, 52–65.

Kahneman, D., P. Slovic, and A. Tversky (eds) (1982), *Judgment under Uncertainty: Heuristics and Biases*, Cambridge: Cambridge University Press.

Kahneman, D. and J. Snell (1990), 'Predicting utility', in R.M Hogarth (ed.), *Insights in Decision making*, Chicago, IL: University of Chicago Press, 295–310.

Kahneman, D. and A. Tversky (1973), 'On the psychology of prediction', *Psychological Review*, **80**, 237–51.

Kahneman, D. and A. Tversky (1979), 'Prospect theory: An analysis of decision under risk', *Econometrica*, **47**, 263–91.

Kahneman, D. and A. Tversky (1982), 'The psychology of preferences', *Scientific American*, **246**, 160–73.

Kahneman, D. and A. Tversky (1984), 'Choices, values, and frames', *American Psychologist*, **39**, 341–50.

Kahneman, D. and A. Tversky (1996), 'On the reality of cognitive illusions', *Psychological Review*, **103**(3), 582–91.

Kahneman, D., P.P. Wakker, and R. Sarin (1997), 'Back to Bentham? Explorations of experienced utility', *Quarterly Journal of Economics*, **112**(2), 375–405.

Kamakura, W.A., S.N. Ramaswami, and R.K. Srivastava (1991), 'Applying latent trait analysis in the evaluation of prospects for cross-selling of financial services', *International Journal of Research In Marketing*, **8**, 329–49.

Karniol, R. and M. Ross (1996), 'The motivational impact of temporal focus: Thinking about the future and the past', *Annual Review of Psychology*, **47**, 593–620.

Karoly, P. (1993), 'Mechanisms of self-regulation: A systems view', *Annual Review of Psychology*, **44**, 23–52.

Katona, G. (1951), *Psychological Analysis of Economic Behavior*, New York: McGraw-Hill.

Katona, G. (1972), 'Theory of expectations', in B. Strumpel, J.N. Morgan, and E. Zahn (eds), *Human Behavior in Economic Affairs: Essays in Honor of George Katona*, Amsterdam and New York: Elsevier Scientific Publishing Co., 549–82.

Katona, G. (1975), *Psychological Economics,* New York: Elsevier.

Katona, G. (1979), 'Toward a macropsychology', *American Psychologist*, **34**, 118–26.

Katona, G. (1980), *Essays on Behavioral Economics*, Ann Arbor, MI: Institute for Social Research, University of Michigan.

Kaufman, B.E. (1999), 'Emotional arousal as a source of bounded rationality', *Journal of Economic Behavior and Organization,* **38**,135–144.

Kelley, H.H. (1967), 'Attribution theory in social psychology', in D. Levine (ed.), *Nebraska Symposium on Motivation*, Vol. 15, Lincoln, NB: University of Nebraska Press, 192–238.

Kelley, H.H. (1973), 'The process of causal attribution', *American Psychologist*, **28**, 107–28.

Kelley, H.H. and J.L. Michela (1980), 'Attribution theory and research', *Annual Review of Psychology*, **31**, 457–501.

Kelly, M. (1997), 'Do noise traders influence stock prices?', *Journal of Money, Credit, and Banking*, **29**(3), 351–63.

Kemeny, J.G., A. Schleifer, J.L. Snell, and G.L. Thompson (1962), *Finite Mathematics with Business Applications*, Englewood Cliffs, NJ: Prentice-Hall Inc.

Keynes, J.M. (1930), *A Treatise on Money,* Vols 1 and 2, London: Macmillan.

Keynes, J.M. (1936), *The General Theory of Employment, Interest and Money*, London: Macmillan.

Knight, F.H. (1921), *Risk, Uncertainty, and Profit*, New York: Harper & Row.

Kroll, Y., H. Levy, and A. Rapoport (1988a), 'Experimental tests of the Mean-Variance Model for Portfolio Selection', *Organizational Behavior and Human Decision Processes*, **42**(3), 388–410.

Kroll, Y., H. Levy, and A. Rapoport (1988b), 'Experimental tests of the separation theorem and the Capital Asset Pricing Model', *American Economic Review*, **78**(3), 500–19.

Kryzanowski, L. and H. Zhang (1992), 'The contrarian investment strategy does not work in Canadian markets', *Journal of Financial and Quantitative Analysis*, **27**(3), 383–95.

Kuhl, J. (1985), 'Cognition–behavior consistency: Self-regulatory processes and action versus state orientation', in J. Kuhl and J. Beckmann (eds), *Action Control: from Cognition to Behavior*, Berlin: Springer, 101–28.

Kuhl, J. and J. Beckmann (1985), 'Historical perspectives in the study of action control', in J. Kuhl and J. Beckmann (eds), *Action Control: from Cognition to Behavior*, Berlin: Springer, 89–100.

Langbein, L.I. and A.J. Lichtman (1978), *Ecological Inference*, Sage University Paper Series on Quantitative Applications in the Social Sciences, 07-010, Beverly Hills, CA: Sage Publications.

Langer, E.J. (1982), 'The illusion of control', in D. Kahneman, P. Slovic, and A. Tversky (eds), *Judgment under Uncertainty: Heuristics and Biases*, Cambridge: Cambridge University Press, 231–38.

Latané, B. (1981), 'The psychology of social impact', *American Psychologist*, **36**, 343–56.

Laughhunn, D.J., J.W. Payne, and R. Crum (1980), 'Managerial risk preferences for below-target returns', *Management Science*, **26**(12), 1238–49.

Lazarus, R.S (1984), ' Thoughts on the relations between emotion and cognition', *American Psychologist*, **37**(9) 1019–24.

Lease, R.C., W.G. Lewellen, and G.G. Schlarbaum (1974), 'The individual investor: Attributes and attitudes', *Journal of Finance*, **29**(2), 413–33.

LeBaron, D.G., G. Farrelly, and S. Gula (1989), 'Facilitating a dialogue on risk: A questionnaire approach', *Financial Analysts Journal*, **45**, May–June, 19–24.

Lee, C.M.C., A. Shleifer, and R. Thaler (1991), 'Investor sentiment and the closed-end fund puzzle', *Journal of Finance*, **46**, 75–110.

Lee, I.H. (1998), 'Market crashes and informational avalanches', *Review of Economic Studies*, **65**, 741–59.

Leibenstein, H. (1950), 'Bandwagon, snob, and Veblen effects in the theory of consumers' demand', *Quarterly Journal of Economics*, **64**(2), 183–207.

Lettau, M. and S. Ludvigson (1999), 'Consumption, aggregate wealth and expected stock returns', New York: Federal Reserve Bank of New York.

Levine, J.M. and R.L. Moreland (1990), 'Progress in small group research', *Annual Review of Psychology*, **41**, 585–634.

Lewis, A. and C. Mackenzie (2000), 'Morals, money, ethical investing and economic psychology', *Human Relations*, **53**(2), 179–91.

Lewis, A. and P. Webley (1994), 'Social and ethical investing: Beliefs, preferences and the willingness to sacrifice financial return', in A. Lewis and K.-E. Wärneryd (eds), *Ethics and Economic Affairs*, London and New York: Routledge, 171–82.

Lifson, L.E. and R.A. Geist (eds) (1999), *The Psychology of Investing*, New York and Chichester: John Wiley & Sons, Inc.

Lintner, J, (1965), 'The valuation of risk assets and the selection of risky investments in stock portfolios and capital budgets', *Review of Economics and Statistics*, **47**(1), 13–37.

Lo, A., H. Mamaysky, and J. Wang (2000), 'Foundations of technical analysis: Computational algorithms, statistical inference, and empirical implementation', *Journal of Finance*, **55**(4), 1705-70.

Loewenstein, G. (1992), 'The fall and rise of psychological explanations in the economics of intertemporal choice', in G. Loewenstein and J. Elster (eds), *Choice over Time*, New York: Russell Sage Foundation, 3–34.

Loomes, G. (1988), 'When actions speak louder than prospects', *American Economic Review*, **78**(3), 463–70.

Lopes, L.L. (1982), 'Doing the impossible: A note on induction and the experience of randomness', *Journal of Experimental Psychology: Learning, Memory, and Cognition*, **8**, 626–36.

Lopes, L.L. (1990), 'Re-modeling risk aversion: A comparison of Bernoullian and rank dependent value approaches', in G.M. von Furstenberg (ed.), *Acting under Uncertainty: Multidisciplinary Conceptions,* Dordrecht: Kluver Academic Publishers, 267–99.

Lopes, L.L. (1994), 'Psychology and economics: Perspectives on risk, cooperation, and the marketplace', *Annual Review of Psychology*, **45**, 197–227.

Lovell, M.C. (1986), 'Tests of the rational expectations hypothesis', *American Economic Review*, **76**(1), 110–24.

Lucas, R.E. (1986), 'Adaptive behavior and economic theory', *Journal of Business*, **59**(4), Part 2, S401–S426.

Lupfer, M. (1970), 'The effects of risk-taking tendencies and incentive conditions on the performance of investment groups', *Journal of Social Psychology*, **82**(1), 135–6.

MacCrimmon, K.R. and D.A. Wehrung (1986), *Taking Risks: The Management of Uncertainty*, New York, NY: The Free Press.

Macrae, C.N. and G-V. Bodenhausen (2000), 'Social cognition: Thinking categorically about others', *Annul Review of Psychology*, **51**, 93–120.

Magnusson, D. and B. Ekehammar (1972), 'Subjective confidence and interjudge agreement as functions of amounts of information: A study of interview data', Report from the Psychological Laboratory, University of Stockholm, No. 366, October.

Maital, S. (1979), 'Inflation expectations in the monetarist black box', *American Economic Review*, **69**(3), 429–34.

Maital, S. (1982), *Minds, Markets, and Money*, New York: Basic Books.

Maital, S., R. Filer, and J. Simon (1986), 'What do people bring to the stock market (besides money)? The economic psychology of stock market behavior', in B. Gilad and S. Kaish (eds), *Handbook of Behavioral Economics*, Vol. B., Greenwich, CT: JAI Press, 273–307.

Maital, S. and S.L. Maital (1981), 'Individual-rational and group-rational inflation expectations: Theory and cross-section evidence', *Journal of Economic Behavior and Organization*, **2**, 179–86.

Malhotra, N.K (1984), 'Reflections on the information overload paradigm in consumer decision making', *Journal of Consumer Research*, **10**(4), 436–40.

Mandelbrot, B. (1966), 'Forecasts of future prices, unbiased markets, and "martingale" models', *Journal of Business*, **39**(1), 242–55.

Markowitz, H. (1952a), 'Portfolio selection', *Journal of Finance*, 7(1), 77–91.

Markowitz, H. (1952b), 'The utility of wealth', *Journal of Political Economy*, **60**(2), 151–8.

Marshall, A. ([1890]1990), *Principles of Economics: An Introductory Volume*, 8th edition, London: Macmillan. (first published in 1890).

McCord, M. and R. de Neufville (1986), 'Lottery equivalents: Reduction of the certainty effect in utility assessment', *Management Science*, **32**, 56–60.

McFadden, D. (1999), 'Rationality for economists?', *Journal of Risk and Uncertainty*, **19**(1/3), 73–105.

Mehra, R. and E.C. Prescott (1985), 'The equity premium: A puzzle', *Journal of Monetary Economics*, **15**(2), 145–61.

Mellers, B.A., A. Schwartz, and A.D.J. Cooke (1998), 'Judgment and decision making', *Annual Review of Psychology*, **49**, 447–77.

Metcalfe, J. and W. Mischel (1999), 'A hot/cool system analysis of delay of gratification: dynamics of willpower', *Psychological Review*, **106**, 3–19.

Metrick, A. (1999), 'Performance evaluation with transactions data: The stock selection of investment newsletters', *Journal of Finance*, **54**(5), 1743–75.

Mill, J.S. ([1836] 1988), 'On the definition and method of political economy', in D.M. Hausman (ed.), *The Philosophy of Economics: An Anthology*, Cambridge: Cambridge University Press, 52–69.

Mischel, W. (1984), 'Convergences and challenges in the search for consistency', *American Psychologist*, **39**, 351–64.

Mischel, W., Y. Shoda, and M.L. Rodriguez (1992), 'Delay of gratification in children', in G. Loewenstein and J. Elster (eds), *Choice over Time*, New York: Russell Sage Foundation, 147–66.

Montgomery, H. (1989), 'From cognition to action: The search for dominance in decision making', in H. Montgomery and O. Svenson (eds), *Process and Structure in Human Decision Making*, Chichester: John Wiley & Sons, 23–49.

Montgomery, H. and O. Svenson (1989), 'A think-aloud study of dominance structuring in decision processes', in H. Montgomery and O. Svenson (eds), *Process and Structure in Human Decision Making*, Chichester: John Wiley & Sons, 135–50.

Moon, P., K. Keasey, and D. Duxbury (1999), 'Mental accounting and decision making: The relationship between relative and absolute savings', *Journal of Economic Behavior and Organization*, **38**(2), 145–53.

Morse, W. C. (1998), 'Risk taking in personal investments', *Journal of Business & Psychology*, **13**(2), 281–8.

Moskowitz, T.J. and M. Grinblatt (1999), 'Do industries explain momentum?', *Journal of Finance*, **54**(4), 1249–90.

Müller-Peters, H. (1999), 'Motivation und Risikoneigung privater Geldanleger – Millers Ratten statt Skinners Tauben?' [Motivation and risk attitudes of private investors – Miller's rats instead of Skinner's pigeons?] in L. Fischer, T. Kutsch, and E. Stephan (eds), *Finanzpsychologie*, München und Wien: R. Oldenbourg Verlag, 135–68.

Murphy, G.L. and D.L. Medin (1985), 'The role of theories in conceptual coherence', *Psychological Review*, **92**, 289–316.

Muth, J.F. (1961), 'Rational expectations and the theory of price movements', *Econometrica*, **29**, 315–35.

Nerlove, M. (1983), 'Expectations, plans and realizations in theory and practice', *Econometrica*, **51**, 1251–79.

Niederhoffer, V. (1971), 'The analysis of world events and stock prices', *Journal of Business*, **44**(2), 193–219.

Nisbett, R.E., D.H. Krantz, C. Jepson, and G.T. Fong (1982), 'Improving inductive inference', in D. Kahneman, P. Slovic, and A. Tversky (eds), *Judgment under Uncertainty: Heuristics and Biases*, Cambridge: Cambridge University Press, 445–59.

Norem, J. K.and K.S.S. Illingworth (1993), 'Strategy-dependent effects of reflecting on self and tasks: Some implications of optimism and defensive pessimism', *Journal of Personality and Social Psychology*, **65**(4), 822–35.

Nyhus, E.K. (1996), *The VSB-CentER Savings Project: Data Collection Methods, Questionnaires and Sampling Procedures*, Progress Report 42, VSB-CentER Savings Project, CentER for Economic Research, Tilburg University.

Odean, T. (1998), 'Are investors reluctant to realize their losses?', *Journal of Finance*, **53**(5), 1775–98.

Odean, T. (1999), 'Do investors trade too much?', *American Economic Review*, **89**(5), 1279–98.

O'Donoghue, T. and M. Rabin (1999), 'Doing it now or later', *American Economic Review*, **89**, 103–24.

Ogburn, W.F. and M.F. Nimkoff (1950), *A Handbook of Sociology*, 2nd edition, London: Routledge & Kegan Paul Ltd.

Olsen, R.A. (1996), 'Implications of herding behavior for earnings estimation, risk assessment, and stock returns', *Financial Analysts Journal*, **52**, July–August, 37–41.

Olsen, R.A. (1997), 'Investment risk: the experts' perspective', *Financial Analysts Journal*, **54**, March–April, 10–18.

Osler, C.L. (1998), 'Identifying noise traders: The head-and-shoulders pattern in U.S. Equities Staff Reports', *Federal Reserve Bank of New York*, **42**, 1–39.

Palomino, F. (1996), ' Noise trading in small markets', *Journal of Finance*, **51**, 1537–50.

Pålsson, A.-M. (1996), 'Does the degree of relative risk aversion vary with household characteristics?', *Journal of Economic Psychology*, **17**, 771–87.

Payne, J.W., D.J. Laughhunn, and R. Crum (1980), 'Translation of gambles and aspiration level effects in risky choice behavior', *Management Science*, **26**, 1039–60.

Pinker, S. (1998). *How the Mind Works*, Harmondsworth: Penguin.

Plott, C.R. (1990), 'Rational choice in experimental markets', in K.S. Cook and M. Levi (eds), *The Limits of Rationality*, Chicago, IL: University of Chicago Press, 146–75.

Porter, D.P and V.L. Smith (1995), 'Futures contracting and dividend uncertainty in experimental asset markets', *Journal of Business*, **68**(4), 509–42.

Poterba, J.M. (2000), 'Stock market wealth and consumption', *Journal of Economic Perspectives*, **14**(2), 99–118.

Pound, J. and R.J. Zeckhauser (1990) 'Clearly Heard on the Street: The effect of takeover rumors on stock prices', *Journal of Business*, **63**(3), 291–308.

Prelec, D. and G. Loewenstein (1998), 'The red and the black: Mental accounting of savings and debt', *Marketing Science*, **17**(1), 4–28.

psychonomics GmbH & Capital (1998), *Private Finanzen 2000 – Eine Repräsentativbefragung zu Finanzverhalten und Finanzmentalität der Bundesdeutschen Bevölkerung* [Private finances in 2000 – A representative survey of financial behavior and financial mentality in the federal German population], Köln.

psychonomics GmbH & Capital (1999), *Die Psychologie beim Aktienkauf: Ängste, Hürden, Hemmschwellen – eine represäntative Studie über potentielle Aktien- und Fondansteiger* [The psychology of stock purchasing: Worries, hurdles, inhibition thresholds – a representative study of potential stock and fund buyers], Köln.

Rae, J. ([1834] 1905), *The Sociological Theory of Capital*, New York: Macmillan.

Rainwater, L, R.P. Coleman, and G. Handel (1959), *Workingman's Wife,* New York: Oceana Publications.

Ramaswamy, V., R. Chatterjee, and S.H. Cohen (1996), 'Joint segmentation on distinct interdependent bases with categorical data', *Journal of Marketing Research*, **33**, 337–50.

Read, D. and G. Loewenstein (1995), 'Diversification bias: Explaining the discrepancy in variety seeking between combined and separated choices', *Journal of Experimental Psychology: Applied*, **1**, 34–49.

Reber, A.S. (1985), *The Penguin Dictionary of Psychology*, Harmondsworth: Penguin Books.

Rogers, E.M. (1983), *Diffusion of Innovations*, 3rd edition, New York: The Free Press.

Romer, D. (1993), 'Rational asset-price movements without news', *American Economic Review*, **83**, 1121–30.

Rose, A. M. (1951), 'Rumor in the stock market', *Public Opinion Quarterly*, **15**, 461–86.

Rosnow, R.L. (1991), 'Inside rumor', *American Psychologist*, **46**(5), 484–96.

Roszkowski, M.J., G.E. Snelbecker, and S.R. Leimberg (1989), *The Tools and Techniques of Financial Planning*, Cincinnati, OH: The National Underwriter Company.

Rothman, A,J. and C.D. Hardin (1997), 'Differential use of the availability heuristic in social judgment', *Personality and Social Psychology Bulletin*, **23**(2), 123–38.

Russell, J.C., D.O. Wilson, and J.F. Jenkins (1976), 'Informational properties of jaywalking models as determinants of imitated jaywalking: An extension to model sex, race, and number', *Sociometry*, **39**(3), 270–3.

Samuelson, P.A. (1963), 'Risk and uncertainty: A fallacy of large numbers', *Scientia*, **98**, 108–13.

Samuelson, P.A. (1965), 'Proof that properly anticipated prices fluctuate randomly', *Industrial Management Review*, **6**, 11–50.

Samuelson, P.A. (1989), 'The judgment of economic science on rational portfolio management: Indexing, timing, and long-horizon effects', *Journal of Portfolio Management*, **16**(1), 4–12.

Samuelson, P.A. (1994), 'The long-term case for equities. And how it can be oversold', *Journal of Portfolio Management*, **21**(1), 15–24.

Samuelson, P.A. and W.D. Nordhaus (1992), *Economics*, 14th edition, New York: McGraw-Hill.

Schachter, S., W. Gerin, D.C. Hood, and P.B. Andreassen (1985), 'Was the South Sea Bubble a random walk?', *Journal of Economic Behavior and Organization*, **6**(4), 23–9.

Schachter, S., D.C. Hood, P.B. Andreassen, and W. Gerin (1986), 'Aggregate variables in psychology and economics: Dependence and the stock market', in B. Gilad and S. Kaish (eds), *Handbook of Behavioral Economics*, Vol. B, JAI Press: Greenwich, CT, 237–72.

Scharfstein, D.S. and J.C. Stein (1990), 'Herd behavior and investment', *American Economic Review*, **80**(3), 465–79.

Schelling, T. (1984), 'Self-command in practice, in policy, and in a theory of rational choice', *American Economic Review*, **74**, May, Papers and Proceedings, 1–11.

Schiereck, D., W.F.M. De Bondt, and M. Weber (1999), 'Contrarian and momentum strategies in Germany', *Financial Analysts Journal*, **55**(6), 104–15.

Schlarbaum, G.G., W.G. Lewellen, and R.C. Lease (1978), 'Realized returns on common stock investments: The experience of individual investors', *Journal of Business*, **51**(2), 299–325.

Schwartz, N. and F. Strack (1985), 'Cognitive and affective processes in judgments of subjective well-being: A preliminary model', in H. Brandstätter and E. Kirchler (eds), *Economic Psychology*, Linz: Universitätsverlag R. Trauner, 439–47.

Schwert, G.W. (1990), 'Stock volatility and the crash of '87', *Review of Financial Studies*, **3**(1), 77–102.

Seehusen, K. (1994), 'Watching for chart patterns', *Futures*, **23**, Oct, 18–22.

Severn, A. (1998), 'Closed-end funds and sentiment risk', *Review of Financial Economics*, **7**, 103–19.

Shapiro, H.T. (1972), 'The index of consumer sentiment and economic forecasting: A reappraisal', in B. Strumpel, J.N. Morgan, and E. Zahn (eds), *Human Behavior in Economic Affairs: Essays in Honor of George Katona*, Amsterdam and New York: Elsevier Scientific Publishing Co., 373–96.

Sharpe, W.F. (1964), 'Capital asset prices: A theory of market equilibrium', *Journal of Finance*, **19**, 425–42.

Sheffrin, S.M. (1983), *Rational Expectations*, Cambridge, UK: Cambridge University Press.

Shefrin, H. (2000), *Beyond Greed and Fear: Understanding Behavioral Finance and the Psychology of Investing*, Boston, MA: Harvard Business School Press.

Shefrin, H. and M. Statman (1985), 'The disposition to sell winners too early and ride losers too long: Theory and evidence', *Journal of Finance*, **40**(3), 777–90.

Shefrin, H. and M. Statman (1993), 'Behavioral aspects of the design and marketing of financial products', *Financial Management*, **22**(2), 123–34.

Shefrin, H. and M. Statman 1994), 'Behavioral Capital Asset Pricing Theory', *Journal of Financial and Quantitative Analysis*, **29**(3), 323–49.

Shefrin, H. and M. Statman (1995), 'Making sense of beta, size, and book-to-market', *Journal of Portfolio Management*, **21**(2), Winter, 26–34.

Shefrin, H. and R.H. Thaler (1988), 'The Behavioral Life-Cycle Hypothesis', *Economic Inquiry*, **26**, 609–43.

Shibutani, T. (1966), *Improvised News: A Sociological Study of Rumor*, Indianapolis, IN: Bobbs Merrill.

Shiller, R.(1981), 'Do stock prices move too much to be justified by subsequent changes in dividends?', *American Economic Review*, **71**(3), 421–35.

Shiller, R.J. (1989), *Market Volatility*, Cambridge: MIT Press.

Shiller, R.J. (1990), 'Market volatility and investor behavior', *American Economic Review*, **80**(2), 58–62.

Shiller, R.J. (1995), 'Conversation, information, and herd behavior', *American Economic Review*, **85**(2), 181–5.

Shiller, R.J. (1999), 'Measuring bubble expectations and investor confidence', NBER Working Paper Series 7008, Cambridge, MA: National Bureau of Economic Research.

Shiller, R.J. (2000), *Irrational Exuberance*, Princeton, NJ: Princeton University Press.

Shiller, R.J. and J. Pound (1989), 'Survey evidence on diffusion of interest and information among investors', *Journal of Economic Behavior and Organization*, **12**(1), 47–66.

Shleifer, A. (2000), *Inefficient Markets*, Oxford: Oxford University Press.

Siegel, J.J. (1992), 'Equity risk premia, corporate profit forecasts, and investor sentiment around the stock crash of October 1987', *Journal of Business*, **65**(4), 557–70.

Simon, H.A. (1955), 'A behavioral model of rational choice', *Quarterly Journal of Economics*, **69**, 99–118.

Simon, H.A. (1979), 'Information processing models of cognition', *Annual Review of Psychology*, **30**, 363–96.

Simon, H.A. (1984), 'On the behavioral and rational foundations of economic dynamics', *Journal of Economic Behavior and Organization*, **5**, 35–55.

Simon, H.A. (1990), 'Invariants of human behavior', *Annual Review of Psychology*, **41**, 1–19.

Simon, H.A. (1994), 'The bottleneck of attention: Connecting thought with motivation', *Nebraska Symposium on Motivation*, **41**, 1–21.

Simon, H.A. and F. Gobet (2000), 'Expertise effects in memory recall: Comment on Vicente and Wang (1998)', *Psychological Review*, **107**(3), 593–600.

Sjöberg, L. (1989), 'Mood and expectation', in A.F. Bennett and K.M. McConkey (eds), *Cognition in Individual and Social Contexts*, Dordrecht: Elsevier Science Publishers, 337–48.

Sjöberg, L. (1998), 'Will and success – individual and national', in L. Sjöberg, R. Bagozzi, and D.H. Ingvar (eds), *Will and Economic Behavior,* Stockholm: Economic Research Institute, Stockholm School of Economics, 85–119.

Sjöberg, L. and T. Johnson (1978), 'Trying to give up smoking: A study of volitional breakdown', *Addictive Behaviors*, **3**, 149–64.

Smith, A. ([1759]1982), *The Theory of Moral Sentiments*, edited by D.D. Raphael and A.L. Macfie, Indianapolis, IN: Liberty Classics (first published in 1759).

Smith, A. ([1776]1981), *An Inquiry into the Nature and Causes of the Wealth of Nations*, Vols I and II, edited by R.H. Campbell and A.S. Skinner, Indianapolis, IN: Liberty Classics (first published in 1776).

Smith, V.L. (1991), 'Rational choice: The contrast between economics and psychology', *Journal of Political Economy*, **99**(4), 877–97.

Solnik, B. (1996), *International Investments*, 3rd edition, Reading, MA: Addison-Wesley Publishing Company.

Solt, M.E. and M. Statman (1989), 'Good companies, bad stocks', *Journal of Portfolio Management*, **15**(4). 39–44.

Statman, M. (1999), 'Behavioral finance: Past battles and future engagements', *Financial Analysts Journal*, **55**(6), 18–27.

Statman, M. (2000), 'Socially responsible mutual funds', *Financial Analysts Journal*, **56**, May/June, 30–9.

Stephan, E. (1999), 'Die Rolle von Urteilsheuristiken bei Finanzentscheidungen: Ankereffekte und kognitive Verfügbarkeit', [The role of judgmental heuristics in financial decisions: Anchoring and availability effects], in L. Fischer, T. Kutsch, and E. Stephan (eds), *Finanzpsychologie*, München und Wien: R. Oldenbourg Verlag, 101–34.

Stephan, E. and G. Kiell (1997), 'Urteilsprozesse bei professionellen Akteuren im Finanzmarkt' [Judgment processes of professional agents in the financial market], Working Paper, Universität zu Köln, Institut für Wirtschafts- und Sozialpsychologie.

Stephan, E. and G. Kiell (2000), 'Decision processes in professional investors: Does expertise moderate judgmental biases?', in E. Hölzl (ed.), *IAREP/SABE Conference Proceedings: Fairness and Competition,* Vienna: WUV, Universitätsverlag, 416–20.

Stiglitz, J.E. (1990), 'Symposium on bubbles', *Journal of Economic Perspectives*, **4**(2), 13–18.

Stroebe, W. and B.S. Frey (1982), 'Self-interest and collective action: The economics and psychology of public goods', *British Journal of Social Psychology*, **21**, 121–37.

Strong, N. and X. Xu (1999), 'Understanding the equity home bias: Evidence from survey data', SSRN Working Papers.

Strotz, R.H. (1956), 'Myopia and inconsistency in dynamic utility maximization', *Review of Economic Studies*, **23**(3), 165–80.

Svensson, E., M. Angelborg-Thanderz, L. Sjöberg, and S. Olson (1997), 'Information complexity – mental workload and performance in combat aircraft', *Ergonomics*, **40**, 362–80.

Swallow, S., and M. Fox (1996), 'Investor psychology in New Zealand', *New Zealand Journal of Psychology*, **25**(1), 21–3.

Thaler, R.H. (1980), 'Toward a positive theory of consumer choice', *Journal of Economic Behavior and Organization*, **1**, 39–60.

Thaler, R.H. (1990), 'Anomalies: Saving, fungibility, and mental accounts', *Journal of Economic Perspectives*, **4**, 193–205.

Thaler, R.H. (1992), *The Winner's Curse: Paradoxes and Anomalies of Economic Life*, New York: The Free Press.

Thaler, R.H. (1999a), 'The end of behavioral finance', *Financial Analysts Journal*, **55**, Nov.–Dec., 12–19.

Thaler, R.H. (1999b), 'Mental accounting matters', *Journal of Behavioral Decision Making*, **12**(3), 183–206

Thaler, R.H. and E.J. Johnson (1990), 'Gambling with the house money and trying to break even: The effects of prior outcomes on risky choice', *Management Science*, **36**(6), 643–60.

Tobin, J. (1958), 'Liquidity preference as behavior toward risk', *Review of Economic Studies*, **26**, Feb., 65–86.

Todd, P.M. and G. Gigerenzer (1999), 'What we have learned (so far)', in G. Gigerenzer, P.M. Todd and the ABD Research Group (eds), *Simple Heuristics that Make Us Smart*, Oxford: Oxford University Press, 357–65.

Tuckman, B.W. (1964), 'Personality structure, group composition, and group functioning', *Sociometry*, **27**(4), 469–87.

Tversky, A. and C.R. Fox (1995), 'Weighing risk and uncertainty', *Psychological Review*, **102**(2), 269–83.

Tversky, A. and C. Heath (1991), 'Preferences and beliefs: Ambiguity and competence in choice under uncertainty', *Journal of Risk and Uncertainty*, **4**, 5–28.

Tversky, A. and D. Kahneman (1982a), 'Judgment under uncertainty: Heuristics and biases', in D. Kahneman, P. Slovic, and A. Tversky (eds), *Judgment under Uncertainty: Heuristics and Biases*, Cambridge: Cambridge University Press, 3–20.

Tversky, A. and D. Kahneman (1982b), 'Belief in the law of small numbers', in D. Kahneman, P. Slovic, and A. Tversky (eds), *Judgment under Uncertainty: Heuristics and Biases*, Cambridge: Cambridge University Press, 23–31.

Tversky, A. and D. Kahneman (1982c), 'Causal schemas in judgments under uncertainty', in D. Kahneman, P. Slovic, and A. Tversky (eds), *Judgment under Uncertainty: Heuristics and Biases*, Cambridge: Cambridge University Press, 117–28.

Tversky, A. and D. Kahneman (1982d), 'Evidential impact of base rates', in D. Kahneman, P. Slovic, and A. Tversky (eds), *Judgment under Uncertainty: Heuristics and Biases*, Cambridge: Cambridge University Press, 153–60.

Tversky, A. and D. Kahneman (1982e), 'Availability: A heuristic for judging frequency and probability', in D. Kahneman, P. Slovic, and A. Tversky (eds), *Judgment under Uncertainty: Heuristics and Biases*, Cambridge: Cambridge University Press, 163–78.

Tversky, A. and D. Kahneman (1983), 'Extensional versus intuitive reasoning: The conjunction fallacy in probability judgment', *Psychological Review*, **90**(4), 293–315.

Tversky, A. and D. Kahneman (1992), 'Advances in prospect theory: Cumulative representation of uncertainty', *Journal of Risk and Uncertainty*, **5**, 297–323.

Tversky, A., P. Slovic, and D. Kahneman (1990), 'The causes of preference reversal', *American Economic Review*, **80**, 204–17.

Vanden Abeele, P. (1988), 'Economic agents' expectations in a psychological perspective', in W.F. van Raaij, G. van Veldhoven, and K.-E. Wärneryd (eds), *Handbook of Economic Psychology*, Dordrecht: Kluwer Academic Publishers, 478–515.

van Raaij, W.F. and H.J. Gianotten (1990), 'Consumer confidence, expenditure, saving, and credit', *Journal of Economic Psychology*, **11**, 269–90.

Wärneryd, K.-E. (1994), 'Economic psychology and telecommunications research', in H. Brandstätter and W. Güth (eds), *Essays on Economic Psychology*, Berlin and Heidelberg: Springer Verlag, 133–52.

Wärneryd, K.-E. (1996a), *Personality and Saving,* VSB-CentER Savings Project, Progress Report 39, CentER for Economic Research, Tilburg University.

Wärneryd, K.-E. (1996b), 'Risk attitudes and risky behavior', *Journal of Economic Psychology*, **17**, 749–70.

Wärneryd, K.-E. (1997), 'Demystifying rational expectations theory through an economic–psychological model', in G. Antonides, W.F. van Raaij, and S. Maital (eds), *Advances in Economic Psychology*, Chichester: Wiley & Sons, 211–36.

Wärneryd, K.-E. (1999), *The Psychology of Saving: A Study on Economic Psychology*, Cheltenham, UK and Northampton, MA: Elgar.

Wärneryd, K.-E. (2000a), 'Future-orientation, self-control, and saving behavior', Paper presented at XXVII International Congress of Psychology, Stockholm, July 23–28.

Wärneryd, K.-E. (2000b), 'The psychology of private investing: Stockowners' risk aversion, activity level and diversification of portfolios', Proceedings, IAREP/SABE 2000 Conference, Vienna: WUV Universitätsverlag, 493–7.

Wason, P. (1966), 'Reasoning', in B.M. Foss (ed.), *New Horizons in Psychology*, Harmondsworth: Penguin, 135–51.

Weber, M. and C.F. Camerer (1998), 'The disposition effect in securities trading: An experimental analysis', *Journal of Economic Behavior and Organization*, **33**, 167–84.

Webley, P. and S.E.G. Lea (1993), 'Towards a more realistic psychology of economic socialization', *Journal of Economic Psychology*, **14**, 461–72.

Weil, D.N. (1991), 'What determines savings? A review essay', *Journal of Monetary Economics*, **28**, 161–70.

Weiner, B. (1972), *Theories of Motivation – from Mechanism to Cognition,* Chicago, IL: Rand-McNally.

Weiner, B. (1974), *Achievement Motivation and Attribution Theory*, Morristown, NJ: General Learning Press.

Weiner, B. (1985), 'An attributional theory of achievement motivation and emotion', *Psychological Review*, **92**, 548–73.

Weinstein, N.D. (1980) 'Unrealistic optimism about future life events', *Journal of Personality and Social Psychology*, **39**(5), 806–20.

Wermers, R. and T.J Moskowitz (2000) 'Mutual fund performance: An empirical decomposition into stock-picking talent, style, transactions costs, and expenses', *Journal of Finance*, **55**(4), 1655–1703.

Winnett, A. and A. Lewis (1995), 'Household accounts, mental accounts, and savings behaviour: Some old economics rediscovered?', *Journal of Economic Psychology*, **16**, 431–48.

Winnett, A. and A. Lewis (2000), 'You'd have to be green to invest in this: Popular economic models, financial journalism, and ethical investment', *Journal of Economic Psychology*, **21**(3), 319–39.

Wirth, M. (1874), *Geschichte der Handelskrisen* [History of Trade Crises], Zweite Auflage, Frankfurt a. M.: J.D. Sauerländer's Verlag.

Zajonc, R.B. (1980), 'Feeling and thinking: Preferences need no inferences', *American Psychologist*, **35**(2), 151–75.

Zeira, J. (1999), 'Informational overshooting, booms, and crashes', *Journal of Monetary Economics*, **43**(1), 237–57.

Zelizer, V.A. (1993), 'Making multiple monies', in R. Swedberg (ed.), *Explorations in Economic Sociology*, New York: Sage, 193–212.

Zivney,T.L, W.J. Bertin, and K.M. Torabzadeh (1996), 'Overreaction to takeover speculation', *Quarterly Review of Economics and Finance*, **36**(1), 89–115.

Zuckerman, M. (1979), *Sensation Seeking: Beyond the Optimal Level of Arousal*, Hillsdale, NJ: Lawrence Erlbaum.

Zullow, H.M. (1991), 'Pessimistic rumination in popular songs and newsmagazines predict economic recession via decreased consumer optimism and spending', *Journal of Economic Psychology*, **12**(3), 501–26.

Index